San Francisco

Bay Area & Wine Country

2010

A SELECTION
OF RESTAURANTS
& HOTELS

Manufacture française des pneumatiques Michelin
Société en commandite par actions au capital de 304 000 000 EUR
Place des Carmes-Déchaux – 63000 Clermont-Ferrand (France)
R.C.S. Clermont-Fd B 855 200 507

Dépot légal Octobre 2009

Made in Canada

Published in 2009

MICHELIN
A better way forward

Please send your comments to :

Michelin North America, Inc.
One Parkway South
Greenville, SC 29615 USA
www.michelintravel.com
Michelin.guides@us.michelin.com

Dear Reader

We are thrilled to present the fourth edition of our Michelin Guide to San Francisco.

Our energetic team has spent this year updating our selection to fully reflect the rich diversity of San Francisco's restaurants and hotels. As part of our meticulous and highly confidential evaluation process, our inspectors have anonymously and methodically eaten through San Francisco, the Bay Area, and Wine Country to compile the finest in each category for your enjoyment. While these inspectors are highly trained food industry professionals, we remain consumer driven: our goal is to provide comprehensive choices to accommodate your comfort, tastes, and budget. Our inspectors dine, drink, and lodge as 'regular' customers to evaluate the same level of service you would experience as a guest.

Furthermore, we have expanded our criteria to reflect some of the more current and unique elements of San Francisco dining. "Small Plates" is a new category, introduced to highlight establishments with a distinct style of service, setting, and menu than previously included in our selection. Additionally, new symbols have been created to showcase restaurants with notable specialty cocktail or sake lists—these offerings have grown to be increasingly more impressive over the last four years.

Our company's two founders, Édouard and André Michelin, published the first Michelin Guide in 1900, to provide motorists with practical information about where they could service and repair their cars, find quality accommodations, and a good meal. Later in 1926, the star-rating system for outstanding restaurants was introduced, and over the decades we have developed many new improvements to our guides. The local team here in San Francisco enthusiastically carries on these traditions.

We sincerely hope that the Michelin Guide will remain your preferred reference to San Francisco restaurants and hotels.

Contents

SFCVB/Phillip H.Coblentz

The Michelin Guide

"This volume was created at the turn of the century and will last at least as long".

This foreword to the very first edition of the MICHELIN Guide, written in 1900, has become famous over the years and the Guide has lived up to the prediction. It is read across the world and the key to its popularity is the consistency in its commitment to its readers, which is based on the following promises.

→ Anonymous Inspections

Our inspectors make anonymous visits to hotels and restaurants to gauge the quality offered to the ordinary customer. They pay their own bill and make no indication of their presence. These visits are supplemented by comprehensive monitoring of information—our readers' comments are one valuable source, and are always taken into consideration.

→ Independence

Our choice of establishments is a completely independent one, made for the benefit of our readers alone. Decisions are discussed by the inspectors and the editor, with the most important decided at the global level. Inclusion in the guide is always free of charge.

→ The Selection

The Guide offers a selection of the best hotels and restaurants in each category of comfort and price. Inclusion in the guides is a commendable award in itself, and defines the establishment among the "best of the best."

How the MICHELIN Guide Works

→ Annual Updates

All practical information, the classifications, and awards, are revised and updated every year to ensure the most reliable information possible.

→ Consistency & Classifications

The criteria for the classifications are the same in all countries covered by the Michelin Guides. Our system is used worldwide and is easy to apply when choosing a restaurant or hotel.

→ The Classifications

We classify our establishments using XXXXX-X and 🏨🏨🏨🏨🏨-🏨 to indicate the level of comfort. The ✿✿✿-✿ specifically designates an award for cuisine, unique from the classification. For hotels and restaurants, a symbol in red suggests a particularly charming spot with unique décor or ambiance.

→ Our Aim

As part of Michelin's ongoing commitment to improving travel and mobility, we do everything possible to make vacations and eating out a pleasure.

How to Use This Guide

Where to Eat

Restaurant Classifications by Comfort

More pleasant if in red

X	Quite comfortable
XX	Comfortable
XXX	Very comfortable
XXXX	Top class comfortable
XXXXX	Luxury in the traditional style
🍽	Small plates

The Michelin Distinctions for Good Cuisine

Stars for Good Cuisine

✿✿✿	Exceptional cuisine, worth a special journey
✿✿	Excellent cuisine, worth a detour
✿	Very good cuisine in its category

Bib Gourmand
Inspectors' favorites for good value

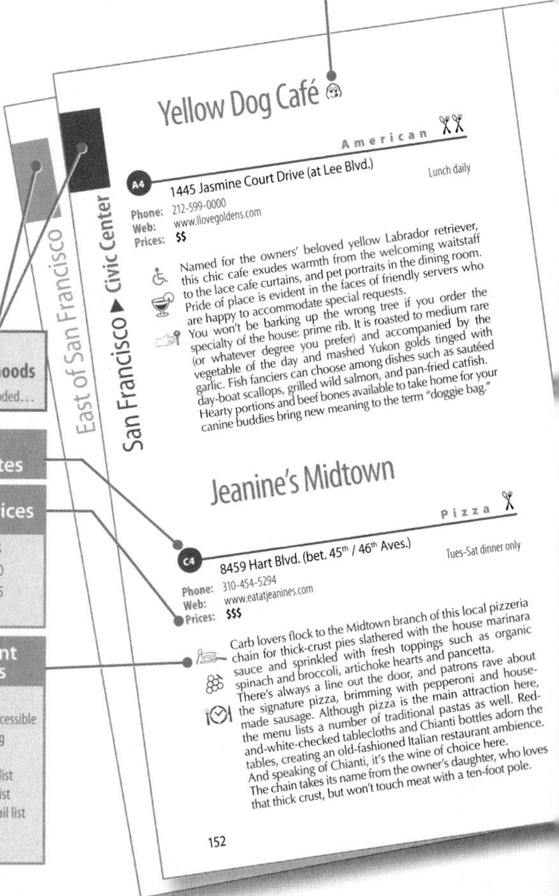

Areas or neighborhoods

Each area is color coded...

Map Coordinates

Average Prices

⊜	under $25
$$	$25 to $50
$$$	$50 to $75
$$$$	over $75

Restaurant Symbols

- Cash only
- Wheelchair accessible
- Outdoor dining
- Brunch
- Notable wine list
- Notable sake list
- Notable cocktail list
- Valet parking
- Late dining

East of San Francisco

San Francisco ▶ Civic Center

Yellow Dog Café

American XX

A4 1445 Jasmine Court Drive (at Lee Blvd.)

Lunch daily

Phone: 212-599-0000
Web: www.llovegoldens.com
Prices: $$

Named for the owners' beloved yellow Labrador retriever, this chic cafe exudes warmth from the welcoming waitstaff to the lace cafe curtains, and pet portraits in the dining room. Pride of place is evident in the faces of friendly servers who are happy to accommodate special requests.

You won't be barking up the wrong tree if you order the specialty of the house: prime rib. It is roasted to medium rare (or whatever degree you prefer) and accompanied by the vegetable of the day and mashed Yukon golds tinged with garlic. Fish fanciers can choose among dishes such as sautéed day-boat scallops, grilled wild salmon, and pan-fried catfish. Hearty portions and beef bones available to take home for your canine buddies bring new meaning to the term "doggie bag."

Jeanine's Midtown

Pizza X

C4 8459 Hart Blvd. (bet. 45th / 46th Aves.)

Tues-Sat dinner only

Phone: 310-454-5294
Web: www.eatatjeanines.com
Prices: $$$

Carb lovers flock to the Midtown branch of this local pizzeria chain for thick-crust pies slathered with the house marinara sauce and sprinkled with fresh toppings such as organic spinach and broccoli, artichoke hearts and pancetta.

There's always a line out the door, and patrons rave about the signature pizza, brimming with pepperoni and house-made sausage. Although pizza is the main attraction here, the menu lists a number of traditional pastas as well. Red-and-white-checked tablecloths and Chianti bottles adorn the tables, creating an old-fashioned Italian restaurant ambience. And speaking of Chianti, it's the wine of choice here.

The chain takes its name from the owner's daughter, who loves that thick crust, but won't touch meat with a ten-foot pole.

152

Where to **Stay**

Average Prices

Prices do not include applicable taxes

$	under $200
$$	$200 to $300
$$$	$300 to $400
$$$$	over $400

Map Coordinates

Hotel Symbols

149 rooms	Number of rooms & suites
♿	Wheelchair accessible
	Exercise room
Spa	Spa
	Swimming pool
	Conference room
	Pet friendly

Hotel Classifications by Comfort

More pleasant if in red

- Quite comfortable
- Comfortable
- Very comfortable
- Top class comfortable
- Luxury in the traditional style

The Fan Inn

D1

135 Shanghai Road, Oakland

Phone: 650-345-1440 or 888-222-2424
Fax: 650-397-2408
Web: www.superfaninnoakland.com
Prices: $$

45 Rooms
5 Suites

San Francisco ▶ Civic Center

Housed in an Art Deco-era building, the venerable Fan Inn recently underwent a complete facelift. The hotel now fits with the new generation of sleekly understated hotels offering a Zen-inspired aesthetic, despite its 1930s origins. soothing neutral palette runs throughout the property, punctuated with exotic woods, bamboo, and fine fabrics. the lobby, the sultry lounge makes a relaxing place for a mixed cocktail or a glass of wine.

linens and down pillows cater to your comfort, while een TVs, DVD players with iPod docking stations, ireless Internet access satisfy the need for modern es. For business travelers, nightstands convert to tables and credenzas morph into flip-out desks. printer, fax or scanner? It's just a phone call away. uest, the hotel will even provide office supplies.

half of the accommodations here are suites, where factor ratchets up with marble baths, spacious , and fully equipped kitchens. Although the inn a restaurant, the nearby blocks hold nearly ou could want in terms of food, from soup haute cuisine.

419

a's Palace

Italian

ther Place (at 30th Street)
309
asfabulouspalace.com

Dinner daily

San Francisco ▶ Civic Center

Home cooked Italian never tasted so good than at this unpretentious little place. The simple décor claims no big-name designers, and while the Murano glass light fixtures are chic and the velveteen-covered chairs are comfortable, this isn't a restaurant where millions of dollars were spent on the interior.

Instead, food is the focus here. The restaurant's name may not be Italian, but it nonetheless serves some of the best pasta in the city, made fresh in-house. Dishes follow the seasons, thus ravioli may be stuffed with fresh ricotta and herbs in summer, and pumpkin in fall. Most everything is liberally dusted with Parmigiano Reggiano, a favorite ingredient of the chef.

For dessert, you'll have to deliberate between the likes of creamy tiramisu, ricotta cheesecake, and homemade gelato. One thing's for sure: you'll never miss your *nonna's* cooking when you eat at Sonya's.

153

Where to Eat

SFCVB photo by Phillip H. Coblentz

San Francisco

Castro

Cole Valley • Haight-Ashbury • Noe Valley

It's raining men in the Castro, the world famous "gayborhood" that launched the career of civil rights icon, Harvey Milk, and remains devoted to celebrating the gay and lesbian community (yes, ladies are allowed here too). The hub for all things LGBT—including Gay Pride in June and the Castro Street Fair each October—the Castro is a constant party with a mélange of bars from shabby to chic and dance clubs that honor the ruling class of one-name wonder women—Madonna, Beyoncé, Bette, Babs, and Cher.

The Castro teems with casual cafés to feed its buzzing population of gym bunnies, leather daddies, and drag queens, as well as a consistent throng of gay out-of-towners on pilgrimage to Mecca. **Café Flore**'s quaint patio is more evocative of its Parisian namesake than the plain-Jane continental fare. But if you go to eat, you're missing the point: This is prime cruising territory with cheap drinks and DJs. There are white napkin restaurants dishing worthwhile cuisine—**Frisée**, **Côté Sud**, and **La Méditerranée**—but the best flavors of the Castro are served on the run.

Thai House and the 24-7 **Baghdad Café** are mainstays for a quick, inexpensive bite, and **Marcello's Pizza** is a satisfying post-cocktail joint. Speaking of booze, San Francisco's first openly gay bar, **Twin Peaks Tavern**, still lures the same gentlemen it did back in the day. The younger hotties, however, sweat it out at **Badlands** and the **Café**. **Café du Nord** draws hipsters for live music in a former speakeasy built in 1907.

The area is chock-full of darling specialty shops. The **Castro Cheesery** pours fresh-roasted gourmet coffees and offers a small selection of cheese; **Samovar Tea Lounge** brews artisan loose-leaf; and **Swirl**, a sleek space brimming with stemware and accessories, offers tastings of boutique wine varietals. Take home a nosh from Italian foods purveyor **A.G. Ferrari**, or indulge your sweet tooth at **Gelateria Naia** or the kitschy kiosk, **Hot Cookie**.

Nearby Cole Valley is home to **Say Cheese**, full of quality international cheeses and a small stock of sandwiches; and **Val de Cole**, with value table wines galore. On Monday nights, dog-lovers treat the whole family to dinner on the garden patio at **Zazie**.

Counterculturalists, of course, have long sought haven in the hippiefied Haight-Ashbury where, despite recent Gap-ification, head shops and record stores still dominate the landscape. Eschew any notions of fine dining here and join the locals at more laid-back hot spots. **Cha! Cha! Cha!** is a groovy tapas bar flowing with fresh-fruit sangria, and **Magnolia Pub & Brewery** serves modern gastropub eats and housemade beers. The morning after, **Pork Store Café** draws a cult following for greasy hash browns and hotcakes.

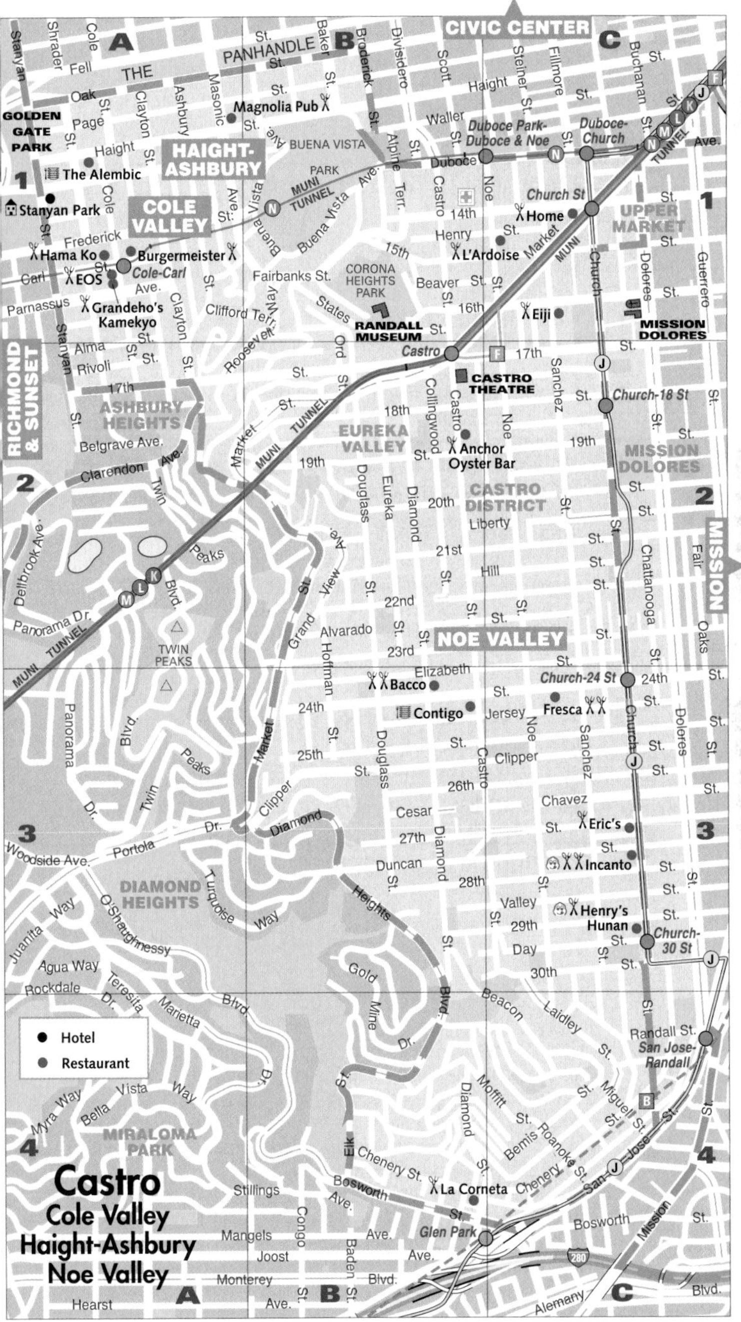

Castro
Cole Valley
Haight-Ashbury
Noe Valley
CIVIC CENTER
MISSION
RICHMOND & SUNSET
GOLDEN GATE PARK
HAIGHT-ASHBURY
COLE VALLEY
THE PANHANDLE
BUENA VISTA PARK
CORONA HEIGHTS PARK
RANDALL MUSEUM
UPPER MARKET
MISSION DOLORES
CASTRO THEATRE
EUREKA VALLEY
CASTRO DISTRICT
ASHBURY HEIGHTS
TWIN PEAKS
NOE VALLEY
DIAMOND HEIGHTS
MIRALOMA PARK
Magnolia Pub
The Alembic
Stanyan Park
Hama Ko
Burgermeister
EOS
Grandeho's Kamekyo
Home
L'Ardoise
Eiji
Anchor Oyster Bar
Bacco
Contigo
Fresca
Eric's
Incanto
Henry's Hunan
La Corneta
Duboce Park-Duboce & Noe
Duboce-Church
Church St
Castro
Church-18 St
Church-24 St
Church-30 St
San Jose-Randall
Glen Park
Hotel
Restaurant

The Alembic

1725 Haight St. (bet. Cole & Shrader Sts.)

Phone: 415-666-0822 — Lunch Fri – Sun
Web: www.alembicbar.com — Dinner nightly
Prices: $$

Featuring a bar topped with boards salvaged from the old Kezar Stadium bleechers, wood floors from a Pennsylvania barn, bare filament lights, fat barstools, and a pressed-tin ceiling, this small tavern exudes big character in the heart of the Upper Haight.

Their revolving menu of small plates takes local ingredients seriously, from bone marrow with garlic confit or bay scallop with coconut curry, to Kobe tongue sliders with hot mustard aïoli.

Tall blackboards behind the bar display hand-written lists of artisan and small batch bourbons, Scotch, and rye. Start the evening or weekend lunch with their creative cocktails, like the Sazerac, (a variation on the Old Fashioned), or the Bee's Knees (a light, sweet blend of Plymouth gin and lavender honey).

Anchor Oyster Bar

Seafood 

579 Castro St. (bet. 18th & 19th Sts.)

Phone: 415-431-3990 — Lunch Mon – Sat
Web: www.anchoroysterbar.com — Dinner nightly
Prices: $$

A neighborhood fixture for over 20 "shucking" years, this pristine little oyster bar is a pearl in the eclectic sea of the Castro. Bivalve lovers pack the long marble-topped counter and the few stainless-steel tables like sardines, while a trophy marlin hanging on the wall surveys the scene.

You don't have to dive very deep to find good oysters here; a board above the bar announces the varieties along with the specials of the day. Fresh-caught oysters may include briny Beausoleil or Kuschi, depending on the season. Slurping them down is half the fun; the other half is starters such as milky New England clam chowder, seafood cocktails, or the abundant salads. Dungeness crab dishes, pasta, and steamed shellfish are specialties of the house.

Bacco

Italian XX

B3

737 Diamond St. (bet. Elizabeth & 24th Sts.)

Phone: 415-282-4969 Dinner nightly
Web: www.baccosf.com
Prices: $$

In honor of the memory of late owner Paolo Dominici, the staff carries on his passion at this Noe Valley trattoria. Many regulars are greeted by name as they enter the warm yellow dining space, where arched openings, terra-cotta tile floors, and Italian ceramics dish up a Tuscan feel.
Homemade potato gnocchi with fontina and black truffles, and prosciutto- and arugula-stuffed chicken breast served with creamy mashed potatoes and wilted Swiss chard are sure to please—but if you're not in a hurry, it's well worth the 30-minute wait for the made-to-order risotto of the day. Come Sunday through Thursday evening for the three-course prix-fixe option that allows diners to mix and match any of the menu items.

Burgermeister

American X

A1

86 Carl St. (at Cole St.)

Phone: 415-566-1274 Lunch & dinner daily
Web: www.burgermeistersf.com
Prices:

This family-owned Cole Valley burger joint is known for its big, juicy half-pound patties, made from humanely raised Niman Ranch beef. Toppings run from the expected, American cheese and chili, to the surprising, including sliced mango or grilled pineapple. Even the crisp fries are kicked up with roasted garlic, chili, or spices. Sure, there are other fine choices on the menu, such as Philly cheesesteak, fish and chips, or grilled chicken, but most come here for a burger. Vegetarians may indulge in a portobello burger with roasted red pepper mayo.
Beyond these offerings, Burgermeister has gone green with all natural products, bio-degradable packaging, and recyclable materials. Look for their other locations in the Castro, North Beach, and Daly City.

Contigo

B3 **Spanish**

1320 Castro St. (at 24th St.)

Phone: 415-285-0250 Dinner nightly
Web: www.contigosf.com
Prices: $$

In Noe Valley, Contigo is a meat market for melt-in-your-mouth, hard-to-get heartbreakers. Minds out of the gutter! We're talking about *jamón ibérico*, the prized imported ham, sliced tissue thin. If the pig's not your type, experiment with other *pica pica*, succulent Spanish teasers like plump oxtail fritters, calamari *a la plancha*, and Catalan flatbreads hot from the wood-burning oven. While the flavors hail from Barcelona, Contigo's sensibility is straight-up California: Dishes are lovingly concocted from local, sustainable products and served on recycled Heath Ceramics dinnerware atop wood tables salvaged from the old Levi Strauss factory on Valencia Street.
The heated patio and organic garden is a comfy spot for a glass of cava.

Eiji

C1 **Japanese** 

317 Sanchez St. (bet. 16th & 17th Sts.)

Phone: 415-558-8149 Lunch & Dinner Tue – Sun
Web: N/A
Prices:

Wooden shingle siding layers the tiny tree-flanked façade, marked by a single oblong flag reading "sushi" on one side and "tofu" on the other. You may have shown up for the well-made sushi, but at Eiji Onoda's eponymous eatery, fresh, homemade tofu's the thing. Go for a bowl of silky, made-to-order *oboro*—delicate curds of tofu just separated from the soymilk (before they take their more recognizable square shape). Or try the ethereal, melt-in-your-mouth *ankake* tofu—cold steamed and topped with a tasty *konbu*-soy sauce.
Top off your tofu with accompanying additions such as julienned *shiso*, scallion rings, and freshly grated ginger. *Sunomono*, seafood casseroles, *yosenabe*, and *misonabe* are also on offer—bring your own bowl if you want either *nabe* to go.

EOS

A1

Asian

901 Cole St. (at Carl St.)

Phone: 415-566-3063 — Dinner nightly
Web: www.eossf.com
Prices: $$

Although it abuts Haight-Ashbury, tiny Cole Valley has its own bohemian charm. Families and young professionals frequent the coffee shops and restaurants along the main drag of Cole Street, where EOS draws diners from all parts of the city.

The restaurant presents two faces, a contemporary dining room and cozy adjoining wine salon, each with separate entrances but serving the same full menu of Asian fare. Order several small portions of tasty Thai salads, curries, or perhaps *poke* rolls (ahi tuna and salmon) and share them family-style. Beverage options include wine flights and inspired sake cocktails.

A dinner here is not complete without a taste of exotic homemade ice cream like Vietnamese coffee, roasted banana, and lychee-coconut sorbet.

Eric's

C3

Chinese

1500 Church St. (at 27th St.)

Phone: 415-282-0919 — Lunch & dinner daily
Web: www.erics.ypguides.net
Prices: ⊜

Eric's in Noe Valley dishes up fresh and flavorful Chinese cuisine at rock-bottom prices, so it is no wonder there is often a wait (they do not take reservations). Large framed mirrors ornament the yellow walls of the small, homey dining room, where lunch specials, including soup and green tea, are under $10. Dinner items are comparably priced, and portions are generous.

Hunan and Mandarin specialties share the menu with other favorites, and none contain MSG. Dishes include fried crabmeat Rangoon, triangular dumplings stuffed with crab and cream cheese, served with hot Chinese mustard and sweet-and-sour sauce; and rainbow fish with bell peppers and pine nuts in a white garlic sauce.

Fresca

Peruvian XX

C3

3945 24th St. (bet. Noe & Sanchez Sts.)

Phone: 415-695-0549
Web: www.frescasf.com
Prices: $$

Lunch & dinner daily

Fresca's airy dining room, sun-yellow walls, arched ceilings, and skylights emanate warmth. The front bar draws cocktail aficionados for Pisco Sours and other Latin libations, while the back of the restaurant highlights the raw bar and open kitchen.
The menu celebrates the cooking of Peru with the likes of *trucha*, skillet-roasted rainbow trout topped with caramelized tiger prawns; or pulled chicken stew with *aji amarillo* cream, Yukon potatoes, hard-boiled eggs, and steamed rice. Seafood starters include raw oysters and an array of ceviches, with combinations available.
For a Fresca fix elsewhere in the city, visit the restaurant's two other locations in the Pacific Heights and West Portal neighborhoods.

Grandeho's Kamekyo

Japanese X

A1

943 Cole St. (bet. Carl St. & Parnassus Ave.)

Phone: 415-759-5693
Web: N/A
Prices: $$

Lunch Tue – Fri
Dinner nightly

Grandeho's original location has satisfied Haight-Ashbury sushi lovers since 1996. A polished light wood sushi bar anchors the intimate dining rooms, while golden walls and a lavender ceiling warmly accent the minimalist décor.
Top quality fish makes big waves here, and the warm, freshly-steamed sushi rice proves that the chefs take their craft seriously. Rather than limiting yourself, consider indulging in the many other fine examples of Japanese cuisine on the menu. Tempura and teriyaki share the limelight with udon or soba noodle bowls and wholesome hot pots, while bento box specials offer economical samplings at both lunch and dinner. Several vegetarian choices are also available.
A sister restaurant resides in North Beach at 2721 Hyde Street.

Hama Ko

Japanese 

A1

108 Carl St. (bet. Cole & Stanyan Sts.)

Phone: 415-753-6808 — Dinner Tue – Sun
Web: N/A
Prices: $$

Wandering a small Japanese village, you won't find a more authentic and unassuming sushi spot than Hama Ko, a mom-and-pop shop run by a charming Japanese couple. He mans the sushi bar, deftly assembling *nigiri* samplers; she serves the handful of tables in the homespun space with a cheerful smile. This feels like the home of the Japanese grandparents you'll wish you had.

The open kitchen is a touch worn, but the food is super-fresh and lovingly prepared. Forget those trendier sushi spots with Americanized fare, and opt for the chef's choice combination platter including melt-in-your-mouth tuna, buttery scallops, and simple maki. While the chef is serious and focused, there will be wide smiles all around when you share how much the meal was enjoyed.

Henry's Hunan

Chinese

C3

1708 Church St. (bet. Day & 29th Sts.)

Phone: 415-826-9189 — Lunch & dinner daily
Web: www.henryshunanrestaurant.com
Prices:

A bargain lover's dream in a tough economy, this Noe Valley newbie ranks as the most stylish of Henry's five locations in the city. The restaurant offers charisma, congenial service, and modern décor, but the food is what deserves the accolades here.

As any capsaicin-junkie will tell you, Hunan cuisine equals spicy—and there are plenty of dishes on the menu to fill that bill. Take, for instance, Henry's Special, a stir-fry of chopped chicken, tender shrimp, delicate scallops, and crunchy vegetables tossed in a zesty bean sauce. For the timid of taste buds, the kitchen will dial it down a bit. No matter which route you go (spicy or mild), the produce is fresh and flavorful, the cooking is spot-on, and the portion sizes will likely warrant a to-go box.

Home

American

C1

2100 Market St. (at Church St.)

Phone: 415-503-0333

Web: www.home-sf.com

Prices: $$

Lunch & dinner daily

All the comforts of home and some of the best people-watching around bring crowds to this spot on the edge of the Castro District. Homespun starters soothe senses with the likes of macaroni and cheese and Sloppy Joe dip with chips. Mom's cooking comes to mind in every wholesome bite of a tender pot roast with mashed potatoes or hearty chicken potpie. Lunch features are reminders of the beauty of leftovers: that pan-fried meatloaf sandwich may be a carryover from the previous evening's bounty, but is newly jazzed with caramelized onions, melted cheddar, and a tomato glaze.

Red banquettes, white tile walls, and black lacquer chairs compose the diner-like décor. On foggy nights, a roaring fire in the enclosed patio coaxes any chill from the air.

Incanto

Italian

C3

1550 Church St. (at Duncan St.)

Phone: 415-641-4500

Web: www.incanto.biz

Prices: $$

Lunch Sun
Dinner Wed – Mon

Chef Chris Cosentino, brings truly rustic, Italian charm to the Noe Valley's quintessential neighborhood spot. Cosentino, who specializes in house-cured meats, leaves no animal part unused, with delicious results. The menu may feature trotter cake with foie gras, apples, and maple syrup; borage and chicken giblet risotto; and pasta dishes with bold flavors and savory richness.

The interior resembles a medieval stone church. A small room towards the back houses a collection of unique, mainly Italian wines. The flourishing rooftop garden provides many of their fresh herbs, which diners may enjoy sprinkled on the duck-fat roasted potatoes.

Also visit Boccalone Salumeria in the Ferry Building, featuring the chef's cured meats, fresh sausages, and cooked specialties.

La Corneta

Mexican

B4

2834 Diamond St. (bet. Bosworth & Chenery Sts.)

Phone: 415-469-8757 Lunch & dinner daily
Web: www.lacorneta.com
Prices:

Set in the quaint neighborhood of Glen Park, this taqueria with its sunshine mural shining upon the clean, upbeat atmosphere transports one to the heart of the multi-cultural Mission. Dishes are assembled fast at the walk-up counter, where meals are tailored to your liking, and servers pile on the fresh, quality ingredients. Tacos, nachos, burritos, and quesadillas—each with a myriad of variations—appear on the menu board in the airy dining room.
The super taco is strictly a knife and fork operation. Be forewarned that anything described with the word "super" is a meal in itself. The super carne asada burrito, brimming with a good balance of rice, beans, meat, cheese, and guacamole, remains intact while eating only because of the skillful wrapping.

L'Ardoise

French

C1

151 Noe St. (at Henry St.)

Phone: 415-437-2600 Dinner Tue – Sat
Web: www.ardoisesf.com
Prices: **$$**

The French accent is thick at L'Ardoise, a petite neighborhood bistro named for the de rigueur chalkboard displaying the daily specials. Dimly lit with antique lamps and awash in burgundy paint, the snug spot draws swish Castro denizens and Noe Valley couples nostalgic for Parisian romance to sit elbow to elbow at zinc-topped tables. Plats du jour might include tiger shrimp ravioli with fresh herbs, or succulent pan-roasted pork tenderloin ready to be washed down with a spicy *Châteauneuf-du-Pape*.
Chef/owner Thierry Clement is to be applauded equally for his knowledgeable, all-French staff and his concise menu of bistro favorites. Savvy locals call ahead for reservations, arrive on the F-Market trolley, begin with charcuterie, and finish with *fromage*.

Magnolia Pub

A1 — **Gastropub**

1398 Haight St. (at Masonic Ave.)

Phone: 415-864-7468

Lunch & dinner daily

Web: www.magnoliapub.com

Prices: $$

This veteran Haight-Ashbury hangout finally got a shave and haircut, perhaps to the dismay of the neighborhood regulars. While black tufted leather now covers the booths and that old psychedelic mural has been muted with a gold-leaf patina, the windows still sweat with the humidity of brewing beer and the air is heavy with the scent of fresh hops late in the week. Magnolia has long been hailed for its draught micro-brews, which are jotted on a blackboard along with each beer's BUs (bitterness units) in keeping with British pub tradition.

Yet these days, its witty gastro-pub fare is a formidable draw, with such twists on bar classics as Scotch quail eggs deep fried to golden brown, or sticky-sweet duck wings—a perfect match for anything on tap.

Good food without spending a fortune? Look for the Bib Gourmand.

Civic Center

Hayes Valley • Lower Haight • Tenderloin

The gilded Beaux-Arts dome of City Hall marks the main artery of the Civic Center, where graceful architecture houses the city's finest cultural institutions, including the War Memorial & Performing Arts Center and the Asian Art Museum. On Wednesdays and Sundays, the vast promenade outside City Hall hosts **Heart of the City**, SF's oldest farmer's market. Priced to attract low-income neighborhood families, the market brims with such rare Asian produce as young ginger, Buddha's hand, and bergamot lemons.

Ground zero for California's marriage equality movement and protests of every stripe, City Hall is also prime territory for festivals, including Love Fest, which brings lavish floats and dance parties each October; the SF Symphony's biennial Black & White Ball; and the Lao New Year Festival in April. This same mall also witnessed the harvest of Alice Waters' Slow Food Nation Victory Garden in 2008.

With an enormous Asian, and particularly Vietnamese, population in the neighboring Tenderloin, there is an incredible array of authentic dining options, especially on Larkin Street. Mom-and-pop shop **Saigon Sandwiches** leads the way with spicy *báhn mì* made with fresh, crusty baguettes. The tasty subs are only three bucks a pop. Nearby, the *pho ga* at **Turtle Tower** is said to be a favorite of Slanted Door's, Chef Charles Phan, while **Bodega Bistro** is a romantic nook with an infusion of French flavors.

Best known for a seedy mess of strip clubs, liquor stores, and drug deals, the Tenderloin is a go-to for both dingy and decadent nightlife. On the site of a former speakeasy, **Bourbon & Branch** is a sexy hideaway with a tome-full of classic and creative cocktails mixed with seasonal ingredients. **Rye** is also known for inventive drinks, but its pool table and smoking patio draw a more laid-back crowd. Ruby Skye is a world-ranked DJ club and a perennial favorite

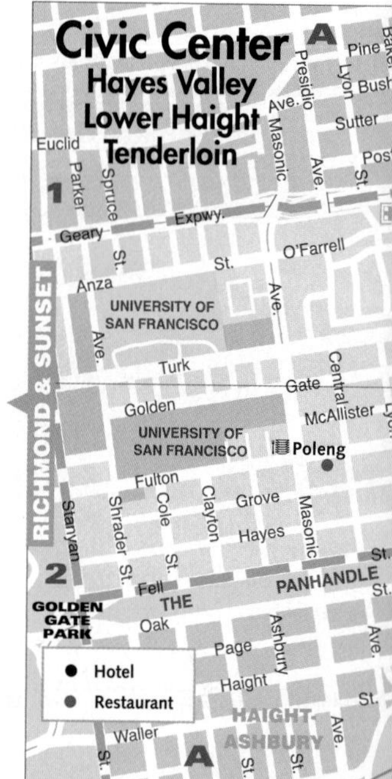

among 20-somethings; next door, sister venue Slide is a more sophisticated playground despite its unusual entrance—that's right, a snaking mahogany slide. West of the Civic Center, Hayes Valley is positively polished, with a coterie of chic design shops and boutiques as well as a mix of stylish restaurants. The concise menu of local, organic fare changes daily at cozy **Bar Jules**, while **Essencia** serves flavorful Peruvian dishes and unique wines in a pumpkin-hued corner space. **Destino** is a mainstay for *"nuevo Latino"* cuisine. **Miette Confiserie** is an impossibly charming old-fashioned style candy store jam-packed with hard-to-find European chocolates, salted licorice, taffy, and gelées. Apostles of **Blue Bottle Coffee** get their daily dose at the kiosk on Linden Alley.

To the West, the Lower Haight draws hipsters for foosball and 21 tap beers at **The Page**, sake cocktails at **Noc Noc**, and live shows at the Independent, but it's the Fillmore Jazz District that lures true music lovers. Settled by African-American GIs at the end of World War II, the neighborhood hummed with such jazz greats as Billie Holiday and Miles Davis. Today, with the attempted resurgence of the jazz district, large restaurants present live music and contemporary stars grace the stage, catering to jazz fans. The Fillmore still echoes with the voices of Pink Floyd, Hendrix, and the Dead, and the annual Fillmore Jazz Festival is also a must-see.

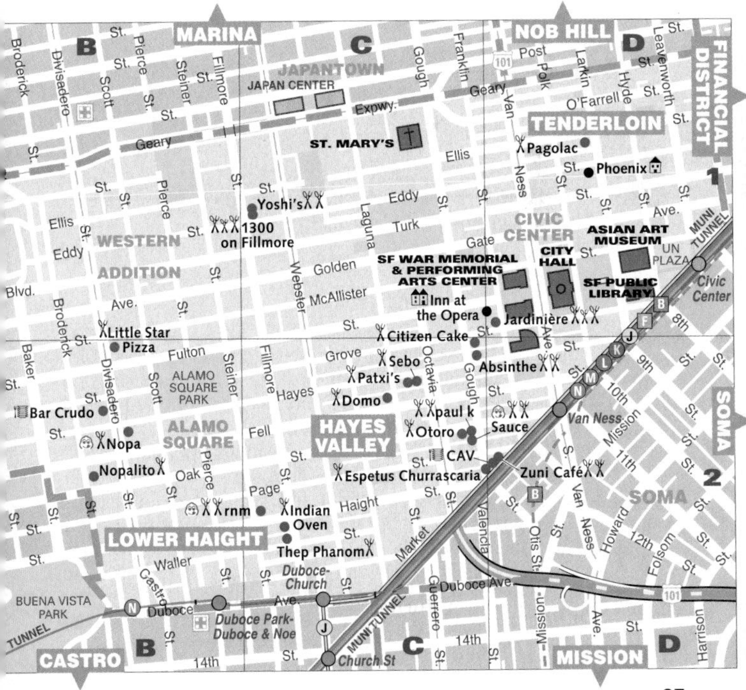

Absinthe

Mediterranean

398 Hayes St. (at Gough St.)

Phone: 415-551-1590 Lunch & dinner Tue – Sun
Web: www.absinthe.com
Prices: $$$

This brasserie is known for its creative cocktails—which, thanks to recent legalization, can now incorporate the restaurant's namesake spirit. (The quaff of choice for artists in mid-19th century France, absinthe was banned in 1912.) Lovers of the arts favor this Absinthe for its corner location near the performing-arts center, where it's a hot spot for a pre- or post-performance meal.

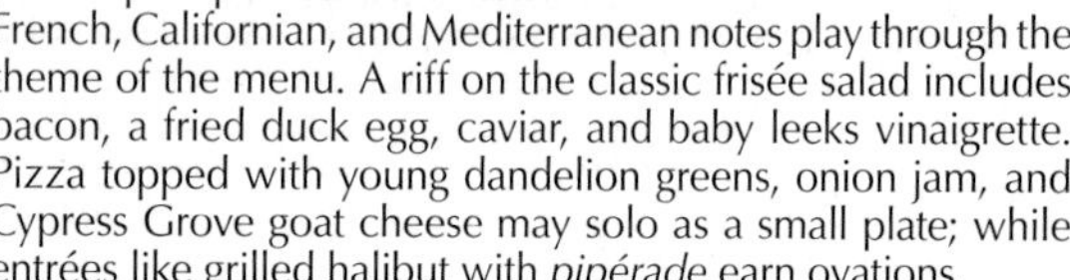

French, Californian, and Mediterranean notes play through the theme of the menu. A riff on the classic frisée salad includes bacon, a fried duck egg, caviar, and baby leeks vinaigrette. Pizza topped with young dandelion greens, onion jam, and Cypress Grove goat cheese may solo as a small plate; while entrées like grilled halibut with *pipérade* earn ovations.

Bar Crudo

Seafood 

655 Divisadero St. (at Grove St.)

Phone: 415-409-0679 Dinner nightly
Web: www.barcrudo.com
Prices: $$

Hailed for raw oysters, clams, crawfish, and Dungeness crabs, Bar Crudo was also known for sardines—or at least for its tin-sized room cramped with folks hooked on fresh seafood. To better accommodate a growing school, Bar Crudo has moved to a larger reef, in NoPa, where beautiful mermaid murals make use of long sought-after wall space.

The menu has also spread its fins with such additions as Arctic char with wasabi *tobiko*, and Anchor Steamed clams with spicy linguiça. There is no dessert but it's all for the best: Artisanal beers pair well with an adventurous octopus salad, or a messy-yet-magical quartet of Louisiana "devil" prawns. Order another round and kick back on the mezzanine, which offers a seagull's view to the zinc bar and open kitchen.

CAV

Mediterranean 

D2

1666 Market St. (bet. Franklin & Gough Sts.)

Phone: 415-437-1770 Dinner Mon – Sat
Web: www.cavwinebar.com
Prices: $$

All varietals of oenophile have a seat at CAV, the modish Upper Market wine bar known for nearly 300 exotic global vintages with discounts on take-home bottles. Bare filament bulbs shaped like test tubes float above zinc-topped tables, lending an intellectual urban vibe sans snoot.

The kitchen also dashes any hope of wine bar ubiquity, luring foodies with unexpected savories designed to complement unusual wines. Melon and grapefruit notes in an Austrian zierfandler coax the flavors from kanpachi *crudo* with briny sea beans. Crispy pig trotters, laden with poached quail eggs, pair with Dubakella pinot noir. Pink peppercorn chocolate cake is rich and simple, but regulars prefer to drink dessert: A selection of "stickies" sweetly caps the night.

Citizen Cake

Californian

C2

399 Grove St. (at Gough St.)

Phone: 415-861-2228 Lunch Tue – Sun
Web: www.citizencake.com Dinner Tue – Sat
Prices: $$

Celebrity chef, Elizabeth Falkner's smile, attitude, and artistry are expressed in her quirky, pun-filled menus and colorful, fresh cuisine. Long known for her prowess with pastry, Falkner expresses her expansive abilities in Citizen Cake's breakfast, lunch, and dinner menus—from the soup du jour, hailed as "a daily creation of a liquid variety from California's bounty," to the crisp, fresh fish tacos, with delicate slices of watermelon radish adding an exotic touch.

The chef's interest in film accounts for the restaurant's name, with a thrilling dessert dénouement that includes a "Tin Roof Sundae" or "Rosebud crème brûlée." Take home one of the signature cakes and enjoy all the applause yourself, from here, or Orson—Falkner's hot spot in SoMa.

Domo

C2 **Japanese**

511 Laguna St. (bet. Fell & Linden Sts.)

Phone: 415-861-8887 — Lunch Mon – Fri
Web: www.domosf.com — Dinner nightly
Prices: 

From the owners of ISA in the Marina, comes this diminutive Hayes Valley eatery. Too tiny for tables, Domo seats 16 along the sushi counter, which wraps around to face the floor-to-ceiling windows in front.

In this bento box-like setting, sushi specials and the fresh fish of the day are noted on the large mirrored wall. Don't overlook other more innovative items on the creative seafood-centric menu devised by Chef Kuo Hwa. Roasted wasabi peas or broiled salmon belly make a good start; while *crudo* selections—two for $5—amount to a bite of bliss in combinations like monkfish liver pâté with ponzu sauce, or a seared scallop with minced yuzu, *tobiko*, and Domo vinaigrette.

Given the limited seating, to-go orders are popular with the locals.

Espetus Churrascaria

C-D2 **Brazilian** 

1686 Market St. (at Gough St.)

Phone: 415-552-8792 — Lunch & dinner daily
Web: www.espetus.com
Prices: **$$**

Have a big appetite for meat? Look for carnivore heaven in the Civic Center area at this *rodizio*-style restaurant. "All you can eat" takes on new meaning here, as waiters clad in *gaucho* garb deliver skewers (*espetus* in Brazil) bearing a myriad of grilled meats—Parmesan pork, homemade sausage, chicken thighs, beef sirloin—to your table. You decide when you've had enough: position the wheel at your table to green if you want "more please"; turn it to red when you are "taking a meat break." As accoutrements, a generous buffet overflows with salads, fresh vegetables, and other side dishes.

Lunch provides a more limited selection, while dinner ups the meat ante as well as the prices. Anytime, a glass of malbec complements the grilled and roasted fare.

Indian Oven

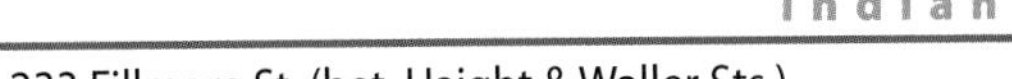

Indian

C2

233 Fillmore St. (bet. Haight & Waller Sts.)

Phone: 415-626-1628 Dinner nightly
Web: www.indianovensf.com
Prices: ⊜

Long a local favorite, Indian Oven dishes up an extensive menu of hearty Northern Indian cuisine. The plate of assorted appetizers makes a good place to start; it teems with large, crisp samosas filled with spiced potatoes and peas; vegetable *pakoras;* and two flavorful *pappadam* wafers served with an array of chutneys and pickles. Entrées encompass classic tandoori chicken; spicy lamb vindaloo; *biryani*; seafood curry; and chicken *tikka masala*, to name just a few.
Tables are cramped in the tiny downstairs dining room (some of the better seats here are next to the open kitchen); for a more intimate ambience, request a table upstairs.
Allow yourself extra time to park, since finding a space can be a nightmare in this Lower Haight neighborhood.

Jardinière

Californian

D1

300 Grove St. (at Franklin St.)

Phone: 415-861-5555 Dinner nightly
Web: www.jardiniere.com
Prices: **$$$$**

Inside this landmark building, Chef Traci Des Jardins and designer Pat Kuleto set the stage for celebration. This bi-level dining room showcases a circular mezzanine, white wrought-iron balustrades, and a golden dome shaped as an inverted Champagne glass rises above the oval bar.
Located one block from the Opera House, Jardinière appeals to a clientele of theatre enthusiasts seeking elegant pre- or post-performance meals. The acoustics can be challenging when the restaurant is crowded, distracting diners from the piano music.
California cuisine is served with French flair, as in the duck confit salad, with butter pears, huckleberries, and candied walnuts. The excellent but expensive wine list highlights the major growing regions of the world.

Little Star Pizza

B2 Pizza

846 Divisadero St. (bet. Fulton & McAllister Sts.)

Phone: 415-441-1118 Dinner Tue – Sun
Web: www.littlestarpizza.com
Prices: ⓢⓢ

As far as pizza goes, New Yorkers and Chicagoans may hold fast to their hometown loyalties, but once they take their first bite of a Little Star pizza, the debate will likely turn to thick versus thin crust—both of which are on the menu here. The Classic deep-dish (sausage, mushrooms, green peppers, and onions) is always a favorite, but lovers of thin crust find their nirvana in the likes of roasted chicken and basil pesto atop a crispy, flakey cornmeal crust.

The dimly lit dining room is always packed, where high decibels prevail against the jukebox. Expect waits during prime time, so consider ordering ahead and taking a pie to-go.

The on-site ATM takes any inconvenience out of the cash-only policy, but there is no helping the tough parking situation.

Nopa

B2 Californian 

560 Divisadero St. (at Hayes St.)

Phone: 415-864-8643 Dinner nightly
Web: www.nopasf.com
Prices: $$

When it opened in 2006, this much-lauded Cal-Med eatery not only revived a neighborhood landmark—a lofty 1920s bank that had fallen into disrepair—it resuscitated the neighborhood itself. Suddenly the residential pocket vaguely known as North of the Panhandle became NoPa, a trendy destination for cross-city hipsters hungry for the latest thing. With a fierce devotion to organic, farm-fresh fare, Nopa dishes such easy crowd-pleasers as an Early Girl tomato salad and a country pork chop wood-fired in the brick oven.

Despite the enormity of the space, which boasts a crowded mezzanine and whimsical local art, Nopa is hailed for friendly service and a boisterous vibe: The after-work crowd shares generous portions at the congenial communal table.

Nopalito

Mexican

B2

306 Broderick St. (at Fell St.)

Phone: 415-437-0303 — Lunch & dinner daily
Web: www.nopalitosf.com
Prices:

Is it a zesty edible cactus? Or, little sister to neighboring Nopa? In name, Nopalito is a double entendre, but the ambiguity stops there.

With vibrant Mexican cuisine served in a mellow space, Nopalito's intent is clear: quality food, no strings attached. Organic décor and walls the shade of salsa verde set an unfussy backdrop for family-friendly meals handcrafted with local, sustainable goods. Start with kicky fried chickpeas on the house, followed by thick *totopos*—corn chips tossed with *chile de arbol* salsa and homemade *cotija* cheese.

A seasonal adobo sturgeon taco, washed down with hibiscus-blood orange soda, makes for a rewarding lunch; while a bowl of posole *rojo*, enjoyed on the heated patio, is a belly-warming cap to a night.

Otoro

Japanese

C2

205 Oak St. (at Gough St.)

Phone: 415-553-3986 — Lunch Mon – Sat, Dinner nightly
Web: www.otorosushi.com
Prices: $$

As any sushi aficionado knows, *otoro* is the Japanese term for the prized yet scarce, melt-in-your-mouth cut of tuna belly that is rich in fat and healthful omega-3 fatty acids. At this tiny new Hayes Valley sushi spot, *otoro* is featured among a wide range of raw, composed, and hot dishes.

Nosh on a plate of perfectly browned gyoza dumplings while checking out the dry-erase board behind the sushi counter for unusual seasonal offerings, such as seared hamachi belly and monkfish liver pâté. Or, feel free to get creative and suggest your own sushi roll ideas here.

A good selection of sake lines the shelves by the entrance, but if you are new to the field of rice wine, rest assured that the list here is well-illustrated and explained for novices.

Pagolac

D1 — Vietnamese

655 Larkin St. (at Ellis St.)

Phone: 415-776-3234 — Dinner Tue – Sun
Web: N/A
Prices: ⊜

San Francisco's Tenderloin district demands quality restaurants like Pagolac to lure folks to this less savory area. The owners of this tiny and very popular family-run business clearly pour their hearts into both the service and the fresh, vibrant Vietnamese food.

The weathered pink awning may not seem enticing, but once inside you'll be embraced by the friendly staff and captivated by the good food at bargain-basement prices. Do-it-yourself cooking and tableside dining are taken to the next level with the "7 Flavors of Beef," a multicourse feast that you prepare using tabletop firepots and a grill—delicious, unforgettable, and just plain fun. The kitchen is equally happy to oblige those seeking less hands-on eating, with claypots and noodle bowls.

Patxi's

C2 — Pizza

511 Hayes St. (bet. Laguna & Octavia Sts.)

Phone: 415-558-9991 — Dinner Tue – Sun
Web: www.patxispizza.com
Prices: $$

Fans of local deep-dish, Chicago-style pizza may draw comparisons, but owner Patxi (say PAH-cheese) Aspiroz's pies are among the city's best.

These hefty Chicago-style pies are stuffed with cheese and your choice of toppings, slathered with tangy (vegan-friendly) tomato sauce atop a rich, two-inch-deep crust. Try "The Californian" featuring low-fat mozzarella, red onions, and spinach over a whole wheat crust; or go for "build your own" toppings on a thin (or extra thin) crisp, cornmeal-crust pie.

Though often loud, the unadorned atmosphere is always family friendly, attended by an eclectic, courteous staff. However, these deep-dish pies can take up to 40 minutes to prepare, so call ahead to pre-order your pizza—or bring patient children.

paul k

Mediterranean XX

C2

199 Gough St. (at Oak St.)

Phone: 415-552-7132 — Lunch Sat – Sun
Web: www.paulkrestaurant.com — Dinner Tue – Sun
Prices: $$

No matter how it is spelled, paul k (an abbreviation for the owner's last name, Kavouksorian) amounts to a trendy stage on which dinner performs nightly; brunch makes a weekend cameo with "bottomless" bloody Marys and mimosas to accompany your smoked lox Benedict. Kavouksorian himself directs the well-choreographed service in the intimate dining room, conveniently located near the Opera House in Hayes Valley.

An array of small plates celebrate Mediterranean, North African, and Armenian heritage in meze of lamb riblets, kebabs, baba ganoush, cucumbers, olives, feta, and yogurt. *Za'atar* (a Middle Eastern herb and spice mix), sumac, and pomegranates are just a few of the more exotic ingredients that co-star with chicken, lamb, and Syrian-spiced duck.

Poleng

A2

1751 Fulton St. (bet. Central & Masonic Aves.)

Phone: 415-441-1751 — Dinner Tue – Sun
Web: www.polenglounge.com
Prices: 

Among NoPa's encroaching marine layer and fading Victorians, a table at Poleng Lounge is a spontaneous passage to the Orient. What region of the Orient isn't quite clear—the décor is Balinese, teas hail from Laos and beyond, and the cuisine is mostly Philippine with a bit of Japanese heritage. But with funky batiks, live palms, and plasma TVs to guide you through terrains from Kuala Lumpur to Machu Picchu, dinner here is a magical mystery tour.

Small plates travel the Asian culinary landscape, from heirloom tomato poke to seared scallop *katsu* and sweet potato fries with banana ketchup. Dine on the late side and stay for a dance: Poleng Lounge lives up to its clubby name when young hipsters converge for tea-infused cocktails and DJ beats after 10:00 P.M.

rnm

American

C2

598 Haight St. (at Steiner St.)

Phone: 415-551-7900 Dinner Tue – Sat
Web: www.rnmrestaurant.com
Prices: $$

Named after Chef/owner Justine Miner's late father, Robert, rnm is a swanky urban spot and culinary diamond in the edgy Lower Haight.

Both the courteous, professional staff and the chef justly honor her father in rnm's creative menu of carefully crafted small plates, celebrating influences of Italy and France. A handful of artisanal pizzas, perhaps topped with wild mushrooms, caramelized onions, fontina, and truffle oil, hold their own against small plates like lobster and mascarapone ravioli with Meyer lemon beurre blanc, or a Parisian-style tuna tartare.

Sophisticated yet unpretentious, the interior features a shimmering stainless steel bar where diners can select a creative cocktail on their way into the warm, inviting main or mezzanine dining space.

Sauce

American

C2

131 Gough St. (bet. Oak & Page Sts.)

Phone: 415-252-1369 Dinner nightly
Web: www.saucesf.com
Prices: $$

In the lively performing arts district, where such dramatic acts as Jardinière and Zuni Café share the stage, Sauce is a quieter number that prefers substance to style. The dining room may be decades overdue for decorating, but the laid-back, old wooden bar and hearty American menu—accented by some lighter, California-style choices—lures a consistent group of neighborhood regulars. Offerings may range from refreshing and savory white peach salad to bacon-wrapped meatloaf.

The kitchen is open until midnight daily, so even late-night snackers can pop in for a "PB&J"—sponge cake layered with strawberry preserves, Frangelico peanut butter, and vanilla ice cream. The bar is open till 2:00 A.M., making Sauce a hit for post-theater nightcaps.

Sebo

Japanese

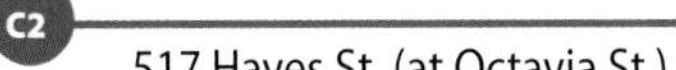

C2

517 Hayes St. (at Octavia St.)

Phone: 415-864-2122 Dinner Tue – Sun
Web: www.sebosf.com
Prices: **$$$**

Serving a great variety of rarely offered fish, including seasonal and sustainably raised seafood, Sebo wins big in Hayes Valley for artfully presented sushi and sashimi. Try to get one of the six seats at the sushi bar in the back of the room and trust your meal to the chefs, who will be happy to describe the evening's fresh catch displayed in a case between the two work stations. The menu lists a different selection of remarkably buttery, delicate sashimi each night, but the wisest gourmets request an entire, personalized omakase. This allows guests to taste the freshest and most delicious cuts of fish as well as maki and hot dishes.

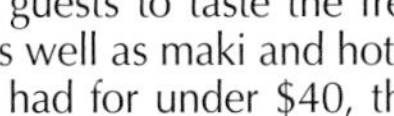

While a meal can be had for under $40, the little portions add up quickly if you are not careful.

Thep Phanom

Thai

C2

400 Waller St. (at Fillmore St.)

Phone: 415-431-2526 Dinner nightly
Web: www.thepphanom.com
Prices: **$$**

Founded in 1986, this little place delivers big flavors. The extensive menu stays true to what the restaurant bills as "authentic Thai cuisine," but also leaves the kitchen leeway to be creative. Thus, the standards like Massaman and Panang curries and pad Thai appear along with "Thaitanic" beef (a spicy stir-fry with a crunch of string beans and green peppers), and "Three's Company" (prawns, scallops and calamari in coconut sauce). The "dancing," "weeping," and "crying" ladies referred to on the Favorites menu are all edible and delicious.

Warmly lit and furnished with simple wood chairs and cloth-covered tables, the small dining room fills up fast. The bar in the back of the room usually bustles with locals coming 'round to pick up carry-out fare.

1300 on Fillmore

American XXX

1300 Fillmore St. (at Eddy St.)

Phone: 415-771-7100 — Lunch Sun
Web: www.1300Fillmore.com — Dinner nightly
Prices: $$$

Here in the Fillmore Jazz Preservation District, Chef David Lawrence plays his own riffs on soul food in a high-brow setting.

Astutely harmonizing his British upbringing and Jamaican ancestry with a touch of southern comfort, the menu features barbecued shrimp tossed in a chopped tomato, onion, and bacon gravy served atop creamy, well seasoned, grits; or silky banana cream pie, with a crisp, flaky pastry shell and delicately balanced lime-caramel sauce. Sides like cornmeal fried okra bring it all down home, without being too heavy.

The serene dining room boasts dark hues under high ceilings. The handsome lounge is a photographic homage to bygone decades when this neighborhood hosted jazz greats Billie Holliday, Duke Ellington, and Dizzy Gillespie.

Yoshi's

Japanese XX

C1

1330 Fillmore St. (at Eddy St.)

Phone: 415-655-5600 — Dinner nightly
Web: www.yoshis.com
Prices: $$$

Music is ringing out again in this Fillmore Street district once known as the Harlem of the West, thanks in part to the Fillmore Heritage Center. At the core of this $72-million structure is the second location of Yoshi's, the restaurant/jazz club that debuted in Oakland more than 30 years ago.

World-class jazz bring patrons to the bi-level amphitheater, but Chef Shotaro Kamio's seasonal riffs on Japanese cuisine merit attention in their own right. Kamio artfully plays with top-quality fish and superb presentations in a hamachi sampler: toro, tartare, carpaccio, and smoked hamachi. The large, well-appointed display kitchen adds vibrance to the sleek, upscale setting. Of course, the waiters will hustle things along if you're holding concert tickets.

Zuni Café

Mediterranean XX

D2

1658 Market St. (bet. Franklin & Gough Sts.)

Phone: 415-552-2522 — Lunch & dinner Tue – Sun
Web: www.zunicafe.com
Prices: **$$**

If you haven't idled away an afternoon slurping oysters and sipping Champagne in a sunny window seat at venerable Zuni Café, you've never lived in San Francisco. A fixture since 1979 and evocative of a European eatery, Zuni remains at the height of local fashion. A recent face-lift made the split-level interior all the more inviting—the revamped mezzanine offers a delicious view.

Serving largely sustainable, ingredient-driven fare, Chef/owner Judy Rodgers seasons her Mediterranean menu with a pinch of California: the rosemary focaccia burger is a favorite; roast chicken is practically famous; and Serrano ham garnished with goat cheese-stuffed black mission figs is divine. On weekends, denim-clad revelers sip aperitifs at the long, copper bar.

Do not confuse X with ✿! X defines comfort, while ✿ are awarded for the best cuisine. Stars are awarded across all categories of comfort.

Financial District

Embarcadero • Union Square

Though San Francisco may be famed for its laid-back image, its bustling business district is ranked among the top financial centers in the nation. On weekdays, streetcars, pedestrians, and wildly tattooed bicycle messengers clog the streets of the triangle bounded by Kearny, Jackson, and Market streets. Lines snake out the doors of the better grab-and-go sandwich shops and salad bars at lunch; both day and night, a host of fine-dining restaurants in this quarter cater to clients with expense accounts. Along Market Street, casual cafés and chain restaurants focus on tourists and shoppers.

Despite all that the area has to offer, its greatest culinary treasures may be within the Ferry Building. This 1898 steel-reinforced sandstone structure was among the few survivors

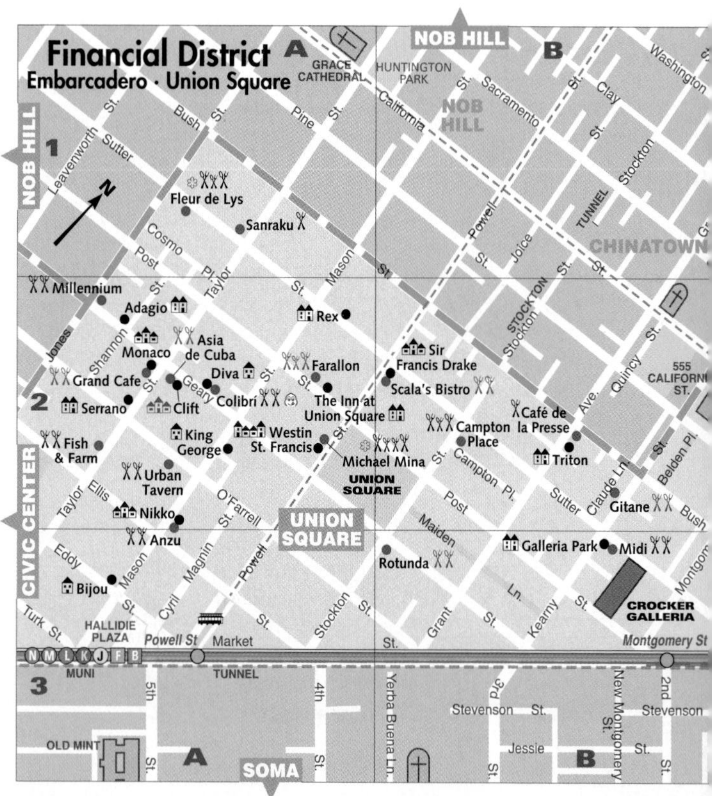

of the 1906 earthquake and fire that destroyed most of the area. It remains a clear neighborhood standout, easily recognized by its 244-foot clock tower rising from Market Street above the waterfront promenade known as the Embarcadero ("boarding place" in Spanish). Renovated in 2004, its soaring interior arcade now makes an architecturally stunning culinary showcase for local and artisanal foods, fine Chinese teas, and everything in between. Known as the **Ferry Building Marketplace,** this is a true foodie pilgrimage.

The marketplace strives to support the local and artisanal food community by highlighting small regional producers. Among these, two of the most popular are the acclaimed **Cowgirl Creamery** farmstead cheeses and the organic breads of Berkeley's **Acme Bread Company.** Discover exotic, organic mushrooms, medicinals, and themed products at **Far West Fungi.** Patient enthusiasts can even purchase logs on which to grow their own harvest. The legendary **Frog Hollow Farms** also has an outpost here, offering luscious seasonal fruit as well as organic chutneys and marmalades. **Rechiutti Confections** elevates

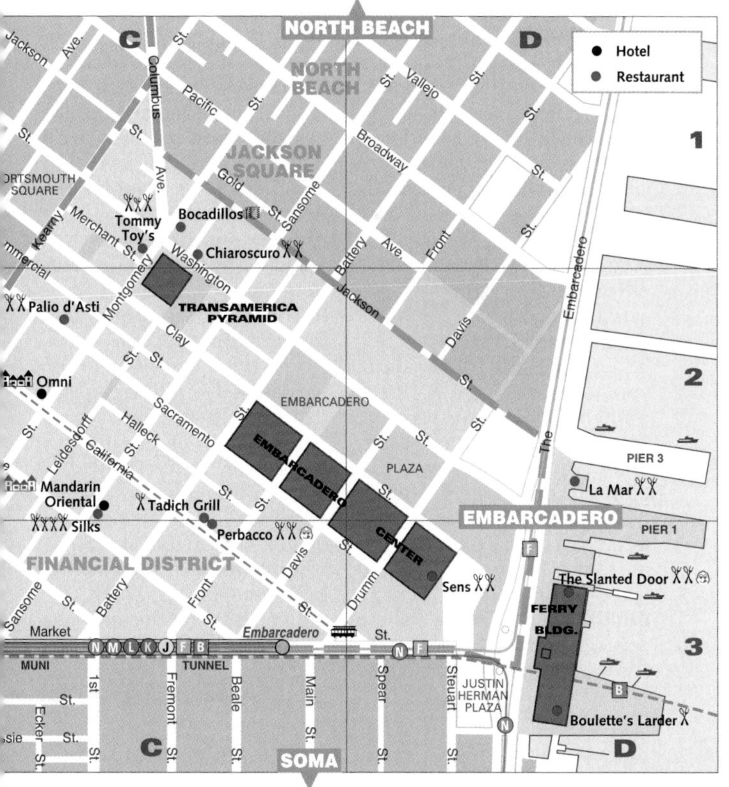

the art of crafting Parisian-style chocolates and caramels to a level that can only be described as heavenly.

Even the retail offerings are food-themed here, with a number of cookware shops and home-design boutiques with northern California flair. **Sur la Table** is among the larger purveyors and remains a favorite for tools of the trade. **The Gardner** focuses on gifts of handmade ceramics or linens that bring artistry to any tabletop.

While this world-class food shopping may whet the appetite, more immediate satisfaction can be found in the building's many casual dining spots. **DELICA rf-1** offers beautifully prepared Japanese fusion foods, from signature sushi rolls to savory croquettes. Grab a seat with the FiDi lunch crowds filling the picnic tables at **Mijita**—run by Traci Des Jardins of Jardinière—to enjoy some Oaxacan chicken tamales or Baja-style fish tacos. Or, take a stool at the bar of the **Hog Island Oyster Company**, whose fresh bivalves are plucked from the Tomales Bay in Marin County—this is a great spot to sit, slurp, and take in the view. For a refined indulgence, visit the **Tsar Nicoulai Caviar Café**, offering a robust selection of caviar to enjoy at the counter with champagne or bring home for more solitary pleasure. Still perhaps the most decadent takeout option may be from **Boccalone Salumeria**, where one can find a full selection of charcuterie that are available for purchase by the platter, pound, or layered in a single-serving "cone" for an unapologetically carnivorous treat.

On Tuesday and Saturday mornings, join the chefs and crowds at the **Ferry Plaza Farmers Market** for organic produce, mouth-watering baked goods, fresh pasta, and more. On market days, stands and tents fill the sidewalk in front of the building and rear plaza that overlooks the bay.

Across from the Ferry Building, the five office towers of the Embarcadero Center span five blocks in the heart of the commercial district. Hordes of FiDi office workers head here to get their mid-day shopping fix in the sprawling three-story indoor mall and to grab a quick lunch in one of the complex's 30-some eateries, which range from chain restaurants to little noodle shops. Here you'll also find two longtime local favorites, **See's Candies** and **Peet's Coffee.**

Any serious shopper in San Francisco makes a pilgrimage to Union Square, the area bordering the formal park (named on the eve of the Civil War) on the FiDi's western edge. Here, upscale department stores like Saks and Neiman Marcus preside over the square. While fashionistas flock to the designers, foodies come for the area's profusion of gourmet restaurants. Eateries in this area are also favored by drama lovers, since they are conveniently located near some of the city's most beloved theaters.

Anzu

Fusion XX

222 Mason St. (bet. Ellis & O'Farrell Sts.)

Phone: 415-394-1100 Lunch & dinner daily
Web: www.restaurantanzu.com
Prices: $$$

Set on the second floor of the Hotel Nikko, Anzu exhibits a minimalist style indicative of Japanese elegance. A lounge area with a long granite bar greets guests, while in the small dining room, low ceilings and a 10-seat sushi bar create an intimate feel.

At lunch, sandwiches and salads hold sway, in addition to a smattering of Asian noodle and seafood selections. In the evening, Anzu breaks out the linens and the raw fish. The kitchen brings new life to hamachi *crudo* with grapefruit, jalapeños, cilantro, and grapefruit-ginger vinaigrette; as well as to hot dishes such as *shiso*- and garlic-crusted rack of lamb.

The hotel validates parking for up to four hours, so you have time to dine and take in a show at one of the nearby theaters.

Asia de Cuba

Fusion XX

495 Geary St. (at Taylor St.)

Phone: 415-929-2300 Lunch & dinner daily
Web: www.chinagrillmanagement.com
Prices: $$$

Just beyond the dramatic lobby of the Clift Hotel, Asia de Cuba dovetails glamorously into its hip environs. Philippe Stark dreamed up this sultry setting, wrapped in soft light from hand-blown Murano glass lamps. Oversized horseshoe-shaped, pebbled-leather booths sit in each corner of the room, and tall arched windows rise above the glitziest communal table in town. Shaped like a cross, this dazzling centerpiece is made from hand-etched Venetian mirrors.

A patchwork of Asian and Latin preparations, the menu might fuse Hoisin duck tacos with kimchi slaw and *pico de gallo*; or miso-cured Alaskan butterfish with Cuban black beans and tempura *shishito* peppers.

Party on in the adjacent Redwood Room, a favorite late-night bar scene.

Bocadillos

C1

710 Montgomery St. (at Washington St.)

Phone: 415-982-2622 Lunch Mon – Fri
Web: www.bocasf.com Dinner Mon – Sat
Prices:

A brick wall painted the color of *piment d'espelette* (a spice made from dried red Basque peppers) illuminated by mounted votives, micro-tiled floors, and a bar running the room's periphery, foster a rustic-meets-metropolitan vibe. The name—Spanish for "little sandwiches"—aptly describes the menu, which focuses on big flavors in bantam sandwiches and tapas. Skillful combinations include chorizo with walnut spread and parsley, or Catalan sausage with arugula and shaved Manchego.

Evenings showcase Chef Gerald Hirigoyen's delectable tapas that stay true to the Spanish traditions, as in prawns with garlic and lemon confit; or oxtail *"tempranillo"* with spring onions. Groups should aim for the communal table near the entrance for conversation's sake.

Boulette's Larder

Californian

D3

1 Ferry Building (at The Embarcadero)

Phone: 415-399-1155 Lunch Sun – Fri
Web: www.bouletteslarder.com
Prices: $$

Think of this little retail business in the Ferry Building as a foodie's version of an apothecary. Here discover everything from wild Italian fennel and rose petal sugar, to lobster stock or squab sauce—and don't forget to pick up Japanese specialty items like bamboo charcoal and freeze-dried yuzu. Beside the esoteric ingredients (pine needle syrup, anyone?), there are composed salads by the pound, soups by the quart, and mouthwatering pastries.

At breakfast, lunch, and Sunday brunch (the only meals served), eat at either the communal kitchen counter or at tables just outside in the busy hall. Choose the former to watch the chefs prepare a daily changing roster of dishes from local, organic, sustainably-raised products—right before your eyes.

Café de la Presse

French 

B2

352 Grant Ave. (at Bush St.)

Phone: 415-398-2680 Lunch & dinner daily
Web: www.cafedelapresse.com
Prices: $$

From the breakfast *crêpes à l'Americaines* (buttermilk pancakes) to a dinner of *coquilles St. Jacques*, everything here is served with French accents. The rattan chairs surrounding marble bistro tables, Gallic staff, patrons consumed in French conversations, and international newsstands authentically compliment the classic bistro fare. Everything here is true to the restaurant's Parisian theme. Naturally, the menu follows suit with classics such as a savory quiche Lorraine; daily specials of *moules frites* or steak tartare; and *pots de crèmes* for dessert.

Run by Chef Laurent Manrique, the café profits from its location on a busy corner across from the Chinatown gate and next to the Hotel Triton—for which it supplies room service.

Campton Place

Contemporary 

B2

340 Stockton St. (bet. Post & Sutter Sts.)

Phone: 415-955-5555 Lunch & dinner daily
Web: www.camptonplacesf.com
Prices: $$$$

Dressed in shades of gold and punctuated by a blooming blown-glass centerpiece, this fine dining room lures socialites to its sleek leather booths. With sinless service and a divine wine culture steered by master sommelier Richard Dean, Campton Place is a culinary mythos.

Chef Srijith Gopinathan commands this artistic kitchen, inside the eponymous hotel near Union Square. Marrying the spice scents of his Southern Indian line with Euro-Californian nuances, his cuisine gallivants the globe. An elaborate prix-fixe dinner offers a sublime dining experience, starring eggplant caponata draped in a creamy basil emulsion and perfect cuttlefish curls; the black cod "Juan Arzak" trickled with a salsa verde; and a sinfully rich "ivorie" chocolate-foie gras ganache.

Chiaroscuro

C1

Italian XX

550 Washington St. (bet. Montgomery & Sansome Sts.)

Phone: 415-362-6012 — Lunch Mon – Fri
Web: www.chiaroscurosf.com — Dinner Mon – Sat
Prices: $$

Poured concrete banquettes softened with snowy pillows put a modern spin on the antique art term for which this *ristorante* is named. Translated as "light and dark," Chiaroscuro's stark white walls and sleek design are illuminated by a flame crackling in the open kitchen, where Roman-style house-made pastas are an artistic achievement. No sense in choosing a favorite: The *trilogia* inspires with tastes of carbonara, *amatriciana,* and pesto *Trapanese*. Carb-conscious diners may opt for olive oil pan-fried chicken or white truffle-scented quail hugged by pancetta.

With a view of the iconic Transamerica building and genuine Italian hospitality, perhaps the real darkness of Chiaroscuro lies in its desserts: The Fuji apple *torta di miele* is exquisitely wicked.

Colibrí

A2

Mexican XX

438 Geary St (bet. Mason & Taylor Sts.)

Phone: 415-440-2737 — Lunch & dinner daily
Web: www.colibrimexicanbistro.com
Prices: $$

Sunny colors, wrought-iron detailing, and wagon-wheel chandeliers bring the soul of colonial Mexico alive in this pleasant bistro. Begin your sojourn at the long tequila bar, where you can catch a vintage Latino movie (with subtitles) while you sip a hand-shaken margarita.

In the cozy dining room, skillfully prepared dishes (*mole poblano* served over chicken; tender marinated pork *carnitas*; pan-seared catch of the day) can be accompanied by sides ranging from *frijoles negros* to a savory *torta* made with cornbread and *chile pasilla*.

Weekend brunch spotlights creative fare such as *huevos ahogados* (eggs baked in a clay pot with tomato-serrano sauce, *panela* cheese, and cactus leaves), as well as more traditional Mexican offerings.

Farallon

Seafood XXX

A2

450 Post St. (bet. Mason & Powell Sts.)

Phone: 415-956-6969 — Dinner nightly
Web: www.farallonrestaurant.com
Prices: $$$

Named for the national wildlife refuge that covers a string of islands off the coast, this undersea fantasy, created in 1997 by Chef Mark Franz and restaurant designer Pat Kuleto, is located near Union Square area shops and theaters. Much of the drama lies inside the restaurant, swimming with flamboyant jellyfish chandeliers, glowing kelp-like columns, scallop-shaped booths, and a school of other aquatic elements.

Move away from the capricious yet classy design to discover true savoir faire in seafood such as a warm Mediterranean octopus confit sprinkled with *fleur de sel*, fresh thyme, and drizzled with fruity olive oil; or crispy seared *branzino* served with truffle-flecked potato ravioli, accompanied by braised leeks and maitake mushrooms.

Fish & Farm

American XX

A2

339 Taylor St. (bet. Ellis & O'Farrell Sts.)

Phone: 415-474-3474 — Dinner Mon – Sat
Web: www.fishandfarmsf.com
Prices: $$

A chef change and mild spiffing up of the dining room has breathed new life into this attractive spot, its narrow space flanked by chocolate-brown leather banquettes and marble tables.

Chef Chad Newton carries on the menu of organic produce and sustainably-raised meat and seafood—all sourced from a 100-mile radius of the restaurant when possible. The likes of a Southern fried Petaluma chicken with cornbread madeleines, and Liberty ale-battered fish and chips made with local cod sing the praises of American products.

One caveat: the valet parking option is only for guests of the adjacent Hotel Mark Twain, so if you're not staying there, you'll have to hunt down your own parking space. The happy hour featuring bites like bacon tater tots is a sheer treat!

Fleur de Lys ✿

French XXX

A1

777 Sutter St. (bet. Jones & Taylor Sts.)

Phone: 415-673-7779 Dinner Tue – Sat
Web: www.fleurdelyssf.com
Prices: **$$$$**

Bill Milne

With a ceiling tented in patterned textile, heavy draperies, indulgent florals, and a grand Murano glass chandelier, Fleur de Lys feels like something from another time and world—perhaps a bit faded in years. Nonetheless, this is an opulent gem. An expert staff has gracious command of the sumptuous dining room, where well-to-do patrons of a certain age and beaming young celebrants enjoy roomy, luxuriant tables.

Everyone here is clearly delighting in the flourish of Fleur de Lys, both in the décor and on the plate. This is, of course, the domain of Chef/owner Hubert Keller, whose excellent Alsatian-style cooking makes good use of pastry technique and Californian flair. Superbly roasted sea bass with olive jus and spicy artichoke is simply perfect, while the Dungeness crab salad, served with caviar, goat cheese, beets, and lobster-infused vinaigrette, is complex and artistically plated. Ornately crafted *mignardises,* from *tuiles* to truffles, offer a sweetly decadent ending.

While the wine list boasts an alluring selection of French and North American vintages, tableside absinthe service, presented in an old-fashioned fountain, puts a touch of bohemian panache into date night.

Gitane

B2

6 Claude Ln. (bet. Bush & Sutter Sts.)

Phone: 415-788-6686 — Dinner Tue – Sat
Web: www.gitanerestaurant.com
Prices: $$

Named for its gypsy spirit, Gitane cooks up a sultry atmosphere in a whimsical multi-level space. It's a much sought-after reservation, so book ahead, and request a table in the avant-garde, hip, and eclectic dining room, which sports a relaxed lounge feel.

Wandering from the Basque country of Spain to the sands of Morocco, Gitane's menu brings together exotic spices and far-flung culinary techniques to the delight of its stylish diners. *Piquillo* peppers stuffed with Dungeness crab pay homage to the former, while a tajine of chicken baked with prunes and vegetables in a piquant cumin- and cinnamon-laced broth transports patrons to North Africa.

Besides their inventive cocktails, Gitane also boasts a respectable selection of sherry and Madeira.

Grand Cafe

French

A2

501 Geary St. (at Taylor St.)

Phone: 415-292-0101 — Lunch & dinner daily
Web: www.grandcafe-sf.com
Prices: $$

"Grand" surely fills the bill given the elegant ambience of this restored turn-of-the-20th-century ballroom in the Hotel Monaco. Art deco splendor abounds, from the whimsical bronze sculptures to the soaring columns and the ornate gilded ceiling.

France provides the inspiration for the cuisine, which the kitchen executes with delicious results. For dinner, roasted wild Chinook salmon may be paired with creamy Brussels sprouts and a julienne of winter vegetables; while duck "coq au vin," cassoulet, and bœuf Bourguignon fill in the Gallic classics. Bistro fare makes a good showing at lunchtime too, between creative pizzas, salads, and steak frites.

Just inside the Geary Street entrance, adjoining Petite Café serves a bar menu all day.

La Mar

Peruvian XX

D2

Pier 1 1/2 (at The Embarcadero)

Phone: 415-397-8880 — Lunch & dinner daily
Web: www.lamarsf.com
Prices: $$

Pisco cocktails and adventurous ceviches are de rigueur at this Pier One-and-a-Half *cebicheria Peruana*, with Bay views and a waterfront breeze on the patio. From Latin American culinary star Gaston Acurio, who owns 10 eateries south of the Tropic of Cancer, La Mar is the chef's first North American foray. A vivacious interior complements the exotic cuisine, which begins with crisp vegetable chips and creamy salsas on the house. *Cebiche mixto* is a spicy, well-balanced mingling of mahi mahi, calamari, and octopus with red onion, Peruvian corn, and yam.

Other delicacies include a tasting of four *causas*—whipped potato cakes, artistically presented—and *aji de Gallina*—a tender chicken stew with *aji Amarillo*, a fruity yellow pepper indigenous to Peru.

Midi

Californian XX

B3

185 Sutter St. (at Kearny St.)

Phone: 415-835-6400 — Lunch Mon – Fri
Web: www.midisanfrancisco.com — Dinner Mon – Sat
Prices: $$

Snappy professionals and professional shoppers flock to see-and-be-seen lunches of tartines, fresh salads, and virgin spritzers at Midi, the sleek hot spot midway between the Financial District and Union Square. The dining room is business chic, with streamlined wood fixtures, leather and chrome accents, alongside pinstriped banquettes. The design, however, is rendered with balance: Pops of hot pink and a flirty, floral mural lend feminine mystique and a certain joie de vivre.

Chef Michelle Mah's seasonal menu offers fresh, Californian bistro fare. The "Midi quartet" makes a stylish lunch at less than $20, while seasonal dinners may include pan-roasted cod or braised spring lamb. For dessert, the bittersweet chocolate mousse is a decadent must.

Michael Mina ✿

Contemporary XXXX

A2

335 Powell St. (bet. Geary & Post Sts.)

Phone: 415-397-9222 Dinner Tue – Sat
Web: www.michaelmina.net
Prices: **$$$$**

Mina Group

Maybe it's fighting your way through the hoi polloi that packs Union Square nightly, or winding your way through the lobby of the outstanding—but equally thumping—Westin St. Francis hotel, but one step into Michael Mina's sophisticated dining room, with its mile-high columns and balcony overlooking the lobby, and you feel it. You, glamorous thing, have arrived.

Of course, so has everyone else. And most nights of the week, you'll find a well-heeled crowd pouring over Mina's impressive wine list, teeming with excellent Californian and French varietals, or being tended to by the polished waitstaff. Mina's signature move here is to do one ingredient, three ways—and his entire menu, carefully prepared by Chef de Cuisine, Chris L'Hommedieu, is set up in trios.

The menu changes often, but might kick off with a super-fresh Dungeness crab rendered three ways—an elegant, three-bite dish of tender poached claw meat, served over endive dressed with garlicky aïoli; whole legs roasted in butter and seasoned with *espelette* peppers, served shell-on alongside a small cup of fragrant broth; and a modern cioppino, an Italian fish stew with backfin meat and tinkerbell peppers.

Millennium

Vegan XX

A2

580 Geary St. (at Jones St.)

Phone: 415-345-3900 — Dinner nightly
Web: www.millenniumrestaurant.com
Prices: $$

Many cultures influence Millennium's vegan cuisine, which bursts with flavor and creativity. A black bean torte with caramelized plantains, pumpkin-honey *papazul*, and English pea samosa may hail from different parts of the world, but all are masterfully made at the hands of Chef Eric Tucker. Even tried and true carnivores trade their steaks for tofu here inside the Hotel California, where the friendly staff is eager to offer advice about the area's best organic markets. Dishes are so tasty that this place is packed most nights, so reserving ahead is advised. Otherwise, hope for a seat at the first-come, first-served bar counter.

Any budget woes will be soothed by the three-course Frugal Foodie menu, offered each Sunday through Wednesday night.

Palio d'Asti

Italian XX

C2

640 Sacramento St. (bet. Kearny & Montgomery Sts.)

Phone: 415-395-9800 — Lunch & dinner Mon – Fri
Web: www.paliodasti.com
Prices: $$$

Colorful banners and coats of arms parade throughout this dining room, commemorating the famed bareback horse race that has been run each year since the 13th century in the Piazza Alfieri in Asti, Italy. Massive concrete pillars in this 1907 building take on a medieval look of their own, while a tiny bar near the entrance pours both Italian and Californian varietals.

The menu celebrates different regions of Italy, depending on the season. Main courses might run from fluffy gnocchi with roasted Muscovy duck to roasted Alaskan halibut with ratatouille. A freewheeling crowd comes in at happy hour for complimentary brick-oven pizzas.

Those in a hurry can grab a panini to-go at the two sister Palio Cafés, nearby at 505 Montgomery Street, or on campus at UCSF.

Perbacco

Italian

230 California St. (bet. Battery & Front Sts.)

Phone: 415-955-0663 — Lunch Mon – Fri
Web: www.perbaccosf.com — Dinner Mon – Sat
Prices: $$

By day, FiDi power-lunchers chew on trade lingo and excellent house-cured *salumi*, diplaying expert craftsmanship and quality. Come evening, the Carrara marble bar buzzes with professional types unwinding over Italian wine and snacks. Over dinner, well-bred couples cozy up at a quiet mezzanine table and share Northern Italian-style seasonal pastas, such as pappardelle with golden chanterelles, sweet corn, and tender *guanciale*.

Whether your purpose is business or romance, pleasure is the heart of Perbacco, whose name means "Good Times" in tribute to the Roman god of vino. Chef Staffan Terje's artisanal cuisine hails from Liguria and Piemonte, with a nod to Provence, and is refreshingly finished by such simple desserts as Meyer lemon semifreddo.

Rotunda

Californian

150 Stockton St. (at Geary St.)

Phone: 415-362-4777 — Lunch daily
Web: www.neimanmarcus.com
Prices: $$$

Upon entering Neiman Marcus from Union Square, cast your eyes skyward to the four-story Belle Époque rotunda. This marvelous architectural opus once crowned the City of Paris department store was built in 1908 on this site. Highlighted in cream and gold with gilded carvings of Poseidon, the soaring oval stained-glass dome bears a nautical theme. The eponymous restaurant that sits under the rotunda looks down on Union Square through large windows.

At midday, Rotunda overflows with well-heeled ladies who lunch; the light menu of American fare caters to their tastes, while the upscale prices aim at the credit cards in their designer bags. Count on a complimentary taste of chicken consommé to begin, along with puffy turnovers paired with strawberry butter.

Sanraku

A1 — **Japanese**

704 Sutter St. (at Taylor St.)

Phone: 415-771-0803 — Lunch Mon – Sat
Web: www.sanraku.com — Dinner nightly
Prices: ⊜

Regulars rave about this sushi spot, which stands out for its fresh fish in the neighborhood around Union Square. Simplicity is the keynote here, where a white wall cut out to form irregular columns divides the dining space from the sushi bar.

Smiling sushi chefs make conversation while they craft high-quality seafood into maki, *nigiri*, and sashimi. For those who want a break from raw fish, the menu also offers a long list of cooked dishes including teriyaki, tempura, udon, and *donburi*. The best bargains at either lunch or dinner are the combination meals.

If you're wandering around SoMa, visit Sanraku's little sister at Metreon, where video gamers meet sushi lovers in an airy space overlooking Yerba Buena Gardens.

Scala's Bistro

B2 — **Italian**

432 Powell St. (bet. Post & Sutter Sts.)

Phone: 415-395-8555 — Lunch & dinner daily
Web: www.scalasbistro.com
Prices: **$$**

Historic charm radiates from this casually elegant bistro, adjacent to the venerable Sir Francis Drake Hotel a block off bustling Union Square. Classy without being stuffy, Scala's conjures the best of the Old World, with tuxedo-clad servers, original murals, and an art deco ceiling.

An open kitchen in back provides a pale brick backdrop dangling with ornamental antique copper cookware. Chef Jennifer Biesty, of *Top Chef* fame and formerly of Coco500, infuses Italian country with Californian flair in *mezzaluna* ravioli stuffed with braised lamb *agrodolce*. On the lighter side, *pizzette* show creativity in toppings like French butter pears, balsamic onions, gorgonzola, and rosemary.

Mini portions of selected desserts allow a last sweet bite.

Sens

Mediterranean XX

D3

4 Embarcadero Center (Sacramento St. at Drumm St.)

Phone: 415-362-0645 — Lunch Mon – Fri
Web: www.sens-sf.com — Dinner Mon – Sat
Prices: $$$

Part of a six-building complex, 4 Embarcadero Center is the tallest—at 45 stories—of its kind. Visit the promenade level for a meal at Sens, the cavernous restaurant that showcases faux-alligator-skin armchairs, flagstone walls, and wood-beamed ceilings draped with fabric. Perhaps best of all, this dining room and its spacious patio enjoy views of the Ferry Building right across the street and the Bay Bridge beyond.
Richly spiced tastes of Turkey, Greece, and North Africa flavor the changing Mediterranean menu. For dessert, honey-cumin *pot de crème* and cocoa-nib panna cotta merely scrape the surface of the sophisticated sweets.
If parking in the garage here, be sure the restaurant validates your ticket or parking may cost as much as the meal.

Silks

C2

222 Sansome St. (bet. California & Pine Sts.)

Phone: 415-986-2020 — Lunch Mon – Fri
Web: www.mandarinoriental.com — Dinner Wed – Sat
Prices: $$$$

Silks plush and stately dining room, set on the second floor of the Mandarin Oriental Hotel, evokes the 13th century journey of Marco Polo along the Silk Road to China. Silk wall treatments, silk draperies, hand-painted chandeliers, and colors inspired by exotic spices imbue the restaurant's décor with traditional elegance.
The contemporary menu continues with this Asian theme, and courses are presented with a sense of grandeur. Chicken may be scented with lemongrass and plated alongside coconut rice; while seared Atlantic salmon may be served with *dashi* ponzu broth and a *shiso*-potato croquette. The lunch menu offers suggestions from the lengthy international wine list, in glass or half-glass portions; dinner offers a sommelier-selected pairing menu.

The Slanted Door

Vietnamese

D3

1 Ferry Building (at The Embarcadero)

Phone: 415-861-8032 Lunch & dinner daily
Web: www.slanteddoor.com
Prices: $$

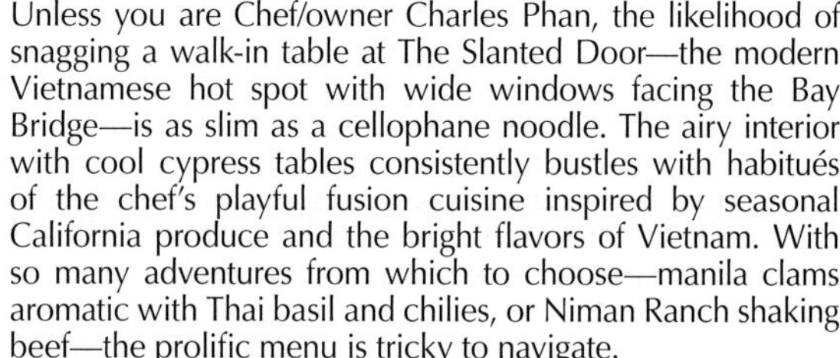

Unless you are Chef/owner Charles Phan, the likelihood of snagging a walk-in table at The Slanted Door—the modern Vietnamese hot spot with wide windows facing the Bay Bridge—is as slim as a cellophane noodle. The airy interior with cool cypress tables consistently bustles with habitués of the chef's playful fusion cuisine inspired by seasonal California produce and the bright flavors of Vietnam. With so many adventures from which to choose—manila clams aromatic with Thai basil and chilies, or Niman Ranch shaking beef—the prolific menu is tricky to navigate.

Luckily, Phan staffs his house with family and loyalists eager to wax poetic about their favorite fare. If reservations elude you, make dinner a party with inventive cocktails in the stylish lounge.

Tadich Grill

Seafood 

C2

240 California St. (bet. Battery & Front Sts.)

Phone: 415-391-1849 Lunch & dinner Mon – Sat
Web: www.tadichgrill.com
Prices: $$

A San Francisco institution since the Gold Rush days, Tadich Grill has long been a family-run operation. The restaurant's precursor was a coffee stand on Long Wharf, started in 1849 by three Croatian immigrants.

A timeless atmosphere brings folks back to this landmark eatery. More than 150 years after it was established, Tadich Grill pays tribute to its history with dark wood paneling and a pressed-plaster ceiling. The noise level is often deafening, the service gruff, and the menu an homage to recipes of yore.

Even so, the products are fresh, and seafood is available in a wide spectrum of preparations, including charcoal-broiled, pan-fried, sautéed, poached, and baked *en casserole*. Carnivores can prospect in the selection of steaks.

Tommy Toy's

Chinese XXX

C1

655 Montgomery St. (bet. Clay & Washington Sts.)

Phone: 415-397-4888 — Lunch Mon – Fri
Web: www.tommytoys.com — Dinner nightly
Prices: $$$

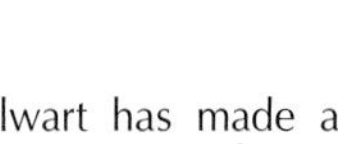

Since 1986, this Financial District stalwart has made an equally elegant choice for power lunches or romantic dinners. Service is gracious and efficient in the formal, softly-lit room, which impresses with shimmering chandeliers, silk draperies, and framed antique tapestries. Porcelain votive lamps, fresh flowers, and silver-plated chargers accent tables.

The late Tommy Toy's menu of "haute cuisine Chinois" succeeds well beyond typical Chinese fare, to remain refreshing, pleasant, and consistently interesting. Wok-fried vanilla-wasabi prawns are complemented by raisins and fresh melon, while Chinese fruits in cassis nectar finish the deep-fried pork tenderloin. Reasonable prix-fixe dining options include the Executive Lunch for less than $25.

Urban Tavern

Gastropub XX

A2

333 O'Farrell St. (bet. Mason & Taylor Sts.)

Phone: 415-923-4400 — Dinner nightly
Web: www.urbantavernsf.com
Prices: $$

Set off the lobby of the large Hilton Hotel, this place is hardly a tavern in the strict sense of the word. However, it is indeed urban; the design is chic and sleek, with warm earthy tones and light wood accents that soften the lines of the room. Tying old and new together is an eye-catching multicolored horse sculpture, cobbled from salvaged automobiles and farm machinery parts.

The inviting bill of fare features classic yet sober pub grub. The Ploughman's board carries a selection of meats and cheese, while a starter of grilled *Caggiano* beer sausage and house-made soft pretzel plays well with beer. Homey entrées include fish and chips; braised short ribs; and the Urban Tavern burger with bacon, white cheddar, grilled onions, and potato-onion fries.

Marina

Japantown • Pacific Heights • Presidio

If San Francisco were a university campus, the Marina would be Greek Row: For what it lacks in diversity and substance, the sunny bayside neighborhood (which sits atop landfill since the 1906 'quake) makes up with the style and energy reserved for affluent youth. The Marina's more sophisticated sister, Pacific Heights, thrives on serious family money and couldn't care less about being edgy.
When the tanned denizens of this beautiful bubble aren't jogging with their golden retrievers at Crissy Field, sipping aromatic chocolate at the **Warming Hut**, or putting at the Presidio Golf Course, they can be seen pushing designer baby strollers in pricey boutiques or vying for parking in Mercedes SUVs.

Perhaps surprisingly, fine dining is not a hallmark of the Marina, whose pristine facades often belie the experience within. Rather, this socialite's calling card is the quick-bite café, like **La Boulange** or the **Grove**; the gastropub, à la **Liverpool Lil's** or the upscale American **Balboa Café**; and the pickup joint once known as a "fern bar"—**Perry's** is said to have been among the world's first. In truth, quality cuisine has little to do with a Marina restaurant's success: The locals are delightfully content to follow the buzz to the latest hot spot, whose popularity seems mandated by the number of pretty people sitting at its tables. However, in the Presidio, where Lucasfilm H.Q. rules, creatives and tech geeks opt for convenience at nearby **Presidio Social Club** and **La Terrasse**.
For the Marina's physically fit and diet-conscious residents, food is mere sustenance to the afternoon shopper and a sponge for the Champagne and Chardonnay flowing at plentiful watering holes. In other words—it's all about the bar scene, baby, and there's a playground for everyone. Oenophiles save the date for the annual ZAP Zinfandel Festival in January. Preppy post-collegiates swap remembrances of European semesters abroad at **Ottimista Enoteca-Café**, **Bacchus Wine Bar**, and **Nectar**. Guys relive their frat

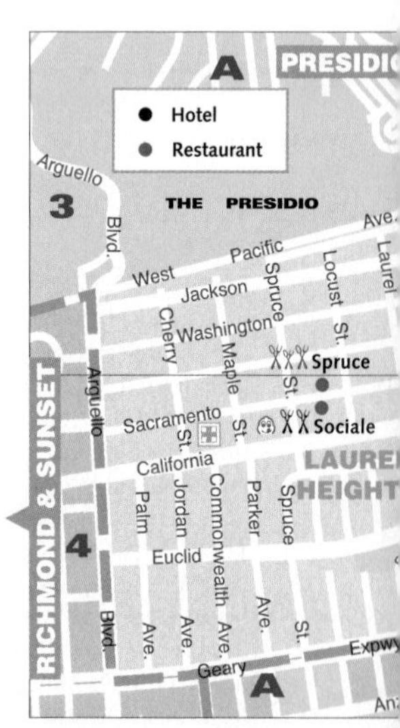

house glory days at **Bayside Sports Bar & Grill** or **Harry's Bar**. Well-heeled singles on the hunt for marriageable meat prefer the fireplace at posh **MatrixFillmore**.

Japantown

With a burgeoning Asian culture, Japantown is the exception to the rule. Hotel Tomo got a cool J Pop overhaul and serves all-you-can-eat shabu-shabu at **Mums Restaurant and Bar**. **O Izakaya Lounge** riffs on the Japanese novelty for baseball; and the fabulous **Sundance Kabuki Cinema** serves noshes in their two full bars.

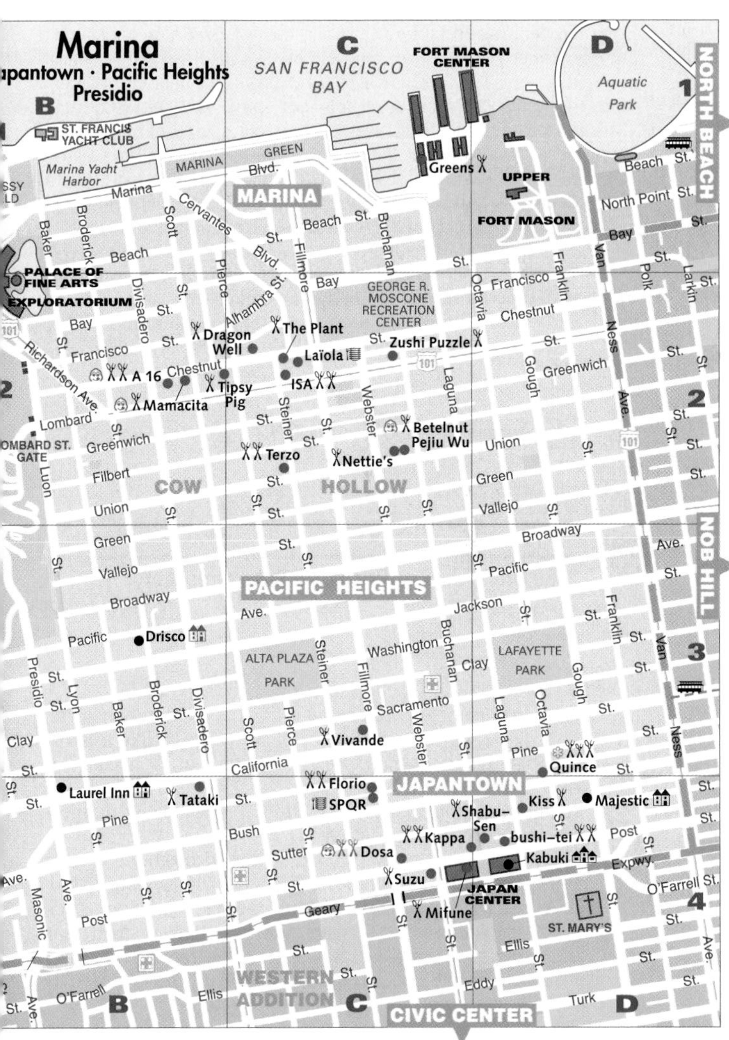

A 16

B2

Italian XX

2355 Chestnut St. (bet. Divisadero & Scott Sts.)

Phone: 415-771-2216 — Lunch Wed – Fri
Web: www.a16sf.com — Dinner nightly
Prices: $$

From a raised table at the bar, the warm dining room, or a counter flanking the open kitchen, there's not a bad seat in this very stylish house. A 16 is that perfect balance between hip and comfortable, lively yet good for conversation—everything one could want in a weeknight meal or weekend destination is here. Lighting is low and casts a warm glow on the packed room. The biggest challenge is making menu decisions, although the knowledgeable, efficient (never stuffy) staff is happy to help. A tasting of La Quercia prosciutto is a tempting starter, as are creative pastas like *cavatelli* with squash blossoms; or rustic entrées, like Duroc pork chop with pear *mostarda* and baby mustard greens.
Look out for their cookbook and a sibling restaurant, SPQR.

Betelnut Pejiu Wu

C2

Asian X

2030 Union St. (bet. Buchanan & Webster Sts.)

Phone: 415-929-8855 — Lunch & dinner daily
Web: www.betelnutrestaurant.com
Prices: $$

From the enameled fire-engine-red bar to the bamboo ceiling fans, this Asian beer house, or *pejiu wu*, feels like a British Colonial movie set. Pull a stool up to the bar for a Tsing Tao or a sake flight, or grab a table in the dimly lit upstairs dining room, where the open kitchen offers counter seating for those who want to view the action.
The kitchen constantly plays to a packed room, serving up small plates that sing with the flavors of the Orient, such as minced chicken and *lup cheong* sausage in lettuce cups; Malaysian curry *"laksa"* with prawns, chicken, mint, and basil; and a host of other choices for the fireproof palate.
Plates arrive at the kitchen's whim and many are designed for sharing, so this is an ideal venue for a group.

bushi-tei

Fusion XX

D4

1638 Post St. (bet. Buchanan & Laguna Sts.)

Phone: 415-440-4959 Lunch & dinner daily
Web: www.bushi-tei.com
Prices: $$$

On a strip of Japantown marked by authentic storefronts and few traces of English, bushi-tei speaks its own language. The performance begins with a glass of "micro-structured electrolysis water with a pH of 8.5-9.5." This is one indication of extreme attention to detail in Chef Seiji Wakabayashi's French fusion kitchen. Dramatic acts include foie gras with *kabocha* squash *pot de crème*, or tender lamb loin balanced atop haricots verts and black rice galette. Chilled sake and interesting wines make witty accomplices. Service is sometimes a flop.

A 16-seat glass communal table hogs the stage, but the candlelit set is actually intimate. Rustic wood wall panels date to 1863 Japan, and a mini mezzanine is ideal for private omakase tastings.

Dosa

Indian XX

C4

1700 Fillmore St. (at Post St.)

Phone: 415-441-3672 Lunch & dinner daily
Web: www.dosasf.com
Prices: $$

Emily and Anjan Mitra's newest Dosa in Pacific Heights outshines its Valencia Street sibling with a larger space and a more opulent contemporary design. Tones of burnt orange, tangerine, chocolate, and mustard dress the urban setting, while the dancing gold deity Shiva oversees it all.

With the expanded space comes a larger selection of Southern Indian cuisine, which includes a reasonably priced four-course tasting menu at dinner. Crisp curls of fennel-studded *pappadam* make a fine introduction to an array of dosas filled with everything from the classic masala (creamy spiced potatoes, onions, and cashew nuts), to mouth-searing habañero-mango chutney. For a unique variation, try the tomato, onion, and chili *uttapam*, and let the flavors seep in.

Dragon Well

C2 — Chinese

2142 Chestnut St. (bet. Pierce & Steiner Sts.)

Phone: 415-474-6888 — Lunch & dinner daily
Web: www.dragonwell.com
Prices: ⊜

Tucked among the posh boutiques and eateries on Chestnut Street, Dragon Well has been a Marina favorite for years. The narrow space, with its worn wooden-plank floor and neat rows of closely spaced tables is lit via skylights by day and pendant lamps by night.

Flavorful Chinese food is Americanized with delicious results. The freshest produce, meats, and seafood flourish in such dishes as Chinese eggplant stir-fried in a brown bean, scallion, and garlic sauce; or lightly battered prawns tossed in a sweet white sauce with a crunch of candied walnuts.

Dragon Well is open from 11:30 A.M. to 10:00 P.M., so shoppers can drop by for a bite—to eat in or carry out—at any time of day. These modest prices will leave cash in your pocket for more shopping.

Florio

C4 — Italian

1915 Fillmore St. (bet. Bush & Pine Sts.)

Phone: 415-775-4300 — Dinner nightly
Web: www.floriosf.com
Prices: $$

Sequestered in a tiny alley in Pacific Heights, this bistro/bar oozes old-world charm with its cozy banquettes, dark wood paneling, black-and-white photographs, and crisp linens. Joseph Graham and Doug "Bix" Biederbeck founded this place in 1998, making it a neighborhood standby for the bustling bar, inviting feel, and simple fare (reservations are recommended).

Bouncing back and forth between Italy and France, the ever-changing menu jumps from pappardelle Bolognese with porcini oil to steak frites as entrées. The likes of chicken-liver pâté with fruit mustard, or locally cured Zoe's prosciutto plated with roasted pear, Grana Padano, and olive oil please palates for starters. Both Old and New Worlds are represented on the fairly priced wine list.

Greens

Vegetarian

C1

Building A, Fort Mason Center

Phone: 415-771-6222 Lunch Tue – Sun
Web: www.greensrestaurant.com Dinner nightly
Prices: $$

Zen is the theme that unites all aspects of this local institution, established in 1979 by disciples of the San Francisco Zen Center. This means inventive organic vegetarian cuisine, with much of the pristine produce coming from the Zen Center's Green Gulch Farm. Recipes from Mexico (black bean chili), North Africa (tagine with couscous, ginger, and saffron), and Asia (stir-fry with grilled tofu) influence the imagination of Executive Chef Annie Somerville. On the unique wine list, labels from boutique, bio-dynamic, and organic vintners vie for attention.

The Zen ambience extends to the dining room, which commands a stellar view of the marina and Golden Gate Bridge. Patrons are strongly encouraged to maintain the mood by turning off their cell phones.

ISA

C2

3324 Steiner St. (bet. Chestnut & Lombard Sts.)

Phone: 415-567-9588 Dinner Mon – Sat
Web: www.isarestaurant.com
Prices: $$

Set on a restaurant-rich block in the Marina, ISA borrows its name from owners Luke and Kitty Sung's daughter, Isabelle. New Age music soothes the sleek space, while candlelight emits a warm glow. For an intimate meal, ask for a table on the covered patio, a quiet space away from the busy open kitchen.

A contemporary French slant infuses Chef Luke's cuisine, which hinges on small plates. Grilled honey-spiced calamari; baked Laura Chenel goat cheese topped with basil pesto and tomato *concassé*; and seared day boat scallops alongside asparagus and potato purée all make good dishes to share. Go Monday through Thursday for the two-course prix-fixe menu; it's a deal at just under $23.

Recently, the Sungs opened a new sushi place, Domo, in Hayes Valley.

Kappa

Japanese XX

1700 Post St. (at Buchanan St.)

Phone: 415-673-6004 Dinner Mon – Sat
Web: www.kapparestaurant.com
Prices: $$$$

Kappa necessitates a call ahead: Not only will you need precise directions to find this obscure Japantown hole-in-the-wall, but the chef only cooks for expected guests. The omakase—an $85 tasting suggested for novices of traditional *koryori* cooking—must be ordered a day in advance. A true mom-and-pop spot, Kappa specializes in intricate small plates with homespun Japanese style.

Served by the lady of the house, who dons a traditional kimono, expect such dishes as bonito atop roasted eggplant in dashi; high-grade sashimi; and fried corn fritters. The à la carte menu, penned in Japanese calligraphy, is tough to discern even in English. Thankfully, the husband/wife duo is happy to guide your experience, with the hope that you will become a regular.

Kiss

Japanese X

1700 Laguna St. (at Sutter St.)

Phone: 415-474-2866 Dinner Tue – Sat
Web: N/A
Prices: $$$

Set on the fringe of Japantown, this matchbox-sized sushi spot stays under the radar, yet it has been run by the same husband-and-wife team for more than a decade. Chef Naka San prepares all the food himself, which is eased by the fact that they only serve three small tables—grab one of the five counter seats to feel like you're in the chef's kitchen.

Kiss is constantly crowded with loyal patrons, who are clearly among the cognoscenti in terms of Japanese food. Forego the regular sushi menu in favor of one of the two omakase offerings. Both feature a delicious culinary trip to Japan: one that lingers over jewels such as a silky warm egg custard in a broth floating with clams and oysters, as well as some of the freshest *nigiri* in the city.

Laïola

Spanish

C2

2031 Chestnut St. (bet. Fillmore & Steiner Sts.)

Phone: 415-346-5641 Dinner nightly
Web: www.laiola.com
Prices: $$

Half bar, half kitchen, and 100-percent busy, Laïola is a lively spot dedicated to the Spanish tapa. On weekends, well-heeled neighborhood types *sin* reservations may be compelled to savor seasonal tender Padrón peppers, drizzled with lemon aïoli and flakes of sea salt, at the first-come, first-served copper-clad bar. No matter. Red glass votives, clamshell *cataplanas*, and a pressed-tin ceiling lend a festive atmosphere throughout.

For those who do score a table, share-worthy small plates of organic Berkshire ham and juicy quail with plump autumn grapes are not to be missed. Nor are the carefully chosen Spanish wines and ingredient-driven cocktails. But don't stop there: Pimentón-spiced *patatas bravas* and saffron rice croquettes are just plain delish.

Mamacita

Mexican

B2

2317 Chestnut St. (bet. Divisadero & Scott Sts.)

Phone: 415-346-8494 Dinner nightly
Web: www.mamacitasf.com
Prices: $$

Lively Latin music sets the pace for bold flavors and fresh Californian accents at this *muy* popular Mexican taqueria. A cool, casual, and young Marina crowd gathers here nightly for margaritas over plates of plump, crisp jalapeño *chile rellenos* stuffed with Yucatan-style black bean hummus in a creamy white pecan salsa; or perhaps a cold Mexican *cerveza* to accompany freshly fried tacos, stuffed with moist, flavorful chicken, lettuce, shredded *queso Oaxaca*, and ancho chile salsa on the side.

The lighting is low, but the volume is high in this upscale taqueria, where small lacquered wood tables huddle under clusters of Moravian star lanterns casting an amber glow on colorful framed photos.

Also try new sibling gastropub, Taverna Aventine, in the FiDi.

Mifune

C4

1737 Post St. (bet. Buchanan & Webster Sts.)

Phone: 415-922-0337 — Lunch & dinner daily
Web: www.mifune.com
Prices:

Oodles of noodles are the star attraction at Mifune, located at the Japan Center. Whether served cold with dipping sauce or in a bowl of steaming-hot broth, the house-made soba and udon noodles here are not to be missed. And if you're thinking that a bowl of noodles is a light meal, think again. You'll change your mind once you experience the massive portions at Mifune. The copious combination lunch, a steal at just over $10, includes sushi, a cut roll or *don*, and choice of soba or udon noodles.

Surrounded by Asian restaurants and gift shops in the Kintetsu Mall, this no-frills eatery is constantly packed. If Mifune is too crowded and you can't get a seat, go next door to little sister Mifune Don, which you'll find on the upper level of Miyako Mall.

Nettie's

Seafood

C2

2032 Union St. (bet. Buchanan & Webster Sts.)

Phone: 415-409-0300 — Lunch & dinner daily
Web: www.nettiescrabshack.com
Prices: $$

With farm tables and weathered cottage chairs, Nettie's is the only "shack" you'll find in this neighborhood. Tables are adorned with mallets and rolls of paper towels for blotting fingers still buttery with the conquest of grilled, local Dungeness crab. While this particular crustacean is king, a messy lobster roll, served with homemade chips, is delish; on Sundays, clambakes or crab feeds bring a smorgasbord of seasonal shellfish with satisfying sides; and barbecue brisket is an option for land-lovers. Don't miss such homespun desserts as caramel apples and s'mores.

The surfer-chic vibe belies the place's pedigree: The shack's namesake, Annette Yang, has worked such fine dining rooms as Spruce; Chef Brian Leitner did five at Chez Panisse.

The Plant

Vegetarian

C2

3352 Steiner St. (bet. Chestnut & Lombard Sts.)

Phone: 415-931-2777 Lunch & dinner daily
Web: www.theplantcafe.com
Prices:

The name has changed, fka Lettus Café Organic, but the concept remains the same at this eco-friendly eatery that aims to keep both their patrons and the planet healthy. Vegetarian and vegan options abound, beginning with a stack of blueberry pancakes for breakfast. Lunch and dinner bring sandwiches, veggie burgers, shiitake mushroom spring rolls, and an array of smoothies. For those who crave more protein, the menu throws in a few meatier choices, such as a mango-lime chicken panini.

The Plant is popular with business people, families, and single diners, who can choose among seats in the simple dining room, at the counter, or at tables on the sidewalk. If time is an issue, grab a pre-packed meal from the to-go cooler, or hit their new Pier 3 location.

Shabu-Sen

Japanese

D4

1726 Buchanan St. (bet. Post & Sutter Sts.)

Phone: 415-440-0466 Lunch & dinner daily
Web: N/A
Prices:

Founded in 1906, San Francisco's Japantown ranks as the oldest Japanese community in the continental U.S.—on this district's main street is Shabu-Sen. With modest décor and prices to match, the restaurant keeps decision-making to a minimum by focusing on two styles of dishes: shabu-shabu and *sukiyaki*. Both come in a half-dozen different combinations: beef, pork, chicken, tiger prawns, sushi-grade scallops, and premium beef.

These preparations derive from the Japanese practice of families gathering in front of a fire to share a meal together. To join in this experience, order shabu-shabu and cook your ingredients in a pot of boiling broth right at the table. Homemade sesame and ponzu dipping sauces are served by helpful and amiable Japanese waitresses.

Quince ✿

Italian XXX

D3

1701 Octavia St. (at Bush St.)

Phone: 415-775-8500 Dinner Tue – Sun
Web: www.quincerestaurant.com
Prices: $$$

Nory Ezo Suzuki

Quince is taking its sweet time to move into the new Jackson Square space (470 Pacific Avenue) they've been talking about for over a year now, but can you blame them for not wanting to rush out of this inviting little spot? Straddling a warm, unassuming corner of a residential pocket in the Marina district, Quince's tinted windows belie a softly lit dining room fitted out with lovely eggshell walls, soft brown fabrics, and gorgeous art deco light fixtures.

Chef/owner Michael Tusk and his wife Lindsay, have a loyal local following for good reason: the sophisticated clientele that pack its dining room most nights of the week know they'll find a warm, polished staff, excellent food, and a short, but carefully assembled, wine list boasting a healthy by-the-glass and half bottle selection.

Though he grew up in New Jersey, Tusk's travels to Southern France and Italy after he finished culinary school are likely the inspiration behind Quince's seasonal, ever-rotating Italian menu, which might include a fresh tangle of homemade *tagliolini*, tossed with fresh zucchini, soft ricotta, and cracked black pepper; or juicy smoked squab, paired with roasted turnips and Santa Rosa plum *mostarda*.

Sociale

Italian

3665 Sacramento St. (bet. Locust & Spruce Sts.)

Phone: 415-921-3200 Lunch Tue – Sat
Web: www.caffesociale.com Dinner Mon – Sat
Prices: $$

Off the beaten path in a posh residential neighborhood that boasts such socialite haunts as Garibaldi's and Spruce, Sociale is positively charming in its rustic Italian setting. Enter from a quaint heated patio, tucked well off the street, into a diminutive dining room that's relaxed at lunch and romantic, if a bit cramped, at dinner. Terra-cotta and butter-yellow walls set the stage for seasonal pastas like ricotta *gnudi* with pea tendrils and Grana Padano, or homemade short-rib agnolotti in a flavorful demi-glace sauce. More serious dishes might include a hearty braised duck with buckwheat penne, tomato, and herbs.

Service is graceful and leisurely (read: slow), the wine list well edited, and the atmosphere friendly with soft tunes in the air.

SPQR

1911 Fillmore St. (bet. Bush & Pine Sts.)

Phone: 415-771-7779 Lunch Sat – Tue
Web: www.spqrsf.com Dinner nightly
Prices: $$

The name may address the *Senatus Populusque Romanus* ("the senate and the Roman people"), but it beckons everyone to join them (and wait in line as there are no reservations to be had) at this Pacific Heights darling. Tables are scarce, so try the bar or chef's counter.

The sensational and talented team of chefs hold power in the kitchen. The simple spirit of Roman cuisine pervades modestly priced seasonal antipasti presented as hot plates of house-made pork sausage with braised fennel; cold salads of wild arugula, roasted carrots, and ricotta salata; or fried specialties rumored to be the winter staples of Pacific Heights residents. House-made pastas and rustic entrées showcasing simple, sensible combinations complete the offerings in this petite place.

Spruce

Mediterranean 

3640 Sacramento St. (bet. Locust & Spruce Sts.)

Phone: 415-931-5100 — Lunch Mon – Fri
Web: www.sprucesf.com — Dinner nightly
Prices: $$$

"If you build it, they will come." And so, the owners of The Village Pub erected a temple to social grandeur, and society mavens jockeyed for reservations.

This former auto garage got a lavish face-lift with Baccarat chandeliers, a proud marble bar, and style emanating from each swanky stitch in the caramel faux-ostrich chairs and deep velvet banquettes. Parisian street art is in edgy contrast to the tony clientele who remain in happy denial of the menu's somewhat less sophisticated fare. Rich dishes, such as local Petrale sole in beurre blanc, are satisfying enough; the Spruce burger, though, has a patronage of its own.

Valet parking and a to-go café are convenient, while legion global wines, encased in towering glass, are highlights for oenophiles.

Suzu

Japanese 

1581 Webster St. (at Post St.)

Phone: 415-346-5083 — Lunch & dinner daily
Web: N/A
Prices: ⊜

A trip to the Japan Center is a lesson in San Francisco's stellar cultural diversity. When you've finished devouring the many Japanese cookbooks and manga at the bookstore, find physical nourishment at Suzu, where regulars slurp their sustenance in the form of fresh soba, udon, and ramen noodles. Thirteen varieties of ramen are cooked al dente, including spicy *mabo* in pork broth and Tokyo ramen with green onion, bamboo shoots, roast pork, and a boiled egg.

Noodled out? Meats are served over rice *donburi* style, and there are a few sushi and sashimi dishes too. Service is brusque, demand is high, and tables are small and sparse. In case of a full house, jot your name on the legal pad at the door. A bowl of buckwheat soba with curry chicken is worth the wait.

Tataki

Japanese

B4

2815 California St. (bet. Broderick & Divisadero Sts.)

Phone: 415-931-1182 — Lunch Mon – Fri
Web: www.tatakisushibar.com — Dinner nightly
Prices: $$

In an area famed for plentiful organic eats, Tataki puts the rest to eco-shame as North America's only "sustainable" sushi bar. Not only are the impeccable rolls and fresh, delicate sashimi thoughtfully prepared, the ingredients are strictly considered in terms of fishing practices—whether diver- or line-caught, netted or trapped, farmed or wild, domestic or imported. Start with a flavorful kampachi or seaweed salad, tossed with paper-thin cucumber and sesame vinaigrette. Top it off with a bowl of soba noodles or an Arctic char and avocado roll that holds together to the perfect finish.

Tataki also pays it forward with take-home sustainability guides from the Monterey Bay Aquarium. This is a bite-size gem with big heart and a teeny footprint.

Terzo

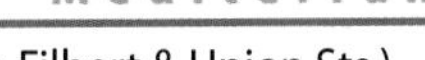

Mediterranean

C2

3011 Steiner St. (bet. Filbert & Union Sts.)

Phone: 415-441-3200 — Dinner nightly
Web: www.terzosf.com
Prices: $$

This third (or "terzo" in Italian) San Francisco restaurant, from proprietor Laurie Thomas and Nice Ventures, features serious cooking and a trendy ambience in a very charming neighborhood.

Warmth permeates the dining space, with its open kitchen, communal tables, and custom-made zinc bar.

Like its North Beach sister Rose Pistola, this Cow Hollow restaurant explores the cuisine of the Mediterranean, wandering far afield to Spain, Portugal, Morocco, and the South of France. The daily-changing menu focuses on small plates like the signature free-range chicken *spiedini*, with a limited selection of entrée-sized dishes and vegetarian choices. All are based on flavorful, local organic products, and preparations exhibit a skilled hand from the kitchen.

Tipsy Pig

Gastropub 

2231 Chestnut St. (bet. Pierce & Scott Sts.)

Phone: 415-292-2300 — Dinner nightly
Web: www.thetipsypigsf.com
Prices: $$

With a name like this, the Tipsy Pig just begs for sophomoric jokes. True, the stylish gastropub resides in a neighborhood that thrives on inherited pork, but you won't find a pig in sight: A pen of spa-fresh 20- and 30-somethings guarantees beer goggles aren't necessary, though you may want to knock back a few to better tolerate the noise. Choose from three beer sizes—the piglet, a pint, and the 20-ounce tipsy pig—then soak up your lager with a pretzel dipped in smoky cheddar or beer-battered onion fritters. More sophisticated dishes like Alaskan halibut with Meyer lemon beurre blanc are nearly superb.

With flat-screen TVs and a vintage saloon vibe, this is very much an adult bar, although there is a special menu for *les petits cochons*.

Vivande

2125 Fillmore St. (bet. California & Sacramento Sts.)

Phone: 415-346-4430 — Lunch & dinner daily
Web: www.vivande.com
Prices: $$

Artisanal produce and authentic Italian products flavor the food in this neighborhood trattoria. Chef Carlo Middione, who opened Vivande in 1981, plumbs his Sicilian heritage for additions to the menu. Made fresh every day, the house fettucine appears at lunch in more than a half-dozen variations. House-made basil pesto; cream, butter, and Parmesan; and fennel sausage, bell peppers, and marinara sauce will give you the mouthwatering idea. The wine list deftly balances offerings from the Northern, Central, and Southern regions of Italy.

Brimming with bottles of olive oil and vinegar; jars of olives and jam; imported cheese and salami; and biscotti and *amaretti*, Vivande's take-out counter invites diners to take a taste of Italy home.

Zushi Puzzle

Japanese

1910 Lombard St. (at Buchanan St.)

Phone: 415-931-9319
Dinner Mon – Sat
Web: www.zushipuzzle.com
Prices: ⊜⊝

Zushi Puzzle's diminutive façade is easy to miss as you're making your way down Lombard Street, but the cognoscenti know to head for this regularly packed Japanese place. Even solo diners are routinely turned away if they don't have a reservation.

What's the lure? Terrific fresh fish, and lots of it. Between the printed menu and the dry-erase board, the restaurant offers more than five dozen maki (think Romeo and Juliet: salmon and avocado topped with thinly sliced scallop, *tobiko*, and spicy sauce). Chef Roger Chong lords it the sushi bar—the best seats in the house—where freshly grated wasabi graces each plate.

Parking in this area can be a hassle, and often there's a line to get in, but a bit of advance planning brings its own reward here.

The sun is out – let's eat alfresco! Look for ⛱.

Mission

Bernal Heights • Potrero Hill

The sun always shines in the Mission, a bohemian paradise dotted with palm trees and home to artists, activists, and a vibrant Latino community. Graffiti murals animate the exterior walls of funky galleries, thrift shops, and bookstores; and sidewalk produce stands burst with Mexican plantains, nopales, and the juiciest limes this side of the border.

In fact, the markets here are among the best in town: **La Palma Mexicatessan** brims with homemade *papusa*, chips, and a range of fresh Mexican cheeses. **Lucca Ravioli** stocks imported Italian goods, while **Bi-Rite** is a petite grocer popular for fresh flowers and prepared foods.

Countless bargain *mercados* and dollar stores might suggest otherwise, but the Mission is home to many a hipster hangout. **Limón** is prized (and packed) for Peruvian and Latin fusion fare, while **Bar Bambino** lures the art house crowd with antipasti and olive oil tastings. **Walzwerk** charms with East German kitsch, and **Bissap Baobab** is *the* go-to for Senegalese eats. Mission pizza reigns supreme—thin crust lovers wait in line at **Pizzeria Delfina**—they serve a wicked pie with crispy edges burnt just so.

To best experience the flavors of the Mission, forgo the table and chairs and pull up a curb on Linda Street, where a vigilante street food scene has incited a revolution on Thursday nights. The **Magic Curry Kart** plates $5 steaming rice dishes, while the **Crème Brûlée Cart** torches fresh custards, some spiked with Bailey's Irish Cream, *à la minute*. The alley buzzes with locals noshing homemade pastries, empanadas, and Vietnamese spring rolls until the grub runs out.

For an affordable dinner in a more civilized fashion, **Mission Street Food** serves an ever-changing menu, prepared by bona fide guest chefs, at **Lung Shan** on Thursdays and Saturdays. Credited with inspiring the area's street food movement, the group donates all profits to such hunger- and food-related charities as La Cocina, the Mission's own "incubator kitchen" that supports aspiring, low-income restaurateurs.

The city's hottest 'hood also offers a cool selection of sweets. A banana split is downright retrolicious when served at the Formica counter of 90-year-old **St. Francis Fountain & Candy**. The sundaes are made with **Mitchell's Ice Cream**, famous in SF since 1953. Modish flavors—think foie gras and salted licorice—are in regular rotation at the newer **Humphrey Slocombe**.

Dance off your indulgences on Salsa Sunday at **El Rio**, the dive bar with a bustling back patio, or join the hip kids for DJs and live bands at **Elbo Room** and **12 Galaxies**. For rooftop imbibing, **Medjool** is unparalleled. The lesbian set shoots pool at the **Lexington Club**.

After the bars have closed, growling stomachs brave harsh lighting at numerous taquerias, many of which are open till 4:00 A.M. Each has a diehard following ready to fight to the death over who makes the best burrito. Stay out of the fray and go see for yourself: Try the veggie burrito at **Taqueria Cancun**; tacos at **La Alteña**; and mind-blowing meats—*lengua* or *cabeza*, anyone?—at **El Farolito**. During daylight hours, **La Taqueria**'s carne asada burrito is arguably the best. And **El Tonayense** taco truck, to quote one blogger, is of course "da bomb!"

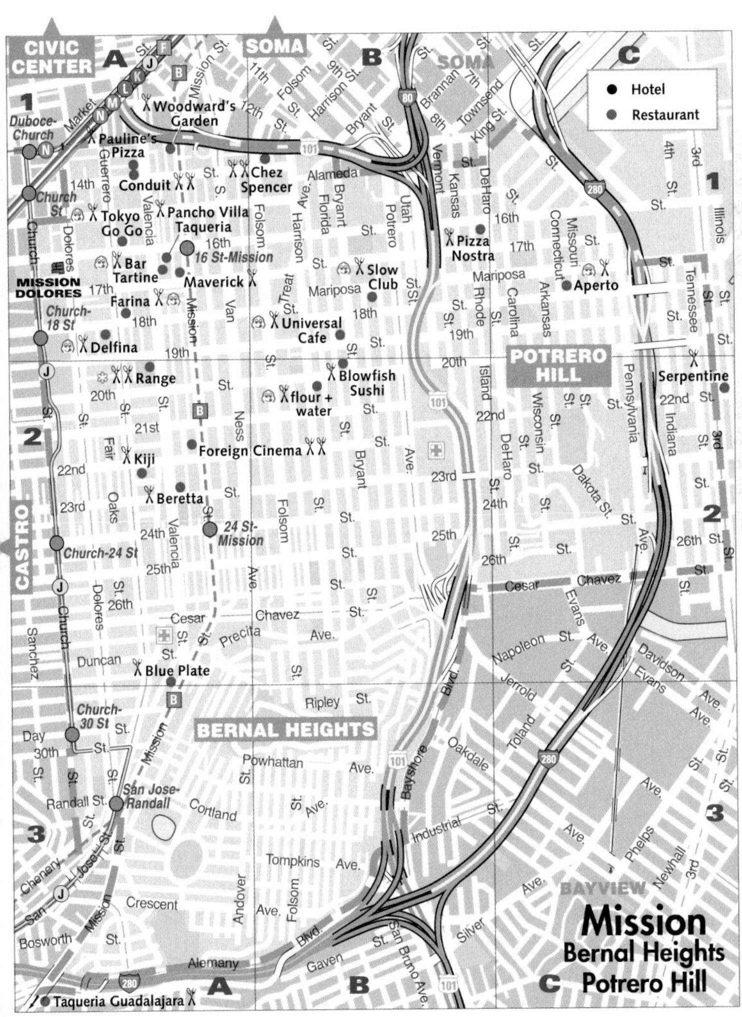

Aperto 

Italian

C1

1434 18th St. (at Connecticut St.)

Phone: 415-252-1625 — Lunch & dinner daily
Web: www.apertosf.com
Prices: $$

With its open kitchen and welcoming staff, this lovely little neighborhood Italian is well suited to its name (*aperto* is Italian for "open"). High-quality local and organic products add Californian touches to the distinctly Italian bill of fare. A chalkboard announces the daily specials, while the creative and sensible menu may list house-made butternut squash ravioli with hazelnut-sage butter and Manchego; or a roasted Fulton Valley chicken with fingerling potatoes, *cipollini* onions, winter greens, and preserved lemons. Dishes are nicely prepared and highlight fresh, well-matched flavors.
Aperto is also happy to accommodate children, with its low-priced option of any shape of pasta served with delicious sauces.

Bar Tartine 

Californian

A1

561 Valencia St. (bet. 16th & 17th Sts.)

Phone: 415-487-1600 — Lunch Sat – Sun
Web: www.tartinebakery.com — Dinner Tue – Sun
Prices: $$

An offshoot of wildly popular Tartine Bakery (nearby at *600 Guerrero St.*), Bar Tartine has developed a following of its own. As parents of both places, Elisabeth Prueitt and Chad Robertson can be justly proud of their two culinary offspring.
The narrow black and white dining room with its elk-antler chandelier has a contemporary bistro-meets-hunting-lodge vibe. Sit near the end of the Carrara marble bar that doubles as a prep area, if interested in cooking tips.
For dinner, enjoy the high quality ingredients and cooking in the likes of braised veal cheeks with heirloom broccoli and horseradish gremolata; or a house favorite: Marin Sun Farms bone marrow and grilled bread with *persillade* and arugula salad. Remember to save room for the delectable desserts.

Beretta

Italian

A2

1199 Valencia St. (at 23rd St.)

Phone: 415-695-1199 — Lunch Sat – Sun
Web: www.berettasf.com — Dinner nightly
Prices: $$

Open late to offer inventive cocktails, artisanal pizzas, and trendy ambience, this Mission spot remains hot, luring locals and nightowls alike until 1:00 A.M. nightly with wine available by the taste, quartino, or bottle.
Beretta occupies the space once filled by the Last Supper Club—the oxidized tin ceiling remains, but a long black communal table adds a hip touch, alongside the inviting bar. In addition to the star attraction—scrumptious thin-crust pizza—there is a slew of antipasti and several variations of *risotti* each evening. Other delicacies may also include lamb osso buco on Thursday, or cioppino on Friday; the selections change per the day of the week.
For a refreshing finale, go with the gelati and *sorbetti*.

Blowfish Sushi

Japanese

B2

2170 Bryant St. (bet. 19th & 20th Sts.)

Phone: 415-285-3848 — Lunch Mon – Fri
Web: www.blowfishsushi.com — Dinner nightly
Prices:

With a name like Blowfish Sushi To Die For, this Japanese eatery is bound to raise expectations. Sit shoulder-to-shoulder at the concrete sushi bar and indulge in arresting items like the Godzilla Roll of sweet shrimp, mango, avocado, cashews, and coconut; the Fiesta Roll pairing tuna, avocado, cilantro, and salsa; or the ménage à trois of salmon, salmon skin, *ikura*, *masago*, *shiso*, and sprouts. Although the titles may sound gimmicky, their creations are exceedingly fresh, flavorful, and well-presented.
The cool Tokyo vibe is enhanced by the hip and young yet professional staff, as well as the multiple screens featuring animé clips and art. Since the original Blowfish Sushi hit San Francisco, multiple outposts have emerged in California and as far away as Auckland, New Zealand.

Blue Plate

American

3218 Mission St. (bet. 29th & Valencia Sts.)

Phone: 415-282-6777 — Dinner Mon – Sat
Web: www.blueplatesf.com
Prices: $$

Opened since 1999, this Bernal Heights bistro is as American as apple pie, starting with the blue neon sign that invites passersby to "EAT." Chef Cory Obenour crafts a new menu daily, focusing on the California formula of high-quality local and organic products. Mediterranean accents pepper a crispy-skinned Sonoma duck breast, fanned over a bed of fresh corn and potato hash with caramelized onions. Sides such as "taco truck" corn on the cob with *queso fresco*, lime, and chile salt; and macaroni and drunken Spanish goat cheese indicate the free-form nature of the kitchen.

If you have a choice, pick a table in one of the dining rooms rather than a seat at the counter facing the kitchen. The latter can get uncomfortably warm on a summer evening.

Chez Spencer

French

82 14th St. (bet. Folsom & Harrison Sts.)

Phone: 415-864-2191 — Dinner nightly
Web: www.chezspencer.net
Prices: $$$

Set amid the warehouses and automotive repair shops of SoMa, this neighborhood darling is easy to miss. Look for the large wooden gate and keep walking through the garden terrace and the covered patio until you reach Chez Spencer's lofty dining room. Under the skylights and soaring arched wooden beams, two kitchens and a wood-burning oven are as integral to the space as the patrons are.

Owned by Chef Laurent Katgely, and named for his son, Spencer, the restaurant dishes up French fare with California freshness. A syrah-roasted rack of lamb paired with coco beans, tomato confit, and tender cubes of braised pork belly will give you the idea.

For French food fast, look for Spencer on the Go "mobile bistro" on the corner of Folsom and 7th streets.

Conduit

Contemporary XX

A1

280 Valencia St. (at 14th St.)

Phone: 415-552-5200 Dinner Tue – Sat
Web: www.conduitrestaurant.com
Prices: $$

Designed by architect Stanley Saitowitz, Conduit is electrically charged with steel and copper pipes that endlessly track the sleek urban resto's ceiling, partitions, eat-in kitchen counter, and bar. The effect is industrial and warm as the metallic tubes reflect fires in two hearths and flames from the exhibition kitchen. Frosted glass stalls in the coed bathroom may leave some feeling chilled, but modern American plates with Mediterranean mojo rekindle the spark.

Menu items are alluringly enigmatic—trust your instincts and you won't be disappointed. With toasted brioche and farm-fresh egg, duck confit is a tender beginning; the game heats up with serious entrées like *sous vide* hen with pea ravioli and wild mushrooms. Elegant desserts seal the deal.

Delfina 

Italian X

A1

3621 18th St. (bet. Dolores & Guerrero Sts.)

Phone: 415-552-4055 Dinner nightly
Web: www.delfinasf.com
Prices: $$

The ambience is comfortably chic, uplifting, and lively (though loud), but Craig Stoll's soul-warming Tuscan cuisine is the reason for the masses at this urban hot spot.

Here, a polite and knowledgeable staff delivers true rustic fare: creamy salt cod *mantecato* with walnut oil and fennel seed flatbread; or roasted Liberty duck with mission figs and Anson Mills polenta. Just remember to save room for their array of tempting desserts. The space is lined with mirrors, tightly spaced zinc tables, soft yellow walls, and wood banquettes—all warmed by the open kitchen and wood-burning oven. Walk-ins can find counter seating, but it is best to reserve in advance.

Next door, Pizzeria Delfina shares the popularity, and has spawned a sibling in Pacific Heights.

Farina

Italian 

3560 18th St. (bet. Guerrero & Valencia Sts.)

Phone: 415-565-0360 — Lunch Fri – Sun
Web: www.farinafoods.com — Dinner Tue – Sun
Prices: $$

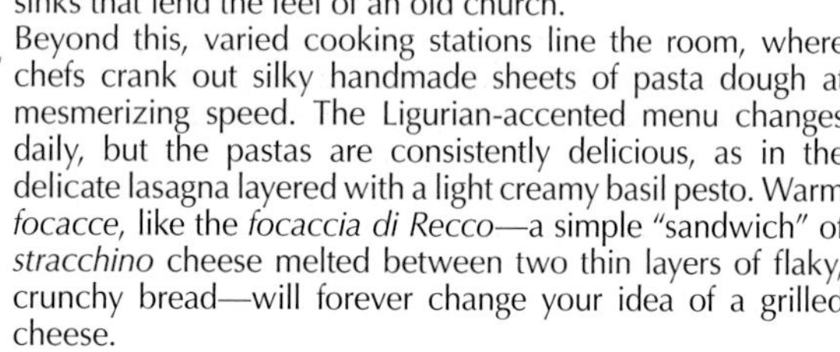

This Mission favorite wows guests. Its curving windowed façade reveals an eclectic design that incorporates elements of old and new in a sleekly contemporary, pleasant space. The bar is enhanced by red button stools and salvaged marble sinks that lend the feel of an old church.

Beyond this, varied cooking stations line the room, where chefs crank out silky handmade sheets of pasta dough at mesmerizing speed. The Ligurian-accented menu changes daily, but the pastas are consistently delicious, as in the delicate lasagna layered with a light creamy basil pesto. Warm *focacce*, like the *focaccia di Recco*—a simple "sandwich" of *stracchino* cheese melted between two thin layers of flaky, crunchy bread—will forever change your idea of a grilled cheese.

flour + water

2401 Harrison St. (at 20th St.)

Phone: 415-826-7000 — Dinner nightly
Web: www.flourandwater.com
Prices: $$

It's easy to sniff out a pizza joint in the Mission, where piquant pepperoni grease saturates the paper plates and the air itself. However, flour + water gives the pie a different spin. In an industrial corner space, high ceilings and concrete floors are expected; meanwhile, an antler light fixture and original artworks that echo the life aquatic are a chic awakening—a must for the Mission's latest culinary darling.

In the kitchen, savory Neapolitans surpass the easy-as-pie implications of flour + water's name: Each is creatively topped and then fire-licked for two minutes in an oven hotter than Hades. The menu's real stars, though, are such seasonal pastas as sweet pea tortellini with mint, and ambitious starters—think warm potato and lamb's tongue salad.

Foreign Cinema

International XX

2534 Mission St. (bet. 21st & 22nd Sts.)

Phone: 415-648-7600 — Lunch Sat – Sun
Web: www.foreigncinema.com — Dinner nightly
Prices: $$

A perennial favorite, Foreign Cinema elevates "dinner and a show" to new cultural heights. Foreign and independent films are screened on the white-washed brick wall of the enclosed courtyard while guests enjoy their meals.

Dinner takes a global slant in such feature presentations as fried Madras curry chicken and sautéed Florida rock shrimp spiked with hot peppers. After the show, many peruse the exhibit in the adjoining Modernism West gallery; others prefer drinks and dancing at adjacent Laszlo bar.

Although no movie is screened at weekend Picnic Brunch, the rough-hewn room is a pleasure in its own right. New Life Farm organic eggs star when served poached with Moroccan-spiced duck breast, or in a Champagne omelet studded with black truffles.

Kiji

1009 Guerrero St. (bet. 22nd & 23rd Sts.)

Phone: 415-282-0400 — Dinner Tue – Sun
Web: www.kijirestaurant.com
Prices:

From the sushi chefs to the servers, a pride of place infuses this Japanese spot, which stands between the Mission District and Noe Valley. Pride shines through in the food as well. Raw offerings such as toro, *nigiri*, or kanpachi carpaccio (Japanese amberjack arranged on a banana leaf and topped with thin slices of jalapeño, a drizzle of olive oil, and a crunch of sea salt) will satisfy sushi lovers; but the extensive menu goes way beyond sushi. Plump, seared Hokkaido scallops, for instance, are flavored with a pleasant ponzu reduction, while black cod is marinated in sweet miso and broiled.

The varnished wood bar is the place to sit and if you want to go completely Japanese, complement your meal with a sampling from the well-stocked sake collection.

Maverick

American

A1

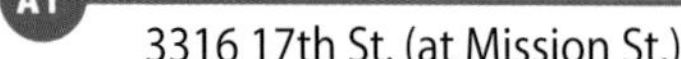

3316 17th St. (at Mission St.)

Phone: 415-863-3061
Web: www.sfmaverick.com
Prices: $$

Lunch Sat – Sun
Dinner nightly

Nonconformity can be a good thing—this is particularly true at Maverick, where innovative regional American cuisine arrives in bold flavors in a mod little neighborhood spot. Take a tour of the menu's playful combinations, from the Baltimore crab fluffs, to Southern fried chicken with Nora Mill "Georgia Ice Cream" grits, or Kurobuta pork cassoulet. With dishes such as duck confit hash; andouille sausage Benedict; and a fried-oyster Po' boy, it is no wonder that Maverick's weekend brunch claims loyal fans.

Old "Maverick" beer cans on tables, and a hanging, backlit abstracted map of the United States offer a masculine, clubby feel to the space, though everyone is treated as a member. Drop by Monday night for 40 percent off any bottle of wine.

Pancho Villa Taqueria

Mexican

A1

3071 16th St. (bet. Mission & Valencia Sts.)

Phone: 415-864-8840
Web: www.panchovillasf.com
Prices: ⊜

Lunch & dinner daily

Located in the heart of the vibrant Mission District, this little taqueria features an extensive menu of fresh Mexican fare. Before you get in line, be sure to peruse the multitude of dishes on the enormous menu board. Once in line, you'll be pressed to make quick decisions on which (of the ten) meats, award-winning salsas, fresh condiments, types of beans, and cheese you want in your burrito. More decisions come at the end of the counter, where soda, *horchata*, *cerveza*, and glass barrels filled with fruit-flavored *aqua fresca* offer to quench your thirst.

The atmosphere is somewhat utilitarian in this dining hall with backless leather stools for seating, but that does nothing to dissuade the swarms of Mission denizens waiting patiently for an empty table.

Pauline's Pizza

Pizza

260 Valencia St. (bet. Duboce Ave. & 14th St.)

Phone: 415-552-2050 Dinner Tue – Sat
Web: www.paulinespizza.com
Prices: $$

Along busy Valencia Street, recognize Pauline's by the crowds sitting on the interior benches, hungry for a delectable pizza and a free table (this popular, budget-friendly hot spot doesn't take reservations). Inside, the spacious upstairs dining room and gallery perfectly accommodate groups.

Thin and crisp yet doughy inside, these handmade crusts may be strewn with "eccentric" toppings ranging from andouille and linguiça sausage to kalamata olives and French goat cheese. Fans of Pauline's crust can even buy a three-pack of frozen shells to-go. The restaurant's Berkeley garden and Star Canyon Ranch provide a year-round supply of greens and vegetables that go into the fresh salads.

Wash it all down with one of Pauline's private-label "pizza reds."

Pizza Nostra

Pizza

300 De Haro St. (at 16th St.)

Phone: 415-558-9493 Lunch & dinner daily
Web: www.pizzanostrasf.com
Prices: ⦻⦻

Who says the French can't do pizza, eh? In a brightly hued corrugated building on Potrero Hill, the mini French empire ruled by Jocelyn Bulow is invading Italy, in cahoots with an award-winning Italian *pizzaiolo* snagged from the Riviera. Counter seating provides an up-close view of the action in the open kitchen, where 12-inch Neapolitan pies are crisped to perfection and turned out with bottles of chili-infused olive oil, an array of antipasti, and a few larger entrées. The thin-crust Calabrese pizza with *salame pepperoncino* and sliced *cipolla* onions is a worthwhile knife-and-fork endeavor.

Dark wood banquettes and an all-European staff add polish to the laid-back space but, on a sunny day, locals prefer to kick back alfresco on the lively patio.

Range ✿

A2 **Contemporary** XX

842 Valencia St. (bet. 19th & 20th Sts.)

Phone: 415-282-8283 Dinner nightly
Web: www.rangesf.com
Prices: $$

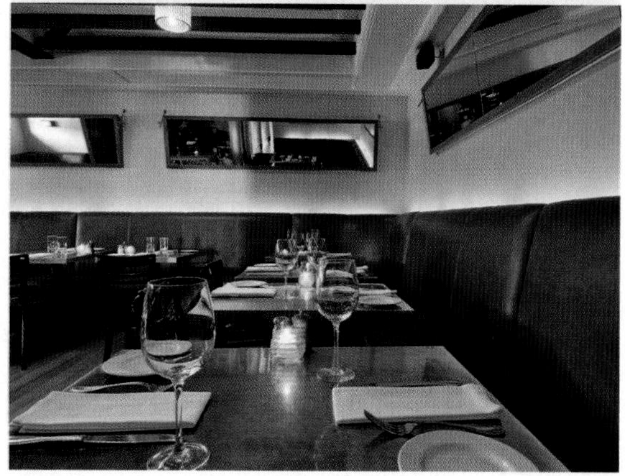

Katherine Emery

On a hipster stretch of Valencia Street chockablock with eclectic shops, one can procure just about anything—from porcupine quills to mermaid repellant—except for a parking spot. (In-the-know foodies take the Muni.) At the heart of it all, Range is a bustling and happening yet pleasant haunt with zinc-topped tables, tubular filament lights, and worn wood floors that lend a funky, urban air.

The concrete front bar is ideal for tasting their interesting selection of specialty drinks or perhaps grabbing a light dinner, while three close-knit dining rooms, tended by a knowledgeable and cordial yet cool staff, provide a relaxed environment for unfussy, sophisticated meals. Chef/owner Phil West's concise menu includes such straightforward fare as rich chicken liver mousse made with a subtle elegance that elevates it high above grandma's more rustic version. Other comforting highlights include a perfectly roasted chicken served with broccoli rabe, toasted almonds, and a sausage bread salad that is pure, homey, and delicious.

For dessert, the expertly prepared bittersweet chocolate soufflé is matched with cinnamon-caramel swirl ice cream, and underscores the simple decadence of meals here.

Serpentine

Californian

C2

2495 3rd St. (at 22nd St.)

Phone: 415-252-2000 — Lunch daily
Web: www.serpentinesf.com — Dinner Tue – Sat
Prices: $$

Located on the flats of the Eastern edge of Potrero Hill, the nine-square-block neighborhood called Dogpatch boasts a long and colorful past. Today, this district still has an industrial feel even while new condos rise on its borders.

Serpentine, an offshoot of Slow Club, named for the layer of rock that forms the foundation for many of the surrounding buildings in the area, retains the stripped-down look of its once industrial space.

The chef at this towering spot, may present his audience with a fresh and flavorful Tombo tuna salad; a moist savory bread pudding; or a delicious lamb meatloaf sandwich at lunch. For dinner he trots out the likes of crispy Hama Hama oysters, and buffalo bone marrow with a parsley and kumquat salad.

Slow Club

Californian

B1

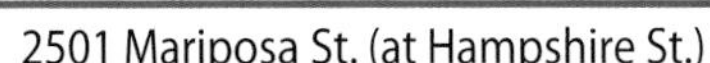

2501 Mariposa St. (at Hampshire St.)

Phone: 415-241-9390 — Lunch daily
Web: www.slowclub.com — Dinner Mon – Sat
Prices: $$

Slow Club's cool vibe and subtle hints (like a "Blue Velvet" curtain) paying homage to the David Lynch film are well suited to this hip SoMa set. They are equally attracted to the very good, simple California cuisine, moderate prices, and urban décor of varnished concrete and exposed black metal beams.

Carefully prepared dishes change daily on the menu but are sure to boast the best of the season. Dishes may be composed of pan-roasted California yellowtail with cranberry beans, baby fennel, cherry tomatoes, peppercress, and citrus vinaigrette; or a grilled Meyer Ranch flatiron steak.

Expect a wait; they take no reservations, and the area lacks many culinary options. Solo diners can grab a perch at the back bar—first-come, first-served.

Taqueria Guadalajara

Mexican

4798 Mission St. (at Onondaga Ave.)

Phone: 415-469-5480 — Lunch & dinner daily
Web: N/A
Prices: ⓈⓈ

Bright painted murals adorn the interior of this tiny taqueria in the Excelsior neighborhood of the Outer Mission. Order at the counter, then claim a seat in the quaint dining area where you can watch Mexican *fútbol* on the flat-screen TV.

Tortillas here are grilled and come in wheat, spinach, and sun-dried tomato; be sure to specify which you prefer, or you'll end up with the plain flour version. Char-broiled meats include carne and *pollo asada*, but regulars rave about the *lengua* (beef tongue) and *cabeza* (beef head). Since it lacks labels, the salsa bar can be a dangerous place. Beware of the orange-hued salsa—it's made with tongue-numbing habañeros.

Taqueria Guadalajara has a sister in the Inner Mission that shows the same quality and consistency.

Tokyo Go Go

Japanese

3174 16th St. (bet. Guerrero & Valencia Sts.)

Phone: 415-864-2288 — Dinner nightly
Web: www.tokyogogo.com
Prices: $$

Hip-hop and techno music set the pace of this cool, young place, styled after an *izakaya*. Chef John Park's menu is chock-full of innovative hand rolls from the sushi bar and hot plates from the kitchen. Baked spicy scallops rolled with wasabi *tobiko* are indeed Dynamite, while the Sunshine roll is brightened by hamachi and cilantro, and is topped with a raw quail egg. Hot entrées separate this place from the typical sushi bar, serving the likes of panko-breaded Tokyo garlic shrimp served with sweet eel *tsume* sauce and chili aïoli; or white tuna *escabeche* plated with shaved fennel, red onion, jalapeño, and Thai chili.

Enjoy $3.50 hand rolls and $3 Kirin or sake during nightly happy hour from 5:30 P.M. to 7:00 P.M., and on Sunday from 5:00 P.M. to 6:30 P.M.

Universal Cafe

Californian

B1

2814 19th St. (bet. Bryant & Florida Sts.)

Phone: 415-821-4608 — Lunch Wed – Sun
Web: www.universalcafe.net — Dinner Tue – Sun
Prices: $$

The cognoscenti once happily kept this sparkling gem a secret on the fringe of Potrero Hill. Now, word has slipped out, and reservations are difficult to attain. Arrive early, or wait elbow-to-elbow at the Carrara marble bar that parallels the open kitchen in this industrial-chic space.

Thanks to Chef/owner Leslie Carr Avalos, who forsakes a traditional toque in favor of a colorful kerchief, creative flavor combinations illuminate the daily menu. The savory and satisfying soups may include a refined combination of heirloom tomatoes and smoked ham, while entrées may include line-caught cod with Dungeness crab rémoulade. Fans of the cafe's brunch come for a sake Bloody Mary or pomegranate mimosa to accompany plates of poached eggs with creamy polenta.

Woodward's Garden

American 

A1

1700 Mission St. (at Duboce St.)

Phone: 415-621-7122 — Dinner Tue – Sat
Web: www.woodwardsgarden.com
Prices: $$$

A diamond in the not-so-rough Mission District, Woodward's Garden, is tucked under the 101 Freeway overpass, where owners Dana Tommasino and Margie Conard have run the quaint place since 1992.

Worn banquettes and small square tables offer an up-close and personal view of the kitchen, which is integrated into the front dining space. The menu serves up down-home comfort in a grass-fed hanger steak, served over a creamy gratin of sliced new potatoes, spring asparagus, and fava beans. Wholesome and delicious describes desserts like a cherry vanilla-bean brown-butter tart nestled in a shortbread crust.

In the mid-19th century, this was the site of an amusement park and gardens—the subject of Robert Frost's poem *At Woodward's Garden.*

Nob Hill

Chinatown • Russian Hill

In company with the Golden Gate Bridge and Alamo Square's "Painted Ladies," Nob Hill is San Francisco at its most iconic. Historic cable cars chug steadily up the dramatic grades that lead to the top, with familiar chimes tinkling in the wind and brass rails checking tourists who dare to lean out and take in the sights. The Powell-Mason line offers a fleeting peek at Alcatraz; the California Street car stops right at the gilded doors of Grace Cathedral.

Once a stomping ground for Gold Rush industry titans whose names grace civic buildings and luxury hotels today, this urbane quarter—sometimes dubbed "Snob Hill"— echoes of mighty egos and ancestral riches. It is home to white-glove buildings, ladies who lunch, and opulent dining rooms that attest to a noble legacy. Named for the 1800s railroad magnates, the **Big Four** is a stately hideaway known for antique memorabilia and nostalgic chicken potpie. Extravagant **Top of the Mark** is beloved for bounteous brunches and panoramic vistas. **Le Club**, a lush supper room and cocktail lounge inspired by the private clubs of yore, is a VIP haunt in an exclusive residential high-rise. For a total departure, kick back with a Mai Tai (purportedly invented at Oakland's Trader Vic's in 1944) at the **Tonga Room & Hurricane Bar**, a tiki bar with a live thunderstorm inside the Fairmont Hotel.

Russian Hill

Downhill toward Polk Street, the vibe mellows as heirloom splendor gives way to Russian Hill, chockablock with boutiques, dive bars, and casual eateries that cater to regular groups of mostly 20-something singles. Good, affordable fare abounds at **Bar Johnny**, **Café Rex**, and **Street**. **Nick's Crispy Tacos**, the tacky taqueria turned nighttime disco, is a perennial fave. For dessert, **Swensen's Ice Cream** flagship parlor is still *so* 1948.

A handful of haute foodie shops whet the palate of resident young professionals. **Cheese Plus** stocks more than 300 international cultures, artisan charcuterie, and chocolate; across the street, the **Jug Shop** is a mecca for micro-brew beer and southern hemisphere wines. Dining at the eternally delish and inexpensive **House of Nanking** is a rare experience. Don't bother ordering from the menu; the owner often takes menus out of diner's hands and orders for them.

Chinatown

For a change of pace, head to Chinatown, whose authentic markets, dim sum palaces, and souvenir emporiums spill down the eastern slope of Nob Hill in a wash of color and Cantonese characters.

Here you'll find some of the city's finest and crave-worthy barbecue pork buns at the area's oldest dim sum house, **Hang Ah Tea Room**, and a bevy of quirky must-sees. Fuel up on oven-fresh 95-cent custard tarts at **Golden Gate Bakery**, but save room for samples at **Golden Gate Fortune Cookie Company**, where you can watch the prophetic little sweets in the making. The Mid-Autumn Moon Festival brings mooncakes, a traditional pastry stuffed with egg yolk and lotus seed paste. Unwind at last at **Imperial Tea Court**, a serene haven that offers proper *gàiwan* and *gongfu* tea presentations and a retail offering of classic accoutrements. Gastronomes inspired to take home a taste of Chinatown, should stop at the **Wok Shop** for Asian cookware, linens, and tools.

Acquerello ✿

Italian XXX

A2

1722 Sacramento St. (bet. Polk St. & Van Ness Ave.)

Phone: 415-567-5432 Dinner Tue – Sat
Web: www.acquerello.com
Prices: $$$

Marty Kelly

Lucky is the diner heading to Acquerello for the first time—for who could guess that tucked behind a small, windowless façade on a plain, workaday street in Nob Hill, sits such a quaint and lovely restaurant.

In its past life, Acquerello was a chapel, and the beautiful wooden beams that supported the steeple remain, hand-painted now, and sloping down into pretty, sunset-colored walls. The soft thrum of classical music drifts down from the speakers, and into a room quietly buzzing with murmuring couples and graceful managers checking in on tables.

There's still a hushed reverence observed in this cathedral, but now it's for Suzette Gresham-Tognetti's clever Italian cooking, which, depending on your appetite, arrives in multiple courses, and might include a creamy risotto, scented with Prosecco and chockablock with tender pink shrimp and fresh slices of scallop; or moist medallions of veal, paired with a soft pile of sautéed chanterelle mushrooms and a savory square of fennel-potato gratin; or a flaky, real-deal strudel stuffed with sautéed apples, apricots, and brandy-soaked raisins, and thumped with a scoop of creamy vanilla ice cream, caramel sauce, and thin apple chips.

Antica Trattoria

Italian 

2400 Polk St. (at Union St.)

Phone: 415-928-5797 Dinner Tue – Sun
Web: www.anticasf.com
Prices: $$

At this charming spot on Russian Hill, the menu shows off the commitment to fresh seasonal cuisine and the Slow Food ideals of its chef and owner, Bergamo-born Ruggero Gadaldi. In true Italian trattoria tradition, the atmosphere is friendly and laid-back in the perpetually packed dining room, where the chef often chats with his guests. Wood paneling, comfy banquettes, and earth-colored walls add warmth.

These dishes are reasonably priced, simple, and very authentic. The menu offerings, accessible to a range of budgets, may include spaghetti *di farro* with Bolognese sauce, or *gamberoni* made with Louisiana white shrimp alongside warm spinach salad. The excellent wine list leans heavily on labels from Italy, but keeps a keen eye on California.

bund

640 Jackson St. (bet. Kearny St. & Wentworth Pl.)

Phone: 415-982-0618 Lunch & dinner daily
Web: N/A
Prices: ⊜

On chilly San Francisco days, Chinatown savants (and a few tourists who wandered in the right direction) slurp belly-warming juicy buns, aka soup dumplings, at bund. Though these particular morsels want an extra kick of ginger, the tender pork and quality dough remind us why they command a cult following. The dining room here is cleaner than its neighbors', the friendly owners are ever-present, and the Shanghainese cuisine is a nice departure from the neighborhood's ubiquitous Cantonese menus. Such dim sum options as a flaky turnip puff make for divine snacking, and vegetarians will rejoice in a spinach stir-fry with fresh bamboo shoots.

Reasonable prices, generous portions, and free two-hour parking (for checks over $40) make bund a no-brainer.

Canteen

817 Sutter St. (bet. Jones & Leavenworth Sts.)

Phone: 415-928-8870 — Lunch Fri – Sun
Web: www.sfcanteen.com — Dinner Tue – Sat
Prices: $$

There's no barrier between chef and guest at Canteen. Patrons who claim a ringside seat at the bright lime-green counter can watch every move Chef Dennis Leary makes. This 20-seat place is reminiscent of a diner, where bare bulbs hanging from the ceiling and walls inset with bookshelves lend the eatery a coffee shop feel.

The regularly changing menu spotlights perhaps a dozen selections total. Straightforward and respectful of good ingredients, the featured shellfish salad might toss crabs, scallops, and prawns with bitter orange and dill; while a moist lamb stew incorporates sun-dried tomatoes, walnut purée, and porcini mushrooms in its robust jus.

Chef Leary also mans the stove at his breakfast and lunch hot spot, The Sentinel, in SoMa.

Crustacean

Asian

A3

1475 Polk St. (at California St.)

Phone: 415-776-2722 — Lunch Sun
Web: www.anfamily.com — Dinner nightly
Prices: $$$

On the third floor of a nondescript Nob Hill building, Crustacean is the kind of place that could be easily overlooked. However, once you discover this stylish and comfortable Vietnamese gem sparkling with secret family recipes, consider yourself a regular.

Matriarch Helene An started out as a princess in Vietnam, but she and her family were forced to leave Saigon in the wake of the Communist invasion in 1975. Their restaurant dynasty, which began in San Francisco with Thanh Long, has branched into three locations of Crustacean. Since its 1991 opening, critics and regulars have been clamoring for the "secret specialties," such as garlic noodles and the whole crab roasted with garlic and spices, both prepared in the locked kitchen within the kitchen.

The Dining Room
at the Ritz-Carlton ✿

Contemporary ✗✗✗✗

600 Stockton St. (at California St.)

Phone: 415-773-6198 Dinner Wed – Sun
Web: www.ritzcarltondiningroom.com
Prices: **$$$$**

Ron Starr/The Ritz-Carlton

Let SoMa have its hip. You'll be expected to don a jacket at The Dining Room at the Ritz-Carlton, thank you very much. Like the exclusive digs it calls home, this legendary beacon of fine dining is decidedly uptown, fitted out in luxurious gold and burgundy fabrics, glowing chandeliers, and china so impeccable it would make a Frenchman blush.

It's almost impossible not to feel a little like Alice in Wonderland, settling into the enormous, cushioned chairs that flank each impeccably-appointed table—all the better position, of course, to soak up the pampering from the professional, polished service staff, with their gracious manner and eye for detail.

Legendary Chef Ron Siegel's creative, contemporary menu rotates seasonally, but might include fresh Dungeness crab, wrapped in thin slices of bright persimmon and paired with lovely little squares of yuzu gelée and a peppercress salad; a perfectly-browned turbot over a Kohlrabi (a type of German turnip) purée, paired with poached candy beets and curried leek gratin; or a silky pumpkin-squash panna cotta, served with two sugared beignets bursting with apricot and raspberry gelée piled over an intense raspberry coulis.

1550 Hyde Cafe & Wine Bar

Californian

A2

1550 Hyde St. (at Pacific Ave.)

Phone: 415-775-1550 — Dinner Wed – Sun
Web: www.1550hyde.com
Prices: $$

Organic is the name of the game at this quaint Russian Hill café. Established in 2003 by Kent Ligget and Peter Erickson, 1550 Hyde fills its Cal-Med menu with sustainably-raised, local, and organic products. Whether you crave grilled Pacific swordfish with farro salad; local sardines with sea beans, olives, and oranges; or a fried Hoffman gamebird chicken, your palate is sure to be pleased.

As for the second part of the restaurant's name, there's a respectable list of more than 150 wines to pair with your meal. Why not be adventurous and introduce yourself to something new via the nightly "Flight Plan," of red and white flights?

With advance planning, you can avoid the parking hassles and play tourist by riding the Powell-Hyde cable car to dinner.

Frascati

Mediterranean

A2

1901 Hyde St. (at Green St.)

Phone: 415-928-1406 — Dinner nightly
Web: www.frascatisf.com
Prices: $$

Big groups or single diners all are welcomed as friends by Frascati's warm staff, as they have been since this charming restaurant opened its doors in 1987. Warm colors abound inside the high-ceilinged space, where those seeking a romantic soirée should request a table on the upstairs balcony.

French, Spanish, and Italian influences show up on the plates, be it in sweet-pea risotto studded with smoked salmon, melted leeks, mascarpone, mint, and gremolata; or an herb-crusted rack of lamb with potato purée, ratatouille, upland cress, mint oil, and lamb jus.

Parking spaces are scarce along these crowded Russian Hill streets. Instead of driving around hoping to find one, hop on the Powell-Hyde cable car, which stops right in front of the restaurant.

Harris'

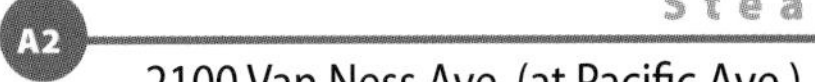

Steakhouse XXX

A2

2100 Van Ness Ave. (at Pacific Ave.)

Phone: 415-673-1888 — Dinner nightly
Web: www.harrisrestaurant.com
Prices: $$$$

Look at the crowds inside this pricey Nob Hill steakhouse and dare to forget there is a recession. Nothing has changed for decades here, including the classic interior with its mahogany wood bar, half-moon-shaped booths, and bustling service. Perhaps that's why Harris' is still so sought-after: when times get tough, folks seek refuge in the tried-and-true.

Steaks are serious business here, as the aged Midwestern corn-fed beef hanging in the display window attest. The meat is as good as ever, the sides of mashed potatoes huge, and the Caesar salads are served with whole anchovies on top.

The Pacific Lounge, where martinis and live jazz are de rigueur, may be the best spot to dine, even if the tables aren't as comfortable as in the main room.

Luella

Mediterranean XX

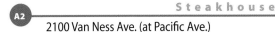

A2

1896 Hyde St. (at Green St.)

Phone: 415-674-4343 — Dinner nightly
Web: www.luellasf.com
Prices: $$

Finding a parking space in Russian Hill may be frustrating, but it's worth the hassle to experience the good food and hospitable service at this family-run restaurant. Ben and Rachel de Vries operate the comfortable hot spot, bedecked with pebbled-leather booths and bamboo-framed mirrors.

Regulars clamor for the Coca-Cola-braised pork shoulder and orange-ricotta fritters, but dishes such as ahi tuna tartare tacos and grilled local halibut with lemon beurre blanc are equally delicious. Bring the kids on Sunday night, when the Little Luella menu caters to diners under 10 with grilled cheese and French fries; chicken pot pie; and ice-cream sundaes for dessert.

Parking note: valet service is available on Polk Street (bet. Green and Union streets).

La Folie ✿

French XXX

A2

2316 Polk St. (bet. Green & Union Sts.)

Phone: 415-776-5577 Dinner Mon – Sat
Web: www.lafolie.com
Prices: $$$$

Dan Peak

Even in these trying times, Chef Roland Passot's house is still hopping most nights of the week—as sure a sign as ever that San Francisco left their heart at this family-run mainstay years ago, and hasn't looked back.

Tucked into the stylish patchwork of hotels and eateries that makes up modern-day Russian Hill, La Folie has earned its keep by turning out expertly-prepared classic French haute cuisine, with a good dose of California sensibility. Enter to find well-heeled patrons lounging on velvet banquettes in a beautiful, wood-paneled room dotted with honey-hued curtains and fresh-cut flowers.

The tasting menu (offered in 3, 4, or 5 courses) spins to the season, but may include a tender, truffle-crusted veal loin, studded with sweetbreads, and laced in a Port-Madeira sauce; roasted Loch Duart salmon on a bed of tender potato gnocchi and soft black trumpet mushrooms, with a lick of sweet onion purée running underneath; or a wicked tarte Tatin with pecan shortbread, flaky apple tart, bourbon ice cream, and caramelized banana. Celebrating their 21st year, the new (and sleek) lounge at La Folie is ideal for lulling over an aperitif or digestif.

Masa's ✿

Contemporary XXXX

C3

648 Bush St. (bet. Powell & Stockton Sts.)

Phone: 415-989-7154 Dinner Tue – Sat
Web: www.masasrestaurant.com
Prices: $$$$

Masa's

Masa's knows it's sexy—can you blame the place for making diners work a bit to track it down? Tucked behind a tiny, blink-and-you'll-miss-it glass awning just north of Union Square, the best way to find this looker is by knowing it's connected to the Hotel Vintage Court. Once inside, you'll find an impeccably sleek lair, gorgeously-appointed in chocolate walls, cushy mohair banquettes, and bright red lampshades.

The good news is that the food is just as pretty, with Chef Gregory Short spinning a wide range of specialty ingredients into his contemporary, French-influenced fare. There is no à la carte, but Masa's recently added a more accessible three-course prix-fixe to tease out recession-spooked clients.

The nightly lineup changes often but might include a warm baby artichoke salad, delicately shaved and tossed with a clutch of bright seasonal vegetables in an excellent extra virgin olive oil; a delicate, roasted *panisse* cake that walks and talks something like a super-creamy polenta, served with blanched Brussels sprouts, glazed red pearl onions, and a gloss of chickpea purée; or a lemon curd tart with fresh citrus, huckleberry *spuma*, and honey *tuile*.

Oriental Pearl

Chinese

C2

760 Clay St. (bet. Grant & Kearny Sts.)

Phone: 415-433-1817 Lunch & dinner daily
Web: www.orientalpearlsf.com
Prices: ⊜

This pearl nestles in the heart of Chinatown, near Portsmouth Square. The stark white second-floor dining room is the place to come for noteworthy Hong Kong-style cuisine and genuinely friendly service—happy to offer unsure patrons a chopsticks lesson. Dive into refreshing, artistically presented dishes on the extensive menu. Choices include the house special chicken meatball, made of chicken, shrimp, mushrooms, and Virginia ham wrapped in an egg-white pancake dumpling. At lunch, try the inexpensive chef's specials, or sample a set dim sum menu designed for two or more.

Mind that the restaurant only accepts credit cards for purchases over $15, as these low prices make it difficult to rack up much of a bill.

Pesce

Seafood

A2

2227 Polk St. (bet. Green & Vallejo Sts.)

Phone: 415-928-8025 Dinner nightly
Web: www.pescesf.com
Prices: **$$**

From Venice, Italy, comes the tradition of *cicchetti*, small appetizers served in wine bars all over that city. Here atop Russian Hill, San Franciscans can savor these little bites too, honestly interpreted by Pesce's Chef and owner, Ruggero Gadaldi (also of Antica Trattoria, down the block).

Here, *cicchetti* arrive either cold or hot—just remember to check the blackboard for daily specials. Refreshing *gamberoni* (white shrimp sautéed with spices) plated with a frisée salad, pecorino, ricotta salata, and mint may be among the cold offerings, while *tonno* puttanesca (herb-crusted tuna in a spicy tomato sauce) is a warm plate highlight. Though meats do appear on the menu, Pesce stays true to its moniker with seafood dishes predominating.

R & G Lounge

Chinese

631 Kearny St. (bet. Clay & Sacramento Sts.)

Phone: 415-982-7877 Lunch & dinner daily
Web: www.rnglounge.com
Prices: $$

Savvy locals have been coming to R & G Lounge for quality Cantonese cuisine since 1985. Décor is contemporary in the deceptively small dining space, where dark wood paneling lines the well-lit room, and a wavy metal "grid" covers the ceiling.

Start with one of the specialty martinis in watermelon, mango, or lychee, to name a few. Then move on to fresh seafood, much of which is scooped live from the aquariums around the restaurant. Chef's recommendations include deep-fried prawns with honey walnuts, and steamed clams with beaten eggs. Entrées like chicken with XO sauce and sautéed steak cubes with macadamia nuts are sure to satisfy. While many bargains abound, be prepared to pay top dollar for a bowl of the controversial shark-fin soup, the most expensive dish on the menu.

Sushi Groove

Japanese

1916 Hyde St. (bet. Green & Union Sts.)

Phone: 415-440-1905 Dinner nightly
Web: N/A
Prices: $$

You can take your pick of cuisine types in the posh residential Russian Hill neighborhood, but you can't beat Sushi Groove for good sushi at reasonable prices. Simple fresh *nigiri* is fine, but don't pass up the creative rolls—like the Jungle Roll with yellowtail, pineapple, and *tobiko*—or the poke salad made with diced ahi tuna, mango, papaya, cucumber, and sesame-chili oil. Be sure to flip the menu over so you don't miss the multitude of other options—including the ever-changing specials—that are listed on the back. A word to the wise: the menu focuses on raw dishes, so if you're looking for cooked fare, you're better off just ordering a glass of sake and enjoying the conversation.

Ask about valet parking when you call to make your reservation.

Tai Chi

A2 — **Chinese**

2031 Polk St. (bet. Broadway & Pacific Sts.)

Phone: 415-441-6758 — Lunch Mon – Sat
Web: N/A — Dinner nightly
Prices:

Neighborhood residents favor this popular, no-frills place for its copious portions of freshly prepared Chinese food and easy-on-the-budget prices. From cashew chicken to chow fun, there are plenty of options here. If your taste buds prefer fiery fare, seek the asterisk-marked menu items, like Mongolian beef (thin pieces of tender flank steak well-infused with heat from dried red chilies, and flavor from minced garlic and oyster sauce, are stir-fried with segments of pungent scallions).

The restaurant's location in residential Nob Hill, coupled with the lack of atmosphere in the plain canteen-style dining room, means that Tai Chi does a big take-out business. Unlike many of the area restaurants, this one is open for both lunch and dinner.

Venticello

B2 — **Italian**

1257 Taylor St. (at Washington St.)

Phone: 415-922-2545 — Dinner nightly
Web: www.venticello.com
Prices: $$$

Concierges in the luxury hotels on Nob Hill never hesitate to recommend this charming restaurant, whose name is Italian for "little breeze." Indeed, this place is a breath of fresh air, from the rustic, cozy dining room that conjures a Tuscan farmhouse, to the menu of well-made Italian favorites.

Chef Martin Parra may be of Mexican descent, but he adheres to the restaurant's decidedly Italian philosophy: *chi mangia bene, vive bene* (he who eats well, lives well). True to this philosophy, everyone is well-fed after polishing off *pizzette* fresh from the cobalt-blue-tiled wood-fired oven, plates of homemade pasta, or outstanding specials.

Parking spaces are precious in this neighborhood at night, so use the valet or take the cable car.

North Beach

Fisherman's Wharf • Telegraph Hill

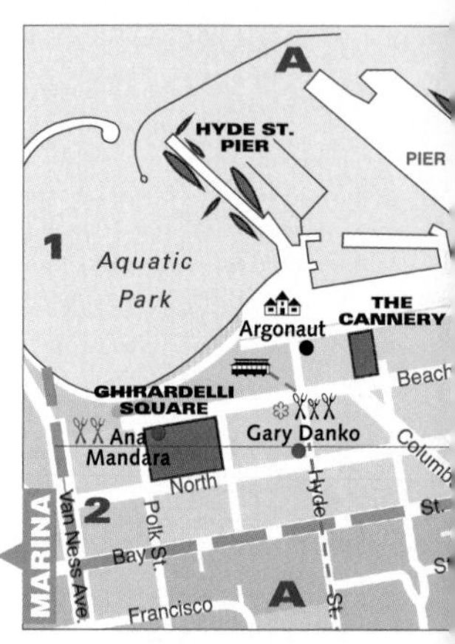

Nestled between bustling Fisherman's Wharf and the steep slopes of Russian and Telegraph hills, North Beach owes its lively nature to the Italian immigrants who settled here in the late 1800s. Many of these were fishermen from the Ligurian coast; the seafood stew they made on their boats evolved into the quintessential San Francisco treat, cioppino—a must-order in this district. Though Italians are no longer in the majority here, dozens of pasta places, pizzerias, coffee shops, and bars in North Beach attest to their idea of the good life. At the annual North Beach Festival in mid-June, a celebrity pizza toss, Assisi Animal Blessings, and Arte di Gesso (chalk art) also nod to the neighborhood's Italian heritage.

Today the majority of North Beach's restaurants and bars lie along Columbus Avenue, which cuts diagonally from the Transamerica Pyramid to Fisherman's Wharf. Be sure to check out the quarter's Italian delis, like **Molinari's**, whose homemade salami has been a local institution since 1896. Pair some imported meats and cheeses with a bottle of wine, and you've got the perfect ingredients for a picnic in nearby Washington Square Park.

Hanging out in North Beach can be a full-time job, which is what attracted a ragtag array of beret-wearing poets to the area in the 1950s. These so-called beatniks—Allen Ginsberg and Jack Kerouac among them—were eventually driven out by busloads of tourists. Beatnik spirits linger on at such landmarks as the City Lights bookstore, founded by poet Lawrence Ferlinghetti in 1953; and next door at **Vesuvio**, the original beatnik bar.

You won't find many locals there, but Fisherman's Wharf, the mile-long stretch of waterfront at the foot of Columbus Street, ranks as one of the city's most popular tourist attractions. Sure, it teems with souvenir shops, street performers, rides, and other attractions, but you should go—if only to feast on a sourdough bread bowl filled with clam chowder, and fresh crabs cooked in huge steamers right on the street.

While you're at the Wharf, sample a piece of edible history at **Boudin Bakery** on Jefferson Street. This old-world bakery may have bloomed into a large modern operation—complete with a museum and bakery tour—but they still make their

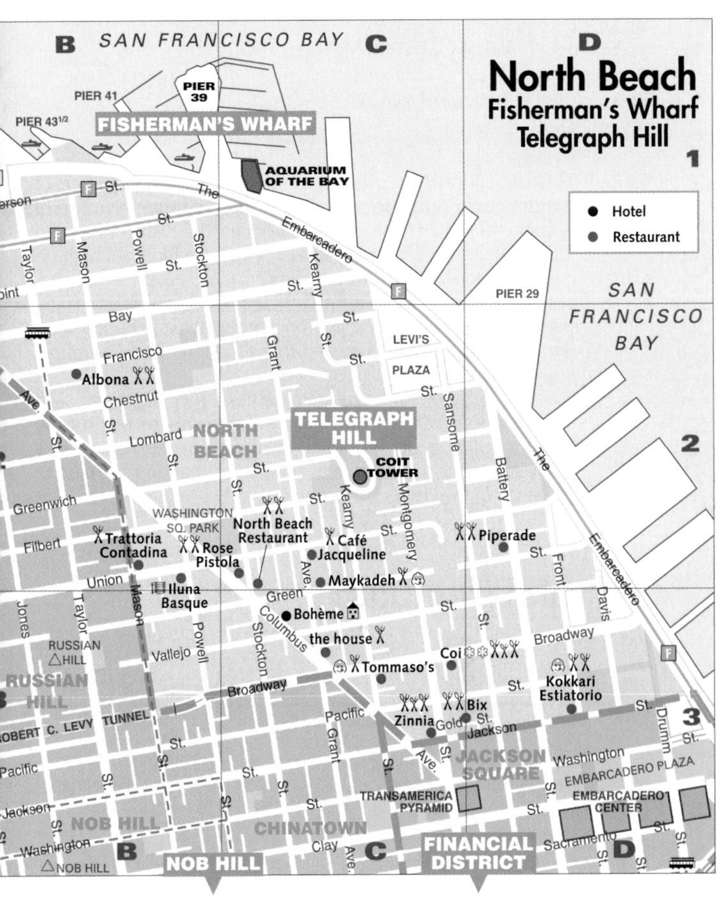

sourdough bread fresh each day, using the same mother first cultivated here from local wild yeast in 1849.

Nearby on North Point Street, Ghirardelli Square preserves another taste of old San Francisco. This venerable chocolate company, founded by Domingo Ghirardelli in 1852, now flaunts its delectable wares at the **Ghirardelli Ice Cream and Chocolate Manufactory**. Here you can ogle the original chocolate manufacturing equipment while you enjoy a hot-fudge sundae. Don't leave without taking away some sweet memories in the form of their chocolate squares.

Albona

B2 — Italian XX

545 Francisco St. (bet. Mason & Taylor Sts.)

Phone: 415-441-1040 — Dinner Tue – Sat
Web: www.albonarestaurant.com
Prices: $$

This old-school charmer, located on a residential block of North Beach, is the place to go for Istrian cuisine. A fusion of Italian and Eastern European influences, the dishes here find their roots in the Croatian town of Albona, which sits high on a cliff overlooking the Adriatic Sea.

Start with Italian, as in a bowl of seafood linguini brimming with fresh mussels, clams, shrimp, and whitefish. The tradition is to follow pasta with a meat dish, perhaps a hearty mustard-crusted rack of lamb.

Closely spaced, linen-topped tables, low lighting, and friendly service fashion an intimate atmosphere favored by local couples. If driving, take advantage of the restaurant's complimentary valet service; otherwise, parking is hard to come by in this area.

Ana Mandara

A1 — Vietnamese XX

891 Beach St. (at Polk St.)

Phone: 415-771-6800 — Lunch Mon – Fri, Dinner nightly
Web: www.anamandara.com
Prices: $$

Situated in the well-tread and touristy Ghirardelli Square area, Ana Mandara is indeed a "beautiful refuge," as its name suggests. Colonial Vietnam comes alive in the Southeast Asian temple décor, replete with silk lanterns, rattan furnishings, trickling fountains, and leafy palms. The upstairs mezzanine lounge, where live music entertains Thursday through Saturday nights, provides a lovely perspective of the scene below.

Courteous servers clad in traditional silk gowns deliver such delicacies as sweet Dungeness crab soup with hand-cut noodles; seared salmon with fresh mango and tamarind sauce; and spicy ginger chicken served atop a bed of snow peas. A quick lunch option for $15 offers the choice of an appetizer and entrée from a limited selection.

Bix

American 

56 Gold St. (bet. Montgomery & Sansome Sts.)

Phone: 415-433-6300 — Lunch Fri
Web: www.bixrestaurant.com — Dinner nightly
Prices: $$$

Hidden in the dark narrow alley known as Gold Street, the brick façade of Doug "Bix" Biederbeck's restaurant would be easy to miss if not for the neon sign that advertises "Bix Here."

Inside, this 20-year veteran shrugs off trendy in favor of a nostalgic supper-club décor recalling 1930s San Francisco. Mahogany paneling, a baby grand piano, plush banquettes, and a long dimly lit bar dress the downstairs; while a sweeping staircase gives way to intimate booths in the mezzanine. Jazz music entertains diners nightly.

Servers clad in white tuxedo jackets and black bow ties deliver the likes of shrimp Louis; house-made pappardelle with short-rib sugo; and steak tartare prepared tableside with an elegant flourish from hand-cut Creekstone Angus beef.

Café Jacqueline

French 

1454 Grant Ave. (bet. Green & Union Sts.)

Phone: 415-981-5565 — Dinner Wed – Sun
Web: N/A
Prices: $$$

Those looking for a quick meal needn't read any further. This café specializes in slow food—soufflés to be exact. Seductively puffed and airy—and sized for two—these savory creations are flavored with ingredients such as Gruyere cheese and white corn; brie and broccoli; and salmon and asparagus. While you're waiting for your soufflé to emerge from the oven, sample a salad or a bowl of the terrific French onion soup. Dessert brings more soufflés, these rich and sweet, heady with intense chocolate or Grand Marnier.

You have to walk through the kitchen on your way to the loo. There you'll see diminutive Chef Jacqueline Margulis passionately whipping up her signature dish—as she has for more than 25 years—kept company by an enormous bowl of fresh eggs.

Coi ✿✿

C3 — Contemporary XXX

373 Broadway (bet. Montgomery & Sansome Sts.)

Phone: 415-393-9000 Dinner Tue – Sat
Web: www.coirestaurant.com
Prices: $$$$

David Wakely

A seasonal 11-course tasting menu is the only option at Coi, but what a glorious option it is—gourmands of all ages book their tables weeks in advance for a brush with this level of foodie perfection.

Tucked into a strip of North Beach better known for late-night bars and pumping strip clubs, Coi (pronounced "kwah") quickly whisks you into an alternate universe—a calm, serene world where a quietly polished staff navigates a super-sleek dining room dressed in soothing earth tones and minimalist lines—the perfect backdrop to let Chef Daniel Patterson's divine creations take center stage.

Known for twisting fresh ingredients into inventive combinations, a spin through the recesses of Patterson's endlessly creative mind unearths a diced pink grapefruit signature starter, topped with fresh tarragon shoots and pepper-dusted dots of ginger syrup, alongside a fragrant drop of Coi oil; a pair of supremely tender asparagus spears with earthy morels, thyme flowers, and ricotta mousse; a rich, slow-cooked farm egg in a decadent foam of brown butter and Parmesan, paired with nutty farro and *erbette* chard; or a lovely caramelized jasmine custard, enhanced by hazelnut *croquant* and cocoa crumble.

Gary Danko ✿

Contemporary

A1-2

800 North Point St. (at Hyde St.)

Phone: 415-749-2060 Dinner nightly
Web: www.garydanko.com
Prices: $$$$

Kingmond Young

Located a souvenir's throw from touristy Fisherman's Wharf and with no views to speak of, this chi-chi mainstay thrives on the distinct signature of its famed chef and owner.

While the name alone may be enough to draw some, the restaurant's accomplished cuisine brings loyal regulars who often order "the usual"—whether it's herb-crusted tuna with crème fraîche spaetzle and arugula; or juicy guinea hen with black truffle gnocchi, jicama, and Brussels sprouts. Patrons can also count on consistently expert service and knowledgeable insight into the kitchen's modus operandi, which offers diners uncommon flexibility. While the offerings change little over time, all are free to compose their own three-, four-, or five-course tasting menu, with each appetizer available in entrée portions and vice versa. There is no shortage of international wines, dessert varietals, and sakes to choose from.

Light jazz and ambient lighting; deep red roses placed on white linen tablecloths; and spacious, curvy booths lend a sexy vibe and encourage close conversation. For a more casual tête-à-tête the bar is ideal, where exotic orchids in luminous glass vases make for a sultry backdrop.

the house

C3 — Asian

1230 Grant Ave. (bet. Columbus Ave. & Vallejo St.)

Phone: 415-986-8612 — Lunch Mon – Sat
Web: www.thehse.com — Dinner nightly
Prices: $$

Opened by Larry and Angela Tse in 1993, this tiny Asian eatery near the busy confluence of Broadway, Columbus, and Grant avenues goes against the predominantly Italian grain of North Beach.

After taking a seat, a small plate of tangy marinated sesame cucumbers will arrive at your table. White shrimp and Chinese chive steamed dumplings with tangy soy-scallion sauce; wasabi house-made noodles with grilled pork; and a deep-fried salmon roll with spicy mustard are staples here—wait for your server to rattle off the slew of specials before making a decision. Copious quantities, colorful presentations, and a good choice of beer and wine by the glass will encourage you to make this house your home for tasty and reasonably priced Asian fare.

Iluna Basque

B2 — Basque

701 Union St. (at Powell St.)

Phone: 415-402-0011 — Dinner nightly
Web: www.ilunabasque.com
Prices: $$

Overlooking Washington Square since 2003 and surrounded by the area's lively nightlife, Iluna Basque is the candlelit brainchild of Chef Mattin Noblia, whose Basque roots shine through in his menu of tapas: a concept of small bites to enjoy with wine.

Like the modest Spanish wine list, the tapas here are appetizing and affordable—dine reasonably on the likes of warm shrimp and potato croquettes with aïoli, *piquillo* peppers stuffed with Spanish salt cod, and roasted mussels. Those seeking larger plates should try the "petites entrées" which include wood-oven baked, spicy Basque chicken with chorizo, and *pipérade* with sautéed Serrano ham and a poached egg.

On weekdays, take advantage of the two-for-one drinks at happy hour (5:30 P.M. - 7:00 P.M.).

Kokkari Estiatorio

Greek

D3

200 Jackson St. (at Front St.)

Phone: 415-981-0983 — Lunch Mon – Fri
Web: www.kokkari.com — Dinner Mon – Sat
Prices: $$

Named for a small fishing village on the Aegean island of Samos, Kokkari transports diners to Greece with its rustic charms. Pick from the eye-catching taverna-style rooms: the front with its cavernous wood-burning fireplace, and the back with its communal table and view of the exhibition kitchen. A large copper urn filled with piping-hot sand stands at one end of the kitchen; it is used to heat pitchers of heady Greek coffee.

Courteous servers deliver the Mediterranean specialties such as grilled whole fish, moussaka, and grilled lamb chops with lemon-oregano vinaigrette. This *estiatorio* fills up fast, and reservations are recommended.

If you're in Palo Alto, Kokkari's successful sister, Evvia, is a good option.

Maykadeh

Persian 

C2

470 Green St. (bet. Grant Ave. & Kearny St.)

Phone: 415-362-8286 — Lunch & dinner daily
Web: www.maykadehrestaurant.com
Prices: $$

Think North Beach is all about Italian food? Think again. This Persian-style tavern (according to the definition of its name) sings a different tune. You'll be off to an excellent start with a copious plate of tender lamb's tongue in a sour-cream-based sauce with saffron and lime. Wonderful products turn a free-range baby chicken into a symphony: the bird cut into pieces; marinated in lime juice, onion, and saffron; roasted until crispy; and lined up artfully across the plate. Don't pass up *bastani* for dessert—the Persian ice cream scented with rosewater and studded with pistachios vies with gelato any day of the week.

Valet parking here is a relief in a neighborhood where finding a place to leave your car nearby always presents a challenge.

North Beach Restaurant

Italian XX

1512 Stockton St. (bet. Green & Union Sts.)

Phone: 415-392-1700 — Lunch & dinner daily
Web: www.northbeachrestaurant.com
Prices: **$$$**

Although oozing with old-world charm, North Beach Restaurant has always been ahead of its time. Partners Lorenzo Petroni and Bruno Orsi have been curing their own precious *salumi* since opening in 1970—years before that practice came into vogue. There is a genuine nostalgic vibe about this place—notice the Italian-American waiters clad in tuxedos, and catering to clients with the warmth typical of a family-run establishment. With its vaulted ceiling and cherry-wood paneling, the main dining room feels formal, yet homey and comfortable.

The menu consistently focuses on simple, satisfying classics like veal saltimbocca; flavorful minestrone; chicken Marsala; lasagna made to order; and salmon poached in white wine with a lemon butter sauce.

Piperade

D2

Basque XX

1015 Battery St. (at Green St.)

Phone: 415-391-2555 — Lunch Mon – Fri
Web: www.piperade.com — Dinner Mon – Sat
Prices: **$$**

Named for the traditional stew made with tomatoes, garlic, and sweet bell peppers (served here with Serrano ham and poached egg), Piperade celebrates Chef Gerald Hirigoyen's roots in this Basque cuisine. The vibrant Basque region (straddling Northwestern Spain and Southwestern France) comes alive, in the likes of sautéed calamari in ink sauce *"txipiroa"* or roasted pork tenderloin with braised cabbage and figs. Savor the carefully chosen wine list of labels predominantly from France, Spain, and California.

The humble space also recalls the Basque countryside, where a communal farm table sits beneath an inverted cone holding empty wine bottles. The clientele is animated, very casual, and clearly enjoying their excellent, authentically prepared meals.

Rose Pistola

Italian

532 Columbus Ave. (bet. Green & Union Sts.)

Phone: 415-399-0499 Lunch & dinner daily
Web: www.rosepistolasf.com
Prices: $$$

A city favorite for over a decade, Rose Pistola has freshened its Northern Italian fare with the help of Executive Chef Pablo Estrada, who took the reigns in June 2008. The kitchen draws inspiration from the coastal region of Liguria, the area that spawned the earlier generations of North Beach. The ever-changing menu focuses on seafood, featuring products from independent farmers and fishermen, such as Monterey calamari, chunks of grilled octopus, whole *branzino*, and roasted Blue Nose sea bass. The wine selection leans heavily toward Italy, with the addition of some fine California labels. Classy and comfortable, the dining space enjoys a view of the wood-burning oven in the exhibition kitchen, which runs the length of the room.

Tommaso's

Italian

1042 Kearny St. (bet. Broadway St. & Pacific Ave.)

Phone: 415-398-9696 Dinner Tue – Sun
Web: www.tommasosnorthbeach.com
Prices: $$

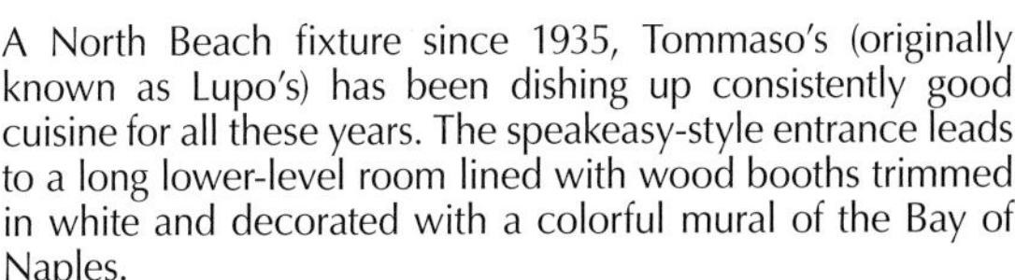

A North Beach fixture since 1935, Tommaso's (originally known as Lupo's) has been dishing up consistently good cuisine for all these years. The speakeasy-style entrance leads to a long lower-level room lined with wood booths trimmed in white and decorated with a colorful mural of the Bay of Naples.

Specials change monthly, but other than that, the menu touts Neapolitan stalwarts—such as baked fresh *coo-coo* clams; homemade ravioli with marinara sauce; and stuffed manicotti with meatballs or sausage—as it has for more than 70 years. Locals in the know keep their eyes on the pies here, since Tommaso's lays claim to introducing wood-fired pizza to San Francisco. Toppings ranging from chicken and artichokes, to sausage and prosciutto are offered.

Trattoria Contadina

Italian

1800 Mason St. (at Union St.)

Phone: 415-982-5728 — Dinner nightly
Web: www.trattoriacontadina.com
Prices: $$

For a neighborhood trattoria where the décor is rustic, the vibe is lively, and the staff is universally welcoming, look no further than the corner of Mason and Union streets. Inside, linoleum floors and signed photographs of celebrities create a homey feel, while outside you can hear the clanging of cable cars on the Powell-Mason line—which stops right outside the restaurant.

The food is equally honest and appealing, pleasing patrons as it has since opening in 1984. Classic preparations of veal and chicken on the menu may not veer from tradition, but they guarantee generous portions and consistent quality. Count on a few daily specials to round out the selection, as well as pasta entrées that are also available in half-orders as appetizers.

Zinnia

Contemporary 

500 Jackson St. (bet. Columbus & Montgomery Sts.)

Phone: 415-956-7300 — Dinner Tue – Sat
Web: www.zinniasf.com
Prices: $$

His former venture, Myth, is now the stuff of legend, but Chef Sean O'Brien has lived to serve another day. The hero's talents are on display in the old Scott Howard space (a challenged location, according to some). Since its 2008 opening, his reinvigorated devotees are eager to gather in the familiar dining room, where a mix of patterns creates graphic whimsy and the warm palette evokes the many spirits that seem to glow behind the bar. Also glowing are the locals' raves over the ground chuck and chorizo burger, housed in a Dutch crunch roll. The contemporary menu carries global appeal—as in the perfectly poached *jidori* egg or subtly seasoned Alaskan black cod in savory miso broth.

The lounge is a perfect spot to raise a glass to new beginnings.

COLVMBVS

Richmond & Sunset

Here in the otherworldly outer reaches of San Francisco, the foggy sea washes up to the historic Cliff House and Sutro Baths; in spring, cherry blossoms blush at the breeze in Golden Gate Park; and whimsical topiaries wink at pastel row houses in need of fresh paint. Residents seem inspired by a sense of Zen not quite found elsewhere in town, whether you happen upon a Japanese sushi chef or a Sunset surfer dude.

A melting pot of settlers forms the culinary complexion of this quiet urban pocket. The steam wafting from bowls of piping hot *pho* is nearly as thick as the marine layer, while many of the neighborhoods' western accents hail from across the pond—the pubs **Pig & Whistle** and the **Plough & the Stars** are English and Irish, respectively.

The Richmond, however, has earned the nickname "New Chinatown" for a reason. A bazaar for the adventurous cook, Clement Street bursts with cramped sidewalk markets where clusters of bananas sway from the awnings and the spices and produce are as vibrant as the nearby Japanese Tea Garden in bloom. While the Bay Area mantra "eat local" doesn't really apply here, sundry international goods abound—think kimchi, tamarind, eel, live fish, and pork buns for less than a buck. Curious foodies find global delicacies: This is the place to source that 100-year-old egg.

There is a mom-and-pop joint for every corner and culture. The décor is nothing to write home about and, at times, the restaurants feel downright seedy. But you're here for the cuisine, which is usually authentic: Korean barbecue at **Brothers Restaurant**; Burmese at **B Star Bar**; *siu mai* at **Shanghai Dumpling King** and **Good Luck Dim Sum**; as well as an intoxicating offering of tequila and mescal at **Tommy's Mexican Restaurant**. For

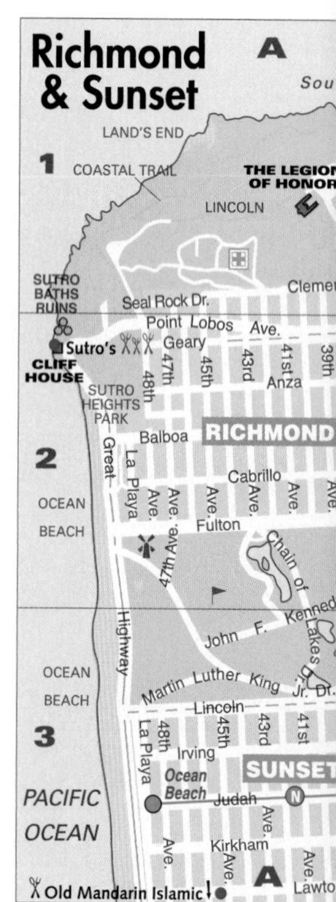

dessert, it's Asian kitsch: **Polly Ann Ice Cream** has served such flavors as durian, jasmine tea, and taro for years, while young club kids nibble Hong Kong–style sweets late night at **Kowloon Dessert Café**.

Sunset

A touch more gentrified than neighboring Richmond, Sunset—once a heap of sand dunes—retains a small-town vibe that's groovy around the edges. In the early morning, locals line up for fresh bread and pastries at **Arizmendi Bakery**, then wash down their scones at the **Beanery** around the corner. **Katana-Ya** and **Hotei** offer soul-warming bowls of handmade noodles for lunch. While tourists taking in the sights at the DeYoung Museum or the Academy of Sciences might grab a bite at the **Academy Café**, loyalists to **L'Avenida Taqueria** take their burritos to the park. Don't miss dinner at the **Moss Room**, the new hot spot from Chefs Loretta Keller and Charles Phan.

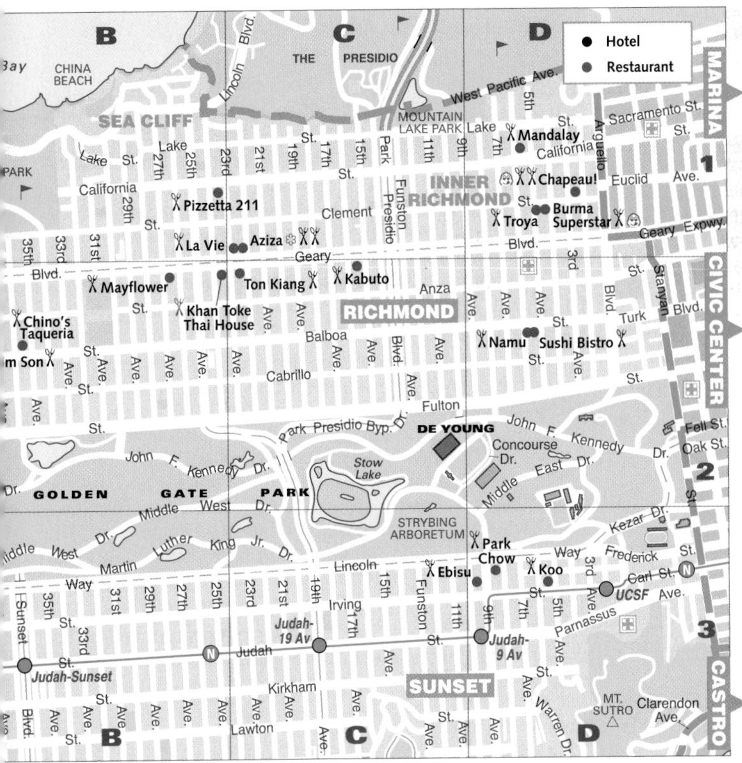

Aziza

Moroccan

C1

5800 Geary Blvd. (at 22nd Ave.)

Phone: 415-752-2222 Dinner Wed – Mon
Web: www.aziza-sf.com
Prices: $$

Mo Gorjestani

Even the tangerine- and saffron-hued walls burst with flavor at Aziza, the Richmond's most ambitious culinary exploit. A delish departure from the area's low-key noodle shops, Aziza is a visual feast with elaborate Moorish architecture, inlaid wood tables, mosaic lighting, and azure suede banquettes—not to mention the ceramic-tiled bar shakes exhilarating, seasonal drinks,

Once a discreet local love, Aziza has visibly risen as Mourad Lahlou, the restaurant's self-made chef/owner, has continued to sharpen his skills. Start his excellent culinary tour with perfectly sautéed squid tossed with a haunting medley of flavors, and you will begin to comprehend how Lahlou's cuisine, with provocative indigenous spices and artistic preparations, is deeply grounded in North Africa. Then take a stroll through glorious entrées that may include a plate of spicy house-made merguez with *harissa* goat yogurt, or roasted rabbit with sweet paprika glaze and parsnip purée.

The five-course tasting ($55) is a tour de force and an easy way to sample the best the chef has on offer each evening. For dessert, hazelnut madelines are warm and divine. Service may be slow, but Lahlou's patrons don't seem to mind.

Burma Superstar

Burmese

D1

309 Clement St. (bet. 4th & 5th Aves.)

Phone: 415-387-2147 — Lunch & dinner daily
Web: www.burmasuperstar.com
Prices: ⊜

A little piece of Burma (now known officially as Myanmar) hides under an orange awning at the corner of Fourth Avenue. Blending in among the Asian restaurants that pack this part of Richmond, Burma Superstar always seems to draw a crowd. The attentive and genuinely helpful staff is happy to assist guests unfamiliar with Burmese cuisine in navigating the exotic menu. Pumpkin-pork stew, chili lamb, and the rainbow salad—with 22 ingredients (including four types of noodles) that play off each other in a perfect symphony of flavor—represent authentic dishes. Since Myanmar borders India, China, and Thailand, also uncover those influences in the shareable dishes here.
Success has spawned a little sister in Oakland, and B Star Bar down the street.

Chapeau!

French

D1

126 Clement St. (bet. 2nd & 3rd Aves.)

Phone: 415-387-0408 — Dinner nightly
Web: www.chapeausf.com
Prices: $$

Recently relocated Chapeau! keeps the tradition of hospitality alive, with owner Philippe Gardelle working the room to make sure his patrons are happy. A shiny copper-topped bar, decorative wall sconces, and off-white color scheme enhanced by green trim decorate the subtle room.
Don't be surprised by the revamped menu which may echoe the likes of porcini-crusted veal sweetbreads; spinach- and mushroom-stuffed leg of Sonoma rabbit; and delicious honey-glazed guinea hen. At meal's end, the bill is fittingly presented in a fedora (*chapeau* may translate as "hat" in French, but when used as an exclamation, means "wow!").
Come early for the bargain three-course dinner menu; it's served from 5:00 P.M. to 6:00 P.M. Monday through Thursday.

Chino's Taqueria

Mexican

3416 Balboa St. (bet. 35th & 36th Aves.)

Phone: 415-668-9956 — Lunch & dinner daily
Web: www.chinostaqueria.com
Prices:

Big flavors at small prices draw the masses to Chino's. Burritos take center stage, bulging with ingredients such as spicy chicken, carne asada, and chile verde. Additional toppings include beans, rice, guacamole, sour cream, or all of the above. Cheese-lovers should request it right away, so the staff can warm it on the tortilla before the stuffing begins. Last, but not least, opt for either the mild green tomatillo sauce or the tongue-tingling red sauce, and dig into the tidy, foil-wrapped result, which bursts with flavor in each juicy bite. Just save room for that brown bag of crispy chips.

There is some seating in the sunny yellow room, but we recommend grabbing a burrito or a jumbo quesadilla to-go, and heading west to enjoy it on the beach.

Ebisu

Japanese

1283 9th Ave. (at Irving St.)

Phone: 415-566-1770 — Lunch & dinner Tue – Sun
Web: www.ebisusushi.com
Prices:

After operating Ebisu for nearly 30 years, Steve Fujii and his wife Koko, decided it was time for a makeover. Fans spent long months pining for their favorite sushi, but they recently celebrated Ebisu's return. A complete remodel of the interior reveals a new polished wood sushi bar and sleek wood accents throughout; the effect is sophisticated and contemporary.

The menu, too, has benefited from an overhaul. Lovers of wacky rolls know this is the place to experiment. With names like Potato Bug (cucumber and freshwater eel inside-out roll), and Tootsie Roll (deep-fried halibut wrapped in soybean paper), these creations push the limits of tradition.

Premium imported sakes have high prices to match, but less expensive sake samplers are also available.

Kabuto

Japanese

C2

5121 Geary Blvd. (bet. 15th & 16th Aves.)

Phone: 415-752-5652
Web: www.kabutosushi.com
Prices: $$

Lunch Tue – Sat
Dinner Tue – Sun

Behind this tiny storefront façade hides some intriguing sushi creations. All the raw-fish dishes are made with pristine seafood, simply, and beautifully presented. However, it's the special sushi selections that set Kabuto apart. Regulars make a beeline here for such items as the Hot Apple (seared scallop, apple, and fruity mustard), the Ono grape (wahoo topped with grapefruit and basil cream), and the 16-20 Kiss (black tiger shrimp and avocado wrapped in paper-thin radish slices served with *abuto* chocolate sauce). The vast menu also cites a plethora of cooked dishes, from tempura to teriyaki.

Sit at the varnished blonde wood sushi bar for access to all the artistic action. You might even pick up a hint or two from the smiling *itamae* (sushi chef).

Khan Toke Thai House

Thai

B2

5937 Geary Blvd. (bet. 23rd & 24th Aves.)

Phone: 415-668-6654
Web: N/A
Prices: ©©

Dinner nightly

This slice of old Siam treats diners to authentic Thai food, music, and culture. Before entering, guests are asked to remove their shoes; sit cross-legged on floor cushions; or have their legs dangling in wells below the hand-carved wooden tables.

Extensive, diverse, and unique, the menu travels through Thailand in the likes of *tom yam* soup with chicken, lemongrass, and cilantro; and *pong pang*, a combination of seafood sautéed with lemongrass, hot chilies, and the chef's secret spicy sauce. Neatly dressed servers can help guide you on your journey.

The ambience, set about with Thai artifacts and a lovely Asian garden out back, makes a perfect romantic rendezvous. Reasonable prices will leave you with enough money to tip the shoeman when you leave.

Kim Son

B2 — Vietnamese

3614 Balboa St. (bet. 37th & 38th Aves.)

Phone: 415-221-3811 — Lunch & dinner daily
Web: N/A
Prices: $$

After a day at Ocean Beach, a piping-hot bowl of *pho* from Kim Son is a surefire way to melt the San Franciscan summer chill. Handwritten on dry erase boards, the daily Vietnamese specials, such as the fresh raw beef with a squeeze of lemon (a Southeast Asian version of carpaccio) augment the enormous menu, and are well worth a try. Barbecued pork chops with an omelet over broken rice are delightful—especially when dipped in sweet-and-sour sauce.

Hanging paper lanterns and a few potted plants are the only embellishments to speak of, but the hospitality and efficiency of this family-run eatery makes up for the lack of aesthetic. Seven-dollar lunch specials are an unbeatable deal—with portions so hearty you may even have leftovers for dinner.

Koo

D3 — Japanese

408 Irving St. (bet. 5th & 6th Aves.)

Phone: 415-731-7077 — Dinner Tue – Sun
Web: www.sushikoo.com
Prices: $$

Located in quiet, and often foggy, Inner Sunset, Koo's tiny sushi counter and tastefully minimalist dining space fills on a regular basis with a coterie of connoisseurs.

Rolls, sized to be easily managed with chopsticks, such as the Tokyo Crunch (hamachi, *unagi*, cucumber, and *tobiko* covered by spicy *tenkatsu*), and the Best Roll (tempura asparagus and avocado wrapped in salmon and thinly sliced lemon) illustrate the tasteful tweaking at which Chef Kiyoshi Hayakawa excels. Tried-and-true plates of beef *tataki* and miso-marinated black cod are meant for sharing, while selections from the grill—marinated artichokes; jalapeño stuffed with hamachi and served with a side of lime aïoli—add a non-traditional twist not normally found in local sushi haunts.

La Vie

Vietnamese

C1

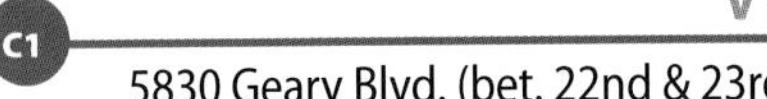

5830 Geary Blvd. (bet. 22nd & 23rd Aves.)

Phone: 415-668-8080 Lunch & dinner Tue – Sun
Web: N/A
Prices: $$

A tank full of playful koi greets visitors to this unassuming Vietnamese spot in the Outer Richmond. In the back of the sparsely decorated room, tanks swim with Dungeness crabs, whose immediate future is rather dim, but all the brighter for diners who order them roasted whole with garlic noodles. This dish may be a bit on the pricey side, but split among friends it becomes a delicious—if messy—party. The menu of moderately priced fare includes the likes of crunchy salt and pepper calamari; tender five-spice chicken with tangy tamarind sauce; steaming bowls of *pho*; cold noodle salads; and loads of vegetarian dishes.

Parking in this area can be a nightmare, so do as many locals do, and take advantage of La Vie's thriving take-out service.

Mandalay

Burmese

D1

4348 California St. (bet. 5th & 6th Aves.)

Phone: 415-386-3895 Lunch & dinner daily
Web: www.mandalaysf.com
Prices: $$

Opened in 1984 in Inner Richmond, Mandalay lays claim to being the oldest Burmese restaurant in the city. Today it is experiencing resurgence in popularity, so be prepared to wait for a table.

Familiar fans of authentic Burmese cuisine will find plenty to please their palates here, reveling in these zesty, spicy, and tangy dishes that often include catfish or coconut. For something completely different, discover the Burmese salad—a virtual cacophony of flavor, with pickled mango, cucumber, and toasted garlic in one version; crunchy tea leaves, roasted peanuts, plum tomatoes, jalapeño peppers, and crispy fried lentils in another.

Holiday decorations displayed year-round add kitsch to a large dining room lined with tropical plants, trees, and fresh flowers.

Mayflower

B2

Chinese

6255 Geary Blvd. (at 27th Ave.)

Phone: 415-387-8338

Web: N/A

Prices: 

Lunch & dinner daily

Easterners outnumber Westerners in this Cantonese dim sum house, and that's a good thing. That means that no matter their background, lovers of authentic Chinese regional cuisine will find marinated duck tongues and cold seasoned white chicken feet on the menu alongside tamer dishes such as steamed barbecue pork buns and crispy spring rolls. Much of the seafood here swims in the aquarium tanks that flank the entrance.

Be aware that the pot of tea which appears on your table without you requesting, is not complimentary. Overall, however, prices are inexpensive, especially considering the copious portions (keep this in mind as you're ordering, in case your eyes are bigger than your stomach).

Visit Mayflower's other locations in Milpitas and Union City.

Namu

D2

Asian

439 Balboa St. (bet. 5th & 6th Aves.)

Phone: 415-386-8332

Web: www.namusf.com

Prices: $$

Lunch Sat – Sun
Dinner nightly

This tale of three brothers began with a food cart named Happy Belly in Golden Gate Park. From there, Dennis, David, and Daniel Lee opened Namu in Inner Richmond. Slate, bamboo, and wood combine to create the modern surroundings in this Zen oasis. The name means "tree" in Korean, a fitting moniker for a spot where the bar is fashioned from a fallen cypress tree that once stood in Golden Gate Park.

The versatile menu focuses on Japanese and Korean cuisine. Dinner is divided into categories that range from "raw" offerings of scallop carpaccio to, "crispy" vegetable tempura and "comfort" foods, as in bowls of Namu ramen. Catch their Korean tacos; short ribs, rice, daikon, kimchi-mayo, and teriyaki sauce wrapped in nori at the Ferry Plaza's Thursday market.

Old Mandarin Islamic

Chinese

A3

3132 Vicente St. (bet. 42nd & 43rd Aves.)

Phone: 415-564-3481
Web: N/A
Prices: ⊜

Lunch Fri – Mon & Wed
Dinner nightly

On a cold day in the fog-shrouded area of the Outer Sunset known as "The Avenues," tucking into a Beijing-style hot pot at this popular place is guaranteed to help shake off the chill. In keeping with what is Halal, or permissible to eat under Islamic law, ingredients range from slices of beef and lamb to fish, but no pork or alcohol. Feel free to add vegetables like spinach, cabbage, and rice noodles, all simmering in a pot of broth placed over an open flame—making this the perfect meal for a group. There's a small charge for the extra-spicy broth, which pays homage to the piquant cuisine of Northern China's Muslim communities. Beyond hot pots, the menu covers a world of offerings; those in the know go for the lamb dishes, or beef and green onion pancakes.

Park Chow

American 

D3

1240 9th Ave. (bet. Irving St. & Lincoln Way)

Phone: 415-665-9912
Web: www.chowfoodbar.com
Prices: $$

Lunch & dinner daily

Next door to Golden Gate Park, this branch of the Chow chain (which has three other locations in the area) is the quintessential neighborhood restaurant. On sunny days, locals fill the sidewalk tables, while others head up to the deck with its retractable roof.

From wontons to pork chops to chicken strips and burgers for "Good Little Kids," the eclectic menu offers something for every member of the family. Three homey, healthy meals a day, with service all day long, means you can drop in for organic farm-fresh eggs for weekday breakfasts, daily changing sandwiches at lunch, or wood-oven-baked lasagna and grilled entrées for dinner. End meals comfortably by digging into a flaky, homemade apple pie while gazing into the crackling fire.

Pizzetta 211

Pizza

211 23rd Ave. (at California St.)

Phone: 415-379-9880 — Lunch Wed – Sun
Web: www.pizzetta211.com — Dinner nightly
Prices: ⊜

Devotees of thin-crust pizza continue to pack this quaint, stripped-down pizza shop in Outer Richmond. It's a tiny hideaway, with the limited indoor seats at a premium on a cool, foggy day—though a few sidewalk tables help accommodate overflow.

The place prides itself on supporting local organic growers and producers, though no one is exactly pampered here. Place an order at the small counter, pick up your own utensils, napkins, and search for a seat during the five short minutes until the pizza arrives. Artisanal pies change combinations frequently, swinging from simple (tomato, mozzarella, basil pesto, and pepperoni) to sophisticated (baby chard, potatoes, garlic confit, and Gruyère). Fresh-baked desserts beckon from their display stands on the bar.

Sushi Bistro

Japanese 

445 Balboa St. (at 6th Ave.)

Phone: 415-933-7100 — Dinner nightly
Web: www.sushibistrosf.com
Prices: $$

An excellent value for the money, Sushi Bistro is still a hit after several years. The restaurant sits on a quiet block in the Inner Richmond, where a young and boisterous clientele fills the sunny room's closely clustered tables.

Unique rolls are the main draw here. Expertly done, these signature offerings take on a pleasing Latino and Caribbean twist. Names reflect the chef's sense of humor, as in the Magic Mushroom (chopped salmon and yellowtail mixed with macadamia pesto and topped with mushrooms, then flash-fried); and the Monster-in-Laws (chopped spicy albacore, cucumber, and green onion topped with yellowtail, jalapeño, and ponzu sauce). Pleasure-seeking purists will be equally satisfied by the relatively large portions of sashimi and *nigiri*.

Sutro's

Californian

A2

1090 Point Lobos Ave. (at Ocean Beach)

Phone: 415-386-3330 — Lunch & dinner daily
Web: www.cliffhouse.com
Prices: $$$

There is no better vantage point in town for watching the waves breaking along the shoreline than Sutro's. Set atop a bluff on the city's westernmost point, the restaurant resides at the most recent incarnation of the 1909 Cliff House. This is as close as anyone can get to the Pacific, short of walking down the hill to Ocean Beach, where many find parking.

Multistory-windowed walls highlight the airy, yacht-club décor, while framing some incredible ocean views. Chef George Morrone has refocused the menu on contemporary and elegant Californian fare, with a good balance between seafood and meat. Long a favorite with visitors, this restaurant also welcomes a healthy number of locals who love to show off this landmark to relatives and friends.

Ton Kiang

Chinese

C2

5821 Geary Blvd. (bet. 22nd & 23rd Aves.)

Phone: 415-752-4440 — Lunch & dinner daily
Web: www.tonkiang.net
Prices:

Upstairs or down, the focus here is on dim sum and Hakka cuisine. The Hakka people migrated across their country from Northern China, many of them settling in the Guangdong Province near the Ton Kiang, or East River.

Once seated at a round table, equipped with a lazy Susan for sharing dishes, you'll be bombarded by a flurry of female servers proffering steamed, fried, blanched, and roasted miniature delights with little explanation (though there is a diagram on each table to help you identify your choices). The density of the crowd, which gets chaotic on weekends, dictates the level of service.

No prices are posted for dim sum, but never fear; the total bill here may well add up to less than what you'd pay for just an entrée elsewhere.

Troya

Mediterranean

D1

349 Clement St. (at 5th Ave.)

Phone: 415-379-6000
Web: www.troyasf.com
Prices: ⊜

Lunch Fri – Sun
Dinner nightly

Chef Randy Gannaway (a former sous-chef at Aziza) took Troya's helm and has steered the menu well beyond kebabs. Though his culinary journey still respects the Turkish traditions of the restaurant's original concept, the new chef has embarked on a more adventurous trek through the Mediterranean at large.

While the likes of chicken and lamb kebabs, or Turkish flatbread still hold their own here, *dolmas* (grape leaves stuffed with currants, pine nuts, and creamy feta); grilled sardines over local cress with sweet onions; and chicken *güvec* (crispy leg and thighs served with a spiced almond coriander sauce, parsnips, eggplant, and olives) illustrate how far the menu has traveled.The six-seat bar is the perfect perch for a mid-afternoon meze break.

Feast for under $25 at all restaurants with ⊜.

1063
F
MARKET
& WHARVES
CASTRO
167

SoMa

Peek behind the unassuming doors of the often-gritty facades prevalent in SoMa, the neighborhood South of Market, and you're bound to discover a not-so-secret trove of creative talent. While you won't find the oodles of sidewalk cafés and storefronts ubiquitous to more obviously charming enclaves, SoMa divulges gobs of riches—from artistic diamonds in the rough to megawatt culinary gems—to the tenacious urban treasure seeker.

Residential Mix

A diverse stomping ground that defies definition at every corner, SoMa is often labeled "industrial" for its hodgepodge of converted warehouse lofts. Or, with a mixed troupe of artists, photographers, architects, dancers, and designers now occupying much of SoMa's post-industrial real estate, you might also call it "artsy."

In reality, dynamic SoMa wears many faces: Youths in concert tees navigate their skateboards around the pitfalls of constant construction, fueled by "Gibraltars" from cult classic **Blue Bottle Café**. On game days, sports fans of a different sort converge for Giants baseball and **Crazy Crab'z** sandwiches at AT&T Park. In the Sixth Street Corridor, an immigrant population enjoys tastes of home at such authentic dives as **Tu Lan**, the Vietnamese hole-in-wall favored by the late Julia Child. Just blocks away, a towering crop of luxury condominiums draws a trendy Yuppie set keen to scoop up modern European furnishings at the SF Design Center and dine at equally slick restaurants—think **Sushi Groove South** and **Roe**, which doubles as an after-hours nightclub.

Arts

Since SoMa is perhaps most notable for its arts scene—this is home to the San Francisco Museum of Modern Art, countless galleries, Yerba Buena Center for the Arts, and the Daniel Libeskind–designed Contemporary Jewish Museum—neighborhood foodies crave stylish culinary experiences to match their well-rounded worlds. Art and design play a key role in the district's most unique dining and nightlife venues; and naturally, the neighborhood is fast welcoming new and avant garde restaurant concepts. Not far from the Jewish Museum, is **Mint Plaza**—step into this charming gathering spot for a bite, perhaps a respite, or to simply read a book. Post-dinner, art evangelists hit **111 Minna**, a gallery turned late-night DJ bar, or the wine bar at **Varnish Fine Art**. Down the street, **Ducca** plays on a Venetian theme with a lush lounge and whimsical paintings of the ducal couple.

Speaking of Ducca, the restaurant inside the Westin Market Street, hip hotel restaurants and bars are prolific in SoMa, in part because of proximity to Moscone Convention Center. While there is a myriad of upscale watering holes to choose from, a batch of casual joints has sprung up of late. **Good Pizza**, inside the Good Hotel, offers crispy artisan pie by the slice, while **Custom Burger/Lounge**, at Best Western Americana, piles gourmet toppings such as Point Reyes Blue Cheese and black olive tapenade onto patties of Kobe beef, salmon, and lamb. **Perry's**, the "meet market" made famous in Armistead Maupin's *Tales of the City*, is enjoying a second home in the Hotel Griffon on Steuart Street. At the InterContinental San Francisco, **Bar 888** pours more than 100 grappas to taste.

SoMa is home to a veritable buffet of well-known restaurants with famous toques at the helm. But the fact that these boldface names can also be found in the food court at the mall is testament to the area's democratic approach to food: There is high-quality cuisine to be had at workaday prices. Here, wondrous things can be found between two slices of bread. Tom Colicchio's **'WichCraft** is a popular lunch among area professionals, and former Rubicon star Dennis Leary can actually be spotted slinging sandwiches at **The Sentinel**. Chef Charles Phan has expanded his empire of Asian eateries in the neighborhood to include **Out the Door**, in Westfield San Francisco Centre, that dishes up tantalizing Vietnamese fare in a flash.

For budget gourmands, SoMa brims with cheap eats. Westfield Centre houses an impressive food court with plenty of international options. Nearby, museumgoers can refuel with a fragrant cup of tea at **Samovar** or try a micro-brew beer at **Thirsty Bear Brewing Company**. In South Park, the **Butler and the Chef** is a Gallic go-to for crêpes and *croques*, while at **Mexico au Parc**, the *sopes* run out by noon. Ballpark denizens get their burger fix at brewpub **21st Amendment**.

Nightlife

This is all to say little of SoMa's buzzing nightlife, whose scene traverses the red carpet from sports bar to DJ bar, hotel lounge to ultra-lounge, and risqué dinner theater that runs the gamut from drag (at **AsiaSF**) to Dutch: The Amsterdam import **Supperclub** serves a racy mixed plate of performance art and global cuisine—in bed. Oenophiles should definitely pop by **Terroir**, the witty little wine bar on Folsom that stocks more than 700 organic old-world varietals. For more boisterous imbibing, **Bossa Nova** bursts with the flavors of Rio. Soak up your *cachaça*, SoMa style, with a Nutella banana pancake from the 11th Street trailer, **Crêpes a Go-Go**.

SoMa
Hotel
Restaurant
NOB HILL
MISSION
MARINA
CIVIC CENTER
CHINATOWN
UNION SQUARE
TENDERLOIN
CIVIC CENTER
Four Seasons
Palomar
Fifth Floor
Tropisueño
Zazil
The Mosser
Lark Creek Steak
Chez Papa Resto
OLD MINT
MOSCONE CENTER WEST
54 Mint
Luce
InterContinental
Heaven's Dog
Basil Canteen
Manora's Thai Cuisine
ASIAN ART MUSEUM
CITY HALL
SF PUBLIC LIBRARY
UN PLAZA
SF WAR MEMORIAL & PERFORMING ARTS CENTER
Powell St
Civic Center
Van Ness

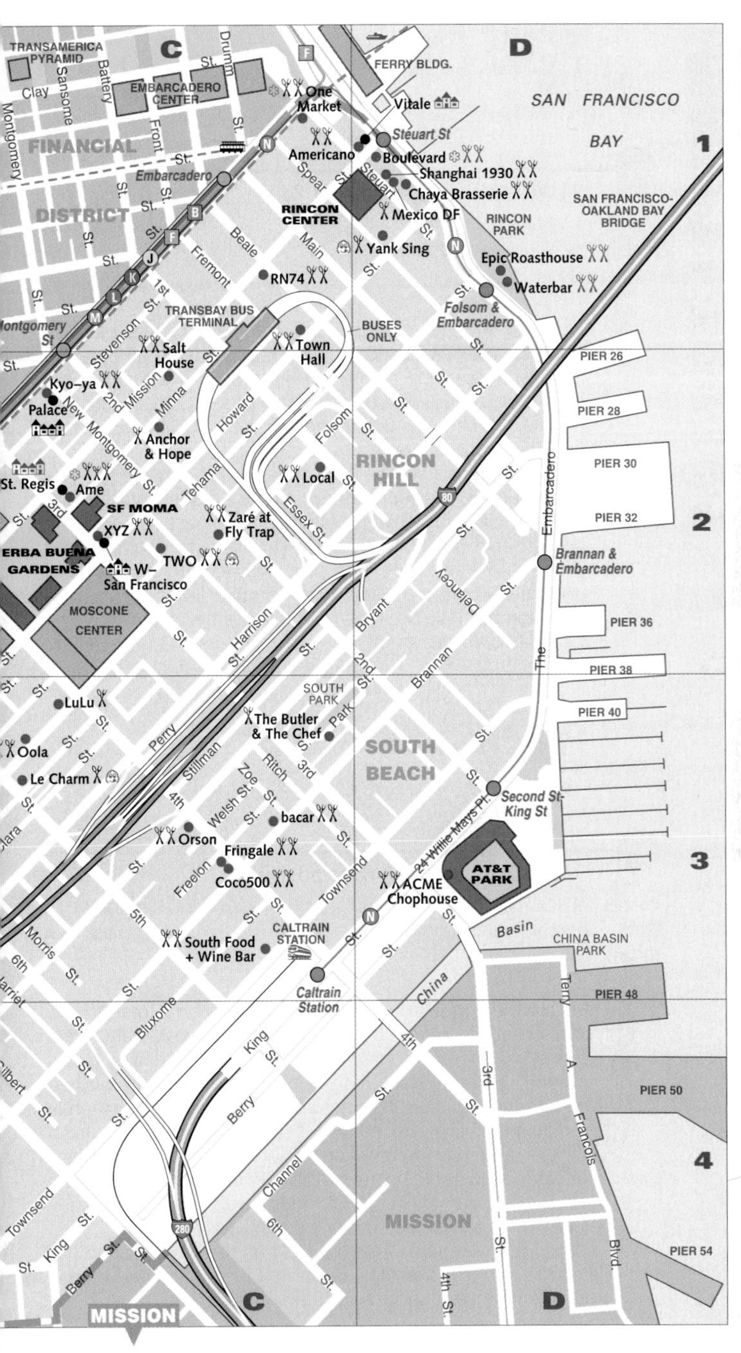
C
D
TRANSAMERICA PYRAMID
EMBARCADERO CENTER
FERRY BLDG.
SAN FRANCISCO BAY
FINANCIAL DISTRICT
One Market
Vitale
Steuart St
Americano
Boulevard
Shanghai 1930
Chaya Brasserie
Mexico DF
RINCON CENTER
RINCON PARK
SAN FRANCISCO-OAKLAND BAY BRIDGE
Yank Sing
Epic Roasthouse
Waterbar
RN74
Folsom & Embarcadero
TRANSBAY BUS TERMINAL
BUSES ONLY
Town Hall
Salt House
Kyo-ya
Palace
Anchor & Hope
PIER 26
PIER 28
PIER 30
PIER 32
PIER 36
PIER 38
PIER 40
PIER 48
PIER 50
PIER 54
St. Regis
Ame
SF MOMA
Local
RINCON HILL
XYZ
Zaré at Fly Trap
TWO
W-San Francisco
YERBA BUENA GARDENS
MOSCONE CENTER
Brannan & Embarcadero
LuLu
SOUTH PARK
The Butler & The Chef
SOUTH BEACH
Oola
Le Charm
bacar
Second St-King St
Orson
Fringale
Coco500
ACME Chophouse
AT&T PARK
South Food + Wine Bar
CALTRAIN STATION
Caltrain Station
CHINA BASIN PARK
MISSION
1
2
3
4

ACME Chophouse

Steakhouse XX

D3

24 Willie Mays Plaza (at AT&T Park)

Phone: 415-644-0240 — Lunch Tue – Fri
Web: www.acmechophouse.com — Dinner Tue – Sat
Prices: $$$

Deep in the belly of the San Francisco Giants baseball stadium (aka AT&T Park), ACME Chophouse hits a home run for anyone seeking a posh ballpark meal. Managing Chef Traci Des Jardins (of Jardinière fame) provides seating for 175 people, which helps accommodate the huge fan base when the Giants play at home.

For those purists whose idea of game-day eats are peanuts and popcorn, the menu offers a house-made pistachio-nut caramel corn for dessert. Otherwise, expect more classic upscale fare: risotto with Maine lobster and ricotta-stuffed squash blossoms; beef short ribs; grass-fed filet mignon; and pristine fresh fish. There's nothing quite like listening to a rendition of "Take Me Out To The Ballgame" while sipping a Grand Cru Bordeaux.

Americano

Italian XX

D1

8 Mission St. (at The Embarcadero)

Phone: 415-278-3777 — Lunch Mon – Fri
Web: www.americanorestaurant.com — Dinner Mon – Sat
Prices: $$$

Located on the ground floor of the stylish Hotel Vitale, Americano is much more than a hotel restaurant. Pass through a circular lounge area to enter the dining room, draped in earthy hues, and serving Italian cuisine meshed with Californian flair. The menu focuses on authenticity while remaining stylish and current. Dishes highlight clean, fresh flavors, and fine preparation of local ingredients, perhaps in starters of *arancini* stuffed with Prather Ranch shortribs; or entrées like grilled lamb sirloin with artichokes, Ruby Crescent potatoes, and lemon verbena salsa verde.

When the weather is fine, opt to sit on the spacious outdoor terrace, order a specialty Bellini made with puréed prickly pear, and drink in the views of the Bay Bridge.

Ame ✿

Contemporary XXX

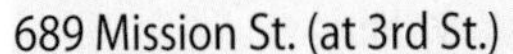

C2

689 Mission St. (at 3rd St.)

Phone: 415-284-4040 — Dinner nightly
Web: www.amerestaurant.com
Prices: $$$

Joe Fletcher

A tony brick and glass façade announces the entrance to Ame, the New American dining room inside the posh St. Regis Hotel, offering its own unique sense of urban chic. Ame reflects its cultured environs with an alluring aesthetic and inventive cuisine enhanced primarily by the flavors of Asia, while paying frequent homage to Italy. End-grain wood floors span the L-shaped dining room, wrapping around the custom-designed sashimi bar and past the exhibition kitchen, offering an impression of minimalist elegance.

Polite and efficient, the staff is knowledgeable about the menu of Chefs Hiro Sone and Lissa Doumani, who turn out a worldly cuisine where seafood dishes shine brightly. Look for such offerings as the luxurious bigeye tuna, adeptly prepared with delicate sake-marinated foie gras and ponzu vinaigrette. Rustic yet sophistated, the braised lamb shanks are fork-tender, served with winter vegetables and rich ricotta dumplings. Desserts are equally indulgent, as in the chocolate mousse served on a base of peanut butter praline, swathed in chocolate sauce.

A global selection of wines is available, but an ample array of sakes and creative cocktails may best suit this modern mood.

Anchor & Hope

C2 — Seafood

83 Minna St. (at 2nd St.)

Phone: 415-501-9100 — Lunch Mon – Fri
Web: www.anchorandhopesf.com — Dinner nightly
Prices: $$

This East Coast-style fish house joins Town Hall and Salt House as testimony to the success of the brothers Rosenthal and Doug Washington. High spirits and higher decibels join under the 30-foot ceiling of this converted early 20th century auto-repair shop, now draped with thick ropes from weathered beams. Behind the long dining counter, a tongue-in-cheek Darwinesque mural reminds us that it is a fish-eat fish world.

Nibble on some "fries with eyes" (fried smelts with remoulade) or try some "angels on horseback" (smoked bacon-wrapped oysters), while perusing the chalkboard list of oysters and shellfish. Mains include spicy mussel and monkfish stew with saffron and chorizo.

Everything on the wine list is available by the glass, half-bottle, or bottle.

bacar

C3 — Californian

448 Brannan St. (bet. 4th & Zoe Sts.)

Phone: 415-904-4100 — Lunch Sun
Web: www.bacarsf.com — Dinner Mon – Sat
Prices: $$

Though not quite the buzzing destination it was in the dot-com boom, bacar is a local favorite with something for everyone. An urbane streetfront bar lures business types for happy hour; live jazz in the subterranean lounge brings a hipster crowd on weekends; and the lofty dining room with brick walls, modern art, and industrial accents lends itself to convivial dinners among friends.

The seasonal Californian menu reflects both creativity and skill without becoming pretentious, but at times is uneven. Admirable courses may include house-made rabbit sausage, creamy rilettes, and perfectly cooked loin; or a delicious roulade of stuffed quail. Sweet and fun desserts may include a coconut rice pudding with cashew brittle in a bed of salted caramel.

Basil Canteen

Thai

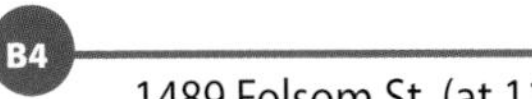

B4

1489 Folsom St. (at 11th St.)

Phone: 415-552-3963 — Lunch Mon – Fri
Web: www.basilcanteen.com — Dinner nightly
Prices:

Exposed brick and steel I-beams dominate the interior of this former 1912 Jackson Brewery building, where the industrial vibe is all SoMa and the flavors are otherworldly. More exotic than piquant, the spices used here lend inspired creativity to Bangkok-style street food. Grab a seat at the long, communal table (quiet types will prefer the mezzanine), and sip a crisp lemongrass cocktail while you peruse the casual yet complex menu. *Satay* selections far outshine the more conventional chicken-on-a-stick; Chinese sausage and star anise plum sauce add zest to a blue crab roll; and pork lovers will not want to miss the *khao moo daeng*, crispy house-cured pork belly and roast pork with star anise gravy.
Fiery condiments are available for heat seekers.

Chaya Brasserie

Fusion 

D1

132 The Embarcadero (bet. Howard & Mission Sts.)

Phone: 415-777-8688 — Lunch Mon – Fri
Web: www.thechaya.com — Dinner nightly
Prices: $$

Opened in 2000 as the San Francisco satellite of a small chain of restaurants whose cousins live in Los Angeles and Venice Beach, Chaya fuses Asian cuisine with European elements. The bill of fare skews toward Japanese, with a substantial selection of sushi and rolls, but entrées like roasted King salmon with cardoons, or red-wine-braised oxtail ravioli demonstrate continental notes. Desserts, such as warm chocolate croissant bread pudding, play a modern tune.
A long zinc-topped bar gives way to a formal carpeted back room. Local business folks favor this brasserie, and its bay views, for lunch.
Although the address is The Embarcadero, the valet stand is on Steuart Street, and a rear entrance at 131 Steuart Place is more readily accessible.

Boulevard ✿

Californian ✗✗

D1

1 Mission St. (at Steuart St.)

Phone: 415-543-6084
Web: www.boulevardrestaurant.com
Prices: $$$

Lunch Mon – Fri
Dinner nightly

Boulevard Restaurant

It's good to be the Boulevard. It ought to be ancient news by now at over a decade and a half old (it's best to think of restaurant years in terms of cat years) and yet Nancy Oakes' beloved SoMa restaurant is still the apple of Frisco's eye.

It's hard to pinpoint just one thing that makes the place so darn popular, but let's give it a whirl. It could be the sweet corner location, occupying the ground floor of the Audiffred Building and offering killer views of the Bay Bridge. It could be the easy, art deco-like charms of the interior design, or the crackerjack waitstaff, which always manages to stay a step ahead of the game.

But our money's on Oakes' delicious seasonal Californian menu, which, rendered under the careful watch of Chef Pam Mazzola, might include a fresh batch of early-season Dungeness crab, formed into two creamy-as-sin crab cakes topped with aïoli, arugula, and a dot of bacon, and submerged in a tangy tomato purée; or succulent, perfectly-browned boneless chicken thighs paired with a beautiful, garlic-studded tangle of organic broccoli and a single, fat *raviolo*, bursting with goat cheese and kabocha squash, and drizzled in warm brown butter and toasted hazelnuts.

Chez Papa Resto

Mediterranean XX

B2

414 Jessie St. (bet. Market & Mission Sts.)

Phone: 415-546-4134 Lunch & dinner Mon – Sat
Web: www.chezpapasf.com
Prices: $$

Part of the expansive Jessie Street face-lift, this newest outpost of Chez Papa is within a landscaped urban space framed by historic architecture and restaurants. More chic than its Potrero Hill sister, this SoMa darling possesses a warm, lively ambience with an unpretentious vibe and a clear touch of class.

The owners grew up in the south of France; thus the simple, expertly prepared dishes offer authentic accents. Chestnuts, chanterelles, bacon, and garlic might accompany sautéed sweetbreads, while a mound of artichoke *barigoule* makes a bed for crispy-skinned fillets of sautéed *dorade*. Whether it was the ambience, service, cuisine, or ample array of pastis displayed behind the bar, you are sure to come away feeling better than when you arrived.

Coco500

Californian XX

C3

500 Brannan St. (at 4th St.)

Phone: 415-543-2222 Lunch Mon – Fri
Web: www.coco500.com Dinner Mon – Sat
Prices: $$

This casually hip SoMa spot continues to draw hefty crowds for lunch and dinner, as the loud buzz from happy patrons in the minimalist setting will attest. Chocolate, blue, and caramel tones color a room decorated with work by local artists, while the handsome teak and Italian glass-tile bar beckons with cocktails made from freshly squeezed organic juices.

Chef/owner Loretta Keller has cobbled a Californian menu with dinner selections broken into six whimsical categories. For example, "Small Starts" include the ever-popular deep-fried green beans; "Leaf" lists tasty salads; *"a la Plancha"* means fish and meat quick-cooked with little oil; and "California Dirt" stars tasty vegetable sides. Lunch items favor sandwiches, soups, and wood-oven pizzas.

Epic Roasthouse

Steakhouse XX

D1

369 The Embarcadero (at Folsom St.)

Phone: 415-369-9955 — Lunch Sun
Web: www.epicroasthousesf.com — Dinner nightly
Prices: $$$

Modeled after the saltwater pumping station used during the 1906 earthquake, this power steakhouse does designer and co-owner Pat Kuleto proud with its wheel-shaped booths, exposed pipes, and old wood beams. Large windows frame fabulous views of the Bay Bridge and blue water, making the outdoor terrace truly superb.

As focal points, the custom-built wood-fired grill and oven are eye-catching, but the dishes of whole roasted fish or pressed organic chicken that emerge are more to the point. Still, the main focus here is classic steakhouse fare, though the New York Strip with coriander, black peppercorns, and coffee beans shows innovative twists. After dinner, the wine bar upstairs is a convivial spot to drink in the incomparable waterfront vista.

54 Mint

Italian XX

B2

16 Mint Plaza (at Jessie St.)

Phone: 415-543-5100 — Lunch & dinner Mon – Sat
Web: www.54mint.com
Prices: $$

Amid the towering walls of the historic Old Mint, 54 Mint evokes a distant *ristorante* overlooking an ancient piazza. Its shelves, stocked with artisanal olive oil, spices, and hanging hams guarding a jumbo wheel of Parmigiano-Reggiano, complete the allusion. Still, this is a passionately run, contemporary space with brick and whitewashed walls, streamlined furnishings, and leather-clad stools at the granite-topped bar.

On the menu, antipasti invite you to savor the simplicity in aged cheeses and house-cured meats. Fresh, house-made pastas abound, from linguini and ravioli to gnocchi with rich meat ragù. Abundant seafood offerings, like crisp *arancini* purple with squid ink, and pleasant game dishes complete the frequently changing menu.

Fifth Floor ✿

French XXX

B2

12 4th St. (at Market St.)

Phone: 415-348-1555 Dinner Mon – Sat

Web: www.fifthfloorrestaurant.com

Prices: **$$$$**

Justin Lewis

Atop the Palomar Hotel, Fifth Floor requires a dramatic entrance: Past the valet and through the chic lobby, hail the elevator to five and follow the marquetry floor to an ambient lounge dotted with cocktail tables. Here, find guests, cozy couples, and business colleagues capping the day.

The reception stand signals entrée into a dark, sexy bar that leads to a swank dining room, where cream leather club chairs contrast with deep wood finishes, and tables are illuminated with soft candlelight. Service is elegant and mesmerizing—the better to highlight this very serious cuisine. For such refinement, the vibe is unexpectedly lively and relaxed. Sit back and be dazzled by a sampling of expertly prepared amuse-bouche and a wine list that deftly leans both fancy and French.

Culinary expert Chef Jennie Lorenzo's creativity and complexity shine in every bite; the à la carte and tasting menus are redolent with the flavors of Gascony—think foie gras terrine with beautifully candied kumquats and toasted challah; *sous-vide* guinea hen with foie gras and black truffle bouillon; and terrific loin of lamb with a parsley, breadcrumb, and mustard crust, served atop a silky white bean purée.

Fringale

French

C3

570 4th St. (bet. Brannan & Bryant Sts.)

Phone: 415-543-0573 — Lunch Tue – Fri
Web: www.fringalesf.com — Dinner nightly
Prices: $$

The currently reinvigorated SoMa restaurant scene can take a lesson from Fringale, which owes its longevity to friendly service, consistency, and just plain good food. Though the Basque cuisine features French accents (and a certain, undeniable romance), there is no fussiness here; dishes continue to be unpretentious and approachable, despite the near-constant chef changes over the past year.

Spicy Monterey calamari cooked *a la plancha* with jalapeños and chorizo, and an organic roasted chicken breast served with *pommes gaufrettes*, chayotes, and thyme sauce embrace bold flavors and rustic quality inspired by Basque traditions. It is no wonder that this small dining room is typically jammed at night, with a line of diners stretching out the door.

Heaven's Dog

Chinese

B3

1148 Mission St. (bet. 7th & 8th Sts.)

Phone: 415-863-6008 — Lunch Mon – Fri
Web: www.heavensdog.com — Dinner nightly
Prices: $$

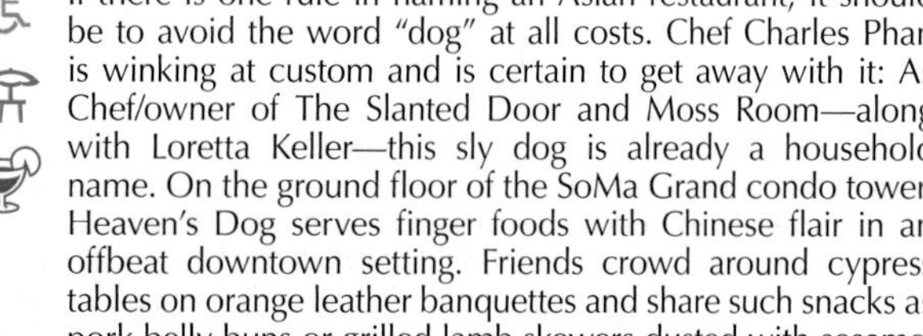

If there is one rule in naming an Asian restaurant, it should be to avoid the word "dog" at all costs. Chef Charles Phan is winking at custom and is certain to get away with it: As Chef/owner of The Slanted Door and Moss Room—along with Loretta Keller—this sly dog is already a household name. On the ground floor of the SoMa Grand condo tower, Heaven's Dog serves finger foods with Chinese flair in an offbeat downtown setting. Friends crowd around cypress tables on orange leather banquettes and share such snacks as pork belly buns or grilled lamb skewers dusted with sesame, cumin, and chilies.

Snacks pair well with designer cocktails or a grassy sauvignon blanc. Noodle soups for the soul are ladled at the bar overlooking the exhibition kitchen.

Kyo-ya

Japanese XX

2 New Montgomery St. (at Market St.)

Phone: 415-546-5090 Lunch & dinner Mon – Fri
Web: www.kyo-ya-restaurant.com
Prices: $$$

Despite its separate entrance at the corner of Jessie Street, Kyo-Ya is part of the 1909 Palace Hotel. The space is serene and tastefully done, with tables scattered throughout the nooks and crannies of the room. If you choose one of the seats at the sushi bar, you'll be dazzled by Master Sushi Chef Akifusa Tonai's deft knife skills as he prepares his trademark rolls. Many of these, such as the Celebration and the Volcano Ano, are wrapped with soy bean skin instead of the usual nori.

Kyo-ya's proximity to the Financial District may influence its prices, but the selection and quality of the fish merit the higher price tag. The room is a bit quiet to discuss confidential business—unless the extensive sake list comes into play.

Lark Creek Steak

Steakhouse XX

845 Market St. (bet. 4th & 5th Sts.)

Phone: 415-593-4100 Lunch & dinner daily
Web: www.larkcreeksteak.com
Prices: $$$

Set off the rotunda on the fourth floor of the Westfield Centre, Lark Creek Steak appeals to savvy shoppers who save money on the sales so they can splurge on a meal here. Farm-fresh American fare and a good wine list add up to this perfect respite from rifling through the racks at Nordstrom.

Local farms and ranches provide many of the ingredients for Chef John Ledbetter's seasonal à la carte menu. Easily the best steaks found in a Bay Area mall, Lark Creek's grass-fed boneless ribeye and certified Angus filet mignon—among other choices—come with house-made sauces like red wine butter, creamy fresh horseradish, or the signature steak sauce. Vanilla cheesecake with Crackerjack crust will furnish the sugar rush for a few more hours of shopping.

Le Charm

C3

315 5th St. (bet. Folsom & Shipley Sts.)

Phone: 415-546-6128 — Lunch Tue – Fri
Web: www.lecharm.com — Dinner Tue – Sun
Prices: $$

True to its name, this high-ceilinged spot is a perennial charmer. A tiny copper-topped bar sits off the foyer, while butcher-paper-covered tables cluster in the small dining room. On the outdoor courtyard, umbrellas shade the sun-dappled space cradled by walls laced with trellised vines.

The open kitchen is the domain of Chef Lionel Balbastre of Toulouse, France, who took over in fall 2008. Peering out over his satisfied diners, the chef sticks to the classics (coq au vin; grilled *bavette* steak; tarte Tatin) that even novices to French cuisine can appreciate. Balbastre's Provençal heritage adds more vegetables and Mediterranean *plats du jour* to the menu. And in these trying economic times, Le Charm's prices reflect the good value of simpler days.

Local

Italian

C2

330 1st St. (bet. Folsom & Harrison Sts.)

Phone: 415-777-4200 — Lunch Tue – Fri & Sun
Web: www.sf-local.com — Dinner Tue – Sun
Prices: $$

On Local's menu, Italian dishes exhibit a good dose of California savoir fare, from pizza decked with shrimp and pesto to organic rotisserie chicken with panzanella. The desserts showcase brightly flavored gelati, panna cotta of the day, and other delicious offerings not often seen.

Yet to appreciate all this, guests must first navigate the quizzical behemoth of a heavy, Mondrian-style door to enter this chic post-industrial offering from Swede, Ola Fendert (also of Oola and Chez Papa). Inside, polished concrete floors form the base for white walls and abundant right angles. A high communal table gives guests a front-row seat near the open kitchen and pizza oven.

Stop in at the adjoining wine shop to stock up on wine and gourmet items to-go.

Luce ✿

Contemporary XX

B3

888 Howard St. (at 5th St.)

Phone: 415-616-6566 — Lunch & dinner daily
Web: www.lucewinerestaurant.com
Prices: **$$$**

InterContinental Hotels/Rien van Rijthoven

On the ground floor of the InterContinental San Francisco, Luce is, upon first glance, a ubiquitous hotel dining room. Enter the spacious marble lobby and pass through the bustling Bar 888—a grappa-centric lounge for a pre-dinner or post-work drink. Beyond this lies a rather stunning dining room with hand-blown Italian glass bubble lamps and tricolore marble floors. Floor-to-ceiling windows highlight the neutral palette with crystal and metallic accents.

Bumbling service, a noisy lobby, and international wines that sometimes miss the mark, however, can interfere with the overall experience. But make no mistake; Chef Dominique Crenn's contemporary cuisine leaves little to complain about. Dinner is the much more sophisticated meal here—Crenn's perfectly seared foie gras is superbly garnished with a de-boned quail leg, Granny Smith apple, crispy sage, and brioche, then finished with rich duck consommé. *"Le Jardin du Printemps"* is a stunning display of seasonal vegetables (not necessarily spring) simply steamed and arranged in an artistic presentation over a bed of crispy "soil."

Tuesday through Saturday, foodies may feast on the chef's tasting of eight to ten courses.

LuLu

Mediterranean

C3

816 Folsom St. (bet 4th & 5th Sts.)

Phone: 415-495-5775 — Lunch & dinner daily
Web: www.restaurantlulu.com
Prices: $$

With its soaring space, wide-open kitchen, and wood-burning oven plus rotisserie as a centerpiece, LuLu has nothing to hide from the hip studio crowd that frequents this former warehouse.

Wood-fired meats and fish cast enticing aromas around the room, tempting diners with the likes of rosemary-scented chicken and suckling pig with baby dandelion, roasted onions, and fig balsamic vinaigrette. A different rotisserie special is offered each day. Fresh oysters and seafood platters kick off the menu, while the bartender mixes great cocktails; and a separate wine bar boasts one of the more extensive and interesting wine selections in the area.

If you're in a hurry, check out LuLu Petite in the Ferry Building for gourmet produce and deli items to-go.

Manora's Thai Cuisine

Thai 

A4

1600 Folsom St. (at 12th St.)

Phone: 415-861-6224 — Lunch Mon – Fri
Web: www.manorathai.com — Dinner nightly
Prices:

Open for more than 20 years, this unpretentious place still packs 'em in for good Thai food and rock-bottom prices. One of the better bargains in the city is Manora's lunch combination: a cup of lemon chicken soup; Thai fried jasmine rice; and a choice of two main-dish items for under $9. Chef's favorite dinner entrées include the Pooket skewer (char-broiled scallop, prawn, and fish with veggies and two spicy sauces), and *Kai Yad Sai*, Thai-style omelets filled with crab, shrimp, and chicken with a mixture of aromatic Thai herbs.

Though the dining room is small, there's a bar up front that accommodates solo diners, and no matter where you sit, the colorfully clad and convivial staff proffer efficient service. Call ahead to avoid a wait for a table.

Mexico DF

Mexican

139 Steuart St. (bet. Mission & Howards Sts.)

Phone: 415-808-1048 — Lunch Mon – Fri
Web: www.mex-df.com — Dinner nightly
Prices: $$

Mexico DF evokes the *Distrito Federal* (known North of the border as Mexico City), and complements this restaurant-rich strip along The Embarcadero. This is where Chef Roberto Aguiar finds inspiration for many of his dishes.

From the colorful, modern dining room, watch the *cocina* turning out fresh tortillas and many versions of creamy guacamole, including *classico*, mango, or shrimp and bacon. Tacos tempt appetites with the likes of barbecue goat and *nopales* (cactus); while succulent pork *carnitas* come by the half or full pound accompanied by a brightly flavored trio of house-made condiments.

And, yes, those digital pictures on the wall *do* actually change . . . but easy on the bar's ample selection of tequila, anyway. Takeout is available at the counter.

Oola

Californian

860 Folsom St. (bet. 4th & 5th Sts.)

Phone: 415-995-2061 — Dinner nightly
Web: www.oola-sf.com
Prices: $$

This industrial-chic SoMa hot spot, with its sultry lighting and animated bar, appeals to the young and hip. Named for its Chef/owner, Ola Fendert (an original partner in Chez Papa, Chez Maman, and Baraka), Oola divides its soaring brick-walled space between booths on the ground floor and table seating on the mezzanine.

Market-fresh organic and sustainably-raised products drive the menu, which focuses on sensible creations such as goat-cheese-stuffed salmon roulade, and coffee-roasted duck breast atop diced pears and fingerling potatoes. A long list of crafted cocktails with a separate section just for "shots" will start—or end—the evening with a bang.

Check out Fendert's other venture, Local Kitchen & Wine Merchant.

One Market ✿

C1 — Californian ✗✗

1 Market St. (at Steuart St.)

Phone: 415-777-5577 — Lunch Mon – Fri
Web: www.onemarket.com — Dinner Mon – Sat
Prices: $$$

John Benson

Think of One Market as a spacious corner office in a sea of cubicles—perhaps inaccessible to neophytes, but just like home to the seasoned executive and society VIP. Presiding over the end of Market Street with views of the Ferry Building and Embarcadero, One Market is a preferred address among power-lunching professionals. Mind you, this bustling brasserie is nothing fancy—stone-tile floors and a few contemporary accoutrements provide the perfectly unassuming décor.

Nevertheless, it is always packed with a loyal patronage that appreciates impeccable service and the consistent market-fresh fare crafted by Chef Mark Dommen. Mediterranean flavors enhance the California cuisine in such savories as fresh Atlantic black cod, poached in olive oil and floating on a bed of *gigante* beans, carrot, fennel, and pine nuts. A wild mushroom potpie is presented tableside in a mini All-Clad pot, its buttery *pâté feuilletée* doused with earthy fungi in a creamy roux-based sauce. The bar is attentively staffed to accommodate guests sans reservations (and is an elegant spot to catch the game).

Wherever you sit, don't miss dessert: One Market's sweet trios and assortment platters always hit the spot.

Orson

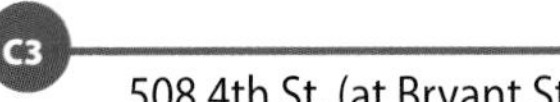

Contemporary XX

C3

508 4th St. (at Bryant St.)

Phone: 415-777-1508 — Dinner Tue – Sat
Web: www.orsonsf.com
Prices: $$

The epitome of industrial-chic, Orson continues to evolve, though the thirty-somethings crowd clustering around the oval bar still revels in the pumping club music. It's an up-tempo vibe that mirrors contemporary cuisine by Chef/owner Elizabeth Faulkner (of Citizen Cake fame).

There is less menu emphasis on small plates now, though entrées such as a pork loin and spare ribs with spiced root beer sauce are sized for sharing. Ever popular, the duck fat fries served with brown butter béarnaise make a perfect mate for one of the bar's crafted cocktails.

Faulkner's fans know not to skip dessert here. Whimsical sweets might include "mesh and lace," a licorice-spiked sponge cake animated by touches of pineapple and lime—and a scoop of buttermilk ice cream.

RN74

Californian XX

C1

301 Mission St. (at Beale St.)

Phone: 415-543-7474 — Lunch Mon – Fri, Dinner nightly
Web: www.rn74.com
Prices: $$$

Housed in Millennium Tower and named for Burgundy's main *route nationale*, Michael Mina's RN74 is an intoxicating spot with a singular wine experience. A handful of rare labels beckon from an old-school train station schedule board. When a wine sells out, the letters flip to reveal another curious bottle. Market wines are displayed on additional boards where a white light signals someone in the room is drinking a particular vintage. A vaulted ceiling, iron rafters, and antique lanterns further evoke the style of a European train station.

If you think the $4.5 million space is sleek, so is the buzzing clientele. The concise menu is carefully considered, while lounge acts include such interesting bites as sautéed sweetbreads and sea urchin carbonara.

Salt House

C2

Contemporary XX

545 Mission St. (bet. 1st & 2nd Sts.)

Phone: 415-543-8900 — Lunch Mon – Fri
Web: www.salthousesf.com — Dinner nightly
Prices: $$$

In a loft-style setting evocative of New York City—think exposed brick, iron girders, and local art—Salt House is the trendier younger sister of Town Hall, just around the corner. A bona fide hot spot given proximity to such SoMa nightspots as Harlot and 111 Minna, Salt House serves contemporary American fuel to well-heeled scenesters on their way to the dance floor. Lunch is popular among neighborhood tech geeks. California nuances inform simple dishes such as wild Coho salmon with cranberry beans and spicy *pimentón* jus. Dessert is stylized southern: Cheddar cheese pecan streusel is topped with vanilla ice cream and huckleberry coulis. Wash it all down with a carafe of house wine and don't mind the noise: Salt House is foremost about buzz.

Shanghai 1930

D1

Chinese XX

133 Steuart St. (bet. Howard & Mission Sts)

Phone: 415-896-5600 — Lunch Mon – Fri
Web: www.shanghai1930.com — Dinner Mon – Sat
Prices: $$

Near the Embarcadero, Shanghai 1930 recalls the opulence of that city in the period between the two World Wars. The place takes on an underground nightclub feel, beginning with the staircase that leads down from the street. A long blue-lit bar and live jazz nightly take you back to the 1930s.
The menu roams the regions of China, bringing diners the different cooking styles of that vast country. At lunch, the set combinations are your best deal, but ask to see the à la carte menu too. Available all day, this bill of fare provides more variety. Firecracker chicken (presented in a mini wok); tangerine beef with celery hearts; and Sichuan braised chili fish will surely tempt your taste buds.
The wine list brags of more than 800 international labels.

South Food + Wine Bar

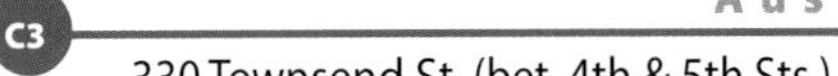

C3 Australian XX

330 Townsend St. (bet. 4th & 5th Sts.)

Phone: 415-974-5599 — Lunch Mon – Fri
Web: www.southfwb.com — Dinner Mon – Sat
Prices: $$$

In this ambitious SoMa restaurant and lounge, celebrity chef Luke Mangan and "mates" educate diners and oenophiles on the pleasures of Australian and New Zealand gastronomy. Lunchtime sandwiches may star the wonderfully flavored and textured Maori bread (a cross between a biscuit and *ciabatta*) encasing the likes of soft-poached eggs. Victorian lamb, West Australian barramundi, and Rozelle spices inspire the dinner fare. To drink, South's exciting wine program complements the menu with unique Australian, New Zealand, and South African labels not typically available in the U.S. The small, boxy room's chic décor mixes Maori-inspired floors; large, striking basket lamps of woven wood; stark white contemporary chairs; and black-faux ostrich skin banquettes.

The Butler & The Chef

C3 French X

155A South Park St. (bet. 2nd & 3rd Sts.)

Phone: 415-896-2075 — Lunch Tue – Sun
Web: www.oralpleasureinc.com
Prices: ⊜

Take a late morning stroll through South Park, the urban green surrounded by studios and neighborhood eateries, and you'll stumble upon vintage enamel tables crowding the sidewalk in front of The Butler & The Chef, a devil-may-care café with a sunny façade and blue awning. There's probably a pooch enjoying the shade beneath an outdoor bistro chair, adding to the convincingly Parisian air of this quaint spot, billed as "the cheapest roundtrip to France."
Try fresh-baked pastries for a *petit dejeuner*. Lunch brings savory stuffed crêpes, *croques*, and fluffy, golden quiches with daily ingredients, like shrimp and spinach. Channel your inner francophile and savor it with a glass of Champagne. Or join the locals and take your hot dog gratiné to the park.

Town Hall

C1 — Contemporary XX

342 Howard St. (at Fremont St.)

Phone: 415-908-3900 — Lunch Mon – Fri
Web: www.townhallsf.com — Dinner nightly
Prices: $$

Exposed brick walls, original local art, and broad windows cast an engaging sheen on this timeless SoMa hot spot. Town Hall rolls out the welcome mat for casual power lunches; come nightfall, a lively happy hour in the grand bar spills over into noisy suppers in the dining room and at the communal table.

Dating to 1907, the narrow space retains a historic charm thanks to eclectic antique furnishings, white beadboard wainscoting, classic soul tunes, and good old-fashioned hospitality. Cajun-inspired cuisine also hits the spot. Crispy oysters or buttermilk biscuits with ham and red pepper jelly kick-start the main event, where tender duck enchiladas are topped with bright tomatillo salsa and short ribs are killer when paired with a robust cabernet.

Tropisueño

B2 — Mexican X

75 Yerba Buena Ln. (bet. Market & Mission Sts.)

Phone: 415-243-0299 — Lunch & dinner daily
Web: www.tropisueno.com
Prices: ⊜

Shaded by the dramatic, blue steel wing of the Contemporary Jewish Museum, Yerba Buena Lane is becoming a foodie destination for local art junkies and tourists alike. In 2008, Tropisueño opened with something for everyone. At lunch, a taqueria-style counter serves tacos and *tortas* to professionals on the run; for those with time for a knife and fork, the super burrito *mojado* is a saucy siesta-inducer.

The restaurant dresses up a bit for dinner, delivering Latin American dishes like ceviche and tender chicken with *mole poblano*. A small salsa bar brims with jalapeños, sliced radishes, and tangy tomatillo salsa to pile on the mercifully thin chips.

But that's nothing compared to the expansive mahogany bar that oozes fine tequila and top-shelf margs.

TWO

American

C2

22 Hawthorne St. (bet. Folsom & Howard Sts.)

Phone: 415-777-9779 Dinner Mon – Sat
Web: www.two-sf.com
Prices: $$

Although TWO is the second restaurant to occupy this unexpected space tucked off a narrow lane, it is owned and operated by the same chef duo who founded its predecessor, Hawthorne Lane. Bridget Batson and David Gingrass keep things simple with market-fresh produce and locally raised meat and seafood. Thus an heirloom melon salad crowned by a lightly breaded and pan-fried disk of goat cheese might make a fitting prelude to grilled salmon boldly spiced with cumin, smoked paprika, and chile powder. Budget-conscious diners can opt for roasted butternut squash pizza, or pastas such as handkerchief noodles with veal sugo, pecorino, and ricotta.

TWO's bar is often packed with the SoMa/FiDi set, who come to enjoy libations after a hard day at the office.

Waterbar

Seafood

D1

399 The Embarcadero (at Harrison St.)

Phone: 415-284-9922 Lunch & dinner daily
Web: www.waterbarsf.com
Prices: $$$

The famed designer Pat Kuleto brings opulent Waterbar to the waterfront, just south of the Ferry Building. Although tall windows provide a great view of the Bay Bridge, there is plenty beneath these towering arched brick ceilings to hold your attention. Twin 19-foot-tall cylindrical aquariums and a hand-blown glass "caviar" chandelier paint an elegant picture over the raw bar's piles of fresh oysters and antique absinthe dispenser. Still, nothing should distract from the seafood bounty flown in from around the globe.

Chef and co-owner Mark Franz serves the likes of fresh sea scallop ceviche, tossed in citrus marinade over delicate rounds of sweet potatoes with smoked sea salt; or crisply seared and moist haddock over chorizo and tender butter beans.

XYZ

C2 — **Californian** XX

181 3rd St. (at Howard St.)

Phone: 415-817-7836 — Lunch daily
Web: www.xyz-sf.com — Dinner Mon – Sat
Prices: $$$

This restaurant in the W San Francisco manages to serve both a trendy setting and excellent, creative cuisine—while remaining a SoMa hot spot. The sleek décor features high-backed circular booths, contemporary canvases, artful floral compositions, seasonal accents, and two-story windows framing Third Street.

Taste modern Californian flair and Mediterranean influence in the kitchen's talented touch, which coaxes bright, bold flavors from top-of-the-line local products. Wild salmon, for example, pan-seared and served on white corn risotto enriched with Parmesan cream, expresses the chef's true devotion to superlative seasonal cooking.

"W" could also stand for wine, as in the more than 600 international labels on the excellent list.

Yank Sing

D1 — **Chinese** X

101 Spear St. (bet. Howard & Mission Sts.)

Phone: 415-957-9300 — Lunch daily
Web: www.yanksing.com
Prices: $$

Housed in an airy urban space with floor-to-ceiling windows, Yank Sing remains the gold standard for dim sum in San Francisco. One need only survey the strictly orchestrated staff, outfitted with earpieces and microphones, to know this place takes dim sum seriously—no wonder it is always packed at lunch. Service is rapid-fire with a procession of carts brimming with steamed and fried delights.

Luckily, the point-and-order method works like a charm. Just beware: With so many tempting options—sublime soup dumplings; pork-and-scallion potstickers; shrimp or snow pea dumplings; and barbecue pork buns—these mostly moderate prices add up quickly. Take heart in the fact that the restaurant is happy to validate your parking in its subterranean garage.

Zaré at Fly Trap

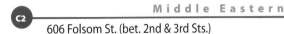

Middle Eastern XX

606 Folsom St. (bet. 2nd & 3rd Sts.)

Phone: 415-243-0580 — Dinner Mon – Sat
Web: www.zareflytrap.com
Prices: $$

Sliding into the Fly Trap, the 1906 eatery with tin ceilings and antique accents, downtowners can't help but feel at home at the end of a long day. That's just how Chef/owner Hoss Zaré felt when he bought the place in 2008: This was the first kitchen to hire Zaré when he arrived from Iran in 1986.

Today, though the historic vibe remains, the chef is infusing the Fly Trap with savory flavors from his home—think cinnamon-braised lamb tongue or sumac couscous with Dungeness crab. "Meatball Mondays" are a vegan's nightmare, with well-spiced two-pound beef and veal balls, stuffed with a meaty surprise. Try pairing it with a heady Lebanese red.

For dessert, crispy milk *torrijas* are plated with rosewater-scented hot chocolate and homemade marshmallows.

Zazil

Mexican 

845 Market St. (bet. 4th & 5th Sts.)

Phone: 415-495-6379 — Lunch & dinner daily
Web: www.zazilrestaurant.com
Prices: $$

A wavy banquette in aquatic shades of blue beneath mounted renderings of fish defines the theme at this seafood-centric restaurant located on the fourth floor of Westfield Centre mall. The name means "clear water" in Mayan, so naturally, the coastal cuisine of Mexico and Latin America anchors the menu.

Guacamole is prepared tableside, paired with fresh warm tortillas and a trio of salsas (crispy chips are also available, upon request). Follow this with ceviche tostadas, spicy crab soup, or maybe tuna *carnitas*, to experience this authentic, upscale fare not often found stateside.

Though Chef Sarah Rocio Gómez once served as the executive sous-chef for former Mexican President Vicente Fox, patrons here enjoy the more casual side of presidential treatment.

MICHELIN

East of San Francisco

East of San Francisco

Berkeley is legendary for its liberal politics and university campus that launched the 1960s Free Speech Movement. Among foodies, the free-thinking borough is a Garden of Eden—it sprouted American gastronomy's leading purist, Alice Waters, and continues to be a place of worship for the local food movement; the term "locavore" was coined here. In recent years, Water's Chez Panisse Foundation has nurtured the Edible Schoolyard, an organic garden and kitchen classroom for students; in 2008, she founded Slow Food Nation, the country's largest festival of slow and sustainable foods.

Since Waters is credited with developing California cuisine, her influence can be tasted in restaurants far and wide. But really, one needn't look much further than Berkeley's Gourmet Ghetto: The North Shattuck corridor is aromatic with fresh-roasted joe from **Village Grounds** and fabulous takeout options at **Grégoire** and **Epicurious Garden**.

The Ghetto is also stuffed with worker-owned co-ops including the **Cheese Board Collective**, which also bakes fresh pastries and breads; the **Cheese Board Pizza Collective**; and the **Juice Bar Collective**. On Thursday afternoons, the **North Shattuck Organic Farmers Market** bursts with local produce rain or shine.

For breakfast, **900 Grayson** is prized for a decidedly un-Belgian buttermilk waffle and farm fresh eggs; **La Note**'s brioche *pain perdu* is lovely; and **Tomate Café** serves Cuban breakfast on a pup-friendly patio; **Caffe Mediterraneum** is the SF birthplace of the caffe latte. Berkeley is also home to foremost artisan baker, **Acme Bread Company**, and Chef Paul Bertolli's handcrafted **Fra'mani Salumi**.

Oakland doesn't quite carry the culinary panache of neighboring Berkeley, but the workaday city has seen a revival of its own with new businesses and condos cropping up downtown. **Jack London Square**, on the waterfront, is the area's chief tourist destination for movies, dining, nightlife, and a **Sunday Farmers and Artisan Market**. With broad patios and Bay views, **Miss Pearl's Jam House** serves island-inspired cuisine and refreshing Cruzan Jello shots. A point of interest—Jack London himself was once a regular at the 1883 cash-only tavern **Heinold's First and Last Chance Saloon**.

Taco junkies congregate on International Boulevard where a two-mile stretch serves as a parking lot for taco trucks; **Tacos Sinaloa** and **Mariscos Sinaloa** are known for chorizo and fish tacos, respectively. Downtown, professionals nosh fried oyster Po'boys at **Café 15**; in Temescal, **Bakesale Betty** serves crispy chicken sandwiches atop ironing board tables. After work, the **Trappist** pours more than 160 Belgian and specialty beers. On Sundays, oyster mongers line up at **Rudy Figueroa's**, at the **Montclair Farmers Market**, for bivalves shucked to order. In August, the Art & Soul Festival brings a buffet of world flavors, as does the Chinatown Streetfest with tropical juices, curries, and barbecue meats. Year round, Chinatown buzzes with Asian restaurants and grocers.

In Rockridge, the quaint shopping district between Oakland and Berkeley, boutiques and eateries abound. **Cactus Taqueria** is popular for its burrito **mejor**. **Tara's Organic Ice Cream** serves cool flavors, like chile pistachio or basil, in compostible cups. **Market Hall** is a gourmet shopper's paradise with sustainable catch at **Hapuku Fish Shop**, specialty groceries at the **Pasta Shop**, a bakery, produce market, and coffee bar.

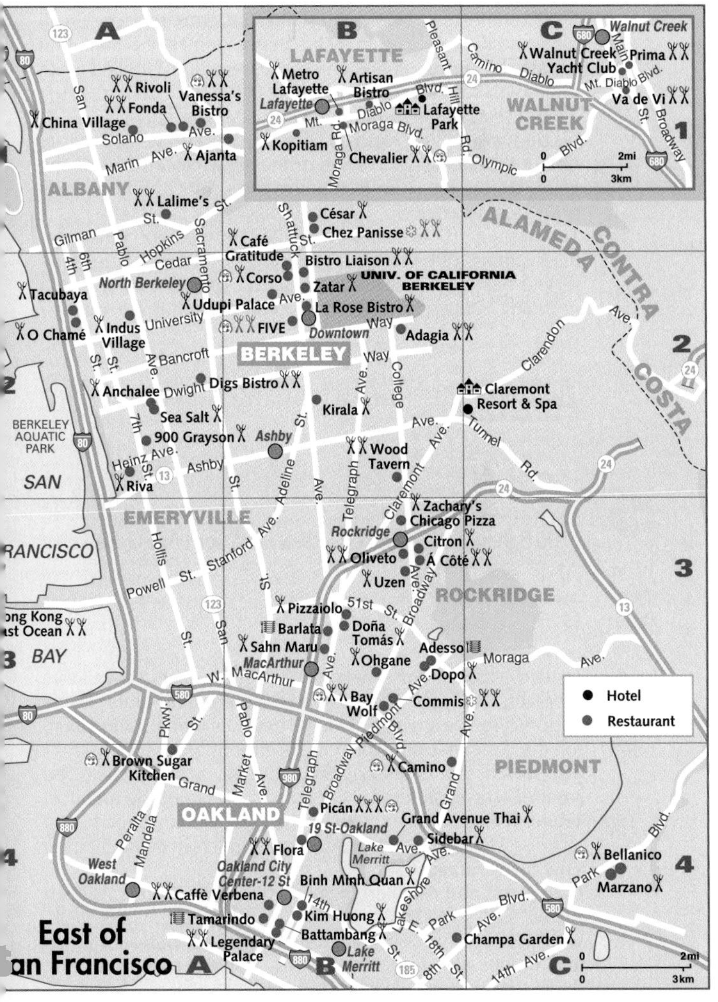

À Côté

Mediterranean XX

B3

5478 College Ave. (at Taft Ave.), Oakland

Phone: 510-655-6469 Dinner nightly
Web: www.acoterestaurant.com
Prices: $$

Rockridge residents love this convivial place, where Mediterranean cuisine pairs with courteous service. Small plates hold sway here, in incarnations such as ricotta-stuffed squash blossoms; grilled duck sausage; and smoked trout salad with baby red mustard.

Take a seat at the communal table near the kitchen and its blazing wood-fired oven, or nosh at the bar while you sip one of the specialty cocktails or the 40 wines offered by the glass. During the warmer months, the sunny patio becomes prime real estate.

The restaurant sets aside a limited number of tables for reservations, but seating is primarily on a first-come, first-served basis. No worries: the adjacent blocks are chock-full of trendy boutiques to occupy you until your table is ready.

Adagia

Californian XX

B2

2700 Bancroft Way (bet. College & Piedmont Aves.), Berkeley

Phone: 510-647-2300 Lunch Tue – Fri
Web: www.adagiarestaurant.com Dinner Tue – Sat
Prices: $$

Leaded-glass windows, wrought-iron chandeliers, the massive fireplace, and the custom-made communal table inside Tudor-style Westminster House create a fitting atmosphere for the academic crowd from neighboring U.C. Berkeley—just beware that eavesdropping here may actually make you smarter. This restored 1926 landmark designed by architect Walter Ratcliff is still owned by the Presbyterian Church, and its Great Hall, where the minister once entertained dignitaries, now holds Adagia.

Californian and Mediterranean compositions here earn high marks, as in grilled chile- and oregano-marinated flank steak, with oyster mushrooms and crispy potatoes. Between lunch and dinner, the restaurant serves a snack menu, enticing those seeking a stately place to study.

Adesso

Italian

B3

4395 Piedmont Ave. (at Pleasant Valley Rd.), Oakland

Phone: 510-601-0305 Dinner Mon – Sat
Web: N/A
Prices: $$

Carnivores rejoice: This is a meaty restaurant. Sister to nearby Dopo, Adesso boasts more than 30 varieties of house-made salumi, a selection of artisanal pâtés—served in thick slices—and jars of creamy rillettes just begging to be spread over toasty croutons. Antipasti, panini, and *piadina* (flatbread wraps) are all made with talent, quickly served, and priced to please.

Its wraparound bar, flat-screen TV, foosball table, high windows overlooking Piedmont Avenue, and chill, watering hole vibe lure a consistent afterwork crowd. Try an original cocktail with freshly muddled fruit, or opt for a dusky red that pairs well with meat. Then again, you'll have time to try both while waiting for a coveted table at this first-come, first-served eatery.

Ajanta

Indian

B1

1888 Solano Ave. (bet. The Alameda & Colusa Ave.), Berkeley

Phone: 510-526-4373 Lunch & dinner daily
Web: www.ajantarestaurant.com
Prices: ⓈⓈ

In an area of Berkeley where Indian restaurants abound, Ajanta stands out for its pleasant, traditional, well-crafted regional cuisine. "As you like it" describes the heat levels here, which are adjusted to your preference—go for "hot" if you fancy spicier food. From Punjab comes tandoori game hen, marinated in yogurt, lemon juice, ginger, garlic, and spices; lamb *do pyaza*, a stew made with cubes of boneless Niman Ranch leg of lamb, hails from New Delhi; green catfish curry, a recipe from Mumbai, simmers in a sauce made with coconut milk, green chillies, herbs, and cashew powder. The menu, which adds new dishes each month, specifies the origin of each entrée.

Enthusiasts can pick up a copy of Ajanta's cookbook and create some of these dishes at home.

Anchalee

Thai

A2

1094 Dwight Way (at San Pablo Ave.), Berkeley

Phone: 510-848-4015 — Lunch & dinner daily
Web: www.anchaleethai.com
Prices: ©©

Catering to its colorful college set, Berkeley is rife with cheap ethnic eateries, but Anchalee's fresh, flavorful fare deems it a worthy stand out. Wooden tables perch on hard wood floors, while olive green walls, exposed brick, and pendant lights create a calm vibe. This is quality Thai where creative dishes like basil squid and garlic salmon fried rice make for exciting picks alongside trusty standbys like pad Thai and satay. And almost every item—except for seafood—is under ten dollars. Tuck into the *yum nuer,* a tender beef salad with mint and cilantro; or the spicy red curry green bean chicken (opt for the nutty brown rice).

Herbivores rave about the steamed radish cakes and green papaya salad. Wash it all down with a creamy Thai iced tea.

Artisan Bistro

Californian

B1

1005 Brown Ave. (at Mt. Diablo Blvd.), Lafayette

Phone: 925-962-0882 — Lunch & dinner Tue – Sun
Web: www.artisanlafayette.com
Prices: **$$$**

Located east of Berkeley, the upscale town of Lafayette is named for the French Marquis who aided America during the Revolutionary War. Were he still around, Lafayette would certainly find nostalgia for his homeland in Artisan's straightforward bistro fare. Seasonal ingredients headline in the likes of a flaky piece of halibut served over wilted spinach and sautéed morels, with English peas adding a sweet note. A luscious Meyer lemon tart crowned with fresh blackberries and candied lemon zest provides the pièce de résistance.

The bistro's craftsman-style cottage includes a spacious brick patio strewn with umbrella-shaded tables. Inside, the space is divided into several small rooms, where the majority of loyal patrons seem to know each other.

Barlata

4901 Telegraph Ave. (at 49th St.), Oakland

Phone: 510-450-0678 Dinner nightly
Web: www.barlata.com
Prices:

Canned food gets a bad rap. So in the tradition of so-wrong-it's-right culinary phenomena, Barlata celebrates the *lata*—which is, you guessed it, a can. Still, there's nothing lowbrow about Chef/owner Daniel Olivella's Spanish tapas, many of which are presented in recycled tins and priced around $8 a pop. The Catalan native, who also owns B44 in San Francisco, conjures the Iberian Peninsula with nearly 40 savory small plates like seafood *piquillo* peppers or fennel sausage stuffed with baby squid. Inventive dishes include lamb meatballs with squid, chocolate, and tomato sauce. Thematic artwork also tributes the tin, and hanging imported hams lend authenticity to the eclectic vibe.

Canned tuna, *pimenton*, anchovies, and the like are available to-go.

Battambang

850 Broadway (bet. 8th & 9th Sts.), Oakland

Phone: 510-839-8815 Lunch & dinner Mon – Sat
Web: N/A
Prices:

Named for Cambodia's second largest city, Battambang is beloved by foodies with a taste for authentic cooking—which, oddly, is tough to find among the area's many Asian eateries. Fresh orchids and perky yellow walls enliven the modest room, where charming servers are proud and knowledgeable of the cuisine. Thai and Vietnamese influences are evident across the extensive menu; though these well-seasoned dishes are less spicy, that jar of garlic-chili sauce on each table allows self-spice gratification.

Expect the likes of charbroiled meats, pan-fried lemongrass catfish, and the vegetarian favorite *trorb aing* (smoky roasted eggplant in spicy lime sauce), as well as specialties that some may find intimidating, but others are sure to find delicious.

Bay Wolf

Californian

3853 Piedmont Ave. (at Rio Vista Ave.), Oakland

Phone: 510-655-6004 — Lunch Tue – Fri
Web: www.baywolf.com — Dinner Tue – Sun
Prices: $$

An Oakland icon, Bay Wolf pinpoints the sophisticated simplicity of seasonal Californian cuisine. Michael Wild, a former teacher with early exposure to haute French cuisine, opened this charmer with a few friends in the early 1970s. Seating is split between two narrow dining areas flanking a small central bar, and the large enclosed, heated patio at the entrance.

Always delicious, the ever-changing menu of comfort food may start with a chilled potato, cucumber, and fava bean soup; followed by oxtail ravioli and butternut squash; and an Anaheim pepper stuffed with spicy black beans and rice. Save room for dessert—a homey apple crisp or a luscious caramel *pot de crème* complemented by a butterscotch brownie are reminders of pleasure in simplicity.

Bellanico

Italian

4238 Park Blvd. (at Wellington St.), Oakland

Phone: 510-336-1180 — Lunch & dinner daily
Web: www.bellanico.net
Prices: $$

Named for their daughters Gabriella and Nicoletta, Bellanico is the culinary child of Chris Shepherd and Elizabeth Frumusa (the duo behind Aperto). The lightly decorated space, once a flower shop, features rust-colored walls and a granite-topped bar.

Meals here may begin with *cicchetti* (snacks) of fried green Sicilian olives, *baccalà mantecato*, *crostini Toscani*, or perhaps a combined plate of all three. *Primi*, like house-made pastas, and *secondi*, such as slow-braised short ribs, demonstrate the success of simple Italian food prepared with care and skill. Accompany meals with a respectable offering of mainly European wines, many served by the glass or flight.

While family friendly with pasta options for kids, this gem also attracts sophisticated foodies.

Binh Minh Quan

Vietnamese

B4

338 12th St. (bet. Harrison & Webster Sts.), Oakland

Phone: 510-893-8136 Lunch & dinner daily
Web: N/A
Prices: ⊜

First-timers are wise to bring their reading glasses and a hearty appetite to appreciate this very authentic view of Vietnam. The sprawling menu features more than 130 items, including 30 dishes with super-sticky, nutty "broken" rice; soups that surpass expectations; and specialties seasoned with mounds of fresh, exotic herbs. Culinary adventurers are bound to relish delicacies like curried frog and grilled wild boar, while couples and larger groups can delight in sharing the seven-course beef tasting prepared in fire pots at the table. Even timid diners should explore the curious drinks selection of fruit shakes made with durian, jackfruit, and soursop.
Bamboo wainscoting and mini-tiki hut roofs fashion a comfortable, unembellished setting.

Bistro Liaison

French

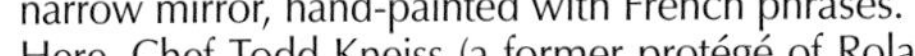

B2

1849 Shattuck Ave. (at Hearst Ave.), Berkeley

Phone: 510-849-2155 Lunch & dinner daily
Web: www.liaisonbistro.com
Prices: $$

The concept of a bistro developed in Paris as a small restaurant serving simple, inexpensive meals in a modest setting. Bistro Liaison follows this time-honored model with its L-shaped banquette that runs along the back wall below a narrow mirror, hand-painted with French phrases.
Here, Chef Todd Kneiss (a former protégé of Roland Passot) approaches simplicity with a deft hand to create "French food for the soul" that celebrates its most traditional dishes. His *ris de veau*, coq au vin, *bouillabaisse*, or steak frites are sure to elevate the mood of any expat. Dessert and cocktail selections are rubber-stamped on the white butcher paper that covers each table.
For regulars and Berkeley residents, a wine club and periodic cooking classes are also offered.

East of San Francisco

Brown Sugar Kitchen

American

2534 Mandela Pkwy. (at 26th St.), Oakland

Phone: 510-839-7685 Lunch Tue – Sun
Web: www.brownsugarkitchen.com
Prices:

From afar it looks as if a giant wedge of sweet potato pie landed smack in the center of industrial West Oakland. This slice of "new style down home" goodness is French trained Tanya Holland's opus—where organic and soul foods meet in a heavenly convergence of sheer belly bliss. Even if you have to wait for a table, think you can resist the brown sugar pineapple-glazed baby back ribs, or smoked chicken and shrimp gumbo? We doubt it. Try the talented chef's take on a beloved Harlem classic: crispy buttermilk fried chicken, perfectly done, nestled aside a delicate, crunchy cornbread waffle kissed with brown sugar butter and apple cider syrup. The smart wine list features mainly African-American vintners and the bounty of rustic desserts changes frequently.

Café Gratitude

Vegan 

1730 Shattuck Ave. (at Virginia St.), Berkeley

Phone: 415-824-4652 Lunch & dinner daily
Web: www.cafegratitude.com
Prices:

On the restaurant-rich strip of Shattuck Avenue known as the "gourmet ghetto," Café Gratitude keeps Berkeley's bohemian spirit alive and well—quite literally, since this healthful cuisine is completely vegan and mostly raw.

Rest assured that before the organic elixirs and the likes of zucchini lasagna layered with cashew "ricotta" have the opportunity to comfort you, the waitstaff will. When presenting, the servers offer menu affirmations such as "you are divine." Quirky and cute the first time, by the end of a multicourse meal—when you are also "fabulous," "insightful," and "lovely"—you will either be at a higher level of self-affirmation, or totally over the kitsch.

Spreading the love in Santa Rosa is a relatively new, freshly sprouted sibling.

Caffè Verbena

Italian XX

B4

1111 Broadway (bet. 11th & 12th Sts.), Oakland

Phone: 510-465-9300 — Lunch & dinner Mon – Fri
Web: www.caffeverbena.com
Prices: $$

The Oakland Convention Center attendees are drawn with good reason to this spacious restaurant for Italian fare. Bright flavors highlight the Caffè's take on classic lasagna: three roulades of lasagna are napped with basil pesto and tangy tomato sauce. Traditional selections of antipasti, pizza, pasta, meat, and fish dishes round out the menu.
The large size of the restaurant and its location on the lobby level of the APL Building in downtown Oakland give it the feel of a hotel dining room. Even so, courtyard views outside the window-lined space feature a pleasant, grassy garden, enhanced by contemporary sculptures and a stone waterfall. After work, Caffè Verbena's bar brings in a lively crowd who sip cocktails and unwind.

Camino

B4

3917 Grand Ave. (at Sunny Slope Ave.), Oakland

Phone: 510-547-5035 — Lunch Sat – Sun
Web: www.caminorestaurant.com — Dinner Wed – Mon
Prices: $$

Courtesy of a Chez Panisse graduate, Camino fills its Basque-style dining room with pressed-tin ceilings, enormous wrought-iron chandeliers, and communal tables fashioned from salvaged redwood trees that blew down in the Mendocino area. Exposed brick walls and dark wood beams add to the homespun feel.
Along a brick wall, the expansive open kitchen provides evening-long entertainment with cooks shelling fresh beans before adding them to bubbling pots over the fire, or turning a roasting leg of lamb over the flames, adding smoked-tinged flavors to the air. Chef Russell Moore's menu changes each night, featuring typically less than 10 dishes, such as grilled duck breast with a crisp salad or plump and tender roasted rockfish set upon farro and rapini.

César

Spanish

1515 Shattuck Ave. (bet. Cedar & Vine Sts.), Berkeley

Phone: 510-883-0222 Lunch & dinner daily
Web: www.barcesar.com
Prices: $$

César was founded in 1998 by three Chez Panisse alumni, so it is no coincidence that this lively "gourmet ghetto" Californian tapas bar lives next door to its famous neighbor—and that its name is an homage to the same trilogy of films by Marcel Pagnol.

In the same spirit of offering incomparably fresh ingredients, César tempts with the likes of portobello mushroom *bocadillos* and fire-grilled shrimp *a la plancha*. Even the most ardent carb-counters will find it hard to resist the perfect mountain of fried potato ribbons dusted with herbs and sea salt, and accompanied by tangy garlic aïoli. A minimal and simple selection of sweets are also available.

A second, much larger, branch of César sits in Oakland and is equally popular and buzzing.

Champa Garden

B4 Asian

2102 8th Ave. (at 21st St.), Oakland

Phone: 510-238-8819 Lunch & dinner daily
Web: www.champagarden.com
Prices: $$

Couched in a residential area of Oakland's edgy San Antonio neighborhood, Champa Garden lures locals inside with its aromatic Southeast Asian cuisine, inexpensive prices, and courteous service. The setting may not impress, but authentic tastes of Vietnam, Laos, and Thailand infuse the appealing dishes.

An abundant offering of noodle soups, pan-fried noodles, seafood entrées, fried rice, and curries pack the value-driven menu. Starters standout in the fried rice ball salad (*nam kaow*), where a symphony of flavor and texture reveals itself in this blend of crispy fried rice, crumbles of preserved pork, green onions, chillies, and lime juice. To eat it, wrap the rice mixture in the Romaine leaves provided, along with some fresh mint and cilantro.

Chevalier

French

B1

960 Moraga Rd. (at Moraga Blvd.), Lafayette

Phone: 925-385-0793 — Lunch Tue – Fri
Web: www.chevalierrestaurant.com — Dinner Tue – Sat
Prices: $$

This little Lafayette neighborhood spot captures the warmth and charm of Southern France in its joie de vivre and delightful seasonal dishes. Ignore the strip-mall location and request a seat on the enchanting semi-circular patio, which winds around a fragrant garden stocked with herbs, flowers, and hedges for privacy. With white-clothed tables and French music crooning softly in the background, the patio encourages romantic dinners on a warm evening.

The chef's passion fires the authentic fare, with appetizers of buttery escargots flavored with garlic and parsley. Entrées may include *noix de Saint Jacques*—plump, golden, pan-seared scallops dusted with spicy *piment d'espelette*, presented with a tender, aromatic vegetable ragout swimming in pesto.

China Village

Chinese

A1

1335 Solano Ave. (at Pomona Ave.), Albany

Phone: 510-525-2285 — Lunch & dinner daily
Web: N/A
Prices: 

High tolerance for tongue-numbing, lip-scorching spice? China Village will happily oblige. Local Chinese diners flock to this Albany spot for fiery, authentic Mandarin and Sichuan style cuisine, where classics like Kung Pao share the menu with more exotic offerings like thousand chili chicken and boiled kidney. For another spicy spectacle, try the West Sichuan style fish fillet: bedecked with a startling number of dried red chilies, the server filters them out, leaving a moderately piquant soup of delicate whitefish, cellophane noodles, and tasty broth.

The modest space, divided into a few pleasant, banquet style dining rooms with artfully decorated tables and tanks of live Dungeness crabs, is ideal for large groups and families.

Chez Panisse ✿

B1 **Californian** XX

1517 Shattuck Ave. (bet. Cedar & Vine Sts.), Berkeley

Phone: 510-548-5525 Dinner Mon – Sat
Web: www.chezpanisse.com
Prices: $$$$

Aya Brackett

If Alice Waters is the fairy godmother of the locavore movement, then Chez Panisse is her castle. Sheltered in a spectacular old bungalow in artsy Berkeley, this iconic restaurant swung open its doors in 1971, kick-starting a concept what would quickly come to define California cuisine—employ premium ingredients from local farmers, ranchers, and fisherman, and only serve whatever is market-fresh that day. Four decades later, the movement is still on fire.

Those lucky enough to score a reservation (a bustling upstairs café welcomes walk-ins, but reservations for the main room should be made well in advance) will find a warm welcome into this beautiful old wood-paneled home, and a tour of the bustling, open kitchen is a must-do for any newbie.

The four-course menu (three-courses on Mondays) rotates nightly, but might include bright green asparagus bathed in a fragrant vinaigrette touched with crispy pancetta shards, golden beets, and a perfectly soft-boiled farm egg; local petrale sole, laced with beurre blanc, kumquat, and fried chervil; or roasted and grilled Laughing Stock pork with a green garlic purée, surrounded by fresh favas, tender peas, and earthy morel mushrooms.

Citron

Contemporary

B3

5484 College Ave. (bet. Lawton & Taft Aves.), Oakland

Phone: 510-653-5484 — Lunch Tue – Sun
Web: www.citronrestaurant.biz — Dinner nightly
Prices: $$

International is too broad a label to put on a cuisine that jumps from Mediterranean to French to Californian. No matter its origins, the food here is fresh, expertly cooked, and full of flavor. At lunch, country pork pâté with dried cherries makes a worthy prelude to potato gnocchi with wild mushrooms, white corn, and Parmesan; or even a barbecue pulled-pork sandwich with house-made *gaufrette* chips. A three-course prix-fixe meal offers good value for the budget-conscious.
Dinner reveals the same variety à la carte, featuring Creole-spiced prawns, or grilled lamb sirloin with fall greens bread salad. Three- to five-course chef's tastings are also available. White linens, sultry jazz, and blues music complement the upscale Rockridge neighborhood.

Corso

Italian

B2

1788 Shattuck Ave. (bet. Delaware & Francisco Sts.), Berkeley

Phone: 510-704-8003 — Lunch & dinner daily
Web: www.trattoriacorso.com
Prices: $$

In the birthplace of California cuisine, Berkeley's Corso is a journey to Tuscany. The rustic little eatery bears the stamps of travel: framed trattorie menus and wine lists offer a glimpse at co-owner Wendy Brucker's extensive "research," collected during her wanderings in the Renaissance city, Florence. In the homey dining room, a granite-topped bar offers a view to the open kitchen where Florentine specialties are testament to Brucker's quest for authenticity. Savory pizzas are thin and true to traditions, while the *pollo al burro*—crispy skin-on chicken sautéed liberally in butter—is revelatory. The wines, of course, are all Italian and available by the carafe.
At brunch, toasted *panettone* with butter and jam is a sweet start to the weekend.

Commis ✿

B3 — Contemporary XX

3859 Piedmont Ave. (at Rio Vista Ave.), Oakland

Phone: 510-653-3902 — Dinner Wed – Sun
Web: www.commisrestaurant.com
Prices: $$$

Aaron Stienstra

The name of this buzzing new spot means "trainee chef" in French—a position Chef James Syhabout might know a thing or two about, having worked his way through many talented kitchens like El Bulli, The Fat Duck, Manresa, and PlumpJack Café. With Commis, he now ventures into his first solo project—and Oakland is all the more delicious for it.

Housed in the former Jojo space, the narrow interior boasts a centerpiece kitchen that makes every table in the sleek, sparsely-decorated room feel like a chef's table. It helps that Syhabout himself occasionally trots the food over to the tables with an explanation of the dish—a nice touch that we're hoping won't go away anytime soon. Hardcore foodies will want to sit at the polished wood bar, which offers great views of the small crew of cooks, each of them sporting the blue pin-striped *commis* apron.

The compact menu is tight, but super creative, with dishes like a soft-cooked farm fresh egg mixed with braised pork jowl, potatoes, black garlic purée, and purple allium blossoms; or a velvety slip of Morro Bay cod, seasoned with *fleur de sel* and browned to a lovely crisp, then paired with an English pea purée.

Digs Bistro

American

A2

1453 Dwight Way (bet. Sacramento St. & San Pablo Ave.), Berkeley

Phone: 510-548-2322 Dinner Thu – Mon
Web: www.digsbistro.com
Prices: $$

Word of mouth draws Berkeleyites to this unpretentious bistro, which started out as an "underground" restaurant in the manager's home. Now housed in a converted residence, Digs is a quaint spot for an evening out. Its four-seat zinc bar and small dining area are accented by arched openings and avocado-green tables; a beehive-oven fire adds warmth in the winter months.

One can measure a kitchen staff by how well they roast a chicken, and here the cooking is spot on. Digs' version turns out succulent, with a crispy skin and a rich chicken jus studded with baby shiitake mushroom caps.

Parents love the first Monday of every month, when the bistro staff will supervise their kids so the adults enjoy a peaceful dinner—though the scene can get chaotic.

Doña Tomás

Mexican

B3

5004 Telegraph Ave. (bet. 49th & 51st Sts.), Oakland

Phone: 510-450-0522 Dinner Tue – Sat
Web: www.donatomas.com
Prices: $$

Oakland's answer to Berkeley's "gourmet ghetto" (home to sibling Tacubaya) is this sexy senorita in the Temescal district. Upbeat Latin music pulses through the restaurant, where an evening may begin with a margarita or *mojito* at the small bar in the corner of the room, and end with coffee on the inviting courtyard out back. The later it gets, the higher the decibel level climbs in the dining room.

Regional Mexican and Californian cuisines offer seasonal flair and fuse here into favorites like *carnitas* with large chunks of slow-cooked pork; and fish tacos filled with sautéed halibut cheeks, onions, chiles, and garlic. While the price tag is higher than that of a local taco truck or neighborhood taqueria, quality is what stands out here.

Dopo

Italian 

4293 Piedmont Ave. (at Echo St.), Oakland

Phone: 510-652-3676 — Lunch & dinner Mon – Sat
Web: N/A
Prices: **$$**

Locals may come here for the artisanal Neapolitan pies, but Dopo is much more than a pizza place. Thank Oliveto veteran Jon Smulewitz. His concise daily menu holds to the basic tenet of Californian cuisine: simple, fresh, and local. Diners who stand in line to eat here—despite an expansion a few years ago that doubled the seating capacity—agree that a panini filled with a breast of fried Hoffman Farm hen, and house-made pasta or pâté are worth the wait. Then again, the namesake Dopo pizza (tangy tomato sauce, oregano, mozzarella, Pecorino Romano, chile flakes, and optional anchovies) always wins raves.

Claim a seat at one of the closely-spaced pine tables, or at the aqua-tiled dining counter that wraps around the bar from the open kitchen.

FIVE

American

2086 Allston Way (at Shattuck Ave.), Berkeley

Phone: 510-845-7300 — Lunch & dinner daily
Web: www.five-berkeley.com
Prices: **$$**

Housed in the extensively renovated Hotel Shattuck Plaza, FIVE's dining room is a stylish feast for the eyes with towering columns, discreet jewel tones that sparkle throughout the bright space, and a glossy checkered floor that leads the way. The sophisticated setting is relaxed and comfortable; but taste is assuredly where the efforts of Chef Scott Howard will sate one's senses.

His comforting menu features top-notch ingredients and preparations as in the delicate house-smoked salmon atop a Yukon Gold potato cake with julienned Granny Smith apple and horseradish cream; crispy skinned chicken paired with mac and cheese starring orzo and topped with tangy tomato jam; and homespun butterscotch pudding accompanied by salted peanut brittle clusters.

Flora

American

B4

1900 Telegraph Ave. (at 19th St.), Oakland

Phone: 510-286-0100 Lunch & dinner Tue – Sat
Web: www.floraoakland.com
Prices: $$

Flora finds its name in its location, inside the 1931 Oakland Floral Depot Building. An art deco gem, the structure is faced in cobalt blue terra-cotta with silver trim that drips down the façade like water. It makes a nostalgic setting for the restaurant's black and cream dining room and long curving bar.

Organic ingredients from local growers pepper the menu. If the likes of a slow-roasted pork shoulder with creamy polenta and *broccoli de ciccio* sounds good, you're in for a treat. And speaking of treats, save room for the caramel pudding, kicked up by a sprinkle of *fleur de sel*.

Run by Dona Svitsky and Chef Thomas Schnetz—the folks behind Doña Tomás (Oakland) and Tacubaya (Berkeley)—Flora proves that this team can reach well beyond Mexican fare.

Fonda

Latin American

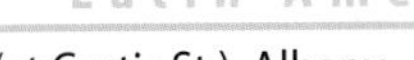

A1

1501 Solano Ave. (at Curtis St.), Albany

Phone: 510-559-9006 Lunch Sat – Sun
Web: www.fondasolana.com Dinner nightly
Prices: $$

Part of the restaurant realm owned by Haig and Cindy Krikorian (of Lalime's and Sea Salt, both in Berkeley), this festive Albany hot spot showcases creative Latin American cuisine and drinks to match. A long inviting bar offers views of the open kitchen, while the upstairs mezzanine sports a comfy lounge-like feel with its upholstered chairs. Mavens of the late-night scene drop in for happy hour, which starts here after 9:00 P.M. every night.

Fonda now also serves weekend brunch, spotlighting favorites such as duck tacos, fish *à la plancha*, and *chilaquiles verdes* (a Mexican scramble with tortilla strips, salsa verde, and Anaheim chiles). Or, drop in Friday through Sunday for an afternoon "siesta" menu featuring rum cocktails and a selection of tapas.

Grand Avenue Thai

Thai

B4

384 Grand Ave. (bet. Perkins St. & Staten Ave.), Oakland

Phone: 510-444-1507
Web: www.grandavenuethai.com
Prices:

Lunch Mon – Sat
Dinner nightly

This chic yet unassuming neighborhood favorite just steps from Lake Merritt fills daily with the Oakland workaday crowd looking for a lunchtime pick-me-up. Brightly hued walls don vivid oil paintings created by a friend of the chef, and each table is topped with fresh, cheerful flowers.

This is a comfortable atmosphere for sampling contemporary Thai cuisine, but spice lovers may be disappointed—the kitchen turns down the heat to suit the American palate. Dishes are nonetheless packed with flavor: A lemongrass tilapia is pan-fried with Thai basil and sweet red chili sauce, while green chicken curry is redolent with coconut milk and kaffir lime. Straightforward service and attention to detail makes this an ideal spot for a quick but satisfying bite.

Hong Kong East Ocean

Chinese

A3

3199 Powell St., Emeryville

Phone: 510-655-3388
Web: www.hkeo.us
Prices:

Lunch & dinner daily

Cantonese dishes, fresh seafood, and dim sum are the main reasons crowds flock to this massive pagoda-roofed restaurant that flanks the Bay. Here, diners enjoy fantastic views of the nearby marina, Bay Bridge, and San Francisco skyline through the large windows that define the space.

This place is meant for family-style dining, so bring a few relatives or friends and try the special set menu available for four, six, or eight. Or choose from the regular bill of fare, which includes fish from the massive tanks along one wall. At lunchtime, opt for dim sum; check off a sampling of items from the written list, and moments later they parade from the kitchen one by one.

Plenty of banquet rooms accommodate groups from business meetings to birthday parties.

Indus Village

Indian

1920 San Pablo Ave. (bet. Hearst & University Aves.), Berkeley

Phone: 510-549-5999 Lunch & dinner daily
Web: N/A
Prices: $$

With carefully crafted curries, tasty lamb dishes, tandoor specialties, and Indian and Pakistani recipes at bargain-basement prices, Indus Village is the answer to any foodie seeking a casual and inexpensive South Asian meal.

Regulars check out the day's specials on the whiteboard at the entrance, walk up to the counter, place their order, and seat themselves in the bright, ornate chairs; food is delivered to them when it is ready. There is table service too, but it's brisk and no-nonsense, keeping the focus on the food rather than formality. Vibrant and evocative wall murals depict the desert life of India and Pakistan.

Next door, the restaurant's grocery is well-stocked with all the items you need to re-create your favorite dishes at home.

Kim Huong

304 10th St. (at Harrison St.), Oakland

Phone: 510-836-3139 Lunch & dinner Wed – Mon
Web: N/A
Prices: $$

Set at the intersection of 10th and Harrison streets, Kim Huong corners the market on good, light Vietnamese fare in this area. There may not be much that is noteworthy about the large, airy, sunny-hued room, but the food is another matter.

Great care shines through in a beef noodle broth, or *pho*, studded with pieces of gelatinous tripe, sheets of beef flavored with just a bit of sweet fat, and beef balls redolent with aromatic herbs. Quickly sautéed slices of white meat chicken are brightened with pungent ginger, while tart green papaya, sweet mango, and dried shrimp are tossed with fried shallots, cilantro, soy sauce, and lemongrass to fashion a perfect salad.

The staff is friendly and attentive, under the watchful eye of the charming owner.

Kirala

Japanese

B2

2100 Ward St. (at Shattuck Ave.), Berkeley

Phone: 510-549-3486 — Lunch Mon – Fri
Web: www.kiralaberkeley.com — Dinner nightly
Prices: $$

Playing world beats and named for Mother Nature, Kirala is a natural selection for Berkeley types craving sushi and *robata* delicacies. Daily market specials are displayed on a whiteboard above the bar, which is staffed by experts who take great care in their perfectly steamed sticky rice—topped with hamachi or blood-red *maguro*—steaming bowls of soba and udon, and robust grilled items such as skewered baby lobster tails, bacon-wrapped asparagus, and chicken-stuffed mushrooms.

True to Japanese form, the dining room is restrained yet sophisticated, and the service is pleasant. Their eclectic music selection (reggae, jazz, and Latin) peps up the sophisticated vibe.

Kirala is also a stone's throw from Berkeley Bowl, the neighborhood's market mecca.

Kopitiam

Singaporean

B1

3647 Mt. Diablo Blvd. (bet. Dewing Ave. & Mountain View Dr.), Lafayette

Phone: 925-299-1653 — Lunch & dinner Tue – Sun
Web: www.kopitiamrestaurant.com
Prices: $$

It's not every day that you stumble across a good Singaporean restaurant, but this casually chic eatery easily fills the bill. Kopitiam's organic chicken rice is the chef's signature and a must-try. It's a comfort food staple in Singapore and after diving into the fluffy mound of chicken broth-infused jasmine rice you'll understand why. It's topped with a swirl of dark soy sauce and crowned with exquisitely tender pieces of steamed chicken and garnished with a julienne of carrots, shaved scallions, and cilantro leaves to add a little crunch. It's more savory than spicy, but if heat is what you're after, a dab of chili-and-garlic-rich sambal will liven things up.

Accompany any meal with a *kopi* or *teh*, with or without sweetened condensed milk.

Lalime's

International XX

A1

1329 Gilman St. (bet. Neilson & Peralta Aves.), Berkeley

Phone: 510-527-9838 — Dinner nightly
Web: www.lalimes.com
Prices: $$

This craftsman-style cottage blends into Berkeley's residential Westbrae neighborhood. Behind its picture-window façade, find the best of both worlds: a lively bar greets guests at the entrance, while a lower dining room fosters cozier meals *à deux*.

Cuisine at Cynthia and Haig Krikorian's place (whose relatives include Sea Salt and Fonda) celebrates the seasons with a menu that mixes numerous cultural influences, all with California flair. In summer, heirloom tomatoes could star with equal aplomb in a salad paired with tuna confit, or grilled in a soup with bacon and garlic croutons. A poblano chile stuffed with chunks of zucchini in savory *fromage blanc*, or a grilled Berkshire pork chop accented by apple-pear chutney is satisfying fare for cooler days.

La Rose Bistro

French

B2

2037 Shattuck Ave. (at Addison St.), Berkeley

Phone: 510-644-1913 — Lunch Mon – Fri
Web: www.larosebistro.com — Dinner nightly
Prices: $$

Painted with pastel hues and pastoral murals, La Rose is equally good for a casual lunch, a family get-together or a romantic evening out. Hai and Quynh Nguyen's laid-back bistro is located in Berkeley's theater district, so it attracts drama lovers as well.

A meal here still begins with fresh-baked French bread and an herbaceous cilantro pesto for dipping. Then come consistently well-prepared French classics, such as entrecote frites and duck confit with Madeira sauce. California touches stand out in succulent roasted medallions of pork, laid on a bed of honeyed apples and rosemary jus.

At lunch a full complement of main courses is on hand, along with sandwiches that might include a pain *bagnat* stuffed with tuna, olives, anchovies, and egg.

Legendary Palace

B4 Chinese XX

708 Franklin St. (at 7th St.), Oakland

Phone: 510-663-9188 Lunch & dinner daily
Web: N/A
Prices: ⊜

In the heart of Oakland's Chinatown, this restaurant boasts two floors of dining space and seats more than 600. The building, which dates back to 1917, was remodeled as a literal palace of Chinese cuisine. Inside, the restaurant is surprisingly elegant; gold curtains frame floor-to-ceiling windows, and sparkling chandeliers dangle overhead.

At lunchtime, dim sum carts circulate amid the closely spaced tables on both levels, offering a treasure trove of tasty little gems that do not disappoint, including dumplings, noodles, meats, and pastries. For dinner, the à la carte selection spotlights Cantonese specialties, and seafood (Pacific lobster, geoduck clams, Chinese ling cod) fresh from the aquarium tanks that line the back corners of the main room.

Marzano

C4 Pizza X

4214 Park Blvd. (at Glenfield Ave.), Oakland

Phone: 510-531-4500 Lunch Sat – Sun
Web: www.marzanorestaurant.com Dinner nightly
Prices: **$$**

Make a reservation at Marzano, the cozy neighborhood pizza joint that bursts with as much local flavor as the tomatoes for which it is named. Reclaimed wood chandeliers and antique glass wine casks hang from the exposed-beam ceiling above the rustic dining room, where personal space is at a premium. While there are a few entrées like pan-roasted Alaskan cod and chicken *all' arrabiata* (all under $15), the blistered pies are the true draw. Blazed to a crisp in minutes in the 800-degree wood-fired brick oven, pizzas range from a classic Margherita to such seasonal creations as spring onion with pecorino, pancetta, and rosemary.

Nibbles like Meyer lemon and green garlic *arancini* are simply lovely, as is Strauss soft-serve ice cream for a *dolce* finish.

Metro Lafayette

Californian

3524 Mt. Diablo Blvd. (bet. 1st St. & Oak Hill Rd.), Lafayette

Phone: 925-284-4422 — Lunch & dinner daily
Web: www.metrolafayette.com
Prices: $$

With an upscale clientele, relaxed atmosphere, and straightforward cuisine, this neighborhood hot spot serves both small town atmosphere and big city food. The mood is boisterous at the front bar, where locals gather for evening cocktails. More subdued are the sleek indoor dining room and the umbrella-shaded outdoor terrace. Vine-covered walls and potted trees ensconce this spot teeming with families and friends.

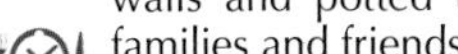

Seasonal and local are the watchwords for this California-style cuisine. French and Asian influences energize dishes such as duck confit spring rolls with spicy lime dipping sauce, and Penn Cove *moules frites* with white wine, garlic, and herbs. At dinner, a three-course fixed menu offers value and numerous options for each course.

900 Grayson

American

900 Grayson St. (at 7th St.), Berkeley

Phone: 510-704-9900 — Lunch Mon – Sat
Web: www.900grayson.com
Prices: ©©

A noteworthy stop on the East Bay hamburger circuit, 900 Grayson makes their version from all-natural beef, topped with double-smoked bacon, white cheddar, shoestring onions, and homemade barbecue sauce. Herbed fries come on the side. Elsewhere on the menu, the Demon Lover—a take on the Southern favorite fried chicken and waffles—coats a boneless chicken paillard in a peppery breading and plates it alongside a buttermilk waffle, with your choice of country-style gravy or Vermont maple syrup. Accompanying bottles of hot sauce give it the final kick. Vegetarians are just as happy to substitute seitan for the chicken.

This quaint family-friendly café, with its raspberry-colored façade and tree-shaded back patio, serves breakfast, lunch, and brunch.

O Chamé

A2 — Asian 

1830 4th St. (bet. Hearst Ave. & Virginia St.), Berkeley

Phone: 510-841-8783 — Lunch & dinner daily
Web: N/A
Prices: $$

This upscale noodle house is the go-to place for savvy locals. Those in the know order off-the-menu bento boxes; this lunchtime treat, available on a first-come, first-served basis, consists of fluffy white rice, pickled vegetables, and an entrée such as grilled salmon. If dining in, earthenware dishes come arranged with satisfying starters like sweet white corn and green onion pancakes, or seared tuna with braised leeks. Noodle bowls are the highlight among main courses. Hearty and healthy, these attractive bowls swim with the likes of buckwheat soba noodles and plump roasted oysters; or thick udon, pork tenderloin, spinach, and *takuan* (a pickle made from daikon radishes).

The pleasant outdoor patio is great for people-watching on a nice day.

Ohgane

B3 — Korean

3915 Broadway (bet. 38th & 40th Sts.), Oakland

Phone: 510-594-8300 — Lunch & dinner daily
Web: www.ohgane.com
Prices:

Lovers of Korean food in Oakland pop over to Ohgane during their midday break for a tasty bargain: the bounteous lunch buffet priced at around $10. Extensive and constantly refilled, the buffet features items from fried mackerel and *bi bim bap* to buckwheat noodles. Their barbecued meats, cooked over mesquite wood, are a specialty of the house and a favorite with the local Korean crowd. Accompaniments include soups, salads, noodles, rice, and assorted kimchi such as crunchy cubed daikon, fiery with vinegar, red chili paste, and garlic. Sliced fruit finishes off the meal.

In addition to the buffet, a large selection of à la carte dishes rounds out the menu at both lunch and dinner. Diners cook many of the meats themselves on the tabletop grills.

Oliveto

B3

5655 College Ave. (at Shafter Ave.), Oakland

Phone: 510-547-5356 — Lunch Mon – Fri
Web: www.oliveto.com — Dinner nightly
Prices: $$$

Oliveto's menu celebrates the time of year, showcasing each season's bounty in specially designed dinners such as a white truffle menu in November, a tomato menu in August, and the ever-popular whole hog dinner in February.

Located in the European-style Market Hall in Rockridge, Oliveto offers guests a choice of dining venues. Downstairs, nosh on a panino or sip an espresso any time of day in a convivial café styled as an Italian trattoria. Up the winding staircase, the dining room offers more seclusion and elegance, holding to regional Italian traditions while bringing sophisticated dishes to life in beautifully composed salads of red cabbage, pancetta, and walnuts; or penne topped with a ragù of Magruder Ranch milk and grass-fed veal.

Picán

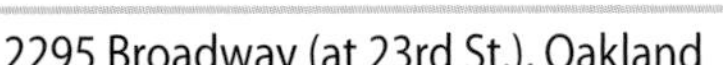

B4

2295 Broadway (at 23rd St.), Oakland

Phone: 510-834-1000 — Dinner nightly
Web: www.picanrestaurant.com
Prices: $$

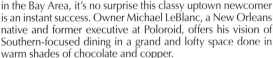

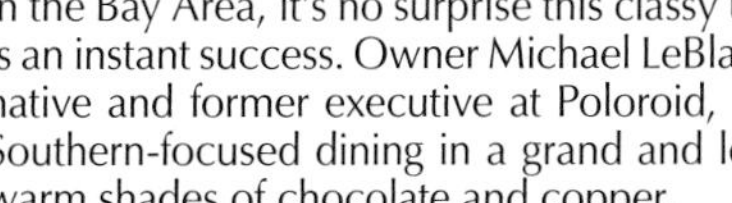

Showcasing a menu of down-home favorites given a distinctive California touch and the largest bourbon portfolio in the Bay Area, it's no surprise this classy uptown newcomer is an instant success. Owner Michael LeBlanc, a New Orleans native and former executive at Poloroid, offers his vision of Southern-focused dining in a grand and lofty space done in warm shades of chocolate and copper.

A mouthwatering tour of the South sizzles in a delightful range of specialties from Atlanta transplant Chef Dean Dupuis, and includes the temptation of plump Gulf shrimp sauced with Worcestershire garlic gravy, on a creamy pool of stone ground grits; or bourbon and molasses lacquered duck breast with sautéed collards and a crispy, gooey white cheddar fritter.

Pizzaiolo

Pizza

5008 Telegraph Ave. (bet. 49th & 51st Sts.), Oakland

Phone: 510-652-4888 — Dinner Mon – Sat
Web: www.pizzaiolooakland.com
Prices: $$

Couples and small groups populate Pizzaiolo's main room, while solo diners line the polished wood bar at this perennial East Bay favorite. All come for the blistered, thin-crust pizzas piled with toppings that epitomize California. Combinations suit the seasons, as in a warm-weather version touting summer squash with pounded parsley, garlic oil, and Grana Padano. As you would expect from an alumna of Chez Panisse, founder Charlie Hallowell updates his menu daily.

A peek into the open exhibition kitchen reveals the wood-burning oven that turns out those mesmerizing pies. Outside, two spacious patios are just right for playing a game of bocce by day, or basking in the moonlight come nightfall. Some say the staff has moxie; others call it attitude.

Prima

Italian

1522 N. Main St. (bet. Bonanza St. & Lincoln Ave.), Walnut Creek

Phone: 925-935-7780 — Lunch Mon – Sat
Web: www.primaristorante.com — Dinner nightly
Prices: $$$

At the heart of Walnut Creek's downtown shopping district sits this stalwart and its adjoining wine shop. Diners may choose from the front space anchored by a large wood-burning oven, a room next to the wine cellar, and a back bar area. Setting the sultry mood are skylights, fireplaces, and flickering candlelight. Outside, a large enclosed patio overlooks the sidewalk.

Prima remains a local favorite for Italian fare—with good reason. The market-fresh menu focuses on as the likes of asparagus, baby beets, and quail eggs combined winningly with Meyer lemon vinaigrette. This may be followed by tender sheets of spinach pasta filled with fresh herb-infused ground lamb. Exceptional and extensive, the wine list revels in Italian reds.

Riva

800 Heinz Ave. (at 7th St.), Berkeley

Phone: 510-649-5075 — Lunch Tue – Fri
Web: www.rivacucina.com — Dinner Tue – Sat
Prices: $$

Translated as the point where land and water meet, Riva marries Italian hospitality with Berkeley industrial chic. The interior echoes a former spice factory with exposed brick and ductwork, but owners Massi and Jennifer Boldrini have warmed the space with citrusy paint and velvet curtains. The Northern Italian fare is crafted with mostly local, organic ingredients—even the restaurant's patio is redolent with fresh herbs and vegetables. (The planters also serve as lessons in healthy eating for the nearby preschool.) If this sounds very California, it is: these influences can be seen in such dishes as free-range chicken in Dijon, lemon, and herbs.
For a more authentic taste of Italy, opt for handmade pastas like tagliatelle with *ragù alla Bolognese*.

Rivoli

Californian

1539 Solano Ave. (bet. Neilson St. & Peralta Ave.), Berkeley

Phone: 510-526-2542 — Dinner nightly
Web: www.rivolirestaurant.com
Prices: $$

Named for the Parisian *rue* where owners Roscoe Skipper and Wendy Brucker spent their honeymoon, Rivoli is a pleasant Berkeley *boîte*—and a certified green business to boot. A wine bar greets guests as they enter the little house, and a narrow hallway leads into the square dining area, lined with floor-to-ceiling windows.
Northern California products rule the menu, which is duly peppered with Italian gusto. The season dictates whether your feast will feature goat cheese soufflé with grilled persimmons, roasted chestnuts, and arugula; or perhaps grilled salmon with snap pea and leek risotto; before finishing with warm apple and cranberry crêpes, vanilla ice cream, and cinnamon crème anglaise.
Sibling Corso trattoria also offers an intimate dining experience.

Sahn Maru

Korean

4315 Telegraph Ave. (bet. 43rd & 44th Sts.), Oakland

Phone: 510-653-3366 — Lunch & dinner Wed – Mon
Web: N/A
Prices: $$

The Korean translation of Sahn Maru, "top of the mountain," is more indicative of its status than location; of the neighboring Korean restaurants, it is pricier yet far more unique than the rest. Still, this quaint, homey, and casual spot impresses with quality ingredients and skillful recipes that cannot be found anywhere else—proof is in the black goat stew served in a stoneware pot with lovely, pungent dipping sauce. Further proof is the the fact that the majority of guests converse with the servers in Korean. *Banchan* such as kimchi and marinated mushrooms lead to heartier entrées like braised pork with dates and sweet potato.

As if to reinforce the authenticity, Korean TV plays in the background, and Korean tchotchkes adorn the walls.

Sea Salt

Seafood

2512 San Pablo Ave. (at Dwight Way), Berkeley

Phone: 510-883-1720 — Lunch & dinner daily
Web: www.seasaltrestaurant.com
Prices: $$

Cousin to Lalime's and Fonda, operated by Haig and Cindy Krikorian, Sea Salt serves some of the area's finest seafood. Arrive between 3:00-6:00 P.M. daily for the $1 oyster special. Follow this with a bowl of exceptional white clam chowder, featuring fresh clams in a light, well-seasoned broth. The young, attentive staff is informative and well-versed in the menu, which changes seasonally but remains fresh and delicious. Dishes may include a crispy, pan-roasted Alaskan black cod paired with white corn, cranberry beans, chanterelles, and tarragon crème fraîche.

Weekend brunch reels in such favorites as seared trout with red flannel hash and sunny-side-up eggs; or steamed lobster on a torpedo roll served with sweet butter and house-made potato chips.

Sidebar

Gastropub

542 Grand Ave. (bet. Euclid Ave. & MacArthur Blvd.), Oakland

Phone: 510-452-8500 — Lunch Mon – Fri
Web: www.sidebar-oakland.com — Dinner Mon – Sat
Prices: $$

Amber pendant lamps, pumpkin walls, and a copper-topped bar cast a warm glow on Sidebar, the casually sophisticated Lake Merritt spot with Mediterranean verve. Friendly patrons crowd the communal table or grab at a seat at the counter for a view into the open kitchen, where upscale pub grub draws influence from Italy, France, and Spain. Run by husband-wife team Barbara Mulas and Mark Drazek, Sidebar is resplendent with homespun hospitality.

At lunch, opt for dressed-up sandwiches or a crisp polenta cake with Manchego and Parmesan; dinner brings more wholesome fare like baked pastas and grilled Hawaiian swordfish. Late afternoon brings "in between" bites, like well-bred burgers topped with fried egg or Maytag blue, served with oven-baked fries.

Tacubaya

Mexican 

1788 4th St. (bet. Hearst Ave. & Virginia St.), Berkeley

Phone: 510-525-5160 — Lunch daily
Web: www.tacubaya.net — Dinner Wed – Mon
Prices: 

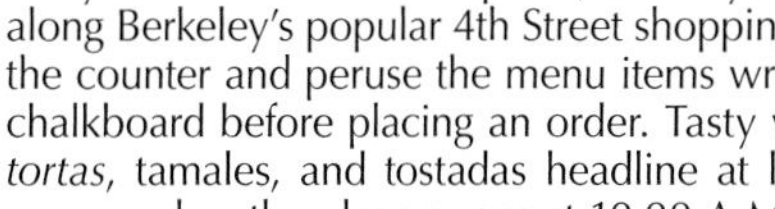

Not your run-of-the-mill taqueria, Tacubaya occupies a corner along Berkeley's popular 4th Street shopping area. Line up at the counter and peruse the menu items written on the large chalkboard before placing an order. Tasty varieties of tacos, *tortas*, tamales, and tostadas headline at lunch. Better yet, come early—the place opens at 10:00 A.M. for *desayuno*—and start the day with chorizo and eggs, *chilaquiles*, and churros (Mexican doughnuts).

A sibling to Doña Tomás in Oakland, this colorful spot is painted in bright red, pink, orange, and blue shades. Take a seat at the long wood bar, and watch the cooks press fresh tortillas as they prepare your meal. Cookie jars and cake plates near the register display homey sweets to tempt you for dessert.

Tamarindo

Mexican

468 8th St. (at Broadway), Oakland

Phone: 510-444-1944 Lunch & dinner Mon – Sat
Web: www.tamarindoantojeria.com
Prices:

A downtown Oakland storefront façade hides this cheery Mexican *antojeria*, which translates as "place of little cravings." With friendly service, a sunny dining room, and terrific Mexican fare, this fave is sure to entice.

Perfect for sharing, *antojitos* ("little whims") are Mexican street food, made by hand, shrunk in portion, yet elevated in presentation and flavor. Savor the likes of an *ahogado torta*—a fresh grilled baguette stuffed with tender pork *carnitas* and beans, then drenched in a piquant salsa made with *chile de arbol*—this delicacy demands a knife and fork!

Chef Gloria Dominguez and family opened this restaurant in 2005, after 16 years of running a taqueria in Antioch; the slightly more sophisticated dinner menu here is still hugely popular.

Udupi Palace

Indian

B2

1901 University Ave. (at Martin Luther King Jr. Way), Berkeley

Phone: 510-843-6600 Lunch & dinner daily
Web: www.udupipalaceca.com
Prices:

For those unfamiliar with the dosa, the sheer size of these thin, crispy, rice and lentil-flour pancakes here is a wonder to behold. Flavorful fillings may include the likes of turmeric-spiced potatoes and creamy spinach. This vegetarian and vegan menu goes on to list Southern Indian specialties that dig much deeper than the standard potato- and pea-stuffed samosas. Breads are reinvented again when presented as puffed pillows of poori or *batura*, and paratha stuffed with a choice of ingredients.

Udupi Palace shies away from calorie-dense ghee, and the students from U.C. Berkeley who frequent this place appreciate the lighter fare that results—as well as the take-out option. Their location in the Mission gives popular competition a run for their money.

Uzen

Japanese

5415 College Ave. (bet. Hudson St. & Kales Ave.), Oakland

Phone: 510-654-7753 — Lunch Mon – Fri
Web: N/A — Dinner Mon – Sat
Prices: $$

Blending into a line of identical storefronts in Rockridge, tiny Uzen is easy to overlook. Inside the quiet, narrow space, rows of pew-like banquettes line the walls alongside a diagonal bar that serves wonderfully fresh seafood. Absent are the long lists of gimmicky rolls. Here, fresh, bright fish is skillfully cut, delicately prepared and best enjoyed as sushi. Several hot teriyaki dishes mollify those that prefer their fish cooked, and steaming bowls of thick udon noodles in savory broth, garnished with crisp tempura, make the ideal antidote for a gray, chilly day.

By day, skylights illuminate the diminutive space with natural light; at night, the bar's pendant lights flicker over the fresh fish. Note the $15 minimum charge if paying by credit card.

Va de Vi

Fusion

1511 Mt. Diablo Blvd. (near Main St.), Walnut Creek

Phone: 925-979-0100 — Lunch & dinner daily
Web: www.vadevi.com
Prices: $$

When denizens of Walnut Creek crave a light nosh paired with global wines, they head to the lusciously fresh Va de Vi—a hugely hip spot around town. With more than 16 different varietals available by the glass, the taste (3 ounces), or in flights of three, this über-popular yet relaxed bistro's focus on wine is true to its Catalan moniker.

Dishes like the wonderfully flavored anise-scented duck confit, or a crispy *chile relleno* filled with melted *queso fresco*, sweet corn, and fresh cilantro, demonstrate the international menu's tone and scope.

An oak-barrel ceiling covers the long room, accented by wood cabinetry and tile floors. Outdoor seating lines the sidewalk, but the back patio is near majestic, with tables surrounding a venerable oak tree.

Vanessa's Bistro

Vietnamese

A1

1715 Solano Ave. (at Tulare Ave.), Berkeley

Phone: 510-525-8300 Dinner Wed – Mon
Web: www.vanessasbistro.com
Prices: $$

Chef Vanessa Dang keeps a hands-on approach in her Berkeley kitchen, crafting an innovative and unique menu of French-accented Vietnamese tapas cuisine that is at once all her own. What appears on the plate stays true to its mouthwatering menu description, as in crisp, succulent honey-marinated quail; flavorful and refreshing duck confit lettuce wraps; and perfectly fried salt and pepper prawns. For beverages, check out the bamboo-lined bar's cocktail selection (lychee martini, anyone?), and be sure end any meal with a Vietnamese coffee.

This is a hospitable place for sharing with friends. In fact, bring a large group with the hope of conquering more of the menu. Just be sure to make reservations, as this intimate dining room fills up fast.

Walnut Creek Yacht Club

Seafood

C1

1555 Bonanza St. (at Locust St.), Walnut Creek

Phone: 925-944-3474 Lunch & dinner Mon – Sat
Web: www.walnutcreekyachtclub.com
Prices: $$$

Despite its lack of both water and yachts, the (landlocked) Walnut Creek Yacht Club does manage to serve some of the best seafood in the East Bay area. The chef's brother-in-law owns Osprey Seafood Company, guaranteeing that everything at this casual seafood favorite is superbly fresh.

Start with raw oysters or a pound of steamers while perusing the menu of expertly prepared, boldly seasoned, and simply great seafood. Creative combinations may include the silky-rich yellowfin tuna, seared and fanned over a refreshing jicama salad and chili-lime cream. Less ambitious palates can opt for the "Dockside" fish selection, where items are prepared to your liking with a choice of sauces and sides. Save room for the all-American peanut-butter chocolate tart.

Wood Tavern

Gastropub

B2

6317 College Ave. (bet. Alcatraz Ave. & 63rd St.), Oakland

Phone: 510-654-6607 — Lunch Mon – Sat
Web: www.woodtavern.net — Dinner nightly
Prices: $$

In the mix of chic specialty shops signature to Rockridge, Wood Tavern is undeniably fab and fabulously unpretentious. It's the kind of place with a casual vibe where everybody knows your name (if you happen to be one of many regulars). Skylights cast a glow on the olive-hued dining room adorned with simple wood tables and a copper-topped bar. Fans of artisanal charcuterie chow crispy pork belly and prosciutto-wrapped *guanciale* terrine from the "Butcher Block."

Dig into American brasserie-style comfort fare, including a tender, pan-roasted half chicken and a "wicked good seafood stew." The warm and delish chocolate cake topped with a dollop of hazelnut ice cream is sinfully divine.

Owners Rebekah and Rich Wood hail from Rubicon, Farallon, and Scala's.

Zachary's Chicago Pizza

Pizza

B3

5801 College Ave. (at Oak Grove Ave.), Oakland

Phone: 510-655-6385 — Lunch & dinner daily
Web: www.zacharys.com
Prices:

Every pie is delivered with pride at this employee-owned pizzeria, which recently celebrated its 25th anniversary. Lovers of Chicago-style deep-dish pizza don't mind waiting 30 to 40 minutes for the cheesy, gooey, calorie-laden Nirvana that is Zachary's signature stuffed pie. Many of the combinations of toppings that are slathered over tangy tomato sauce are also available on a thin cornmeal crust—though not the favorite spinach and mushroom.

Great for families, this no-frills place is always bustling (there are other locations in Berkeley and San Ramon). Consider calling ahead to place your order to cut down the wait for a table once you arrive. Another way to avoid the wait is to order a "half-baked" pizza to take away and cook in your oven at home.

Zatar

B2 — Mediterranean

1981 Shattuck Ave. (bet. Berkeley Way & University Ave.), Berkeley

Phone: 510-841-1981 — Lunch Fri
Web: www.zatarrestaurant.com — Dinner Wed – Sat
Prices: **$$**

Though it is set in Berkeley, Zatar transports diners to the Mediterranean with the colorful murals and collection of hand-painted ceramic platters that adorn the walls. Husband-and-wife team Waiel and Kelly Majid do Berkeley proud in their certified green business by harvesting vegetables from their organic garden, composting raw kitchen scraps, and feeding any vegetarian food remains to their laying hens.

Zatar's name refers to the traditional Middle Eastern spice mixture—made from sesame seeds, oregano, thyme, and sumac—used here in a variety of dishes. The dinner menu recites a litany of vegetable spreads and dolmas to start; grilled leg of lamb, pistachio and spring herb chicken, and sea bass with sesame-*harissa* sauce make satisfying entrées.

Remember, stars (✿✿✿...✿) are awarded for cuisine only! Elements such as service and décor are not a factor.

SFCVB photo by Phil Coblentz

North of San Francisco

North of San Francisco

Journey north of the Golden Gate Bridge and entrée the sprawling North of San Francisco. Draped along the breathtaking Highway 1, coastal climates hallow this region with abounding agricultural advantages. Snake your way through the gigantesque ground, and you will find that food oases are spread out. But when fortunate to 'catch' them, expect fresh and luscious seafood, oysters, and cold beer...slurp! Farm-to-table cuisine is the par in North Bay and they boast an avalanche of local food purveyors.

Begin with the prodigious cheese chronicles. Visit the quaint and rustic **Cowgirl Creamery** where "cowgirls" make delicious, distinctive, and artisan cheeses. By producing only farmstead cheese, they help refine and define artisan cheesemaking...respect! Turn the leaf to cheese wizard **Laura Chenel**. Her baby, chevre, is a scrumptious goat cheese full of nuance and zing. For a more lush and heady blue cheese, dive into the divine 'Original Blue' at **Point Reyes Farmstead Cheese Co**. The cheese conte continues at **Adante Dairy**, where they churn out every type of cheese imaginable; and the fertile process at **Bellwether Farms** uses first-class milk to produce a quintessential cheese. These driving and enterprising cheesemakers live by *terroir*. Restaurants here follow the European standard and offer cheese before, or in lieu of a dessert course. The ideal is simply magical...end of story!

From tales of cheese to Ranch romances, **Niman Ranch** is at the crest. They tell the story of environmentally sustainable farming, and provide the most wholesome and finest tasting meats to a sweeping nexus of establishments from farmers and grocery stores, to a plethora of stellar restaurants. Although petite in comparison, **Marin Sun Farms** is towering. A magnified butcher shop, their heart, hub, and soul lies in the production of local and natural-fed livestock for the hamlet.

Ravenous after hours of scenic driving and the ocean waft? Rest at **The Pelican Inn**. Their hearty stew of English country cooking and wide brew of the English 'bar' will leave you craving more of the bucolic. Carry on your hiatus and stroll into the olive tree orchard **McEvoy Ranch** a dairy farm reincarnated into olive oil utopia. The piece de resistance here is their rich and peppery extra virgin olive oil in the Tuscan style. Like most thirsty travelers, let desire lead you to **Three Twins Ice Cream**. A lick of their organically produced creamy goodness will bring heaven to earth.

Waters off the coast here provide divers with exceptional hunting ground, and restaurants across the country seek the same including lush oysters, clams, and mussels. The difficulty in obtaining a hunting permit, as well as the inability to retrieve the large savory mollusks, makes red abalone a treasured species, especially in surrounding Asian restaurants. Yet, despite such hurdles, seafood is the norm at most restaurants in Marin County. One such gem is **Sam's Anchor Café** known for their superb seafood and glorious views. If seafood isn't your thing, entice your palate with authentic Puerto Rican flavors at **Sol Food**; or opt for a more clean dining experience at **Cottage Eatery** with their crisp and seasonal delicacies.

North of San Francisco is known for its deluge of local organic ingredients carried in the numerous farmers' markets. The marriage of food and wine is best expressed at Sausalito's own "Tour de Cuisine" and The Marin County Tomato Festival. Marin County, with its panoramic views, is one of the most sought after locales and celebrities abound. Thus, some diners may have a touristy mien; however, it is undeniable that restaurants and chefs are blessed with easy access to the choicest food and local food agents.

Boca

Steakhouse XX

B1

340 Ignacio Blvd. (bet. Alameda Del Prado & Enfrente Rd.), Novato

Phone: 415-883-0901 — Lunch Mon – Fri
Web: www.bocasteak.com — Dinner nightly
Prices: $$

Jersey boy George Morrone heads this ranch-style steakhouse. A Northern California restaurant with a South American twist, Boca ("mouth" in Spanish) honors the chef's Argentinean heritage from its cuisine to the music. Grass- and grain-fed beef form the core of the menu in a variety of cuts that are grilled over blazing hardwood, served with basil and smoked paprika *chimichurri* sauces, and accompanied by piping-hot baked potatoes. A good selection of fresh seafood entrées is also available. For lunch, "Boca dillios"— sandwiches with duck-fat fries will satisfy any hungry cowpoke.

Boca's ranch-like ambience employs timber, rawhide, and leather placemats to create a home on the range. Ride over on Tuesdays to take advantage of half-price wine bottles.

Buckeye Roadhouse

American XX

A2

15 Shoreline Hwy. (west of Hwy. 101), Mill Valley

Phone: 415-331-2600 — Lunch & dinner daily
Web: www.buckeyeroadhouse.com
Prices: $$

Cross the Golden Gate Bridge and take the Highway 1 exit for Stinson Beach to practically run into this comfortable and enjoyable roadhouse, tucked into the side of a mountain in Mill Valley. Sounds of the busy highway melt away as you follow the winding tree and flower-lined path to this cozy 1937 lodge. Inside, the dark cocoon-like bar area gives way to a lofty dining room.

The high quality of this cooking results in consistent, very good food. Entrées may range from the house-smoked, orange-glazed Sonoma duck with balsamic red-wine sauce and mushroom goat-cheese pudding, to the half-pound hamburger, "fully garnished" with fries.

Delectable sweets like the towering wedge of fluffy coconut-cream pie are reminders to save room for dessert.

Bungalow 44

American

B2

44 E. Blithedale Ave. (at Sunnyside Ave.), Mill Valley

Phone: 415-381-2500 Dinner nightly
Web: www.bungalow44.com
Prices: $$

Little Mill Valley is resplendent with trendy boutiques, cute shops, and great restaurants like this local favorite. In the evening, the vibrant bar scene is jammed with young couples who leave the kids with the nanny and congregate here for a night out. Their lively conversations can overwhelm the space, so those seeking a quieter evening should shoot for a table in the tented dining area or in the main room past the open kitchen.

The menu plays with American dishes, so mouths water for cayenne-spiced onion rings and artichoke fritters with tarragon aïoli; while the signature kickin' fried chicken draws fans of its own. Salad aficionados feast on the smoked-duck Cobb; heartier appetites may favor a Kobe beef burger cooked on the wood-fired grill.

Cucina

Italian

B2

510 San Anselmo Ave. (at Tunstead Ave.), San Anselmo

Phone: 415-454-2942 Dinner Tue – Sun
Web: www.cucinarestaurantandwinebar.com
Prices: $$

For a case of the warm fuzzies along this quaint main strip of San Anselmo, try this charming and welcoming trattoria, where the staff greets everyone with a smile, and hails regulars by name.

Sunny walls, terra-cotta floors, and a blazing wood-burning oven warm the dining room, which brims with families and friends. Garlicky tomato bruschetta offers a tasty start, served compliments of the house. Depending on the ever-changing menu, dinner may feature rustic dishes such as *pollo saltimbocca* or gnocchi with asparagus, fontina cheese, and white truffle oil. These homey preparations are simple, genuine, and uncomplicated. Kids love the pizza Margherita, and few folks turn down the tiramisu.

The wine bar at back is a perfect post-dinner spot.

El Paseo

French

B2

17 Throckmorton Ave. (bet. Blithedale & Sunnyside Aves.), Mill Valley

Phone: 415-388-0741 Dinner Wed – Sun

Web: www.elpaseorestaurant.com

Prices: $$$$

Grand Vin Inc.

This petite brick cottage is tucked down a winding lane a safe distance from the bustle of downtown Mill Valley. Meander through the paved maze to enter this series of very charming, old-world dining rooms. Rustic exposed beams, high-backed leather chairs, and a crackling fireplace lend a romantic air that draws both mature foodies and starry-eyed couples finding that perfect moment to pop the question.

Featuring elegant service to complement highly creative cuisine with heavy French and occasional Japanese accents, El Paseo is both grand and seductive. Chef Keiko Takahashi infuses Asian sensibilities into these classically French three-, four-, or six-course prix-fixe menus. Even when her creativity falters, this chef's impeccable technique shows gifts and talent. Unique and versatile dishes like the foie gras and sea eel terrine, or cherry blossom-smoked Muscovy duck may be among the best preparations you've ever had. Decadent, smooth, and the perfect balance between flavors and texture, the ice cream here is a necessary pleasure.

The gracious sommelier is cordial and dedicated—he is genuinely enthusiastic and eager to enhance your meal with his vast knowledge of fine wine.

Fish

Seafood

A3

350 Harbor Dr. (at Bridgeway), Sausalito

Phone: 415-331-3474 — Lunch & dinner daily
Web: www.331fish.com
Prices: $$

Fish bone to funny bone—fall hook, line, and sinker for Sean Connery's rendition of *What's Love Got to Do with It* (on the restaurant's voice mail) before tasting the fresh 'catch' at Fish. From chowders and ceviche, to Tuscan white bean and house-poached tuna salad, dishes here are creative and plentiful. Place your order at the counter, grab a number, and take a seat. Then tuck into classic, cornmeal-crusted Po'boys, filled with local Miyagi oysters or Louisiana catfish; or peruse the daily blackboard specials. You can even buy fish to cook at home.

The outdoor dining is sublime. Despite the kitschy picnic tables and beverages in Ball jars, this grand Sausalito harborside set amid yachts emanates sheer luxury.

An on-site ATM eases the cash-only policy.

Frantoio

Italian

A2

152 Shoreline Hwy. (Stinson Beach exit off Hwy. 101), Mill Valley

Phone: 415-289-5777 — Dinner nightly
Web: www.frantoio.com
Prices: $$

What this restaurant lacks in location—just off Highway 101 next to a Holiday Inn Express—it makes up for with its delicious Northern Italian cuisine. Frantoio, Italian for "olive press," makes its very own olive oil on-site in November and December. Two granite wheels, weighing in together at 3,200 pounds, are used to crush organic olives; you can watch the process behind a large window in back of the dining room.

On busy nights, the high ceilings reverberate with the sounds of animated conversations over spinach gnocchi, pan-seared day boat scallops, or perhaps a wood-oven-roasted leg of lamb. Olive oil, of course, finds its way into many of the dishes. For a finale, the moist chocolate tower cake wins raves, as does the tiramisu spiked with grappa.

Insalata's

B2 **Mediterranean** XX

120 Sir Francis Drake Blvd. (at Barber Ave.), San Anselmo

Phone: 415-457-7700 Lunch & dinner daily
Web: www.insalatas.com
Prices: $$

In both name and spirit, this establishment pays homage to Chef Heidi Krahling's father, Italo Insalata. The ivy-covered exterior welcomes guests to an airy dining room filled with larger than life paintings of fruit—reminders that this restaurant exalts a familial love of cooking with fresh, local products.

Care and pride in the preparation of healthy food was instilled in this chef at an early age—Marinites rejoice that she learned her lessons well. Tastes of the Mediterranean sparkle in the chilled avocado and cucumber soup, or roasted honey-glazed pomegranate duck breast. Herbivores relish in the Middle Eastern-inspired vegetarian platter, a seasonal mélange served with Turkish yogurt and couscous, regularly emerging from the open kitchen.

Left Bank

B2 **French** XX

507 Magnolia Ave. (at Ward St.), Larkspur

Phone: 415-927-3331 Lunch & dinner daily
Web: www.leftbank.com
Prices: $$

Roland Passot of La Folie fame operates this small chain of restaurants, which extends from Larkspur to San Jose. This spacious location, in the c.1913 Blue Rock Inn on the quaint main street in the storybook village of Larkspur, features pressed-tin ceilings, a lengthy bar, and large colorful posters. This may be a far cry from the Rive Gauche in Paris, but French comfort food here stays as true to tradition as anywhere along St. Germain des Près.

With Northern Californian accents, the classic menu retains an intense focus on seasonal ingredients. Thus tarte flambée is topped with glorious heirloom tomatoes and basil pistou; and *crevettes* Provençal uses Fisherman's Daughter Wild Sonora Coast shrimp, finished off with Pernod and crisp, lacey frisée.

Le Garage

Mediterranean

85 Liberty Ship Way #109, Sausalito

Phone: 415-332-5625 — Lunch daily
Web: www.legaragebistrosausalito.com — Dinner Mon – Sat
Prices: $$

Don't let the fire-engine red doors and servers clad in mechanic getups fool you. As the name suggests, Le Garage is an old carport with Provençal polish. Perched at the tip of Liberty Ship Way—picturesque with palms, bobbing dinghies, and a briny sea breeze—this is a feel-good bistro serving simple Mediterranean eats both inside and on a cozy heated patio. The owners hail from San Francisco's Chez Papa, and the food reflects this heritage.
Start with mussels *du Mistral* or Loch Duart salmon atop sautéed green onions and Niçoise olives. Finish with Nutella panna cotta dusted with bittersweet chocolate, delight in the French staff, and conjure visions of an evening at water's edge in Nice.
Limited seating and irresistible charm make reservations a must.

Marché aux Fleurs

Mediterranean

23 Ross Common (off Lagunitas Rd.), Ross

Phone: 415-925-9200 — Dinner Tue – Sat
Web: www.marcheauxfleursrestaurant.com
Prices: $$$

In the tiny hamlet of Ross in Marin County, Marché aux Fleurs evokes the farmers' markets in the South of France that inspired the restaurant's name. Look for the hand-painted sign and manicured shrubbery outside. A Provençal décor colors the interior, while the brick patio lures diners to tables dappled by rays of sunlight that shine through the canopy of trees overhead.
Chef Dan Baker, who runs the place with his wife, Holly, favors seasonal products from small local growers in entrées such as crispy Sonoma duck confit and house-made spinach pappardelle with Bellwether Farms ricotta meatballs. Thursday is hamburger night, when a half-pound burger topped with Carmody cheese, bacon, and grilled onions rings up at less than $15.

Marinitas

B2 Latin American

218 Sir Francis Drake Blvd. (bet. Bank St. & Tunstead Ave.), San Anselmo

Phone: 415-454-8900 Lunch & dinner daily
Web: www.marinitas.net
Prices: $$

Rustic antlers, a warm stone fireplace, and exposed wood beams crisscrossing lofty ceilings give Marinitas, named for *la gente* of Marin, a cozy cantina feel. Focusing on seasonal ingredients, Chef/owner Heidi Krahling cooks authentic Mexican and Latin American dishes just like *tia* used to make. Juicy carne asada tacos burst with flavor and vegetable enchiladas are bold and savory in green *pepian* mole. A dash of ancho chili spices up moist chocolate cake.

Upbeat Latin tunes encourage festive imbibing at the long, friendly bar, where the wine list features mostly South American varietals. Fresh-squeezed juices and house sweet-and-sour mix add zest to margaritas concocted with specialty tequilas. Homemade corn chips and salsas are on the house.

Nick's Cove

A1 Seafood

23240 Hwy. 1 (near Miller Park), Marshall

Phone: 415-663-1033 Lunch & dinner daily
Web: www.nickscove.com
Prices: $$$

On the reinvigorated shores of Tomales Bay, Nick's Cove has reinvented this 1930s settlement. The restaurant, an hour north of the Golden Gate Bridge, is far from everything but oysters. This is a boon to the menu; the briny bivalves, a specialty of the house, are harvested fresh from Tomales Bay. Beyond oysters, there are Monterey sardines and Bodega Bay Dungeness crab; as well as refined dishes made from the likes of Washington arctic char, Maine diver scallops, and Cape Cod clams.

This nostalgic spot, recreated by designer Pat Kuleto, retains a hunting-lodge feel along with great bay views. For those who would rather not jump back on the winding coastal highway, Nick's offers 12 rustic (on the exterior) beach cottages, available for overnight visits.

Murray Circle ✿

Californian

A3

601 Murray Circle (at Fort Baker), Sausalito

Phone: 415-339-4750 Lunch & dinner daily
Web: www.murraycircle.com
Prices: $$$

Kodiak Greenwood

Patrons here are treated to culinary theater in a superb Fort Baker colonial that boasts a well-seasoned chef and history in its trappings. Artfully renovated with a neutral palette, plush carpets, and velvet draperies, Murray Circle tips a hat to its heyday with nostalgic black-and-white photography, leaded-glass windows, wainscoting, and pressed-tin ceilings.

In the kitchen, however, the farm-to-table California culinary philosophy is fully mastered and au courant thanks to Chef Joseph Humphrey. Guests may sample a four-course menu, perhaps including perfectly baked crab cakes topped with sunflower seeds; peppery mizuna salad with seared *magret* of squab; or a wood-roasted bison ribeye. Or, feast on the unabridged eight-course menu, paired with wines from an international list with loving focus on Northern California vintages. Either way, the experience is sure to satisfy with clean, carefully balanced dishes that highlight unique combinations and subtle preparations of local, seasonal ingredients. A well-choreographed team of youthful servers delivers each course in perfect time, right to the last *pâté de fruit* and *mignardises*.

The clubby bar is a refined post for an aperitif.

Olema Inn

Californian XX

10000 Sir Francis Drake Blvd. (at Hwy. 1), Olema

Phone: 415-663-9559 — Lunch Sat – Sun
Web: www.theolemainn.com — Dinner nightly
Prices: **$$$**

Olema Inn sits high above Highway 1, in a tiny blip of a town (population: 55) that caters to folks headed for Point Reyes National Sea Shore. Owners John and Carole Wiltshire took the space over in 2007, beautifully renovating the quaint 19th century farmhouse, and handing the culinary reins over to her son, Chef James Wong.

The bulk of his ingredients—Hog Island oysters served eight different ways, succulent Marconi Cove mussels, or a fresh steak from Marin Sun Farms—are caught or grown within 50 miles of the Inn. But he's been known to let a few delicious exotic ingredients slip in here and there. A fittingly relaxed approach for a place where sitting on the shady porch and enjoying the country breeze for hours on end is de rigueur.

Om

Indian X

1518 4th St. (at E St.), San Rafael

Phone: 415-458-1779 — Lunch & dinner Mon – Sat
Web: www.omcuisine.com
Prices:

Patrons at this family-run spot focus their attention on the food, knowing that all their senses will delight in Om's fragrant rice-based South Indian cuisine. They might begin with the bright red chicken *anjappa*—yummy cubes of boneless meat marinated in yogurt and spices, then deep-fried—and move on to dosas. Made from rice and lentil flour, dramatic dosas come sliced and easy to eat. A pancake-like *uttapam* is smaller and more delicate, studded with a variety of components. Sambar and coconut chutney accompany just about everything.

The all-you-can-eat lunch buffet is wildly popular, and bargain-priced ($8.99) for Marin County. If you have time to spare, order off the menu; the service will be slower, but the dishes will be worth waiting for.

Paradise Bay

A3 American XX

1200 Bridgeway (at Turney St.), Sausalito

Phone: 415-331-3226 Lunch & dinner daily
Web: www.paradisebaysausalito.com
Prices: $$

Aptly named, this casual dining room overlooks Sausalito's placid harbor (with a dock available for short-term boat "parking"), with retractable doors opening onto a heated waterfront patio.

Despite its bayside location, the restaurant broadens its menu of contemporary American cuisine to include options as varied as Buffalo burgers; lemongrass-marinated chicken breast; or grilled pork Porterhouse with Calvados cream sauce, apples, fennel, and sweet potato spring roll. Cornmeal-battered halibut fillets served with fresh coleslaw and garlic fries; squid ink linguini; Paradise Bay cioppino; and a lobster maki roll assure a sea-loving component.

Cure whatever may ail you with a weekend brunch on the waterfront deck in the open, salty air.

Picco

B2 Contemporary XX

320 Magnolia Ave. (at King St.), Larkspur

Phone: 415-924-0300 Dinner nightly
Web: www.restaurantpicco.com
Prices: $$

For the optimum Picco experience, dine with a group of friends to relish the range of Chef/owner Bruce Hill's contemporary small plates menu. Amid the exposed rafters, brick, and redwood accents, small plates and dishes are graciously placed in the middle of the table to ease and encourage sharing. Although the menu changes frequently, satisfying and skillfully prepared offerings may include the likes of sunchoke soup with celery-leaf pesto; farro-dusted Florida prawns; or mini burgers. New on the menu: Marin Mondays, when a special bill of fare features local products from area farms.

Those who prefer not to share can visit Pizzeria Picco next door for wood-fired thin crust pie and Straus Family Creamery soft-serve ice cream all for themselves.

Poggio

A3 — Italian XX

777 Bridgeway (at Bay St.), Sausalito

Phone: 415-332-7771 — Lunch & dinner daily
Web: www.poggiotrattoria.com
Prices: $$

The Casa Madrona Hotel houses this Northern Italian restaurant, with its mahogany-lined archways, plush booths, terra-cotta tiles, and buzzing bar. Dining here is pure joy in warmer months, when French doors swing open to offer views of the serene Sausalito yacht harbor across the street.

Having cooked in the Italian regions of Tuscany and Lombardy, Chef Peter McNee brings authenticity to a menu that incorporates the freshest products of California. Hand-pulled mozzarella with heirloom melon and *Prosciutto di Parma* is served alongside dishes featuring herbs and greens from the restaurant's terraced garden. Wafer-thin pizzas emerge from a wood-burning oven.

Poggio, as its name translates, is indeed a "special hillside place."

Spinnaker

A3 — Seafood XX

100 Spinnaker Dr. (at Anchor St.), Sausalito

Phone: 415-332-1500 — Lunch & dinner daily
Web: www.thespinnaker.com
Prices: $$

Panoramic views of Richardson Bay, Tiburon, Belvedere Island, Alcatraz, and the Bay Bridge alone merit the price of admission at this Sausalito dowager (a $14 minimum charge discourages those seeking only to indulge in the spectacular scenery).

Picture windows lining three sides of the dining room are the most noteworthy aspect of the décor. This place draws crowds of tourists who love to capture the marine backdrop on film.

Steady as she goes, the time-honored menu brims with seafood, from rich bowls of spaghetti with prawns; flavorful crab pot stickers on a bed of frisée; to a petrale sole sauté. Smartly dressed servers keep a friendly mien, no matter how packed the place may become. Every table here gets a warm sourdough baguette, butter, and a view.

Sushi Ran

Japanese

A3

107 Caledonia St. (bet. Pine & Turney Sts.), Sausalito

Phone: 415-332-3620 — Lunch Mon – Fri
Web: www.sushiran.com — Dinner nightly
Prices: $$

A favorite among foodies and tourists north of the Golden Gate, Sushi Ran is a convivial eatery with pan-continental inspirations. The restaurant's twin wood bungalows (one house is open daily; the other is reserved for dinner and private parties) are situated on a main neighborhood drag, and feel pure Sausalito. The interior, though, feels strongly Japanese, with a sushi bar dominating the dining room, while more intimate tables are tucked at the back.

Innovative maki and tempura reflect influences from the Pacific Rim, California, and beyond: New Caledonia blue prawn, Canadian sweet shrimp, and Golden State sea urchin grace a sushi assortment.

Bento boxes are hot options at lunch, while dinner brings chicken teriyaki and miso-glazed black cod.

Tavern at Lark Creek

American

B2

234 Magnolia Ave. (at Madrone Ave.), Larkspur

Phone: 415-924-7766 — Lunch Sun
Web: www.tavernatlarkcreek.com — Dinner nightly
Prices: $$

After twenty years in the restaurant business, the exterior of Tavern at Lark Creek is the same as it always was—a charming yellow Victorian shaded by majestic redwoods. Inside, however, it has a new lease on life with a young chef; much more casual, pared-down interior; and an eclectic menu of comfort foods all under $15. The motto here could be "light on the wallet, full in the belly" with offerings like *panko*-crusted mac 'n' cheese croquettes served with cheddar fondue; and Spanish chorizo in the sweet company of a Mexican chocolate crostini.

While change is clear throughout, it remains a local favorite, with a bustling bar serving creative cocktails and value wines on tap. The patio outside is a great spot to enjoy this farm-to-table fare.

Vin Antico

881 4th St. (bet. Cijos St. & Lootens Pl.), San Rafael

Phone: 415-454-4492 — Lunch Tue – Fri
Web: www.vinantico.com — Dinner Tue – Sun
Prices: **$$**

With rich fabrics, noir leather, and plentiful candles ablaze, Vin Antico exudes big city sophistication in a small town setting. Perhaps inspired by Tuscany's venerable reputation for art, museum-quality works by local painters adorn the brick walls. Meanwhile, Northern Italian culinary masterpieces are crafted in the exhibition kitchen—solo diners should grab a seat at the chef's counter for maximum viewing pleasure. The atmosphere is laid-back and the meals are satisfying, with such gourmet ingredients as smoked duck breast and hazelnut-rolled goat cheese topping seasonal *pizzetines*. Homemade pastas might include organic parsley fettuccine or leek- and lobster-stuffed ravioli. The small wine bar is a jovial spot for a glass of Italian vino.

Look out for red symbols, indicating a particularly pleasant ambiance.

IN HOC SIGNO VINCES
RAMOS PINTO
Est. 1880

Peter L. Wrenn/MICHELIN

South of San Francisco

South of San Francisco

Known locally as "America's Premier Mountain Appellation," the Santa Cruz Mountains are home to a number of wineries. Not to be outdone by the more well-known vineyards of its northern neighbors, this burgeoning wine region has a great deal of community pride, and many restaurants and wine bars in the South of San Francisco area only offer the grape of the territory. Santa Cruz Mountains Wine Express, an annual springtime event at Roaring Camp Railroad, gathers local vintners and restaurants for an afternoon of wine and food tasting. It's the only chance you'll get to sample all seventy Santa Cruz Mountain wines in one location, after which

you can hop the Santa Cruz Mountains Wine Express for a train ride through the gorgeous redwood forests.

Farmer's markets are a way of life for locals—each city has one and some have several throughout the week. Upscale and specialty markets are also a vital aspect of the culture here. **The Milk Pail Market** in Moutain View is particularly known for its selection of cheeses, supplying over 300 varieties. **Dittmer's Gourmet Meats & Wurst Haus**, a popular, family-owned butcher shop and delicatessan, offers fine meats and homemade sausages. **Draeger's Market** in San Mateo (one of four in the Northern California area) offers a substantial selection of wines, cheeses, breads, produce, and specialty products as well as cooking classes like "Indian Cooking Bootcamp" and "Rustic Italian Breads." Find a sprinkling of Asian markets and bakeries in the area as well; visit one of several **99 Ranch Markets**, a popular Asian

grocery chain in San Jose, Mountain View, Cupertino, and Foster City.

Slow Food, a grassroots movement dedicated to promoting local foods and culinary traditions, has a thriving chapter in The Silicon Valley. In Mountain View, the expansive Googleplex is known to feed its fortunate employees three free meals a day from a variety of cafés and restaurants where organic and sustainable foods from local farms are on offer. **Charlie's Place**, the main eatery on the grounds, serves up a cornucopia of gourmet goods and ethnic eats (sorry employess only!).

Head to Millbrae for authentic dim sum and Chinese food. In San Mateo, locals flock to **Gator's Neo Soul Food** for friendly service and succulent southern fare served up with doses of California health-consciousness. An early morning may be best spent biting into a warm, gooey almond croissant from **Fleur de Cocoa**, a cracker jack patisserie and chocolaterie in Los Gatos. Special occasions call for cakes from **Copenhagen Bakery** in Burlingame. This longstanding favorite has over three decades of baking under its belt, enticing generations of sugar addicts with cakes, pies, and authentic Danish pastries.

Amble through Emma Prusch Farm Park in San Jose where rare fruit orchards and community gardens rented by local residents flourish. Once a working dairy farm, the city owned park hosts the popular Story Road Tamale Festival, a annual day-long nosh fest where buckets of corn husks wait eagerly to be stuffed and sold. (Tamale-lovers take note: the 2009 festival was cancelled due to economic hardship, but will resume in 2010.) San Jose loves its cultural food festivals, and if Mexican grub ain't your thing, hang out for the Japenese Obon Festival in July, The Italian Family Festival in August, or the hugely loved Greek Festival in May. Close out the summer at the Millbrae Art & Wine festival over Labor Day Weekend with fennel-scented sausage, hearty cheesesteaks, cajun corndogs, vanilla pudding crêpes, and frozen lemonade. Grab a cold microbrew or glass of wine and peruse the artisan craft and jewlery stands or sing along with one of the local cover bands. Sight San Jose's sophisticates at Santana Row, an ultra-sleek and chic shopping village with a slew of high end restaurants and stores. This gorgeous outdoor complex has its very own farmer's market, several spas for pampering, and even residential rentals.

Downtown Palo Alto bristles with casual eateries and coffee shops, catering to the students and faculty of Standford University. Locals love **Fraîche Yogurt** for their organic artisan yogurts made onsite out of a small batch pastuerizer. Grab a pint of fresh or frozen yogurt and top off with homemade granola or handshaved Callebaut chocolate. Stop into the **Village Cheese House** for a delicious double decker sandwich or a cheese tasting.

Alexander's Steakhouse

Steakhouse XXX

E3

10330 N. Wolfe Rd. (at I-280), Cupertino

Phone: 408-446-2222 Dinner nightly
Web: www.alexanderssteakhouse.com
Prices: $$$$

A boon for South Bay food lovers, Alexander's is far from your run-of-the-mill steakhouse. The Asian twist that runs through the wide-ranging menu is a creative surprise. Japanese Kobe appears alongside prime beef dry-aged on the premises. Chef Jeffrey Stout, whose heritage is half American and half Japanese, interprets surf and turf—called Cow and Crustacean here—as a petite filet mignon with lobster *kushiyaki* and hon-shimeji mushrooms. Fish is given equal play, in small-plates such as hamachi shots—an intriguing mélange of hamachi sliced sashimi-style with red chili, frizzled ginger, cubes of avocado, and truffled ponzu.

A wall of wine and a decanting area in the middle of the room bear testimony to Alexander's award-winning wine program.

Arcadia

Steakhouse XXX

B1

100 W. San Carlos St. (at Market St.), San Jose

Phone: 408-278-4555 Dinner nightly
Web: www.michaelmina.net
Prices: $$$

Part of Chef Michael Mina's ever-growing restaurant empire, spacious Arcadia is located in the San Jose Marriott. The corner space features an open kitchen with views of a glowing pizza oven and raw bar, overlooking an earth toned dining room in patterned mocha-colored carpeting and dark wood tables set with woven fiber placemats. Natural light floods through glass walls overlooking San Jose Park.

The menu has a contemporary take on steakhouse fare, divided between meat and seafood. While some may opt for chilled shellfish and charcuterie, snacks like foie gras sliders, mini crab Po'boys, and lobster corn dogs are whimsical takes on American classics.

Keeping with the theme, nostalgia inspires a root beer float for dessert.

Bistro Elan

Californian

B3

448 California Ave. (near El Camino Real), Palo Alto

Phone: 650-327-0284 — Lunch Tue – Fri
Web: www.bistroelan.com — Dinner Tue – Sat
Prices: $$

This charming Californian bistro has an inviting dining room with mustard-yellow walls lined with black-and-white photography. Loyal regulars flock to the enchanting back garden, a small but exclusive setting, or dine at the bar with the warm and welcoming bartenders waiting on their every whim.
The seasonally-driven bistro fare has European influences but shines from a commitment to using local Californian ingredients. Imagine satisfying plates like a Sonoma duck confit with risotto, garnished with roasted garlic, Parmesan, and local mushrooms; or chanterelle and Gruyere pancakes topped with a bright cherry tomato salad. Refreshing pomegranate sorbet makes the perfect end to a meal when it's on the frequently-changing dessert list.

Bistro Luneta

Filipino 

C2

615 E. 3rd Ave. (bet. Eldorado & Delaware Sts.), San Mateo

Phone: 650-344-0041 — Lunch & dinner Tue – Sun
Web: www.bistroluneta.com
Prices:

Although San Francisco boasts a wealth of Asian dining choices, Bistro Luneta will have adventurous palates dropping their *dan dan* noodles for the likes of *tapsilog*—a heaping plateful of thinly sliced marinated beef, fried garlic-infused sticky rice, crumbly salt-cured egg, and a side of vinegar jelly. Chef Emmanuel Santos, whose path to the kitchen was initiated by cooking alongside his great-grandmother, prepares unique specialties that include Manila-style barbecued pork skewers with pickled papaya; soy and vinegar sauced chicken adobo; and crème brûlée flavored with Philippine-grown coffee.
Served in a clean and modern dining room, the cooking here takes an upscale and contemporary approach to the traditional dishes of the Philippines.

Cafe Gibraltar

Mediterranean XX

C2

425 Avenue Alhambra (at Palma St.), El Granada

Phone: 650-560-9039 Dinner Tue – Sun
Web: www.cafegibraltar.com
Prices: $$

Delicious and affordable are an enviable duo in today's restaurants, and this oceanside café is beloved by diners on the San Mateo County coast. Borrowing from the Middle East, the décor offers sunny colors and Moorish elements, as well as tented booths along one wall, with low tables where guests sit cross-legged on cushions, North African-style.
For more than a decade, Chef Jose Luis Ugalde has led this open kitchen, turning out a variety of fresh, aromatic dishes that hail from almost every country along the Mediterranean Sea. From Lebanon comes vegan moussaka, slowly cooked in a clay pot, then baked in the wood oven. *Pollastre amb cepes* claims Catalan roots, its mixture of boneless chicken and wild mushrooms is served in a traditional tagine.

Cantankerous Fish

Seafood 

420 Castro St. (bet. California & Mercy Sts.), Mountain View

Phone: 650-966-8124 Lunch Mon – Sat
Web: www.thecantankerousfish.com Dinner nightly
Prices: $$

Showcasing contemporary seafood dishes in a large welcoming space, the restaurant features a lengthy granite bar and cocktail lounge, where small plates complement the discounted happy hour libations. Large, colorful canvases on the walls swim with a variety of denizens of the deep.
"Fresh Feisty Fish," as the menu bills its offerings, emerge from the open kitchen in preparations that would make Neptune proud. Bold creations could include spicy salmon fried wonton rolls; shellfish, and seafood corn dogs; and crab-encrusted Idaho trout. "More Grounded" dishes like the chicken breast milanese are available for those who prefer that their food have four legs.
The front patio reels in schools of diners when the weather permits.

Cascal

Spanish

400 Castro St. (at California St.), Mountain View

Phone: 650-940-9500 Lunch & dinner daily
Web: www.cascalrestaurant.com
Prices: $$

Cheery and casual, this popular restaurant in Mountain View occupies a voluminous space on the main floor of an office building. Adorned in Spanish style with arched openings, wrought-iron fixtures, and a high coffered ceiling, Cascal draws a large business crowd for lunch and after-work cocktails. Vivid splashes of red, gold, blue, and green kick up some Latin panache in the room.

Tapas top the menu, which also features entrées, like paella, that are meant for sharing. Either way, Latin American flavors will tango with your taste buds in such vibrant dishes as a pair of bowl-shaped masa *sopes*, both filled with a base of earthy black beans. Spicy chicken *picadillo* crowns one, while moist Cuban-style roasted pulled pork caps the other.

Cin-Cin

International

368 Village Ln. (at Saratoga Los Gatos Rd.), Los Gatos

Phone: 408-354-8006 Dinner Tue – Sun
Web: www.cincinwinebar.com
Prices: $$

Tucked down a tiny lane in downtown Los Gatos, this bungalow hides a neighborhood hot spot for the local happy-hour set. Though it bills itself as a wine bar, Cin-Cin boasts a large dining room incorporating recycled items amid the green walls and wine-themed artwork that sets the scene for shareable small plates.

Flavors from many nations influence the menu. Peppercorn ahi tuna *crudo* roams to Asia, while duck confit served over a bed of creamy cannelini beans pays homage to the cuisine of France. Addictive *tostaditos* topped with shredded lamb and striped with a smoky chipotle sauce, avocado crème fraîche, and tangy tomatillo salsa salute Mexican flavors. Featured wine flights make it easy to sample your way through the international list.

Chez TJ ✿

Contemporary XX

E2

938 Villa St. (bet. Bryant & Franklin Sts.), Mountain View

Phone: 650-964-7466 Dinner Tue – Sat
Web: www.cheztj.com
Prices: **$$$$**

Mark Leet

After 27 years, Chez TJ still has it. Built in 1894, the historic Victorian home only grows more charming with each passing day on its quiet provincial lane. TJ's multiple intimate dining rooms may feel a bit worn with age, but the old-fashioned mirrors, Tiffany-style lamps, cozy fireplace, and antique furnishings feel nonetheless nostalgic and quaint. Well-spaced tables, some of which have garden views, preserve privacy among couples celebrating special occasions.

The prolific Chef Bruno Chemel masters traditional French technique and crafts contemporary cuisine with exceptional ingredients and refined flavors. The food here is delicious and complex, if at times fussy. Dinner may begin with canapés, such as beet rounds topped with creamy goat cheese and air-dried buffalo. The beautifully presented courses that follow range from the likes of tender Napa cabbage rolls, generously filled with sweet Dungeness crab, to velvety sliced duck set atop braised endive glazed with vanilla bean.

The small, über-professional staff demonstrates expertise, though at times can be a touch zealous. Then again, such imaginative culinary experiences do inspire enthusiasm.

Consuelo

A1 — Mexican XX

377 Santana Row (bet. Olin Ave. & Olsen Dr.), San Jose

Phone: 408-260-7082 — Lunch & dinner daily
Web: www.consuelomexicanbistro.com
Prices: $$

In a lively yet professional atmosphere, hospitality rules the attentive and efficient staff at this authentic Mexican spot, located in the upscale Santana Row shopping center.

From *pipián* to a filling *torta de elote*, this reasonably priced menu is ambitious and unapologetically traditional—without any nods to the nachos set. Layers of flavor stand out in each regional Mexican dish, and there's no holding back on the heat. A meal here may begin with warm house-made tortillas, accented by mango, tomatillo, and toasted-chile salsas.

A festive mood prevails in the evening, when friends gather for margaritas, or to enjoy the impressive tequila list. For those who prefer their drinks non-alcoholic, Consuelo features a different *agua fresca* daily.

Crouching Tiger

D2 — Chinese XX

2644 Broadway St. (bet. El Camino Real & Perry St.), Redwood City

Phone: 650-298-8881 — Lunch & dinner daily
Web: www.crouchingtigerrestaurant.com
Prices:

In Redwood City, Crouching Tiger is a hidden dragon—a real fire breather, as evidenced by the red chili pepper icons heating up the menu. Sichuan lovers can scorch their palates and sweat their brows with a dish of *Xingjian* lamb, which is stir-fried with dried red chilies and sliced jalapeños. It's hotter than Hades, but wickedly delicious. Sizzling dishes are also just as they sound, so shyer tongues are wise to opt for such widely appealing Mandarin and Hunan classics as pot stickers, fried wontons, and sweet-and-sour pork.

If things get too hot, take solace in the cooling effect of the trickling fountain and flatscreens looping aquatic images and slideshows of mouthwatering delicacies. Note that the service is efficient but can be a bit cold.

Dio Deka

Greek XX

E3

210 E. Main St. (bet. Fiesta Way & Johnson St.), Los Gatos

Phone: 408-354-7700 — Lunch Sun – Fri
Web: www.diodeka.com — Dinner nightly
Prices: $$$

Tucked into the Hotel Los Gatos on Main Street, Dio Deka is a lovely Greek tavern with a big, open kitchen, a crackling fireplace, and a whole lot of Greek hospitality. The brainchild of five Greek restaurateurs, the menu is a seamless blend of Greek and Mediterranean, with a heavy influence on fish and lamb.
Hunker down at the big communal table, and sink your teeth into grass-fed lamb chops. Served with lemony potato wedges and a scoop of silky spinach, the chops are a study in harmonious flavors—perfectly grilled and boasting a mouthwatering outer crust of spices. Don't forget to carefully peruse the extensive wine book with well over 1,000 labels; the selections of Greek wines and Ouzo are particularly noteworthy.

Donato Enoteca

Italian XX

D2

1041 Middlefield Rd. (bet. Jefferson Ave. & Main St.), Redwood City

Phone: 650-701-1000 — Lunch & dinner daily
Web: www.donatoenoteca.com
Prices: $$

Executive Chef Donato Scotti brings the cuisine of his native Northern Italy to this newcomer in Redwood City. Located next to City Hall, the *enoteca* has already proven itself to be a popular addition to the town's dining scene. When the weather is warm, locals love to eat on the alluring and spacious outdoor patio, shaded by umbrellas and decorated with potted plants. Indoor options include the chic but rustic main dining room and the lounge-like wine bar.
A bowl of house-made agnolotti stuffed with ground sausage and veal is as appealing as a wood-fired pizza or a sautéed Mediterranean sea bream. The menu changes weekly, according to the market and the chef's whim.
Compact and well-chosen, the wine list offers a solid range of Italian varietals.

Evvia

B3 Greek XX

420 Emerson St. (bet. Lytton & University Aves.), Palo Alto

Phone: 650-326-0983 Lunch Mon – Fri
Web: www.evvia.net Dinner nightly
Prices: $$

Equally popular sister to Kokkari Estiatorio in San Francisco, Evvia mirrors the delectable Greek fare, rustic ambience, and friendly service of its big-city sibling. The casual dining room recalls a country inn with wooden beams, a stone fireplace, copper pots, handmade pottery, and retractable floor-to-ceiling windows.

Daily offerings of fresh whole fish are served grilled or roasted. Lamb, a Mediterranean staple, comes in incarnations ranging from grilled riblets with lemon and oregano, to shank braised with aromatics. End meals on an authentic note with Greek coffee cooked over hot sand. Request it *sketo* (no sugar), *metrio* (medium sugar), or *glyko* (sweet); however you like it, mind the grounds at the bottom of the cup before taking that last swig.

Flea Street

A3 Californian XX

3607 Alameda de las Pulgas (at Avy Ave.), Menlo Park

Phone: 650-854-1226 Dinner Tue – Sun
Web: www.cooleatz.com
Prices: $$$

The name may not evoke appetizing cuisine, but this classy café is Menlo Park's darling. Housed in a white cottage-like structure, the restaurant boasts a pretty patio that provides outdoor seating on warm days. The building sits on a slope, so there are also several tiers of dining space inside. Low lighting and closely spaced, linen-topped tables create an intimate ambience equally conducive to celebrating a special occasion or staging a first date.

Savory courses make up the high points here. Locally grown, seasonal, and primarily organic products lend their simple clean flavors to the café's Californian cuisine: think fork-tender braised grass-fed short ribs, and delicate black pepper gnocchi balanced by earthy cubes of roasted yellow beets.

Fook Yuen Seafood

Chinese

195 El Camino Real (at Victoria Ave.), Millbrae

Phone: 650-692-8600 — Lunch & dinner daily
Web: N/A
Prices: $$

Despite its name, Fook Yuen Seafood is foremost a dim sum restaurant. Servers parade the room with trays and carts displaying an ever-changing variety of steamed buns, fried dumplings, noodle dishes, barbecue, and stir-fried offerings. Be quick, decisive, and prepared to point and nod, for once an item has passed the table, it is unlikely to be seen again. Those who like to eat where patrons of the same culture flock should note that this is Chinese for the Chinese.

Arrive early to grab a seat and to be assured to see the full array of freshly prepared fare. Although there is no readily available price list, most dim sum items are priced under $5. In the evening, larger entrées range from braised abalone to sautéed scallops and roasted crispy suckling pig.

Higuma

Japanese 

540 El Camino Real (bet. Hopkins & Whipple Aves.), Redwood City

Phone: 650-369-3240 — Lunch Mon – Fri
Web: N/A — Dinner Mon – Sat
Prices: $$

A meal in this popular neighborhood sushi spot housed in a cute little bungalow on El Camino Real is a straightforward affair, and one that caters to midday crowds of Japanese businessmen and the local high-tech and medical industry. Friendly service, reasonable prices, and good ingredients ensure that the place stays packed for weekday lunch.

The chef's sushi assortment emerges as an ungarnished array of neat packages of fresh fish placed atop rice. A large bowl of fragrant and spicy miso ramen makes a fine meal on its own.

Seats at the tiny sushi bar are at a premium here, but small tables that huddle close together are also available in the dining room. Echoing the restaurant's name, images of Japanese brown bears (*higuma*) decorate the space.

Hong Kong Flower Lounge

C1

Chinese

51 Millbrae Ave. (at El Camino Real), Millbrae

Phone: 650-692-6666 Lunch & dinner daily
Web: N/A
Prices:

Crowds pose no challenge to this wildly popular green-tile-roofed restaurant. With 400 seats, Hong Kong Flower Lounge can easily accommodate the predominantly Asian clientele that pours into the place at peak meal times, creating a buzz that suggests the city for which the lounge is named.

Dim sum is the main attraction for lunch. Servers bearing trays and rolling carts stream out of the kitchen with a parade of jewel-like treats: potstickers; fluffy dumplings filled with the likes of barbecued pork or steamed shrimp; or Chinese broccoli steamed tableside. Eager and adventurous foodies are rewarded with items like marinated duck tongue; jellyfish in chili bean sauce; or cold chicken feet. Look for servers in pink jackets if you don't speak Cantonese.

Hunan Home's

D2

Chinese

4880 El Camino Real (at Showers Dr.), Los Altos

Phone: 650-965-8888 Lunch & dinner daily
Web: www.hunanhomes.com
Prices:

This restaurant's name may seem to be lost in translation, but the value here is the same in any language. Run by the Yuan family, who own the original in San Francisco's Chinatown, Hunan Home's dishes up speedy, courteous, and friendly service along with an extensive menu.

Lunch brings the best bargains; midday specials include a choice of soup, salad or spring roll, entrée, steamed rice, dessert, and tea for less than $10. Dinner is also reasonable, with an almost overwhelming array of items running the gamut from shredded pork to sizzling platters—and everything in between. Keep in mind the complimentary dishes, or you may end up with more food than you can eat.

Large tables in the middle dining room easily accommodate families and other groups.

Iberia

Spanish XX

B2

1026 Alma Ave. (at Ravenswood St.), Menlo Park

Phone: 650-325-8981 — Lunch Mon – Sat
Web: www.iberiarestaurant.com — Dinner nightly
Prices: $$

Housed in a cozy bungalow on a quiet street across from the train station, Iberia celebrates the best of Spanish cuisine. Offerings showcase a large selection of tapas, in addition to ever-changing specials, and more ambitious seafood entrées—as in the deboned Idaho trout, enhanced with flavors from a reduction of fresh citrus and Spanish olives. Fixed menus like the Harvest Table and Sunday's Roast Dinner are available for the entire table only, though no matter what you order, a 19 percent service charge is included in your check.

The tree-shaded patio makes a perfect spot to sip a glass of the house sangria on a warm day. Next door, The Rock of Gibraltar Comestibles sells quality Spanish ingredients, as well as a sampling of dishes to-go.

John Bentley's

Contemporary XX

D2

2915 El Camino Real (bet. Berkshire Ave. & E. Selby Ln.), Redwood City

Phone: 650-365-7777 — Lunch Mon – Fri
Web: www.johnbentleys.com — Dinner Mon – Sat
Prices: $$$

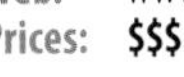

Just off the seemingly never-ending corridor of El Camino Real, John Bentley's is an oasis of elegance. Whereas the original John Bentley's in Woodside centers on its historic setting in a c.1920s firehouse, the newer location displays an urban refinement. The comfortable dining space, with dark wood and colorful artwork, expands into several distinct sections.

Chef/owner John Bentley focuses on premium organic produce, sustainably-raised meats, and environmentally sound seafood. Seasonal dishes are precisely prepared, as in the likes of seared foie gras teamed with sweet and sour cherries and candied kumquats; Dungeness crab artfully arranged atop slices of blood orange and avocado; or peppercorn-crusted ahi with pickled ginger soba noodles.

Junnoon

Indian XX

B3

150 University Ave. (at High St.), Palo Alto

Phone: 650-329-9644 Lunch Mon – Fri
Web: www.junnoon.com Dinner nightly
Prices: $$

Pink and orange sheers filter a mysterious glow into Junnoon's Palo Alto dining room. Here, Chef Kirti Pant (formerly of Tamarind in New York City) infuses contemporary Indian cuisine with passion, energy, and obsession, as the restaurant's name (in Hindi) infers. During lunch, the "Junnoon Tiffin" offers guests a light combination meal for less than $20, and remains popular at this hot spot near Stanford University. Fans line up for the likes of aromatic spice-infused *aachaari* chicken served with black lentils, mint *raita,* and rosemary naan; or creative, well-spiced Indo-Asiatic combinations, like Darjeeling-steamed wontons.

A house signature, the moist tandoori halibut tempts taste buds with a delicious coconut-ginger sauce and curry leaf semolina.

Kaygetsu

Japanese XX

A3

325 Sharon Park Dr. (at Sand Hill Rd.), Menlo Park

Phone: 650-234-1084 Lunch Tue – Fri
Web: www.kaygetsu.com Dinner Tue – Sun
Prices: $$$$

Owned by sushi chef, Toshio Sakuma and his wife, Keiko, this "beautiful moon" (as the name translates from Japanese) hangs in the corner of the Sharon Heights shopping center. Here, the *kaiseki* menu shines, amid the variety of sushi, *nigiri,* and maki. Harmonious balance of flavors, preparations, and artistry characterize this traditional meal, which has origins in the Zen tea ceremony.

Those who indulge in this option should plan to spend two to three hours feasting on a series of small sensuous courses. Flowers imported from Tokyo may grace the parade of items ranging from roast duck with apple and tamari, to impeccably fresh sashimi and house-made yuzu citrus sorbet, all arranged on an attractive array of dishes, baskets, and platters.

The Kitchen

Chinese

C1

279 El Camino Real (at La Cruz Ave.), Millbrae

Phone: 650-692-9688 Lunch & dinner daily
Web: N/A
Prices:

Parked in a largely Asian locale, The Kitchen unfolds top-notch dim sum and delicacy-laden Cantonese specialties to a knowledgeable Asian crowd. Step into their professionally-run dining room freckled with large tables and fish tanks, then merely take a whiff. Rest assured, you will want to return with many friends and family to sample their abounding offerings.

Let the Cantonese chronicles at lunch begin with the a tasting from the well-versed chef's classic or inventive dim sum such as chive dumplings; a cilantro bean curd salad; and a giant sharks fin soup dumpling. Or turn a leaf to the sizeable dinner menu—think of wasabi-tossed chicken with pork belly or sautéed squab with foie gras and shredded lettuce—and let your palate absorb the rest.

Koi Palace

Chinese

C1

365 Gellert Blvd. (bet. Hickey & Serramonte Blvds.), Daly City

Phone: 650-992-9000 Lunch & dinner daily
Web: www.koipalace.com
Prices:

Koi Palace can seat 400 guests, and the ample parking lot often overflows with cars having to be stationed on the surrounding streets. This phenomenon bespeaks the restaurant's popularity—mostly with a local Chinese clientele who flock here for dim sum at appealing prices.

Walk through the moon gate to spot aquarium tanks swimming with the day's catch; koi ponds in the dining room add aesthetic appeal for grown-ups and provide little ones with entertainment. Try to snag a seat on an aisle for the best service. From here, you can more easily hail the servers who hurry by with a staggering array of items. Offerings include everything from familiar *siu mai* with diced mushrooms or barbecue pork, to exotic fare like poached queen's clam and soya duck tongue.

La Forêt

French XX

21747 Bertram Rd. (at Almaden Rd.), San Jose

Phone: 408-997-3458 — Lunch Sun
Web: www.laforetrestaurant.com — Dinner Tue – Sun
Prices: $$$

Built in 1848 as a boarding house for miners working to extract a local vein of cinnabar (quicksilver), this unassuming two-story structure is quietly tucked into a rather rural residential area south of downtown San Jose. Today the building houses a uniquely charming restaurant, La Forêt, named for the leafy surroundings visible through walls of windows. Here, an old-school approach to French cuisine inspires dishes such as pan-seared foie gras with sauternes sauce or tournedos of beef with chanterelles, herbs, ginger, and brandy.

Although some sections of the restaurant may seem dated, the atmosphere is better defined by the personal attention received from this well-informed, accommodating staff rather than modern accents or trendy design.

Lavanda

Mediterranean XX

185 University Ave. (at Emerson St.), Palo Alto

Phone: 650-321-3514 — Lunch Mon – Fri
Web: www.lavandarestaurant.com — Dinner nightly
Prices: $$$

Palo Alto goes Mediterranean at this pleasant spot, where white-cloth-draped tables huddle close together, light jazz animates the room, and a coterie of locals crowds the wine bar. Windows line the front wall and a lavender-streaked fabric mural decorates the wall opposite.

Start your meal here by mixing and matching a number of small tastes such as Manchego cheese and preserves, shaved artichokes, and Parmesan; or chorizo and clams. The menu offers a choice of any three for $15. Still hungry? Pan-fried rabbit or roasted mahi mahi all sing with the fresh flavors of the lands that border the Mediterranean Sea.

The wine list impresses with its extensive selection of international labels, which includes hard-to-find boutique producers.

LB Steak

Steakhouse XXX

A1

334 Santana Row, Suite 1000 (bet. Olin Ave. & Stevens Creek Blvd.), San Jose

Phone: 408-244-1180 — Lunch & dinner daily
Web: www.lbsteak.com
Prices: $$$

Sister to the Left Bank Brasserie located at the opposite end of Santana Row, LB Steak is a good fit for this tony mixed-use complex. At lunchtime, the patio is the place to be for local business folks to sink their teeth into gourmet burgers and steak sandwiches. In the evening, couples and shoppers stop by for brawny USDA prime steaks and elegant seafood. Dishes get a soupçon of French sophistication courtesy of Chef/proprietor Roland Passot.

When it's time for dessert, look to the pastry cart for more refined offerings than the usual steakhouse sweets. Among the cookies, financiers, and fruit tarts, a raspberry *macaron* filled with vanilla pastry cream and scattered with plump, sweet raspberries does justice to the restaurant's French legacy.

Le Papillon

French 

A1

410 Saratoga Ave. (at Kiely Blvd.), San Jose

Phone: 408-296-3730 — Lunch Fri
Web: www.lepapillon.com — Dinner nightly
Prices: $$$$

Despite changes in Silicon Valley since this restaurant opened its doors in 1977, Le Papillon (French for "butterfly") maintains the tradition of sophisticated French cuisine that has long been its hallmark. Classic Gallic preparations take flight at the hands of Chef Scott Cooper. Tender buffalo tenderloin, for instance, is cooked to medium-rare and garnished with a well-seasoned *marchand du vin* sauce. A tartlet of bone-marrow custard adds a rich note to the dish.

A serious old-world atmosphere complements the food: tables are swathed in white linen, chairs covered with floral tapestry prints, and a lavish floral arrangement forms the room's focal point. Oenophiles' hearts will flutter when reading the lengthy list of French and Californian wines.

Liou's House

Chinese

1245 Jacklin Rd. (at Park Victoria Dr.), Milpitas

Phone: 408-263-9888 — Lunch & dinner Tue – Sun
Web: N/A
Prices:

Looking for authentically fiery Hunan cuisine? Drop by Chef Liou's House, near the Summitpointe Golf Club in Milpitas. This cushy family-run restaurant features a large selection of expertly prepared Hunan fare, as well as a zesty sampling of regional Chinese dishes.

The cognoscenti—a sizeable contingent of Chinese residents among them—know to order from the chef's specialties list, which is an insert in the main menu. These dishes are where the talent of noted Taiwanese chef, James Liou really dazzles. "Addictive" best describes the blisteringly hot—as in spicy—nuggets of chicken coated in ground dried red chilies.

Top off such delicious food with warm, friendly service and you've got a go-to restaurant that's worth the trip to the South Bay area.

Lure

Seafood

204-A 2nd Ave. (bet. B St. & Ellsworth Ave), San Mateo

Phone: 650-340-9040 — Dinner Tue – Sat
Web: www.lurerestaurant.com
Prices: $$$

Black walls and tables glistening with silverware meet sculptural white plaster etched with an undulating motif at this smart urban restaurant. Hip describes the vibe here from the dim lights and contemporary music to the very cool crowd. While other restaurants might rest on this accomplishment, Lure extends its sophistication through to its cuisine.

Bustling and well-staffed, the glassed-in kitchen is stocked with the fresh shellfish offerings of the day, tantalizingly displayed on a mound of ice. Perhaps begin with caviar-topped blinis before moving onto classical preparations of impeccably fresh seafood, such as Hokkaido sea scallops, pan-seared skate, or whole *branzino*. End meals on a deliciously light note, with a trio of seasonal sorbets.

Madera

Contemporary XXX

A3

2825 Sand Hill Rd. (at I-280), Menlo Park

Phone: 650-561-1546 Lunch & dinner daily
Web: www.maderasandhill.com
Prices: **$$$**

Madera sports an elegant ranch-inspired setting complete with a vaulted western red cedar ceiling, picture windows framing panoramic views of the rolling hillside, and an open, wood-fired kitchen. The talented brigade honors sustainable, local, seasonal products to craft a menu that displays an impressive stroke of refinement. A starter of smoky grilled cuttlefish drizzled with paprika oil rests atop a vibrant combination of garbanzos, *piquillo* peppers, and caper berries; while entrées may feature flaky rainbow trout filled with sweet Dungeness crabmeat, slicked with sauce *vierge*—a bright mixture of fragrant olive oil, ripe tomato, fresh herbs, and citrus.

The dining room's idyllic porch is a lovely spot to savor a cocktail or light meal.

Mantra

Indian XX

B3

632 Emerson St. (bet. Forest & Hamilton Aves.), Palo Alto

Phone: 650-322-3500 Lunch Tue – Fri
Web: www.mantrapaloalto.com Dinner nightly
Prices: **$$**

Expect the unexpected in this urban-chic dining room serving exciting East Indian fare with California accents. Elegance and harmony permeate the space, where black stone floors echo the high, open-grid black ceiling, and the walls showcase contemporary Indian artwork.

From the kitchen come quirky dishes such as cinnamon shrimp lollipops, and smoked cumin and pomegranate short ribs. In other preparations, the menu shines with well-balanced classics like chicken curry and Madras shrimp. Naan might come simply flavored with garlic, or innovatively with rosemary pesto or spicy jack cheese. Sophisticated cocktails and a good selection of international wines pair with exotic small plates in the swanky Daru Lounge, which claims Palo Alto's longest bar.

Manresa ✿✿

Contemporary

E3

320 Village Ln. (bet. Santa Cruz & University Aves.), Los Gatos

Phone: 408-354-4330 Dinner Wed – Sun
Web: www.manresarestaurant.com
Prices: $$$$

Pim Techamuanvivit

At the critically-acclaimed Manresa, Chef David Kinch draws his inspiration for his four-course menu (selected by the customer from multiple categories) and more extensive tasting menu from nearby Love Apple Farm. Undoubtedly, the fresh produce he procures from the biodynamic farm is top of the line, but what this innovative chef is able to prepare with those ingredients is absolute artistry.

Squirreled away in a little yellow house tucked down a narrow side street in the trendy shopping area of Los Gatos, Manresa possesses the kind of fresh ranch house charm Northern California is known for, with a sunny dining room framed in silk drapes, exposed wood and oriental rugs, and an outdoor terrace that fills up when the weather's right.

The menu spins to the season, but might include a fresh pile of Nantucket bay scallops, sautéed in a brown butter with cabbage and radish and served with a soft tangle of wilted greens and citrus; perfectly crispy-meets-tender duck with a walnut fondant, preserved Meyer lemon and broken meat jus, paired with wilted fennel; or tender and juicy lamb loin cooked to dazzling, medium-rare perfection and served with glazed fruit and caramelized artichokes.

Marché

Contemporary XXX

A2

898 Santa Cruz Ave. (at University Dr.), Menlo Park

Phone: 650-324-9092 Dinner Tue – Sat
Web: www.restaurantmarche.com
Prices: $$$

This spot continues to be a good choice for fine dining in downtown Menlo Park. Fresh products from local farms harmonize with interesting flavor combinations on Marché's seasonal menu. Mediterranean elements spark the contemporary fare in homemade ricotta gnocchi with blue prawns, and an organic chicken breast plated with braised leg cannelloni and pipérade. Attention to detail pops out in a pancetta-wrapped pork loin and fresh sausage served atop a bed of sweet corn and caramelized onion salsa, with a purée of ginger-infused peaches.

Service is discreet and professional in the dining room, sleek in shades of chocolate brown, with smoked mirrors lining one wall. On the opposite side of the room, large windows provide great views into the kitchen.

Mingalaba

Asian 

C1

1213 Burlingame Ave. (bet. Lorton Ave. & Park Rd.), Burlingame

Phone: 650-343-3228 Lunch & dinner daily
Web: www.mingalabarestaurant.com
Prices: ⓈⓈ

Bamboo wainscoting, modern lighting, and red-gold walls dotted with Asian artifacts add a touch of pretty to this quick-service hot spot in the center of Burlingame. Popular among local business types and afternoon shoppers, a table at Mingalaba is well worth the wait—provided you opt for the bold Burmese fare in lieu of forgettable Mandarin menu options.

Begin with light and crispy vegetarian *samusa* stuffed with potatoes and onion, or an interesting tea leaf salad—mounds of fresh ingredients are mixed at the table to an earthy, crunchy finish. Burmese-style curries are vividly flavored and the black pepper soup with a fresh fish fillet is an unusual delight. Cool down at dessert with a mildly sweet mango pudding served in a leaf-shaped bowl.

Naomi Sushi

A2 Japanese

1328 El Camino Real (bet. Glenwood & Oak Grove Aves.), Menlo Park

Phone: 650-321-6902 Lunch Tue – Fri
Web: www.naomisushi.com Dinner Tue – Sun
Prices: $$

Set on bustling El Camino Real, this modest Menlo Park sushi grill may have an unassuming façade, but duck inside for very well-prepared sushi and sashimi of true quality. The sushi bar, which welcomes patrons as they enter, is the place to park yourself and to enjoy the traditional, reasonably priced omakase offerings. Elsewhere on the menu, Japanese entrées exhibit a clear Californian twist, as in the poached pork loin with shiitake mushrooms, or grilled sea bream with fresh vegetables. Daily specials are worth investigating, as are the sake tastings that change each week.

Two dining rooms recall a rustic seaside tavern, decorated with fishing paraphernalia, a mounted game fish, and murals of the sea. Restaurant guests enjoy private parking.

Navio

C2 Californian

1 Miramontes Point Rd. (at Hwy. 1), Half Moon Bay

Phone: 650-712-7040 Lunch Sat – Sun
Web: www.ritzcarlton.com Dinner nightly
Prices: $$$$

Perched on a bluff above the Pacific, this restaurant sits within the Ritz-Carlton Half Moon Bay. And though the sleek space is well-designed with soft blue hues and a wood-lined barrel-vaulted ceiling, watching the waves roll in over the rocky coast clearly trumps all.

Such natural splendor makes it difficult to focus on the food, but this contemporary fare is worthy of its setting. With a concise, widely appealing menu of both seafood and meat preparations, offerings may include opaque pan-seared dayboat scallops set upon sweet-tart braised Belgian endive, or an Asian-inspired broiled local butterfish served atop shiitake mushrooms and baby bok choy in a warm shiitake broth. California varietals dominate the international library of wine labels.

New Kapadokia

Turkish

D2

2399 Broadway St. (at Winslow St.), Redwood City

Phone: 650-368-5500 — Lunch Tue – Fri
Web: www.newkapadokia.com — Dinner Tue – Sun
Prices:

Named for Turkey's region known for ancient underground cities, New Kapadokia is perhaps the most genuine culinary experience this side of the Aegean Sea. Unlike the average Turkish eatery, this family-run restaurant is proud of its heritage and serves only authentic recipes, many of which were handed down from the chef's mother and grandmother. The uninitiated should rely on the knowledgeable staff and the trays of starters or desserts they bring to you to assist with ordering. Kebabs are wrapped in *lavash* and served with garlicky yogurt, sumac, and spicy sauce, while platters teem with lamb and vegetable stew.

Say hello to gracious owner Celal Alpay, and don't miss the spinning Turkish coffee—its service here is quite the performance!

Nick's on Main

American

E3

35 E. Main St. (bet. College Ave. & Pageant Way), Los Gatos

Phone: 408-399-6457 — Lunch & dinner Tue – Sat
Web: www.nicksonmainst.com
Prices: **$$$**

Size has little to do with sophistication as this shoebox of a bistro attests. As chic as it is tiny, Nick's packs patrons elbow-to-elbow at closely spaced tables. The ladies who lunch don't seem to mind; they keep up a steady flow of chatter as they choose among zippy offerings—such as Chinese chicken salad, mushroom ravioli, and a Dungeness crab melt—on the reasonably priced midday menu. Lucky for everyone, the room's high ceilings help minimize the din of conversations.

The lighting turns down and prices for entrées jump up at dinnertime, when chef and owner Nick Difu concocts comforting dishes like pan-roasted pork filet. A playful touch comes at the end of the meal, when the bill is presented in a worn copy of *The New Food Lover's Companion*.

Pampas

B3

529 Alma St. (bet. Hamilton & University Aves.), Palo Alto

Phone: 650-327-1323 — Lunch Mon – Fri
Web: www.pampaspaloalto.com — Dinner nightly
Prices: $$$

Come hungry to this sophisticated *churrascaria*, where *passadors* circulate throughout the room carrying an unlimited parade of large skewers of spit-roasted meats that they slice at the table.

Quality is there in the *rodizio* dinner, 14 different types of meat, delivered piping hot to the table. Pork, beef, lamb, and chicken are seasoned with Brazilian dry rubs, or spiced with combinations of garlic, ginger, mint, cumin, cracked pepper, paprika, and Parmesan. Linguiça turns out tasty and sweet, while bacon lends a smoky flavor to pieces of turkey breast.

A buffet of side dishes kicks things up with the likes of coconut-whipped sweet potatoes with yucca, ginger-glazed carrots, and a salad of chickpeas and olives.

Pasta Moon

Italian XX

C2

315 Main St. (at Mill St.), Half Moon Bay

Phone: 650-726-5125 — Lunch & dinner daily
Web: www.pastamoon.com
Prices: $$

A taste of Italy comes to the fog-shrouded beach hamlet of Half Moon Bay in the form of Pasta Moon. Regulars have been flocking here for some 20 years for house-made, hand-cut pasta and an exclusively Italian wine list, with many available by the glass. Tourists are learning that both the food and the town merit the winding, half-hour drive down Highway 1 from San Francisco. From first glance, Main Street reveals a tapestry of boutiques in a mix of Southwestern adobe and New England-style façades.

Inside Pasta Moon, cocoa-colored walls cradle tightly packed tables, and heady aromas of garlic and spices fill the air. Seasonal offerings of light, pillowy pumpkin gnocchi are a must during autumn, bathed in Bolognese ragù and shaved Parmesan cheese.

Pizza Antica

A1 — Pizza

334 Santana Row, Suite 1065 (bet. Stevens Creek Blvd. & Tatum Ln.), San Jose

Phone: 408-557-8373 — Lunch & dinner daily
Web: www.pizzaantica.com
Prices: $$

Shoppers and others consistently line up at this bistro-style pizza parlor at lunchtime, eager for a taste of the restaurant's thin-crust pies. Dough proofs for three days before being rolled out cracker-thin, topped with a wide range of artisanal ingredients, and baked in the gas oven. "Our Pizza" features set combinations, while "Your Pizza" allows guests to customize their toppings—from pesto to pepperoni. It is equally worthwhile to explore the full menu of fresh salads, pasta, and entrées like herb-roasted breast of chicken and zinfandel-braised boneless short ribs.

High chairs and a kids menu that doubles as a coloring book make wee diners welcome. On sunny days, everyone clamors for the sidewalk seating in this heart of Santana Row.

Red Lantern

D2 — Asian

808 Winslow St. (at Broadway St.), Redwood City

Phone: 650-369-5483 — Lunch Mon – Fri
Web: www.redlanternrwc.com — Dinner nightly
Prices: $$

A redeveloped area of Redwood City is home to this fresh and flavorful Asian favorite, conveniently situated next to the Caltrain Sequoia Station. A 20-seat communal table and carved Asian artifacts adorn the soaring bi-level space. From the restaurant's high ceiling hangs a collection of huge red silk lanterns—red representing luck, happiness, and prosperity.

Local business people indeed feel lucky to have this place, judging from the crowds that come here for inexpensive lunch combinations spotlighting Southeast Asia. At dinner, the only option is the à la carte menu, where a "Taste of Paradise" might translate to tender, rich lamb curry.

No matter when you go, the food is tasty and satisfying, the atmosphere exotic-chic, and the vibe relaxed.

Plumed Horse ✿

Contemporary XXX

E3

14555 Big Basin Way (bet. 4th & 5th Sts.), Saratoga

Phone: 408-867-4711 Dinner Mon – Sat
Web: www.plumedhorse.com
Prices: **$$$$**

James Fong

Plumed Horse takes its moniker from the 19th century stable that once claimed the land at this beautiful Saratoga location—set along a charming street lined in enormous trees and quaint artisan shops—but there's not a lot of country farm left in this cutting-edge establishment.

And in this case, that's a very good thing. There are six gorgeous, slickly-appointed rooms to take your pick from, including a light-soaked stained-glass room, a beautiful wine cellar, and a private chef's table overlooking the kitchen. No matter where you sit, this is no time to teetotal—the restaurant carries a dizzying selection of wines, with over 24,000 bottles in inventory.

Chef Peter Armellino's seasonal, California-minded menu might include a Parmesan-and-black pepper soufflé, filled tableside with a creamy Dungeness crab and uni fondue; silky slips of fresh Monterey abalone paired with matchbook sticks of Blue Foot chicken confit served on a hot, smooth bed of puréed squash; or a savory loin of seared antelope kissed with a chestnut purée, topped with two pristine Italian chestnuts sprinkled with sea salt, and paired with a rich pile of French lentils, Swiss chard, and garlicky house-made sausage.

Saint Michael's Alley

Contemporary

140 Homer Ave. (at High St.), Palo Alto

Phone: 650-326-2530 — Lunch Tue – Sun
Web: www.stmikes.com — Dinner Tue – Sat
Prices: $$

What's old is new again, as this Palo Alto fixture recently moved to new digs at the corner of High Street and Homer Avenue, though the original Emerson Street location remains open for weekend brunch. The new restaurant packs in a business crowd at lunch, and a cadre of loyal locals for dinner.

An inviting front patio and a series of small rooms weave through the space. Cheery terra-cotta-colored walls, fresh wildflowers, and soft lighting create a charming atmosphere in which to enjoy light, flavorful, and well-prepared dishes. Straightforward describes the fluffy potato gnocchi served in a rich, basil-scented tomato sauce. A bit more modern are ginger prawn lollipops, deep-fried in egg-roll wrappers and paired with a piquant dipping sauce.

Sakae

Japanese

243 California Dr. (at Highland Ave.), Burlingame

Phone: 650-558-9530 — Lunch & dinner daily
Web: www.sakaesushi.com
Prices: $$

Get to know this sushi-ya and Japanese grill, and love it. Formerly called Noboru, the contemporary, popular dining room offers plentiful wood tables and sits amid numerous car dealerships, with abundant parking. There are additional seats at the (exclusively) sushi counter, but beware of a $20 minimum and ordering cooked items (like the superb egg custard, *chawan mushi*) from the broad menu is forbidden.

The real lure of Sakae is fresh, top quality fish sourced from the U.S. and Japan. Expect deep-red and silky tuna, or sweet, buttery salmon among the offerings. While some maki may seem bulky, the seven-course sushi omakase best highlights the seafood, which might include seared fluke fin and amberjack. This may help forgive their uneven service.

Sakoon

Indian XX

E2

357 Castro St. (bet. California & Dana Sts.), Mountain View

Phone: 650-965-2000 Lunch & dinner daily
Web: www.sakoonrestaurant.com
Prices: $$

Bold is as bold does at this Mountain View standout. Start with the dining room, wrapped in a contemporary-chic ambience that flaunts a playful palette of colors and patterns. Neon backs the bar, and hundreds of fiber-optic lights hang from the ceiling, changing color every few seconds. You might think it would be too much, but it works.

Bold, too, are Chef Sachin Chopra's updated Indian dishes. Chopra cut his teeth in New York City before heading west, and he has mastered the complex art of layering flavors and textures in his cuisine. The chef's talent shines brightest at dinnertime in a lovely rack of lamb, crusted in a tangy-sweet glaze spiked with Indian spices and hints of lavender and thyme. Pear chutney polishes off the preparation.

Sent Sovi

Californian XX

E3

14583 Big Basin Way (at 5th St.), Saratoga

Phone: 408-867-3110 Dinner Tue – Sun
Web: www.sentsovi.com
Prices: $$$

On the main street of the charming town of Saratoga, Sent Sovi's entrance is tucked inside a brick-paved terrace. Natural light bathes the room inside, casting a warm glow on the copper wainscoting.

Chef Josiah Slone crafts his cuisine from naturally-raised ingredients that hail from small local farms and ranches. In summer, à la carte items might include smoked-paprika-dusted scallops with Lemon Boy tomato coulis, or Niman Ranch pork tenderloin with yellow wax and Blue Lake beans. Other options include a six-course chef's tasting, a vegetarian menu, and a personalized Grand Tasting—which requires that you pre-order 48 hours in advance.

At times service conveys a degree of attitude and pretentiousness that could rub guests the wrong way.

Seven

American XX

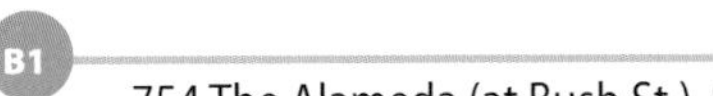

B1

754 The Alameda (at Bush St.), San Jose

Phone: 408-280-1644 — Lunch Mon – Fri
Web: www.7restaurant.com — Dinner Mon – Sat
Prices: $$

The trendy crowd jamming the narrow bar area is the first thing you'll notice upon entering this industrial-chic establishment just across from the HP Pavilion in downtown San Jose. Opened in 2003 by the Valdez twins, Curtis and Russell, Seven maintains the cool urban vibe that lures a young clientele. And the bar serves food until midnight, another draw for those looking for a bite after a concert or a Sharks game.

On the ceiling, a tangle of exposed ductwork and pipes overhangs the polished concrete floors. Curving booths and banquettes alternate in shades of Burgundy and Bordeaux against pale green walls. On the menu, an all-American cheeseburger and a classic chicken pot pie share space with French fare such as steak frites and duck cassoulet.

Shanghai Dumpling Shop

Chinese 

C1

455 Broadway (bet. Hillcrest & Taylor Blvds.), Millbrea

Phone: 650-697-0682 — Lunch & dinner daily
Web: N/A
Prices: ⓢ

Neat red lettering on a tall pale façade spells out the name in both Chinese and English, while inside white tiled floors topped with plain wooden tables set up a no frills vibe. Plumb in the heart of Millbrae amidst a quaint street of shops and businesses, Shanghai Dumpling Shop is a must stop for authentic Shanghainese cuisine. It won't take much persuasion to start with a bowl of savory steamed soup dumplings—*xiao long bao*—just check out the selections of your fellow diners for evidence of the dish's popularity. Move on to one of the tasty Shanghai-style braises—"lion head" meatball, pork rump, fish tail, or gluten puff perhaps?

For a fantastic finale, the sesame rice dumplings with rice wine soup are a lovely sweet and sticky creation.

Shokolaat

B3 Contemporary XX

516 University Ave. (bet. Cowper & Webster Sts.), Palo Alto

Phone: 650-289-0719 Lunch Mon – Fri
Web: www.shokolaat.com Dinner Mon – Sat
Prices: $$

To say that Shokolaat is a fantastic patisserie would be to underestimate the scope of this Palo Alto culinary lounge dedicated to European decadence in many mouthwatering forms. True, a glass pastry case brims with chic little chocolates and elaborate confections, beckoning passersby on the go. But those who take the time to sit down in this sleek former art gallery with a Scandinavian aesthetic receive their just deserts: a surprising menu of ambitious savories ranging from light plates at lunch to heartier Gallic suppers.
Expect such palate-pleasers as tuna tartare with chopped black truffles, shallots, and toasted brioche; gratin of escargots with bone marrow; and duck confit *crépinette*. Ethereal soufflés are a sweet reward for those who wait.

South Legend

E2 Chinese X

1720 N. Milpitas Blvd. (bet. Dixon Landing Rd. & Sunnyhills Ct.), Milpitas

Phone: 408-934-3970 Lunch & dinner daily
Web: www.southlegend.com
Prices:

Ring the alarm—South Legend's bold menu promises "all Szechuan, all the time" and is comprised of bold specialties from China's extra spicy province. The likes of *ma-po* tofu pocked with ground pork, scallions, and fermented black beans; boiled fish in fiery sauce; and twice cooked pork are not for the faint of heart. This is cuisine that will leave you blushing from a flavor-packed smackdown of chili paste, peppercorns, and red chili oil.
A listing of cooling sides like slices of winter melon seasoned with dried shrimp and a selection of dim sum that includes fried yam cakes filled with sweet red bean paste round out the offerings served at this unassuming local favorite found in a busy shopping center occupied by markets and small businesses.

Sushi Sam's

Japanese

218 E. 3rd Ave. (bet. B St. & Ellsworth Ave.), San Mateo

Phone: 650-344-0888 — Lunch & dinner Tue – Sat
Web: www.sushisams.com
Prices: $$

Minimal décor keeps the attention on the wide variety of fresh, high quality fish at this unassuming sushi spot, located on one of the busier blocks of downtown San Mateo. A favorite with local culinary professionals, Sushi Sam's boasts a well-trained team of chefs whose impressive knife skills are entertaining to watch from the three narrow seating areas (including the sushi bar).

Although there are only a few rolls on the menu, they do offer a more extensive array of fish—needlefish, butterfish, briny octopus, to name a few—than many other sushi joints in the area. Noodle bowls and hot specials are popular at lunch, while shrimp and vegetable tempura or beef teriyaki appear on the menu at dinner alongside special sushi combinations.

Tamarine

Vietnamese 

546 University Ave. (bet. Cowper & Webster Sts.), Palo Alto

Phone: 650-325-8500 — Lunch Mon – Fri
Web: www.tamarinerestaurant.com — Dinner nightly
Prices: $$

A high-topped communal table, upholstered horseshoe-shaped booths, and modern music spawns a lounge ambience here. Set on an attractive strip of University Avenue, Tamarine serves as a gallery for a changing display of contemporary Vietnamese art.

This theme also pervades the menu, with updated takes on traditional Asian cuisine. Artfully arranged plates emerge from the kitchen displaying such appetizers as savory shrimp cupcakes or grilled quail salad; and continue the parade in tri-squash scallop curry, clay pot cod, and cumin-spiced duck. Pair your entrée with a choice of aromatic rice from jasmine to empress, the latter dotted with garlic, leeks, ginger, and egg.

Delectable Asian-influenced desserts merit the extra calories.

Thea Mediterranean

Mediterranean XX

A1

3090 Olsen Dr. (at Winchester Blvd.), San Jose

Phone: 408-260-1444 — Lunch & dinner daily
Web: www.thearestaurant.com
Prices: **$$**

Named for the mythical mother of the sun and moon, Thea shines its light on traditional Greek and Turkish specialties at reasonable prices. The 20-foot-tall olive tree in the center of the soaring dining room sets the stage for a delightful culinary journey through the Mediterranean.

Begin your trip with an authentic meze sampler that includes hummus, *tzatziki*, *htipiti*, and *melitzanosalata*, served with homemade pita bread and fruity olive oil. Then explore the region more intimately in entrées such as moussaka, chicken souvlaki, and *garides* (grilled prawns in Greek spices, served over a zucchini cake).

The young, polite staff is swift and efficient—a fact that the corporate Silicon Valley crowd who lunches here no doubt appreciates.

231 Ellsworth

Contemporary XX

C2

231 S. Ellsworth Ave. (bet. 2nd & 3rd Aves.), San Mateo

Phone: 650-347-7231 — Lunch Tue – Fri
Web: www.231ellsworth.com — Dinner Mon – Sat
Prices: **$$$**

At this South Bay darling, warm-toned wood paneling, seasonal flower arrangements, perfectly pressed linens, and a cobalt-blue barrel-vaulted ceiling set the mood. Service that is as polished as the setting is elegant makes this a winner for any special occasion. Simple dishes with abundant flavors fill the seasonal menu. Thus Berkshire pork loin and confit belly sit atop house-made sauerkraut and roasted beets with whole-grain mustard. Note that some offerings can also be prepared in vegan-friendly variations.

As for the restaurant's sizeable wine collection, it stocks an impressive array of Californian labels, as well as some serious old-world wines at sensible prices. A glassed-in cherrywood day cellar near the bar displays some 800 bottles.

Trevese

Contemporary 

E3

115 N. Santa Cruz Ave. (bet. Bean Ave. & Grays Ln.), Los Gatos

Phone: 408-354-5551 — Lunch Fri – Sun
Web: www.trevese.com — Dinner Tue – Sun
Prices: $$$

Chris Schmauch

Housed in a beautiful 19th century Queen Anne Victorian tucked into a boutique-lined street in Los Gatos, Trevese glows with warmth. Inside, couples linger over wine and small groups sing "Happy Birthday," while a pleasant, polished waitstaff hums quietly through a sleek interior accented by flickering candlelight and softly-playing background jazz.

Sound idyllic? You can thank critically-acclaimed Chef Michael Miller and his wife for this lovely little oasis of comfort and style—they opened Trevese in 2007 with the mission to introduce green fine dining to Northern California. And from the moment the 800+ bottle wine list hits your table, you know you're in for a treat.

The menu spins to the season, and might include two sweet and tender sea scallops, perfectly caramelized and garnished with nests of chilled soba noodles and seaweed salad; a succulent pair of bone-in pork loins served over a silky mound of collard greens, served with a raisin-purée puff pastry and finely shaved fennel slaw; or a small block of moist brioche bread pudding, filled with golden raisins and dried cranberries and paired with a quenelle of vanilla ice cream and small vial of warm brandy crème anglaise.

The Village Pub ✿

Gastropub

D2

2967 Woodside Rd. (off Whiskey Hill Rd.), Woodside

Phone: 650-851-9888 — Lunch Mon – Fri
Web: www.thevillagepub.net — Dinner nightly
Prices: $$

Frankie Frankeny

Culinarily blessed are those who can call this their local. Tucked into the adorable moneyed mountain town of Woodside, the sophisticated Village Pub is—despite its pedestrian-sounding name—no average pub. Rather, it's a charming, elegant restaurant outfitted with pristine rounds of white-cloth tables, a giant wood-burning oven, and a clubby, old-school bar lined in glossy mahogany.

The latter practically begs for a pre-dinner cocktail, and drink they do—pouring in come early evening to relax by the crackling fireplace and soak up the irresistible buzz of the room. Over in the dining room, the service staff hums quietly to and fro—always informed and polished, but never too fussy.

Chef Mark Sullivan's rustic menu is decidedly seasonal but may include a Waldorf salad bursting with ripe, fresh-from-the-market fruits and vegetables, glistening in an apple-vinegar vinaigrette with whole grain mustard aïoli; a rich, house-made duck sausage, served with fork-crushed potatoes and sautéed red kale with a whole grain mustard sauce; or a decadent dessert of peanut butter cookies surrounding Valrhona chocolate ice cream, drizzled in chocolate sauce, and topped with a shake of peanut brittle.

Xanh

Vietnamese

E2

110 Castro St. (bet. Evelyn Ave. & Villa St.), Mountain View

Phone: 650-964-1888 — Lunch Mon – Fri
Web: www.xanhrestaurant.com — Dinner nightly
Prices: $$

In early 2008, Xanh moved into the bigger digs of this über-sleek lounge. Club music sets the tone for this audience of twenty- and thirty-somethings who applaud the liberties Chef Thuy Pham takes with Vietnamese cuisine. With a focus on original creations, Xanh's innovative, carefully prepared menu may include "crispy shrimp clouds," featuring miniature rice pancakes with shrimp, green apple, and mint; or "angry crabs" served crisp and spicy with garlic, onions, and basil. Twists on traditional spring rolls, as in the Xanh Deuce (with pork tenders and crispy shrimp) further show off the chef's inventions.

Beaded mesh curtains, smoked-glass partitions, and a trickling waterfall bring a swanky feel throughout the three dining rooms.

Zen Peninsula

Chinese

C1

1180 El Camino Real (at Center St.), Millbrae

Phone: 650-616-9388 — Lunch & dinner daily
Web: www.zenpeninsula.com
Prices: $$

A much-frequented spot for dim sum and banquet dining in Millbrae, Zen Peninsula is regularly jammed with hungry Chinese families. There's not enough space between the closely packed tables in the elegant room for dim-sum carts to maneuver, so waitresses carry platters laden with steaming baskets of dumplings and other delicacies from table to table.

Quality ingredients are evident in rich morsels of barbecue pork, their skins crusted with a satisfying five-spice coating; and crispy fried packets of tofu skin that hold small shrimp, ground pork, ginger, and garlic. Beyond dim sum, the extensive à la carte menu runs from noodles dishes to clay pot creations, and incorporates specialties such as abalone in oyster sauce and braised bird's nest soup.

Peter L. Wrenn/MICHELIN

Wine Country

Wine Country

Napa Valley and Sonoma County

Picnicking on artisan-made cheeses and fresh crusty bread amid acres of gnarled grapevines; sipping wine on a terrace above a hillside of silvery olive trees; touring caves heady with the sweet smell of fermenting grapes: this is northern California's Wine Country. Lying within a hour's drive north and northeast of San Francisco, the hills and vales of Sonoma County and Napa Valley thrive on the abundant sunshine and fertile soil that produce grapes for some of North America's finest wines.

Fruit of the Vine

Cuttings of Criollas grapevines traveled north with Franciscan *padres* from the Baja Peninsula during the late 17th century. Wines made from these "mission" grapes were used primarily for trade and for sacramental purposes. In the early 1830s, a French immigrant propitiously named Jean-Louis Vignes (*vigne* is French for "vine") established a large vineyard near Los Angeles using cuttings of European grapevines *(Vitis vinifera)*, and by the mid-19th century, winemaking had become one of southern California's principal industries.

In 1857 Hungarian immigrant Agoston Haraszthy purchased a 400-acre estate in Sonoma County, named it Buena Vista, and cultivated Tokay vine cuttings imported from his homeland. In 1861, bolstered by promises of state funding, Haraszthy went to Europe to gather assorted *vinifera* cuttings to plant in California soil. Upon his return, however, the state legislature reneged on their commitment. Undeterred, Haraszthy persisted in distributing (at his own expense) some 100,000 cuttings and testing varieties in different soil types. Successful application of his discoveries created a boom in the local wine industry in the late 19th century.

The Tide Turns

As the 1800s drew to a close, northern California grapevines fell prey to phylloxera, a root louse that attacks susceptible *vinifera* plants. Entire vineyards were decimated. Eventually researchers discovered they could combat phylloxera by replanting vineyards with disease-resistant wild grape rootstocks, onto which *vinifera* cuttings could be grafted. The wine industry had achieved a modicum of recovery by the early 20th century, only to be slapped with the 18th Amendment to the Constitution, prohibiting the manufacture, sale, importation, and transportation of intoxicating liquors in the US.

California's winemaking industry remained at a near-standstill until 1933, when Prohibition was repealed. The Great Depression slowed the reclamation of vineyards and it wasn't until the early 1970s that California's wine industry was fully re-established. In 1976 California wines took top honors in a blind taste testing by French judges in Paris. The results helped open up a whole new world of respectability for California vineyards.

Coming of Age

As Napa and Sonoma wines have established their reputations, the importance of individual growing regions has increased. Many sub-regions have sought and acquired Federal regulation of the place names as American Viticultural Areas, or AVAs, in order to set the boundaries of wine-growing areas that are distinctive for their soil, microclimate and wine styles. Although this system is subject to debate, there is no doubt that an AVA such as Russian River Valley, Carneros, or Spring Mountain can be very meaningful. The precise location of a vineyard relative to the Pacific Ocean or San Pablo Bay, the elevation and slope of a vineyard, the soil type and moisture content, and even the proximity to a mountain gap can make essential differences.

Together, Sonoma and Napa have almost 30 registered appellations, which vary in size and sometimes overlap. Specific place names are becoming increasingly important as growers learn what to plant where and how to care for vines in each unique circumstance. The fact that more and more wines go to market with a specific AVA flies in the face of the worldwide trend to ever larger and less specific "branded" wines. Individual wineries and associations are working to promote the individuality of North Coast appellations and to preserve their integrity and viability as sustainable agriculture.

Destination Wine Country

In recent decades the Napa and Sonoma valleys have experienced tremendous development. Besides significant increases in vineyard acreage, the late 20th century witnessed an explosion of small-scale operations, some housed in old wineries updated with state-of-the-art equipment. Meanwhile, the Russian River Valley remains less developed, retaining its rural feel with country roads winding past picturesque wineries, rolling hills of grapevines, and stands of redwood trees.

With easy access to world-class wines, and organic produce and cheeses from local farms, residents of northern California's Wine Country enjoy an enviable quality of life. Happily for visitors, those same products supply the area's burgeoning number of restaurants, creating a culture of gourmet dining that stretches from the city of Napa north to Healdsburg and beyond.

Note that if you elect to bring your own wine, most restaurants charge a corkage fee (which can vary from $10 to as much as $50 per bottle). Many restaurants waive this fee on one particular day, or if you purchase an additional bottle from their list.

Which Food?	*Which Wine?*	*Some Examples*
Shellfish	Semi-dry White	Early harvest Riesling, Chenin Blanc, early harvest Gewürztraminer, Viognier
	Dry White	Lighter Chardonnay (less oak), Pinot Blanc, Sauvignon Blanc, dry Riesling, dry Chenin Blanc
	Sparkling Wine	Brut, Extra Dry, Brut Rosé
	Dry Rosé	Pinot Noir, Syrah, Cabernet
Fish	Dry White	Chardonnay (oaky or not) Sauvignon Blanc, dry Riesling, dry Chenin Blanc, Pinot Blanc
	Sparkling Wine	Brut, Blanc de Blancs, Brut Rosé
	Light Red	Pinot Noir, Pinot Meunier, light-bodied Zinfandel
	Dry Rosé	Pinot Noir, Syrah, Cabernet
Cured Meats/ Picnic Fare	Semi-dry White	Early harvest Riesling or early harvest Gewürztraminer
	Dry White	Chardonnay (less oak), Sauvignon Blanc, dry Riesling
	Sparkling Wine	Brut, Blanc de Blancs, Brut Rosé
	Light Red	Gamay, Pinot Noir, Zinfandel, Sangiovese
	Young Heavy Red	Syrah, Cabernet Sauvignon, Zinfandel, Cabernet Franc, Merlot
	Rosé	Any light Rosé
Red Meat	Dry Rosé	Pinot Noir, Cabernet, Syrah, Blends
	Light Red	Pinot Noir, Zinfandel, Gamay, Pinot Meunier
	Young Heavy Red	Cabernet Sauvignon, Cabernet Franc, Syrah, Grenache, Petite Sirah, Merlot, Blends, Pinot Noir, Cabernet Sauvignon
	Mature Red	Merlot, Syrah, Zinfandel, Meritage, Blends
Fowl	Semi-dry White	Early harvest Riesling, Chenin Blanc, Viognier
	Dry White	Sauvignon Blanc, Chardonnay, Pinot Blanc, dry Riesling
	Sparkling Wine	Extra Dry, Brut, Brut Rosé
	Rosé	Any light Rosé
	Light Red	Pinot Noir, Zinfandel, Blends, Gamay
	Mature Red	Pinot Noir, Cabernet Sauvignon, Merlot, Syrah, Zinfandel, Meritage, Blends
Cheese	Semi-dry White	Riesling, Gewürztraminer, Chenin Blanc
	Dry White	Sauvignon Blanc, Chardonnay, Pinot Blanc, dry Riesling
	Sparkling Wine	Extra Dry, Brut
	Rosé	Pinot Noir, Cabernet, Grenache
	Light Red	Pinot Noir, Zinfandel, Blends, Gamay
	Young Heavy Red	Cabernet Sauvignon, Cabernet Franc, Syrah, Grenache, Petite Sirah, Merlot, Blends
Dessert	Sweet White	Any late harvest White
	Semi-dry White	Riesling, Gewürztraminer, Chenin Blanc, Muscat
	Sparkling Wine	Extra Dry, Brut, Rosé, Rouge
	Dessert Reds	Late harvest Zinfandel, Port

intage	2007	2006	2005	2004	2003	2002	2001	2000	1999	1998	1997	1996	1995
hardonnay arneros	Above Average	Above Average	Above Average	Outstanding	Outstanding	Outstanding	Outstanding	Above Average	Above Average	Average	Outstanding	Above Average	Outstanding
hardonnay ussian River	Outstanding	Above Average	Outstanding	Outstanding	Above Average	Outstanding	Outstanding	Above Average	Above Average	Average	Outstanding	Above Average	Outstanding
hardonnay apa Valley	Above Average	Above Average	Above Average	Above Average	Outstanding	Outstanding	Above Average	Average	Above Average	Above Average	Outstanding	Outstanding	Outstanding
uvignon Blanc apa Valley	Above Average	Above Average	Outstanding	Outstanding	Above Average	Outstanding	Outstanding	Average	Above Average	Average	Outstanding	Above Average	Above Average
uvignon Blanc onoma County	Above Average	Outstanding	Above Average	Outstanding	Above Average	Above Average	Outstanding	Average	Above Average	Average	Outstanding	Above Average	Above Average
not Noir arneros	Above Average	Above Average	Above Average	Outstanding	Outstanding	Above Average	Outstanding	Average	Above Average	Average	Outstanding	Above Average	Above Average
not Noir ussian River	Outstanding	Above Average	Above Average	Outstanding	Outstanding	Outstanding	Above Average	Above Average	Above Average	Above Average	Outstanding	Above Average	Above Average
erlot apa Valley	Above Average	Above Average	Outstanding	Average	Outstanding	Above Average	Outstanding	Above Average	Outstanding	Above Average	Outstanding	Outstanding	Outstanding
erlot onoma County	Above Average	Above Average	Outstanding	Outstanding	Above Average	Above Average	Above Average	Above Average	Above Average	Above Average	Outstanding	Above Average	Outstanding
abernet Sauvignon apa Valley	Outstanding	Outstanding	Outstanding	Outstanding	Above Average	Outstanding	Outstanding	Above Average	Outstanding	Above Average	Outstanding	Outstanding	Outstanding
abernet Sauvignon outhern Sonoma	Above Average	Above Average	Above Average	Outstanding	Above Average	Above Average	Outstanding	Above Average	Above Average	Above Average	Outstanding	Outstanding	Above Average
abernet Sauvignon orthern Sonoma	Above Average	Outstanding	Outstanding	Outstanding	Above Average	Outstanding	Above Average	Above Average	Above Average	Above Average	Outstanding	Outstanding	Above Average
infandel apa Valley	Outstanding	Outstanding	Above Average	Outstanding	Outstanding	Outstanding	Outstanding	Above Average	Above Average	Above Average	Outstanding	Outstanding	Above Average
infandel outhern Sonoma	Outstanding	Outstanding	Above Average	Outstanding	Outstanding	Outstanding	Outstanding	Above Average	Above Average	Above Average	Outstanding	Outstanding	Above Average
infandel orthern Sonoma	Above Average	Outstanding	Above Average	Outstanding	Outstanding	Outstanding	Outstanding	Above Average	Outstanding	Above Average	Outstanding	Outstanding	Outstanding

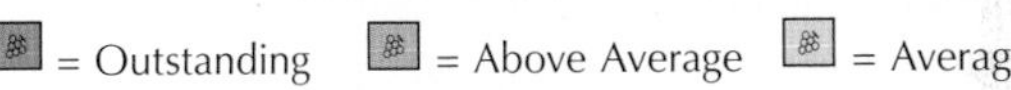

Peter L. Wrenn/MICHELIN

Napa Valley

Wine is the watchword in this 35-mile-long valley, which extends in a northerly direction from the San Pablo Bay to Mount St. Helena. Cradled between the Mayacama and the Vaca mountain ranges, the area boasts some of California's most prestigious wineries, along with a host of restaurants that are destinations in themselves.

Reclaimed 19th century stone wineries and Victorian houses punctuate the valley's landscape, reminding the traveler that there were some 140 wineries here prior to 1890. Today, Napa Valley has 325 producing wineries (and more than 400 brands), up from a post-Prohibition low of perhaps a dozen. They cluster along Route 29, the valley's main artery, which runs up the western side of the mountains, passing through the commercial hub of Napa and continuing north through the charming little wine burgs of Yountville, Oakville, Rutherford, St. Helena, and Calistoga. More wineries dot the tranquil Silverado Trail, which hugs the foothills of the eastern range and gives a more pastoral perspective on this rural farm county. Along both routes, picturesque spots for alfresco dining abound. So pick up some picnic supplies at the **Oakville Grocery** (on Route 29), or stop by either the **Model Bakery** in St. Helena or **Bouchon Bakery** in Yountville for fresh-baked bread and delectable pastries.

Throughout the valley you'll spot knolls, canyons, dry creek beds, stretches of valley floor, and glorious mountain vistas, all of which afford varying microclimates and soil types for growing wine. San Pablo Bay has a moderating effect on

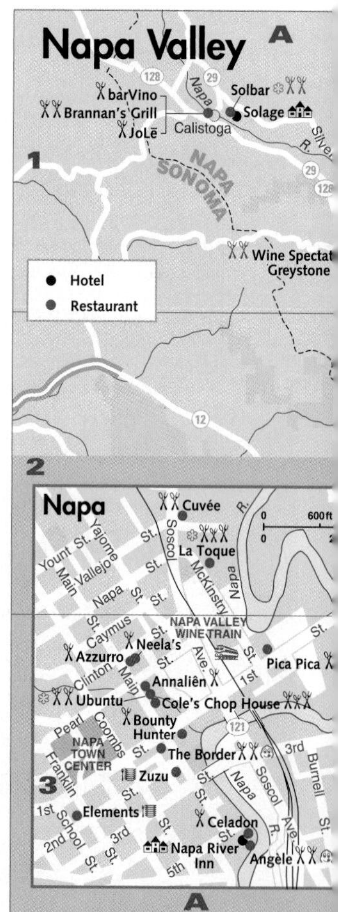

the valley's temperatures, while the influence of the Pacific Ocean—40 miles west—is lessened by the mountains. In the valley, powerfully hot summer days and still cool nights provide the ideal climate for Cabernet Sauvignon grapes, a varietal for which Napa is justifiably famous.

Among the region's many winemakers are well-known names such as Robert Mondavi, Francis Ford Coppola, and the legendary Miljenko "Mike" Grgich. Originally from Croatia, Grgich rose to fame as the winemaker at **Chateau Montelena** when his 1973 Chardonnay took the top prize at the Judgment of Paris in 1976, outshining France's best white Burgundies. This feat turned the wine world on its ear, and put California on the map as a bona fide producer of fine wine. (A bottle of the winning vintage is on display

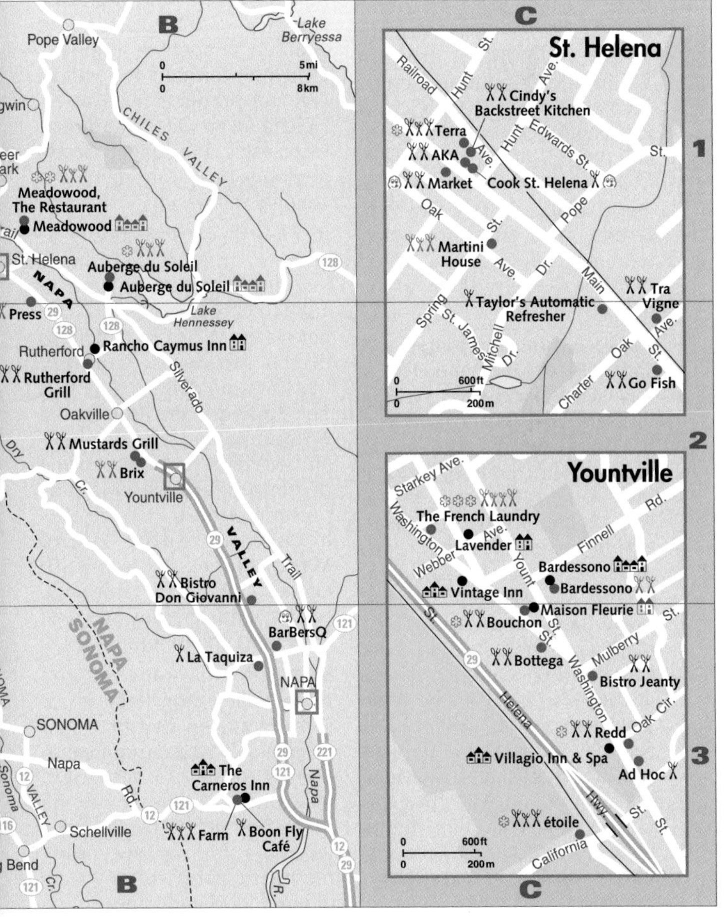

at the Smithsonian National Museum of American History in Washington, D.C.) Since then, Napa's success with premium wine has fostered a special pride of place. Fourteen American Viticultural Areas (AVAs) currently regulate the boundaries for sub-regions such as Carneros, Stags Leap, Rutherford, and Los Carneros.

The boom in wine production has spawned a special kind of food-and-wine tourism: Today tasting rooms, tours, and farm-fresh cuisine are de rigueur here. Along Washington Street, the main drag in Yountville, acclaimed chefs such as Thomas Keller, Richard Reddington, Michael Chiarello, and Philippe Jeanty rub elbows. Many other chefs hail from the Napa Valley—Cindy Pawlcyn, Jeremy Fox, and Hiro Sone, to name a few—have raised their local-legend status to the national level.

Those touring the valley will spot fields of wild fennel, silvery olive trees, and rows of wild mustard that bloom between the grapevines in February and March. The mustard season kicks off each year with the Napa Valley Mustard Festival, which celebrates the food, wine, art, and rich agricultural bounty of the area. Several towns host seasonal farmers' markets, generally held from May through October. These include Napa (held in the Wine Train parking lot Tuesdays and Saturdays); St. Helena (Fridays in Crane Park); and Calistoga (Saturdays on Washington Street). On Thursday nights in the summer, there's a **Chef's Market** in Napa Town Center.

Opened in early 2008, **Oxbow Public Market** is a block-long 40,000-square-foot facility that is meant to vie with the Ferry Building Marketplace across the bay. Oxbow brims with local food artisans and wine vendors, all from within a 100-mile radius of the market. Within this barn-like building you'll find cheeses and charcuterie; spices and specialty teas; olive oils and organic ice cream; and, of course, stands of farm-fresh produce. And there are plenty of snacks after you work up an appetite shopping. Elsewhere around the valley, regional products such as St. Helena Olive Oil, Woodhouse Chocolates, and Rancho Gordo heirloom beans are gaining a national following.

Just north of downtown St. Helena, the massive stone building that was erected in 1889 as Greystone Cellars now houses the West Coast campus of the renowned Culinary Institute of America (CIA). The Culinary Institute has a restaurant and visitors here are welcome to view cooking demonstrations (reservations recommended), as well as browse the **Spice Island Marketplace**, stocked with kitchen equipment, tableware, linens, and shelves stocked thick with cookbooks.

With all this going for the Napa Valley, one thing is for sure: From the city of Napa, the region's largest population center, north to the town of Calistoga—known for its mineral mud baths and spa cuisine—this narrow valley represents paradise for lovers of good food and wine.

Ad Hoc

American

C3

6476 Washington St. (bet. California Dr. & Oak Circle), Yountville

Phone: 707-944-2487 — Lunch Sun
Web: www.adhocrestaurant.com — Dinner Thu – Mon
Prices: $$$

Ad Hoc is the kind of place where its chef, Thomas Keller, might grab a bite after a long day at the stoves. The convivial (if boisterous) bistro is elegantly low-key with a gorgeous farm table and counter seating that is ideal for swirling a glass of Sancerre, from a wine list that highlights small-production, value-driven varietals.
Meticulous attention to detail and top ingredients ensure the mastery of American cuisine. Expect easy-to-share plates of tender, roasted beef skirt steak with braised hearts of Romaine, or cheddar salad with toasted walnuts and Pink Lady apples. Know that this menu is "one-size-fits-all"—every diner gets the same thing. The four-course prix-fixe menu changes daily, and Sunday brunch should indeed be mandatory.

AKA

American

C1

1320 Main St. (bet. Adam St. & Hunt Ave.), St. Helena

Phone: 707-967-8111 — Lunch Wed – Sat
Web: www.akabistro.com — Dinner Tue – Sun
Prices: $$

Look for the vintage neon sign reading "Keller's Meat Market" to find AKA, a casual bistro and wine bar. Inside, pressed-tin ceilings, polished concrete floors, and grapevine-wrapped pendant lamps provide a comfy setting for dinners of build-your-own-burgers. More upscale entrées may include tender grilled pork chops with crispy oven potatoes and a deliciously eclectic medley of accompaniments.
Owner Robert Simon is a fixture in the dining room, though service can be hit-and-miss. Perhaps AKA's best draw is the California-centric wine list. An electronic wine dispensing system has 20 varietals to taste, while a rustic wood tower showcases nearly 600 vintages from mostly local labels. Cured meats and cheese plates are perfect for pairing.

Angèle

A3 — French

540 Main St. (at 5th St.), Napa

Phone: 707-252-8115 — Lunch & dinner daily
Web: www.angelerestaurant.com
Prices: $$

Take a chair at a bistro table set with pressed white cloth and a potted olive sapling, close your eyes, and imagine you are dining seaside in the South of France. True, the water that flows beneath your breezy terrace seat is just the Napa River, but the rustic charm of Angèle, to say nothing of its bilingual menu, is enough to transport even a cynic to a Mediterranean state of mind.

Tucked behind the brick façade of the 1893 Hatt building, once used as a boathouse for the local milling industry, Angèle rises to a magnificent framework ceiling. Below, Californian influences can be seen in such well-prepared French dishes as salad Lyonnaise, sprinkled with crisp bacon bits instead of lardons, and crispy *fromage blanc* gnocchi with roasted wild mushrooms.

Annaliên

A3 — Vietnamese

1142 Main St. (bet. 1st & Pearl Sts.), Napa

Phone: 707-224-8319 — Lunch & Dinner Tue – Sat
Web: N/A
Prices: $$

Annaliên "Anna" Shepley fled to the United States from her native Saigon in 1975, and Napans are glad she did. Today the diminutive chef boasts her culinary heritage to crowds of diners at this cozy namesake restaurant in downtown Napa. Regulars are accustomed to seeing Shepley make the rounds; she is not shy about warmly greeting newcomers and inquiring how they are enjoying their food.

Tasty contemporary Vietnamese dishes reflect both French and Chinese influences, with a focus on pleasing the American palate. Selections may include *Dalat* spicy beef accompanied by a creamy slaw of shredded cabbage, lettuce, mint, and cilantro; or *Ha long* bread, a warm, pan-seared, green-onion-flavored flatbread served with curry dipping sauce.

Auberge du Soleil ✿

Californian XXX

B1

180 Rutherford Hill Rd. (off the Silverado Trail), Rutherford

Phone: 707-963-1211 Lunch & dinner daily
Web: www.aubergedusoleil.com
Prices: $$$$

Auberge du Soleil

Adjoined to a gorgeous luxury inn of the same name, Auberge Du Soleil's management happily likes to remind people that the restaurant opened first (in 1981, as a matter of fact). No wonder—one view of the stunning grounds that the restaurant sits on and you might call "finder's keepers" too.

By day, the main dining room is drenched in sunlight, with an easy country chic dressed in earth tones, exposed beams, and rustic furnishings. As night falls, it simply doesn't get more beautiful than the view from this restaurant's terrace, perched high above Napa Valley's Silverado Trail, where a lingering meal at sunset is positively transformative.

Back on your plate, a different kind of beauty awaits. Chef Robert Curry fills his nightly menus with impossibly fresh farm goodies, and dinner might include an incredibly light potato gnocchi in a foamy Parmesan *nage*, pitted with bright green pea shoots and woodsy sautéed mushrooms; a tender golden fillet of Blue Nose bass with three Manila clams, served over a silky mound of braised escarole decorated with diced chorizo; or a flaky cinnamon apple tart, filled with tangy cream cheese mousse and pooled in an irresistible sun-dried raisin purée.

Azzurro

Pizza

A3

1260 Main St. (at Clinton St.), Napa

Phone: 707-255-5552
Web: www.azzurropizzeria.com
Prices:

Lunch Mon – Fri
Dinner nightly

Chef Michael Gyetvan's Pizza Azzurro outgrew its space on Second Street in 2008, and moved to this corner spot as the first tenants of the new Main Street West complex. The pizzeria's digs are now both comfortable and classy with polished concrete floors, high ceilings, and wine-bottle pendant light fixtures.

In the gleaming open kitchen, a white-tiled oven turns out pies that are justly famous in the Valley for their thin crusts and imaginative combos (sweet onions, gorgonzola, and rosemary; fennel sausage, red onion, tomato sauce, and mozzarella). The expanded menu adds seasonal antipasti, pastas, desserts, and a broader selection of beer and wine.

Be prepared to wait, as this lively, family-friendly scene fills up quickly.

BarBersQ

Barbecue

B3

3900 D, Bel Aire Plaza (at Trancas St.), Napa

Phone: 707-224-6600
Web: www.barbersq.com
Prices: $$

Lunch & dinner daily

Barbecue conjures a certain down-home nostalgia. For those raised in the south, like Chef Stephen Barber, just the smell of pulled pork recalls cinematic memories of vintage truck stops and family trips to the lake. In Napa, BarBersQ puts a sophisticated glaze on the Memphis-style staple but remains true to those down-home roots. A black-and-white photo exhibit, "The People and Places of Napa," graces the dining room, with marble and stainless steel accents.

Deeply satisfying wallet-friendly eats are cooked up from strictly local, organic, and farm-fresh products. Start with an upscale rendition of smoked spicy wings, and save room for Joey Ray's gumbo, free-range fried chicken (Sunday's only), smoked beef brisket and, yes, pulled pork sandwiches.

Bardessono

Californian

C2

6526 Yount St. (at Finnell Rd.), Yountville

Phone: 707-204-6030 — Lunch & dinner daily
Web: www.bardessono.com
Prices: $$$

In the gastronomically rich belly of Yountville, just a baguette's throw from Washington Street, Bardessono stands apart as the greenest spot just off restaurant row. Housed in the new Bardessono Hotel, the earthy dining room is fashioned from 90-percent recycled design.

Redwood wine barrels were repurposed to create the restaurant's doors, tables are made of reclaimed orchard walnut, sconces are recycled glass, and a Monterey cypress, leftover from the hotel's construction, has become a striking communal table. As one would expect, the cuisine is honest Californian sustainable—think Marin Sun Farms beef or Bodega Bay halibut atop oyster mushrooms and watercress coulis.

With shallow ponds and cool bamboo, the shaded patio is an enchanting spot for lunch.

barVino

Italian

A1

1457 Lincoln Ave. (bet. Fair Way & Washington St.), Calistoga

Phone: 707-942-9900 — Dinner nightly
Web: www.bar-vino.com
Prices: $$

Despite being a world-class destination for spa seekers and oenophiles, Calistoga is a pretty sleepy country hamlet. But with red leather booths and such modern metallic accents as a streamlined silver stag's head, barVino is a sigh of relief for displaced city slickers. Open for wine service at 4:00 P.M., this hip little lounge pours rare and limited-production local vintages at the shimmering tiled bar, ideal for lone imbibers and couples. Larger groups gather at round tables to soak up the day's tastes with shared half-portions of Italian-inspired nibbles like pancetta-wrapped dates and fried calamari with *piquillo* pepper aïoli.

For heartier appetites, a grilled hanger steak is well prepared with a side of steamed *broccolini* and Parmesan fries.

Bistro Don Giovanni

B2 — Italian XX

4110 Howard Ln. (at Hwy. 29), Napa

Phone: 707-224-3300 — Lunch & dinner daily
Web: www.bistrodongiovanni.com
Prices: $$

A Napa Valley mainstay, Giovanni and Donna Scala's beloved bistro still pleases droves of tourists and locals with the deliciously pronounced flavors of rustic Italian fare. The large indoor space, warmed by a wood-burning pizza oven and ornamented with gleaming copper pots, meanders into an outdoor terrace with its fountains, playful sculptures, and rosemary-lined gardens. Views are among the best in Napa, stretching across miles of vineyards to the mountains beyond.

Fresh *foccacia* with olive oil for dipping starts your meal, followed perhaps by a salad of beets and haricots verts dressed in Roquefort vinaigrette. Other highlights include their tender, perfectly seasoned meatballs. For dessert, the delicate, classic tiramisu is the hands-down favorite.

Bistro Jeanty

C3 — French XX

6510 Washington St. (at Mulberry St.), Yountville

Phone: 707-944-0103 — Lunch & dinner daily
Web: www.bistrojeanty.com
Prices: $$

Washington Street may seem a touch contrived in its tourist-friendly charm, but this tree-lined avenue's acclaimed foodie haunts are genuine and sincere. Among them, Bistro Jeanty is a quaint spot for a luxuriant, country lunch. With its red-and-white striped awning, simple bistro furnishings, and a scattering of French antiques, Jeanty could as easily be located in Provence. A lazy vibe soaking the sunny patio is transporting.

As expected, the menu is rich with bistro classics—quiche, steak tartare, sole meunière, and *côte de porc*. While some of the meatier fare is a tad heavy for a warm alfresco lunch, it's still tasty. And when paired with a mellow vibe and a glass of crisp rosé, it's impossible to complain.

Boon Fly Café

Californian

B3

4048 Sonoma Hwy. (at Los Carneros Ave.), Napa

Phone: 707-299-4870 — Lunch & dinner daily
Web: www.thecarnerosinn.com
Prices: $$

Straddling the wine-growing areas of Napa and Sonoma, the Carneros region was named by the Spanish for the sheep that once grazed here. It still maintains a pastoral aspect, echoed in the rustic red-barn style of the Boon Fly Café. Part of the Carneros Inn, which sits amid 27 bucolic acres off the Old Sonoma Highway, the café serves breakfast, lunch, and dinner to visitors and locals alike.

Flatbread pizzas and sandwiches, or more meaty fare (a brown-sugar-rubbed pork chop with roasted peach and Port reduction), show up for lunch and dinner. On weekends, folks don't mind relaxing on the porch swings as they wait to indulge in brunch favorites like "Poppa Joe's eggs in a hole," grilled sourdough with center cut-outs for two fried eggs.

The Border

Mexican

A3

1005 First St. (at Main St.), Napa

Phone: 707-258-1000 — Lunch Mon – Fri, Dinner nightly
Web: N/A
Prices: $$

After honing their cooking skills with Michael Chiarello, Donna Scala, and Cindy Pawlcyn, brothers Pablo and Erasto Jacinto struck out on their own in spring 2009. The Border raises the bar on Napa city's dining scene by introducing a welcome diversity and proposing dishes that reflect the bounty of Mexico's different states.

You can taste the brothers' Oaxacan roots in an adventurous starter of *guajillo* masa turnovers stuffed with *huitlacoche* and melted Oaxacan cheese. Entrées tempt with the likes of tequila-braised pork shoulder and beer-battered ling cod tacos.

There's nothing edgy about the spacious and rustic dining room, which seats interested diners at a long counter facing the open kitchen with its mesquite grill and fiery rotisserie.

Bottega

C3 — Italian

6525 Washington St. (near Yount St.), Yountville

Phone: 707-945-1050 — Lunch Tue – Sun
Web: www.bottegaanapavalley.com — Dinner nightly
Prices: $$

Yountville's famed Washington Street is now home to another celebrity, Chef Michael Chiarello. Lured back to helm a new Napa Style store and the kitchen at Bottega, both at V Marketplace, Chiarello seems far removed from the stardom of so many cookbooks and TV specials. Bottega exudes elegance with a warm palette, distressed leather, and Murano glass accents.

Outside, wood-burning stone fireplaces heat a flagstone patio dotted with sofas; inside, two dining rooms and a popular bar burst with the aromas of rustic Italian meals executed in California style.

A grilled octopus salad is tender and flavorful; pastas and cured meats are homemade; and simple delights like pecorino "pudding" remind us why Chiarello commands such an audience in the first place.

Bounty Hunter

A3 — American

975 First St. (at Main St.), Napa

Phone: 707-226-3976 — Lunch & dinner daily
Web: www.bountyhunterwine.com
Prices: $$

Reopened in spring 2008 after a significant kitchen expansion, Bounty Hunter retains much of the same historic warmth to match its worn wooden floors, exposed brick walls, and pressed-copper ceiling. An 1888 building houses this bar and bistro, which serves some 40 wines by the glass and 400 by the bottle. Patrons may choose among different wine flights, with whimsical names like Killer Cabs and Pinot Envy.

Once primarily salads and sandwiches, the lunch menu has blossomed with the addition of a new smoker. Fueled by hickory, apple wood and cabernet barrel staves, it turns out spicy, slow-cooked ribs and brisket all day long—no longer just for dinner. These and signatures like the fantastic beer-can chicken, keep folks coming back for more.

Bouchon ✿

French XX

C3

6534 Washington St. (at Yount St.), Yountville

Phone: 707-944-8037 Lunch & dinner daily
Web: www.bouchonbistro.com
Prices: **$$$**

Bouchon

If you didn't score resos to Thomas Keller's legendary The French Laundry, there's a simpler way to sample the great chef's handiwork if passing through Napa—his decidedly casual Bouchon, a lively, hopping bistro named for a traditionally meat-heavy café found in Lyon.

Outside, you'll find the outdoor terrace packed come summer, with customers happily lingering over Sancerre and oysters. Inside, you'll find a busy dining room, replete with specials scratched out on a chalkboard and waiters happily hustling to and fro. The whole package oozes a kind of haphazard, cozy-sweater Parisian charm, but a closer inspection of the menu reveals Keller's trademark perfectionism: A goldmine of rustic French offerings, refined to sublime perfection by the master chef.

Dinner kicks off with the house's legendary baguettes *épis*, and just gets better from there. Try the soft red wine-poached egg with tender, just-crisped sweetbreads, forest mushrooms, and scallions; and then move onto a silky pan-roasted trout laced with clarified butter and lemon, paired with a silky mound of almond-topped haricots verts; and finish with a world-class tart, fresh as can be, bursting with bright lemon custard.

Brannan's Grill

American XX

A1

1374 Lincoln Ave. (at Washington St.), Calistoga

Phone: 707-942-2233 Lunch & dinner daily
Web: www.brannansgrill.com
Prices: $$

After a soothing mud bath or a healing dip in one of Calistoga's famous mineral springs, a mountain breeze pouring through large screen windows and a blazing fire in the stone hearth could be just what the doctor ordered. And with genuine service and a richly decorated mahogany-paneled dining room that dates to the 19th century, Brannan's Grill is the right prescription for a cushy night out. Live piano or jazz sets the mood for casual American suppers on weekends.

Dishes might include puréed butternut squash soup garnished with blue cheese beignets, or chipotle-glazed pork loin with crispy straw onions. You can't go wrong, however, with a straightforward burger. Cap the night with a glass of pinot noir at the romantic Victorian bar.

Brix

Californian 

7377 St. Helena Hwy. (at Washington St.), Yountville

Phone: 707-944-2749 Lunch & dinner daily
Web: www.brix.com
Prices: $$$

With prolific vegetable gardens, a burgeoning orchard, and an award-winning vineyard, Brix gives new meaning to fresh, local food. Peek out the floor-to-ceiling windows and spot talented Chef Anne Gingrass-Paik with an armful of produce on its way to your plate. Their garden patio may be the most picturesque locale for sipping and savoring Californian cuisine in the wine country. At the restaurant's center, wrought-iron chandeliers preside over a glass-encased wine cellar, which doubles as a dramatic venue for private parties.

The menu is presented in straightforward categories: a "Wood Oven" fires lamb-sausage pizza; the "Charcoal Grill" brings a porcini-rubbed New York steak; and a prosciutto-wrapped halibut is hot from the "Range."

Celadon

International

A3

500 Main St., Suite G (at 5th St.), Napa

Phone: 707-254-9690
Web: www.celadonnapa.com
Prices: $$

Lunch Mon – Fri
Dinner nightly

Nestled in the Historic Napa Mill complex, Celadon presents the globetrotting menu of Chef/owner Greg Cole, who is currently splitting his time here with Cole's Chop House. He can often be found lending a hand in the dining room, chatting with guests in a genuinely caring manner. Dishes travel from sweet coconut fried prawns to Moroccan braised lamb shank, pleasing most every palate.

In addition to the celadon-green dining room, the large adjoining atrium provides covered "outdoor" seating in rain or shine. On cooler days, the atrium is heated and the raised brick fireplace adds coziness.

Be aware that the area around the restaurant has been cordoned off with fencing and detours owing to ongoing development of the Napa riverfront.

Cindy's Backstreet Kitchen

American

C1

1327 Railroad Ave. (bet. Adams & Hunt Sts.), St. Helena

Phone: 707-963-1200
Web: www.cindysbackstreetkitchen.com
Prices: $$

Lunch & dinner daily

Continuing her culinary legacy, Chef Cindy Pawlcyn's second of three Napa Valley restaurants, nestles in an early 19th century house. Set a block off St. Helena's Main Street, Cindy's Backstreet Kitchen boasts flower-bedecked arbors on its terrace, while the modern, bistro-style interior sings with country charm. The long zinc bar attracts a local crowd who nosh on small plates, while they sip creative house cocktails or savor some great Napa Valley wines.

The menu mixes classic and modern American dishes infused with Latin accents, resulting in food with floods of flavor. Daily specials range from the fish of the day to wood-oven duck with potato croquettes and citrus sauce; or "mighty meatloaf" with horseradish barbecue sauce.

Cole's Chop House

Steakhouse

1122 Main St. (bet. 1st & Pearl Sts.), Napa

Phone: 707-224-6328 — Dinner nightly
Web: www.coleschophouse.com
Prices: **$$$$**

Down the street from sibling Celadon, Greg Cole's pricier steakhouse gives locals good reason to dress for dinner in laid-back Napa. With its soaring truss ceiling and towering hand-hewn stone walls (original to this 1886 structure), Cole's departs from the stuffy men's-club tone set by many steakhouses. A large variety of wines are displayed around the room; the sommelier may reach over your table for that luscious bottle of Napa cabernet cached overhead.

On the menu, straightforward classics like oysters Rockefeller; Caesar salad; or formula-fed veal and New Zealand lamb complement the main attraction: prime 21-day-dry-aged Angus beef.

Despite the Main Street address, the entrance is on the creek side, by the valet parking lot behind the restaurant.

Cook St. Helena

Italian 

1310 Main St. (bet. Adams St. & Hunt Ave.), St. Helena

Phone: 707-963-7088 — Lunch Mon – Sat
Web: N/A — Dinner nightly
Prices: **$$**

In downtown St. Helena—-a wine country hamlet lined with posh boutiques—first you shop, then you Cook. Cook St. Helena is one of those restaurants that always gets it right. Locals count on friendly hospitality and satisfying Italian fare at a great value. The small eatery is cramped yet comfortable, with a few antiques and prints of black-and-white vegetables on the walls.

In the kitchen, the fresh produce is vibrantly showcased with Californian sensibility in Chef/owner Jude Wilmouth's all-day menu. Roasted red peppers and mizuna brighten fresh mozzarella, while flavorful broccoli rabe and fingerling potatoes complement pan-fried chicken. Single diners feel at home at the Carrara marble bar, which pours a concise list of Napa and Italian varietals.

Cuvée

American XX

A2

1650 Soscol Ave. (at River Terrace Dr.), Napa

Phone: 707-224-2330 — Lunch & dinner daily
Web: www.cuveenapa.com
Prices: **$$**

What would a trip to Napa Valley be without dinner on a tree-lined courtyard to the tune of live music and old-world-style barrel tastings of California wines? In this sense, Cuvée, at the River Terrace Inn, answers the call. Despite its location in Napa's business district, Cuvée's contemporary dining room, with wall hangings composed of vineyard clippings, provides a charming backdrop for American dishes with a local twist, such as grilled prawns with sweet corn salad, or salmon and rock shrimp potpie. For dessert, a gingered pear crisp arrives hot from the oven. Wednesday evenings bring one of the Valley's best values: three courses for $33.
The restaurant also waives its corkage fee—for wine country tourists fresh from Route 29.

Look for our new symbol, spotlighting restaurants with a notable sake list.

étoile ✿

C3 Californian XXX

1 California Dr. (off Hwy. 29), Yountville

Phone: 707-204-7529 Lunch & dinner Thu – Mon
Web: www.chandon.com
Prices: $$$$

John Benson

Domaine Chandon could have been torn from the pages of a Victorian novel: manicured lawns and vineyards seem to stretch forever; spring-fed ponds, arching foot bridges, and fountains have the air of a watercolor tableau from the estate's grand veranda. Still, Chandon's success is very real and tangible—this is one of the region's largest wineries, complete with a tasting room, gift shop, and first-rate restaurant.

Étoile crafts its contemporary Californian menu around the wine experience and recommends pairings for every dish, both from the property's own label and beyond. The kitchen's accomplishments have a hint of French influence and a flair for originality worthy of its celestial name. Meyer lemon panna cotta topped with herbacious shrimp salad is a creamy and delicious start; champagne gelée and *Prosciutto di Parma* dress the meaty lobster bisque; and crisp, wild striped bass is enhanced by forbidden black rice and lobster consommé.

With a barrel-vaulted ceiling and cork-bound menus, the dining room winks at the refined wine theme. Despite the dining room's comfort, on a sunny afternoon, the patio is the best spot for a sophisticated lunch paired with crisp étoile brut.

Farm

Californian XXX

B3

4048 Sonoma Hwy. (at Old Sonoma Rd.), Napa

Phone: 707-299-4882 — Dinner nightly
Web: www.thecarnerosinn.com
Prices: $$$

Dressed-up farm buildings may punctuate the grounds of the Carneros Inn, but nothing is old-fashioned about fine-dining at the Farm. Chef Jeff Jake's skillful attention to detail comes to the fore in the wonderful tastes of organic and sustainably-raised products, most of which come from within a 150-mile radius of the restaurant. These may be used in refined preparations of Sonoma duck foie gras torchon or wild mushroom risotto. A local thread runs through the wine list as well, focusing on the Napa Valley.

Tall cathedral ceilings and windows allow natural light, while fireplaces inside and out create a cozy vibe. At the hostess counter, an eye-catching, backlit, opaque glass wine display periodically changes colors.

Go Fish

Seafood XX

C2

641 Main St. (bet. Charter Oak Ave. & Mills Ln.), St. Helena

Phone: 707-963-0700 — Lunch & dinner daily
Web: www.gofishrestaurant.net
Prices: $$$

For fresh seafood in Napa Valley, cast your net no farther than Go Fish on Main Street in St. Helena. Here, find Cindy Pawlcyn's (of Mustards) idea of a fish house.

With views of surrounding mountains and vineyards—best enjoyed from a seat on the large outdoor patio—Go Fish highlights its bright white dining room with hues of deep-sea blue, mustard, and brown. Sushi master, Chef Ken Tominaga presides over the long Carrara marble sushi bar, where a large chalkboard depicts a lone docked fishing boat.

A happy-go-lucky vibe pervades the upscale crowd who come here to taste wines and sample the bounty of the sea: from the raw bar offerings or daily chowder, to brandade cakes with Meyer lemon aïoli and local sole with tarragon *verjus* vinaigrette.

The French Laundry ✿✿✿

Contemporary XXXX

C2

6640 Washington St. (at Creek St.), Yountville

Phone: 707-944-2380 Lunch Fri – Sun

Web: www.frenchlaundry.com Dinner nightly

Prices: $$$$

Deborah Jones

How does Thomas Keller still manage—after being fawned over by every critic known to man; after becoming a household name the world over; after winning enough awards to line a football field—to keep it real at his revered Napa Valley restaurant, The French Laundry?

Lord knows, but no one wants to rock this boat, for a meal at what many consider to be one of the best restaurants in the world is just as exquisite and personable an experience as ever—should you be fortunate enough to enter its hallowed, century-old stone walls. The good news is that with advance planning (reservations must be made two months in advance, and jackets are required for men), being one of the chosen few is highly attainable.

The two nine-course tasting menus (one is vegetarian) bring new meaning to the word seasonal, changing by leaps and bounds nightly—each perfect little dish arriving like rolling gifts from the Gods. Yours might unveil butter-poached Maine lobster mitts bursting with sunchokes, dates, and almonds, dancing in Madras curry emulsion; or tender lamb saddle, paired with scrumptious falafel and a delish mix of English cucumber, yogurt, and sweet red *piquillo* peppers.

JoLē

Mediterranean

A1

1457 Lincoln Ave. (bet. Fair Way & Washington St.), Calistoga

Phone: 707-942-5938 — Dinner Tue – Sun
Web: www.jolerestaurant.com
Prices: $$

Set at the north end of Highway 29, the little spa town of Calistoga is often overlooked by wine tourists. It is here, however, that husband-and-wife team Matt and Sonjia Spector are carving out their culinary names.

The restaurant promises "farm to table" fare, and the Spectors prove their devotion to this credo by using locally-raised organic ingredients. A menu of Mediterranean-inspired small plates allows diners to design a multicourse meal, or simply to have a snack and a glass of wine from small producers. Consider a salad of toasted chestnuts, duck, and chicory to precede potato and crab-crusted cod. Leave room for one of Sonjia's homestyle desserts, such as a satisfying apple and cranberry strudel, or a comforting slice of coconut cream pie.

La Taquiza

Mexican

2007 Redwood Rd. (at Solano Rd.), Napa

Phone: 707-224-2320 — Lunch & dinner Mon – Sat
Web: N/A
Prices:

A patio lined with leafy potted palms provides prime seating on this corner of Redwood Plaza, home to this delectable fresh-Mex taqueria. Inside, polished concrete floors, black metal furnishings, and local artwork create a stylish perch any time of year.

Fresh coastal ceviches, chilled seafood *coctels*, and bountiful bowls—or *tazons*—brimming with your choice of meat, seafood, or grilled vegetables prove that this is no mere taco stand. The celebrated fish tacos come either Baja-style (fried) or California-style (flame grilled), making it easy to eat light and still leave satisfied.

The complimentary fresh salsa bar offers varying levels of heat and bold flavors to suit all tastes. A small menu selection for *niños y niñas* (kids) is also available.

La Toque ✿

A2 **Contemporary** XXX

1314 McKinstry St. (at Soscol Ave.), Napa

Phone: 707-257-5157 Dinner nightly
Web: www.latoque.com
Prices: $$$

Melissa Werner, CCS Architecture

After a decade in nearby Rutherford, Chef Ken Frank moved his critically-acclaimed La Toque south, to Napa Valley. Set in the banal Westin Verasa Napa Hotel, a large illuminated toque (or chef's hat) and pretty, timber verandah mark the way into the restaurant's beautiful new digs—a contemporary dining room soaked in soothing earth tones broken up by the occasional bright dot of fresh flowers.

Though La Toque's impressive wine inventory has slimmed down with the move, the list is still wildly on point, as is the wine service—in fact, some might argue that Scott Tracy, who usually weaves an engaging story around each selection, is the best wine director in Napa.

All the better to enjoy Frank's contemporary fare, which spins to the season but might include perfectly-seared foie gras, surrounded by diced mango and paired with a slice of toasted brioche and smear of sweet red wine reduction; a moist, fresh slice of Loch Duart salmon topped with a crispy horseradish crust and set upon a tangle of beet ribbons kissed with leek fondue; or tender, boneless slices of lamb loin over a cumin-spiced carrot purée, and paired with a small stack of chick pea fries.

Market

C1

American XX

1347 Main St. (bet. Adams & Spring Sts.), St. Helena

Phone: 707-963-3799 — Lunch & dinner daily
Web: www.marketsthelena.com
Prices: $$

It has been more than a year since Eduardo Martinez bought this place from the powerhouse team that runs Cyrus, and in that time, Market hasn't skipped a beat. The food is as solid and market-fresh as ever, with a few new dishes (smoked chicken empanadas and fried Green Zebra tomatoes with Romesco sauce) slipped in for good measure. Of course, the cult faves are still here; locals would surely rebel if they couldn't get their fix of mac and cheese with aged *Fiscalini* cheddar, and Champagne-battered fish and chips. A blissfully old-fashioned butterscotch pudding—made with real Scotch—is worth the trip in itself.

An anomaly in these parts, Market doesn't charge a corkage fee; so feel free to bring your latest prize after wine-tasting in the valley.

Martini House

C1

Contemporary XXX

1245 Spring St. (bet. Main & Oak Sts.), St. Helena

Phone: 707-963-2233 — Lunch Fri – Sun
Web: www.martinihouse.com — Dinner nightly
Prices: $$$

From the tree-shaded stone terrace with its vine-covered arbors and bubbling fountain to the lodge-like interior, Martini House exudes charm. Three fireplaces spread warmth throughout the restaurant when it's cold outside, while stained-glass lanterns, Native American textiles, wood beams, and candlelight describe a stylishly Frank Lloyd Wright, yet Old West ambience.

The likes of duck terrine wrapped in bacon and studded with pistachios bring contemporary Californian cooking to the fore. Mushrooms, a favorite ingredient of Chef/partner Todd Humphries, figure prominently on the menu. Downstairs, the Wine Cellar Bar highlights the large list of labels organized under such titles as "What's New in the Old World," and "Women Winemakers We Love."

Meadowood, The Restaurant ✿✿

Contemporary XXX

B1

900 Meadowood Ln. (off Silverado Trail), St. Helena

Phone: 707-967-1205 Dinner Mon – Sat
Web: www.meadowood.com
Prices: $$$$

Meadowood

Founded as an exclusive lodge in 1964, Meadowood's restaurant and forest-wrapped hillside cottages are secluded and fantastical. Though the property evokes a posh country club, its doors are open to affluent urbanites on the lam. Dressed in rich chocolate and milky white, the formal dining room is at once comfortable, elite, and unlike any hotel restaurant. Chef Christopher Kostow's immaculate, textural cuisine is also atypical, where suppers may begin with a quartet of harmonious canapés and amuse-bouche, such as a flatbread puff with creamy *fromage blanc* or corn custard with sweet, fresh kernels.

Two menus—a four-course seasonal ($95) and an eight-course chef's tasting ($155)—are complemented by pairings selected by the skilled sommelier. Seasonal highlights may include the likes of pristine ocean trout, slowly poached in olive oil, surrounded by a beautifully composed spring salad of asparagus, herbs, and a hint of rhubarb. The intricate performance continues with squid prepared four ways and a chocolate "bar" sprinkled with salted caramel. Service is equally thoughtful.

With a fire in the hearth and views of the golf course, the lounge is idyllic for romantic tête-à-têtes.

Mustards Grill

American

B2

7399 St. Helena Hwy. (at Hwy. 29), Yountville

Phone: 707-944-2424 Lunch & dinner daily
Web: www.mustardsgrill.com
Prices: $$

Napa Valley foodies had a scare in early 2009, when a kitchen fire forced Mustards Grill to close. All's well that ends well, though, and owner Cindy Pawlcyn took this opportunity to spruce the place up a bit. Nothing has been drastically altered, but the staff now operates in a remodeled kitchen.

Despite a chef change, the menu sticks to favorites such as the ever popular seafood tostada (the main ingredient of which varies daily); sweet corn tamales; and the Truckstop Deluxe ("always meat, usually potatoes, rarely vegetables").

Long before it was trendy for chefs to farm, Pawlcyn created an organic garden adjacent to the restaurant. That plot is now bigger and more bountiful than ever, supplying Mustards with a cornucopia of just-picked produce.

Neela's

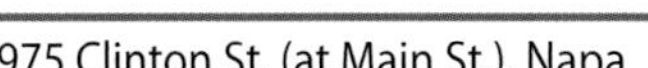

Indian

A3

975 Clinton St. (at Main St.), Napa

Phone: 707-226-9988 Lunch Tue – Fri
Web: www.neelasindianrestaurant.com Dinner Tue – Sun
Prices: $$

With a jewel-toned interior and bar streaming Bollywood music videos, this is as close to Mumbai as wine country gets. Raised in old Bombay, Chef/owner Neela Paniz moved from L.A. to Napa to share her native flavors with a town that lacked an Indian eatery. Now, the scent of fresh-ground spices can be traced to Neela's, serving contemporary fare reflective of India's many culinary styles.

Offerings range from *chaat* to such sophisticated dishes as a "Niçoise" salad with garam masala-crusted ahi; or *sev puri*, wheat crackers topped with potatoes, onions, contrasting chutneys, and crisp chick pea noodles. Super-fresh ingredients guarantee outstanding chicken tikka masala; Thursday "bread nights" are carbo-licious with melty pepper-jack naan.

Pica Pica

Latin American

610 First St. (at McKinstry St.), Napa

Phone: 707-205-6187 — Lunch & dinner daily
Web: www.picapicakitchen.com
Prices:

Fast, fresh, and flavorful Venezuelan cuisine highlights this casual eatery in the Oxbow Public Market (Napa's answer to San Francisco's Ferry Building Marketplace) which cannot be navigated on an empty stomach.

Among these shops selling local produce, seafood, and wine, is Pica Pica—a standout for its delicious food but also one of the building's few fast and easy dining options.

Catering largely to a take-out crowd, this "corn-centric kitchen" centers on the *arepa*, a grilled white-corn flatbread, stuffed with chicken salad and avocado, or shredded skirt steak with fried plantains and black bean paste. Heartier fare includes *cachapas*, a large yellow-corn pancake wrapped around a choice of fillings. Rejuvenate with a refreshing coconut lemonade.

Press

Steakhouse

587 St. Helena Hwy. South, St. Helena

Phone: 707-967-0550 — Dinner Wed – Mon
Web: www.presssthelena.com
Prices: $$$$

The simple warehouse façade visible from Highway 29 hides a posh steakhouse, where vaulted ceilings and natural light flooding through greenhouse-glass panels create an airy, luxurious space. A dark wood wine cabinet towers behind the bar, and an oversized fireplace and rotisserie form the focal point of the dining room. The swanky outdoor patio features long wooden tables and lush foliage.

Most of the beef is hand-selected, USDA Prime Angus, but the prized Japanese Kobe Kuroge Wagyu beef also appears on the menu. Dry-aging for 28 days enhances the taste of the meat—a grill fueled by cherry and almond woods does the rest.

The list of exclusively Napa Valley wines uncovers local gems from well-known vintners and small-batch wineries.

Redd ✿

Contemporary

C3

6480 Washington St. (at Oak Cir.), Yountville

Phone: 707-944-2222 — Lunch Fri – Sun
Web: www.reddnapavalley.com — Dinner nightly
Prices: $$$

MICHELIN

At the southern end of the sleepy Napa Valley town of Yountville, Redd feels more Museum of Modern Art than wine country casual thanks to New York's Asfour Guzy Architects. Stark white walls provide a blank canvas for ever-changing natural light, while immense wood-framed windows overlook Washington Street, and a courtyard with a fountain and fireplace. Gray Gubi-style chairs and minimalist place settings invoke an intellectual urban vibe that draws buzzing groups of denim-clad friends and couples taking respite from wine tasting.

The overall chic tone reflects Chef/owner Richard Reddington's new American cuisine, which is animated by playful Asian flavors and served both à la carte and in tasting menus (four courses at lunch, five at dinner). Seafood here is very fresh and delicately prepared, as in the starter of yellowfin tuna and hamachi tartare with diced apple and avocado over crispy puffed rice—well balanced, flavorful, and fun. Desserts, like peanut butter and chocolate *gianduja* mousse with honeycomb parfait, are elegant and bold without being too sweet.

Stylish locals often take their meals in the more casual bar, which offers a concise menu of playful takes on bar food.

Rutherford Grill

American

B2

1180 Rutherford Rd. (at Hwy. 29), Rutherford

Phone: 707-963-1792 Lunch & dinner daily
Web: www.hillstone.com
Prices: $$

Located at the intersection of Highway 29 and Rutherford Road, this unpretentious oasis has the feel of a suburban ski lodge set amid the wine country. Heady aromas from the hardwood-burning grill and wood-fired rotisserie escape to greet you in the parking lot. Inside, comfort reigns in the cozy confines of red leather booths and exposed ceiling beams.

Comfort can also be found in the hearty grilled steaks, barbecue ribs, fish, and rotisserie chicken with sides of mashed potatoes colcannon and creamy coleslaw. Starters such as a grilled jumbo artichokes play second fiddle to the sweet and buttery skillet corn bread, studded with jalapeños and kernels of fresh corn.

Popular with locals as well as wine-tasting tourists, the Grill usually has a wait.

Taylor's Automatic Refresher

American

C2

933 Main St. (at Charter Oak Ave.), St. Helena

Phone: 707-963-3486 Lunch & dinner daily
Web: www.taylorsrefresher.com
Prices: 

For a quick burger in the wine country, look no farther than this roadside icon. Opened in 1949, long before Napa was renowned for wine, Taylor's has kept pace with the times with its upscale burgers. While the prices may seem high, so is the quality—know that juicy Niman Ranch beef lies between those buns, beneath toppings like grilled mushrooms or guacamole. This wine country cuisine also includes plump hot dogs topped with hearty house-made chili, and sides of crisp sweet potato fries. Taylor's refreshes any thirst with thick milk shakes, draft beers, and local wines by the glass, half-bottle, or bottle.

All three locations (San Francisco's Ferry Building and Napa's Oxbow Public Market) have picnic tables perfect for alfresco family dining.

Solbar ✿

Californian XX

A1

755 Silverado Trail (at Rosedale Rd.), Calistoga

Phone: 707-226-0850 Lunch & dinner daily
Web: www.solagecalistoga.com
Prices: $$$

Solage Calistoga

Modern and glamorous Solbar, at Solage Calistoga, is the hippest sibling in the renowned Auberge family. As testament to its luxe heritage, the resort burgeons with olive trees, towering palms, and fire pits by the swimming pool that beg for a cocktail.

The restaurant, which also serves poolside, keeps a contemporary barn aesthetic with a gas fireplace and vaulted tin ceilings. Meanwhile, a black leather-clad lounge, polished concrete floors, and sleek Cherner chairs evoke San Francisco's savviest design quarters. Bare wood tables are minimally set to highlight creative Californian cuisine and lighter bites designed for a pre- or post-spa nosh. At lunch, this is a relaxed spot to indulge in a gourmet tuna burger.

Dinner focuses a keen eye on freshness and seasonality in an enticing menu that is equally divided into lighter spa cuisine and heartier fare. Guests might expect tender ricotta gnocchi with seasonal English peas and Mendocino morels, or flavorful braised beef short ribs served with potato "gremolata" and sautéed spinach. Whether it is the laid-back service or the bucolic surroundings, Solbar is undeniably chill—you may even spot a few terrycloth bathrobes at brunch.

Terra ✿

Contemporary XXX

C1

1345 Railroad Ave. (bet. Adams St. & Hunt Ave.), St. Helena

Phone: 707-963-8931 Dinner Wed – Mon
Web: www.terrarestaurant.com
Prices: $$$

Hiro Sone

The popularity of this Napa Valley favorite can be attributed to the one-two punch of husband-and-wife restaurateurs Hiro Sone and Lissa Doumani. As head chef, Sone spins out creative, globe-trotting fusion fare like foie gras tortellini, while his wife manages dining room service and oversees the pastry department. The result is foodie nirvana.

Housed in a late 19th century historical foundry tucked behind downtown St. Helena's main drag, Terra's arched windows and old stone walls lead to a romantic interior fitted out with lofty, wood-beamed ceilings, rustic terra-cotta floor tiles, and cozy tables built for lingering. The ample wine list, which pays homage to the local artisanal scene from Dry Creek, Alexander Valley, and the Russian River Valley, offers even more reason to loiter.

Sone's menu spins to the season, but might include a trio of plump abalone, sautéed in their shell and paired with roasted tomatoes, sugar snap peas, woodsy mushrooms, and a sprinkle of bright green parsley; or an exceptionally moist buttermilk fried quail with forest mushroom sauce, served with a silky mound of mashed potatoes and curly strips of smoky, crispy bacon.

Tra Vigne

Italian XX

C2

1050 Charter Oak Ave. (off Hwy. 29), St. Helena

Phone: 707-963-4444 Lunch & dinner daily
Web: www.travignerestaurant.com
Prices: $$$

Few *ristorantes* leave a first impression quite like Tra Vigne. Majestic olive trees twinkle with lights above a Tuscan-style courtyard patio, surrounded by vineyards and heated to ward off the evening chill. A grand neo-Italian dining room boasts a beautifully hand-carved bar and reflects the ambitious Italian menu.

Begin with the house's signature dish—mozzarella "al minuto" with fresh-ground pepper, olive oil, and grilled country bread—then settle in for a rich and savory Liberty Farms duck risotto, slow-cooked with green apple, fresh thyme, and quince-scented *saba*. The prolific wine list features both high-end Italian and Californian labels.

For more casual nibbles among local vintners, order a seasonal pie at adjacent Pizzeria Tra Vigne.

Wine Spectator Greystone

Californian XX

A1

2555 Main St. (at Deer Park Rd.), St. Helena

Phone: 707-967-1010 Lunch & dinner daily
Web: www.ciachef.edu
Prices: $$$

Inside this imposing stone chateau (built in 1889 as Greystone Cellars winery) is the West Coast campus of the Culinary Institute of America, whose restaurant is a destination in itself.

From any of the hand-crafted butcher block tables in the rustic main room, beneath high, wood-beamed ceilings, guests can watch the chefs at work in three exhibition kitchens—don't be surprised to find students pitching in. Their contribution further enhances the preparation of local seasonal products cooked with a Mediterranean spin. Meals here may begin with a lobster and chorizo tart, perhaps followed by a dry-aged strip loin with foie gras-oxtail ravioli.

Lunch on the outdoor terrace, with its bubbling fountain and vineyard view, is a wine country classic.

Ubuntu ✿

Vegetarian XX

A3

1140 Main St. (bet. 1st & Pearl Sts.), Napa

Phone: 707-251-5656 — Lunch Fri – Sun
Web: www.ubuntunapa.com — Dinner nightly
Prices: $$

Elijah Woolery

Nowhere else can you catch a candlelight evening yoga class and then slip downstairs, still in workout gear, for a truly inspired vegetarian dinner. Ubuntu, whose name means "humanity toward others," is a divine addition to downtown Napa. More good feelings await inside the airy restaurant, where stone walls and uplifting wall art are stylish yet serene, and the redwood communal table is always lively.

Minimally dressed, polished wood tables clear the stage for Chef Jeremy Fox's jaw-dropping mastery of the humble vegetable, many of which are harvested daily from Ubuntu's biodynamic garden. Immense care and skill are exhibited in these concoctions, which are artistically plated and meant to be shared. Of course, the exuberant young staff wouldn't mind if you simply had to keep that carrot *gnocchetti*, topped with tarragon and *mimolette* all to yourself. Blessedly, there's no shortage of cheese and butter to liven up the veggies—English pea consommé has a hint of white chocolate, and that "cheesecake in a jar" layered with triple cream and sour cherries soaked in wine is the reason you went to yoga in the first place.

The organic and biodynamic wine list reflects Ubuntu's philosophy.

Zuzu

Spanish

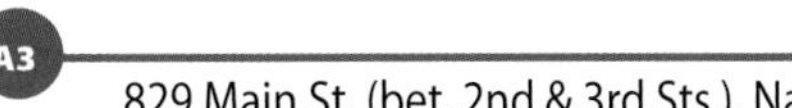

A3

829 Main St. (bet. 2nd & 3rd Sts.), Napa

Phone: 707-224-8555 — Lunch Mon – Fri

Web: www.zuzunapa.com — Dinner nightly

Prices:

As one of the few tapas bars in the Valley, Zuzu was serving small plates before the fad reached its current level of trendiness. The varied fare featuring tastes of Spain, Portugal, and elsewhere in the Mediterranean makes this a great place for a group. Sharing dishes in a casual backdrop is de rigueur and a good way to save a few dollars—although prices here are very reasonable. Niman Ranch grass-fed flatiron steak stands at the higher end of the price spectrum; while a traditional *tortilla Española* (omelet of potatoes and sweet onions), and others ring up at the $6 range.

Zuzu is open later than most downtown Napa restaurants, so you can go to grab a late-night nosh, sway to the beat of the Latin music, and hang out in the well-stocked wine bar.

Your opinions are important to us. Please write to us at: michelin.guides@us.michelin.com

Sonoma County

Often eclipsed as a wine region by neighboring Napa Valley, the county that borders Marin County to the north claims 76 miles of Pacific coastline, as well as 250 wineries that take advantage of some of the best grape-growing conditions in California. Northern California's first premium winery, **Buena Vista**, was established just outside the town of Sonoma in 1857 by Agoston Haraszthy. Today thirteen distinct wine appellations (AVAs) have been assigned in Sonoma County, where vintners produce a dizzying array of wines in an area slightly larger than the State of Rhode Island. Along

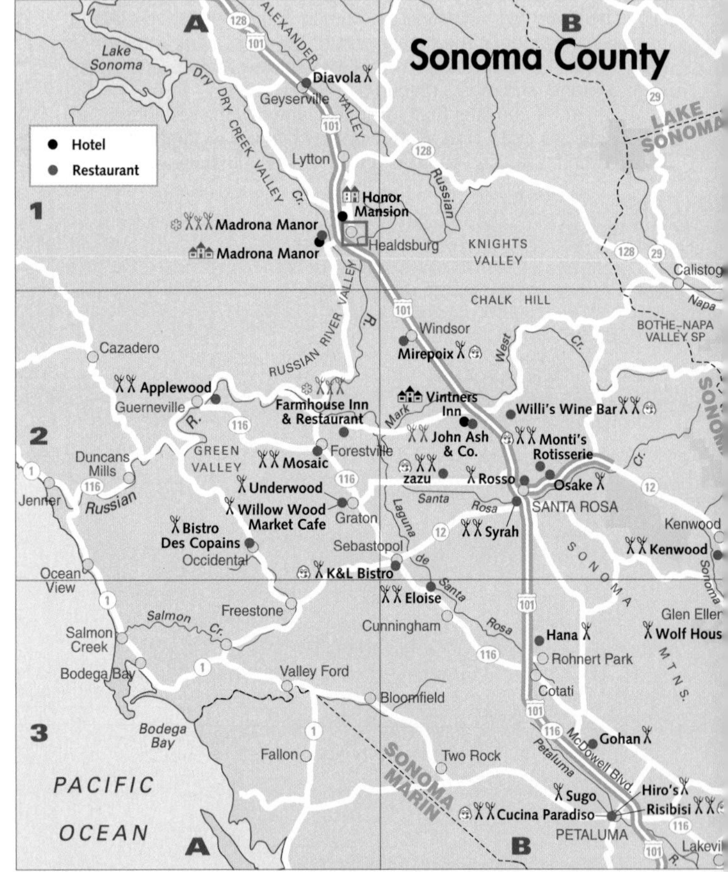

Highway 12, heading north from the town of Sonoma through Santa Rosa to Healdsburg, byroads lead to out-of-the-way wineries, each of which puts its own unique stamp on the business of winemaking.

The Russian River Valley edges the river named for the early Russian trading outposts that were set up along the coast. This is one of the coolest growing regions in Sonoma, thanks to the river basin that offers a conduit for cool coastal air. Elegant Pinot Noir and Chardonnay headline here, but Syrah is quickly catching up.

At the upper end of the Russian River, the Dry Creek Valley yields excellent Sauvignon Blanc, Chardonnay and Pinot Noir. This region is also justly famous for its Zinfandel, a grape that does especially well in the valley's rock-strewn soil. Winery visits in Dry Creek are a study in contrasts. Palatial modern wineries rise up along the same rural roads that have

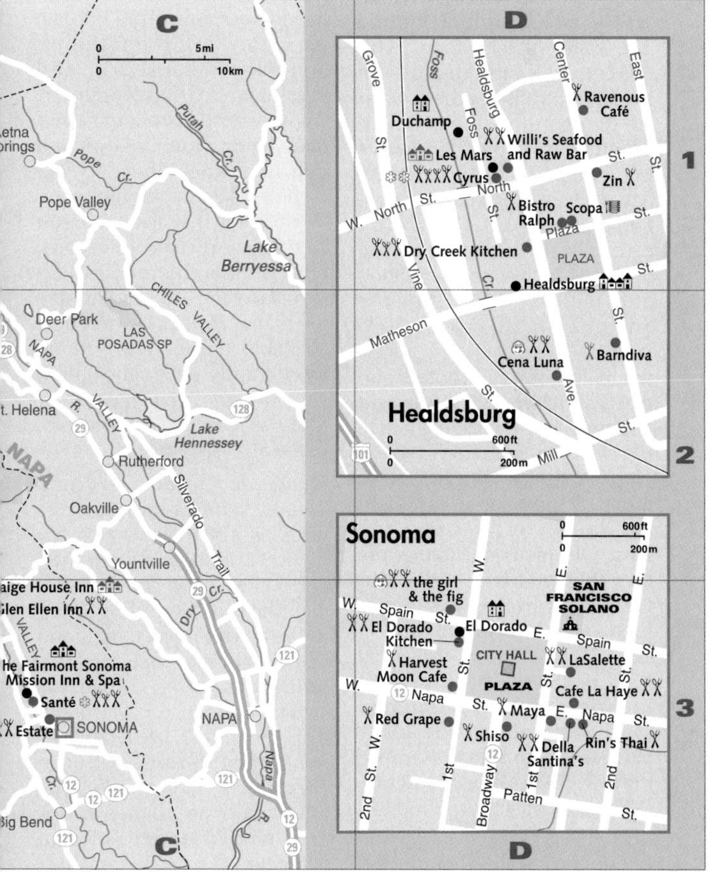

been home to independents for generations, and young grapevines trained into laser-straightened rows are broken up by the dark, gnarled fingers of old vines.

Sonoma County's inlandmost AVAs are Knights Valley and Alexander Valley, the latter named for Cyrus Alexander who planted the area's first vineyard in 1846. These two warm regions both highlight Cabernet Sauvignon.

Nestled between the Mayacamas and Sonoma ranges, the 17-mile-long Sonoma Valley—which writer Jack London dubbed The Valley of the Moon in his 1913 novel—dominates the southern portion of the county. At its center is the town of Sonoma, site of California's northernmost and final mission: San Francisco Solano Mission, founded in 1823. The mission once included a thriving vineyard before secularization and incorporation into the Sonoma State Historic Park system 102 years ago, when the vines were uprooted and transplanted elsewhere in Sonoma. The town's eight-acre plaza is still surrounded by 19th century adobe buildings, most of them now occupied by shops, restaurants, and inns. Of epicurean note is the fact that building contractor Chuck Williams bought a hardware store in Sonoma in 1956. He gradually converted its stock from hardware to French cookware, kitchen tools, and novelty foods. Today **Williams-Sonoma** has more than 200 stores nationwide, and is a must-stop for foodies.

Just below Sonoma lies a portion of the Carneros district, named for the herds of sheep (*los carneros* in Spanish) that once roamed its hillsides. Carneros is best known for its cool-climate grapes, notably Pinot Noir and Chardonnay.

Throughout this bucolic county—called SoCo by savvy locals—vineyards rub shoulders with orchards and farms that take advantage of the area's fertile soil to produce everything from apples and olives to artisan-crafted cheeses. Sustainable and organic are key words at local farmers' markets, which herald the spring (April or May) in Santa Rosa, Sebastopol, Sonoma, Healdsburg, and Petaluma. At these open-air smorgasbords, you can find everything from just-picked heirloom vegetables to sea urchins taken out of the water so recently that they are still wiggling. Artisanal olive oils, chocolates, baked goods, jams, and jellies count among the many homemade products available. In addition, ethnic food stands cover the globe with offerings that have their roots as far away as Mexico, India, and Afghanistan.

Thanks to the area's natural bounty, farm-to-table cuisine takes on new heights in many of the county's restaurants. Some chefs need go no farther than their own on-site gardens for fresh fruits, vegetables, and herbs. With easy access to local products such as Dungeness crab from Bodega Bay, poultry from Petaluma, and cheeses from the **Sonoma Cheese Factory**, it's no wonder that the Californian cuisine in this area has attracted national attention.

Applewood

A2 — Californian XX

13555 Hwy. 116, Guerneville

Phone: 707-869-9093 — Dinner Tue – Sat
Web: www.applewoodinn.com
Prices: $$$

A romantic wine country weekend awaits visitors to the Applewood Inn, located on winding Highway 116. A mile from Guerneville, this tile-roofed B&B sits on a knoll surrounded by manicured gardens and orchards. Dinner guests are welcome at the inn's barn-like restaurant, warmed by soaring stone fireplaces set at either end of the room. An enclosed sun porch affords lovely views of the woodsy environs.

Californian sensibilities marry French and Italian flair in the cuisine of Chef Bruce Frieseke, whose talent speaks for itself in the likes of a fennel-crusted ahi tuna loin nesting on a bed of fava beans, with cilantro blossoms scattered on top.

Call to reserve one of the inn's 19 rooms if you plan to partake in the liquid assets of the wine country.

Barndiva

D2 — Contemporary X

231 Center St. (bet. Matheson & Mills Sts.), Healdsburg

Phone: 707-431-0100 — Lunch & dinner Wed – Sun
Web: www.barndiva.com
Prices: $$$

Despite the name, you'll find no prima donnas here. Instead, a block off Healdsburg's square, Jil and Geoffrey Hales' soaring mahogany barn houses a chic urban boîte with a pastoral soul. Vivid artwork and funky wire sculptures of fish and game cling to the white walls inside. If it's sunny, go straight for the garden terrace, where raked sand and manicured flora beget the feel of a posh country club—*sans* the attitude or dues.

The seasons inspire eclectic dishes that look to local purveyors and food artisans for their ingredients. Dessert adds a graceful ending with such creative contemporary confections as a lemon-black pepper angel food cake with blood orange gelée.

The beauty of this place motivates many couples to hold their nuptials here.

Bistro Des Copains

French

A2

3782 Bohemian Hwy. (at Occidental Rd.), Occidental

Phone: 707-874-2436 — Dinner nightly
Web: www.bistrodescopains.com
Prices: $$

Don your vintage driving gloves, turn up "La Vie en Rose," and imagine yourself on the Côte d'Azur as you wind your way to Occidental, the out-the-way hamlet home to Bistro Des Copains. Delightfully located on Bohemian Highway, the petite green cottage with bright white trim transports you to Provence via the California wine country. Sonoma wines, as well as a few French labels, complement Southern Gallic fare like buckwheat crêpes stuffed with mushrooms and brie, scallops gratiné, and creamy chocolate *pots de crème*.
Reservations are a good idea, especially on Wednesdays when dollar oysters lure locals by the dozen.
The wine bar, warmed by a wood oven in the kitchen and adorned with photos of the owner's ancestral farm, is a cozy spot to wait.

Bistro Ralph

Californian

D1

109 Plaza St. (bet. Center St. & Healdsburg Ave.), Healdsburg

Phone: 707-433-1380 — Lunch & dinner Mon – Sat
Web: www.bistroralph.com
Prices: $$

Chef Ralph Tingle's refined bistro is perched just off Healdsburg's natty central plaza, and blends beautifully with its environs. The warehouse-chic dining room is all blithe, and teems with locals and tourists. The succinct and seasonal menu manifests California cheer laced with French influences. At lunch, comfort classics reign supreme like a smoked salmon BLT on toasted sourdough, or chicken livers with caramelized onions and fried polenta. Dinner entrées may pair Liberty Farm duck confit with figs and balsamic sauce, or grilled wild salmon with chanterelles and creamed corn—*finis* the dining marvel with a glass from their mostly local wine list.
Pre- or post-meal, linger to explore the chic shops, and wine tasting rooms that surround the plaza.

Cafe La Haye

D3 **Californian** XX

140 E. Napa St. (bet. 1st & 2nd Sts.), Sonoma

Phone: 707-935-5994 Dinner Tue – Sat
Web: www.cafelahaye.com
Prices: $$

This quaint and comfortable little café, opened by Saul Gropman, has a charming spirit and strong local following. A rotating selection of work by local artists hangs around the room, giving the place a gallery feel. In the bi-level dining room, butter-yellow walls reflect a soothing light under the exposed beams of the pitched roof. Art lovers and foodies alike flock here to sample items on the concise market-driven menu that focuses on cheeses, vegetables, and meats from nearby farms and ranches.

Complementary ingredients take center stage in roasted pork tenderloin, topped with a bacon-cherry pan sauce, fanned over corn, oyster mushroom, and red pepper ragout. The daily risotto always spotlights the freshest flavors of the season.

Cena Luna

D2 **Italian** XX

241 Healdsburg Ave. (bet. Matheson & Mill Sts.), Healdsburg

Phone: 707-433-6000 Dinner Mon – Sat
Web: www.cenaluna.com
Prices: $$

This family-run Northern Italian eatery is warm and welcoming in all the right ways. Set just off the main square in Healdsburg, Cena Luna (which translates to "dinner moon" in Italian) is the brainchild of co-owners and chefs, Yvette Peline-Hom and Stuart Hom. Together, they envisioned and created a delicious menu, minus the wine country pretension.

Colorful salads filled with roasted beets, oranges, and goat cheese get things started—but save room for one of the house-made pastas, where you might come across tender pockets of veal and duck ravioli; or a soft tangle of chicken and prosciutto fettuccini, laced with preserved lemon and fresh mozzarella. For dinner, try the chicken stuffed with prosciutto and *crescenza*, or roast duck with mascarpone.

Cucina Paradiso

Italian XX

B3

114 Petaluma Blvd. N. (bet. Washington St. & Western Ave.), Petaluma

Phone: 707-782-1130 — Lunch & dinner Mon – Sat
Web: www.cucinaparadisopetaluma.com
Prices: ⚭

From the crusty *focaccia* to the pastas and sauces, everything at this homey Petaluma trattoria is made from scratch, which accounts in part for its devoted following. The other reason is the warm, family-oriented vibe and gracious service that Chef/owner Dennis Hernandez and his wife, Malena, have fostered since they opened the restaurant—which recently relocated just down the road.

Evidence of the chef's culinary training in Italy is everywhere; the arias playing as background music seem perfectly suited to a satisfying and homey plate of house-made veal tortellini, matched with the flavors of a mushroom cream sauce studded with diced prosciutto. Perhaps best of all, the price is a wonderful value for the high quality of the cuisine.

Della Santina's

Italian XX

D3

133 E. Napa St. (bet. 1st & 2nd Sts.), Sonoma

Phone: 707-935-0576 — Lunch & dinner daily
Web: www.dellasantinas.com
Prices: $$

This cozy little Italian dining room exudes hominess, with family photographs and framed lace napkins adorning the walls, and rustic Tuscan dishes that keep fans returning. A sprawling back patio is equipped with heaters and canopies to accommodate alfresco dining on cool days.

The kitchen offers a variety of spit-roasted meats, including duck, chicken, pork, and rabbit; as well as pastas like fresh pappardelle in a hearty rabbit ragù; lasagna Bolognese; or linguini with pesto. Both the *gnocchi della nonna* and the veal *della casa* change daily, and a set four-course dinner delivers good value. The Californian-Italian wine list covers all the bases from A to Z, starting with amarone from the Veneto region to zinfandel from Sonoma County.

Cyrus ✿✿

Contemporary XXXX

D1

29 North St. (bet. Foss St. & Healdsburg Ave.), Healdsburg

Phone: 707-433-3311 Dinner nightly
Web: www.cyrusrestaurant.com
Prices: $$$$

Andy Katz

Like a princess lost in earthier environs, sleek Cyrus offers so much pedigree to Sonoma County's Healdsburg you'll think you've died and gone to *paradis*. There's the mind-reading service staff anticipating your every need; and the beautiful, intimate space, with its cloistered ceilings, curving banquettes, and wooden armoires. Then there's the caviar and Champagne cart, the impeccable wine service, and did we mention jackets are suggested?

Luckily, the food competes with all this perfection thanks to the able hands of Chef Douglas Keane, whose elegant nightly tasting menu, which comes in two prix-fixe menus (five- and eight-course options), is a seasonal, seafood-strewn affair that often dances with Asian influences.

Dinner might kick off with Thai-marinated lobster, layered with creamy avocado, fresh mango, and tender hearts of palm; then quickly digress into perfectly-caramelized foie gras set atop a slice of *pain perdu* and cooked pineapple, doused with flaming pirate rum and cinnamon; and close with the black truffle lamb roulade layered with white root vegetables and béchamel over creamy parsnip purée, garnished with a bright array of parsnip, baby carrots, and baby rutabaga.

Diavola

A1 — Pizza

21021 Geyserville Ave. (at Hwy. 128), Geyserville

Phone: 707-814-0111 — Lunch & dinner daily
Web: www.diavolapizzeria.com
Prices: $$

With the relocation of its sister, Santi, to Santa Rosa in fall 2009, Diavola is the only serious culinary contender for miles around. At mealtime, cars jam the spaces on tiny Geyserville's main drag as their occupants savor rustic fare hand-crafted by Chef Dino Bugica.

Artisanal cured meats, sausages, and wood-fired pizzas get to the heart of the matter here. Bugica has a passion for all things porcine, and pig products figure prominently on the menu—be it in the daily selection of salami; the pizza Sonja with prosciutto, mascarpone, and arugula; or a roasted asparagus salad tossed with pancetta and truffled pecorino.

A former brothel, the building touts its historic charm in the original wood floors, pressed-tin ceilings, and exposed brick walls.

Dry Creek Kitchen

D1 — Californian

317 Healdsburg Ave. (bet. Matheson & Plaza Sts.), Healdsburg

Phone: 707-431-0330 — Lunch Fri – Sun
Web: www.charliepalmer.com — Dinner nightly
Prices: $$$

Downtown Healdsburg is quintessential Sonoma—from the mom-and-pop bakeries to its dynamic restaurant scene. Dry Creek Kitchen is a favorite haunt inspired by its environs, with seasonal potted plants dotting each linen-topped table, soon to be laden with locally baked breads and wines selected from more than 600 Sonoma County all-stars. A spacious bar, heated patio, and occasional live jazz make this a comfy spot for casual tourists and local regulars alike.

Both service and cuisine can be hit or miss, but Dry Creek Kitchen does send out quality fare, as in the flavorful pork rillettes atop savory spinach salad, or perfectly roasted sea bass with vegetable *Basquaise*. For dessert, caramel corn ice cream is a clever complement to a caramelized banana.

El Dorado Kitchen

Californian XX

D3

405 1st St. W. (at Spain St.), Sonoma

Phone: 707-996-3030 Lunch & dinner daily
Web: www.eldoradosonoma.com
Prices: $$

A stone's throw from the grassy Sonoma town square, this casual kitchen is nestled inside the El Dorado Hotel. The urban-chic interior boasts white-washed walls, dark brooding woods, and sage-green accents. In the center of the dining room, two long rectangular hanging lamps illuminate the communal table fashioned from a single plank of wood salvaged from a bridge in Vermont.

Sit at the far end of the room to view Chef Justin Everett in the open kitchen. From here come decidedly Californian preparations, like a warm artichoke tart, crispy fried organic summer squash, and corn agnolotti with chanterelles and black truffles.

The breezy stone courtyard makes a perfect perch for Sunday brunch, especially if you have children in tow.

Eloise

French XX

B3

2295 Gravenstein Hwy. South, Sebastopol

Phone: 707-823-6300 Lunch & dinner Wed – Mon
Web: www.restauranteloise.com
Prices: $$$

As if it were still Sonoma's best-kept secret, locals are possessive of this gem with blue-and-white tiled floors and light-filled windows facing a spectacular wildflower garden. Butcher paper tops small tables lending a country vibe, and lush gardens out back provide much of the kitchen's fresh produce. But don't be fooled: In the hands of Chefs Ginevra Iverson and Eric Korsch, formerly of New York's Prune, the French-influenced fare is perfectly refined, especially with a glass of boutique wine included in the $25 three-course prix-fixe lunch.

Sunset brings pricier fare. Roasted bone marrow with lemony parsley and shallot salad is a rendezvous to remember; entrées such as milk-poached day boat black cod attest to the relaxed polish of the chefs.

Estate

C3

400 W. Spain St. (at 4th St.), Sonoma

Phone: 707-933-3663 — Lunch Sun
Web: www.estate-sonoma.com — Dinner nightly
Prices: $$

With sweeping grounds, masterfully cultivated gardens, a wraparound porch, and sumptuous interiors dressed in burgundy and gold, this former home of General Mariano Vallejo's daughter is worthy of its new name. The historic Victorian was taken over in 2008 by the proprietors of the successful girl & the fig. Today, the mystical manor draws foodies into its art-filled dining rooms for delicious small plates evocative of Southern Italy, like sautéed foraged mushrooms and crisp semolina *gnocchetti* with tender pork, fried sage, and black pepper. Main dishes such as fresh arctic char and leg of lamb are skillfully prepared, and many infuse handpicked ingredients from Estate's edible gardens.
The outdoor fireplace is an alluring spot for a cocktail.

Glen Ellen Inn

Californian XX

C3

13670 Arnold Dr. (at Warm Springs Rd.), Glen Ellen

Phone: 707-996-6409 — Lunch Fri – Tue
Web: www.glenelleninn.com — Dinner nightly
Prices: $$

For a romantic getaway, head for the hamlet of Glen Ellen. The secluded Glen Ellen Inn promotes serenity with a cozy fireplace on the enclosed porch and a trickling waterfall in the back garden. Inside, tones of gold, green and burgundy prevail, and homemade biscuits and *focaccia* get your meal off to a tasty start.
Oysters and designer martinis are a big draw. The former come fire-grilled, crispy fried, or raw on the halfshell. But don't stop there. Artichoke and Stilton ravioli, or Sonoma duck with orange-ginger glaze and soba noodles satisfy as entrées. And don't overlook the seasonal desserts; the likes of spiced pumpkin baked Alaska make a sweet ending indeed.
Can't bear to leave? Book one of the six "Secret Cottages" set alongside a burbling creek.

Farmhouse Inn & Restaurant

Californian

A2

7871 River Rd. (at Wohler Rd.), Forestville

Phone: 707-887-3300 Dinner Thu – Mon
Web: www.farmhouseinn.com
Prices: **$$$**

Kevin Schultz

On six wooded acres off a country road surrounded by vineyard and forest in the Russian River Valley, this two-story yellow farmhouse is the bucolic stuff of dreams. The rustic retreat features a garden, sun porch, swimming pool, and 18 luxury guest quarters—eight of which were added this year.

The restaurant is also enjoying a recently refreshed look, with a contemporary palette, natural fabrics, and mod farm touches such as *faux bois* mirrors and majestic wood chandeliers. The soul of the gracious dining room remains unchanged, with a continued devotion to classic cooking and abundant use of local, sustainable produce. While the family-run staff may feel at times inattentive, there is no denying its expertise: Served in perfect synchronicity, flavorful dishes may include a tender duet of beef with chanterelle butter and horseradish potato purée; or the kitchen's signature, a hearty rabbit trio with bacon, fingerlings, and whole grain mustard sauce. A terrific selection of local and old-world wines is served in lithe stemware by the easygoing yet savvy sommelier.

With classical music and lovely nighttime views, the Farmhouse Inn is an idyllic getaway for sophisticated couples.

Gohan

Japanese

B3

1367 N. McDowell Blvd. (at Redwood Way), Petaluma

Phone: 707-789-9296 — Lunch Mon – Fri
Web: www.gohanrestaurant.com — Dinner nightly
Prices: $$

Some good sushi lies tucked away in the Redwood Gateway strip mall, where Gohan now operates under Chef Takeshige Yahiro.

Despite the untimely death of the original Chef/owner Steve Tam, a little over a year ago, Gohan's team has kept Tam's dream alive. And they've been doing a fine job of it. Among the many meticulously formed and plated makimono rolls, the menu now lists one in Chef Steve's honor: shrimp tempura and snow crab salad wrapped in *maguro* and avocado with a dusting of *togarashi* for extra color and kick. At lunch, the best bargains are in the bento boxes; new-style sashimi (*hirame* with ponzu citrus; albacore with jalapeño) is a bit pricier.

Dinner specials may include a ribeye with zinfandel teriyaki—this is wine country after all.

Hana

Japanese

B3

101 Golf Course Dr. (at Roberts Lake Rd.), Rohnert Park

Phone: 707-586-0270 — Lunch Mon – Sat
Web: www.hanajapanese.com — Dinner nightly
Prices: $$

Despite its unexpected location in the Double Tree Plaza, Hana has been Chef/owner Kenichi (Ken) Tominaga's baby for 15 years. Here, Tominaga and his chefs are known to nurture patrons with their pleasant demeanor, as well as nourishing them with the freshest fish flown in from Japan and the east and west coasts of the U.S.

Feel free to ask questions to the chefs at the bar—they are glad to describe the characteristics of a particular fish, or even display the day's fresh whole catch. The staff's love of food jumps out in their knowledgeable technique; and their exquisite omakase is perfect for those seeking true adventure.

If you miss Chef Ken's smiling face here, he is probably at Go Fish, the restaurant he runs with partner Cindy Pawlcyn in St. Helena.

Harvest Moon Cafe

Californian

487 1st St. W. (bet. Napa & Spain Sts.), Sonoma

Phone: 707-933-8160 — Lunch Sun
Web: www.harvestmooncafesonoma.com — Dinner Thu – Tue
Prices: $$

A relaxed feel and light-hearted approach have put this little family-run place on Sonoma's culinary map. Husband-and-wife team Nick and Jen Demarest's respect for locally grown produce is evident in the handful of appetizers and entrées that comprise the daily changing menu of Californian cuisine. Cooked with care and creativity, the food here is homey and comforting.

Tastes of the Mediterranean enliven the simple yet impressive dishes of long-cooked Monterey Bay squid with grilled bread and spicy rouille; or grilled pork chops with sautéed rapini, soft polenta, and caper sauce.

Set on Sonoma's historic plaza, the serpentine dining space seats about 40 people and is complemented by a large garden patio furnished with tiny red metal tables.

Hiro's

Japanese

107 Petaluma Blvd. N. (bet. Washington St. & Western Ave.), Petaluma

Phone: 707-763-2300 — Lunch Mon – Sat
Web: www.hirosrestaurant.com — Dinner nightly
Prices: $$

Japanese businessman Hiro Yamamoto came to Sonoma County from Japan in 1988, fell in love with the quality of life here, and the rest is history in the making. Set in the heart of downtown Petaluma, Hiro's restaurant serves some of the freshest sushi around.

Sushi and sashimi are plated to please the eye, and innovative maki are presented with a twist (as in a Dynamite roll done with salmon and fresh crab salad baked over a California roll with a creamy piquant sauce). If you don't see a roll you like on the menu, the sushi chefs will customize one for you.

Many nights, Hiro himself works the floor, seeing to the satisfaction of his guests. Unique wood-block prints by Naoki Takenouchi add an artistic element to the room's casual studio feel.

John Ash & Co.

B2 — Californian XX

4330 Barnes Rd. (at River Rd.), Santa Rosa

Phone: 707-527-7687 — Dinner nightly
Web: www.vintnersinn.com
Prices: **$$$**

Set among 92 acres of bountiful vineyards and manicured landscapes at Vintners Inn, John Ash & Co. is California dreamy. A romantic dining room and exquisite solarium encourage a carefree conviviality among guests. The restaurant is also lauded as the first in Sonoma County to promote seasonal cooking with area produce and local wine pairings. And though the kitchen's namesake hasn't cooked here in years, John Ash & Co. continues to celebrate haute Californian cuisine. Homegrown produce is plucked from the property's gardens and graces such dishes as heirloom tomato consommé with goat cheese ravioli and basil.

A grilled rack and cheek of lamb exotically spiced with *ras el hanout*, or a plump *chile relleno* reflect the chef's global musings.

Kenwood

B2 — International XX

9900 Hwy. 12 (at Warm Springs Blvd.), Kenwood

Phone: 707-833-6326 — Lunch & dinner Wed – Sun
Web: www.kenwoodrestaurant.com
Prices: **$$**

Both locals and wine trail travelers (Highway 12 from Sonoma to Santa Rosa) trust Kenwood to dish up country charm with a side of urban sophistication. The bright spacious interior is divided into three distinct areas, including a bar and a private dining room. In the main room, French doors open onto a vineyard landscape bounded by the Sugarloaf Mountains.

Not content to confine itself to one continent, the menu roams from Asia to Europe and back to North America. This may translate into escargots with parsley butter; veal piccata with artichokes atop porcini ravioli; and crisp, rich duck spring rolls with mango salad and tangy ponzu sauce.

A relative rarity in wine country, Kenwood's courteous service, atmosphere, and menu are all kid-friendly.

K & L Bistro

French

119 South Main St. (bet. Burnett St. and Hwy. 12), Sebastopol

Phone: 707-823-6614 Lunch & dinner Mon – Sat
Web: N/A
Prices: $$

A little French bistro with a big heart, K & L is named for its owners, husband-and-wife team Karen and Lucas Martin. This cozy neighborhood spot offers one of the best deals in Sonoma's wine country for fine food seriously prepared and served in generous amounts. The menu is a casual French affair, as in Dover sole in beurre blanc, plated with crispy fries and a frisée salad. For lunch, locals seem to favor American staples like the house burger and a cold beer. Check the blackboard for a list of the day's selection of wines, cheeses, and desserts.

Genuine and friendly, servers quickly come to know the regulars by name here. You'll want to be one too, once you savor a delectable meal in the brick-walled room adorned with work by local artists.

LaSalette

Portuguese

452-H 1st St. E. (bet. Napa & Spain Sts.), Sonoma

Phone: 707-938-1927 Lunch & dinner daily
Web: www.lasalette-restaurant.com
Prices: $$

Fashioned with burlap draperies, hand-painted Portuguese pottery, and tables crafted from Port wine crates, LaSalette, the family-run affair near the Sonoma town square, tips its hat to the vibrant docks of Lisbon. Self-taught Chef/owner Manuel Azevedo and his cuisine, however, hail from the Azores islands 1,000 miles from the capital. LaSalette is named for the chef's mother; his wife, Kimberly, is ready with a smile at the door.

Inside, pumpkin-hued walls echo the heat of a wood-burning oven that cranks out much of the restaurant's fare, including a whole-roasted fish. On the enchanting patio, heaters ward off the evening chill, as do rich seafood and slow-cooked meat stews. Finish with a creamy flan, fresh berries, and a tasting of top-notch Ports.

Madrona Manor ✿

A1 **Contemporary** XXX

1001 Westside Rd. (at West Dry Creek Rd.), Healdsburg

Phone: 707-433-4231 Dinner Wed – Sun
Web: www.madronamanor.com
Prices: $$$

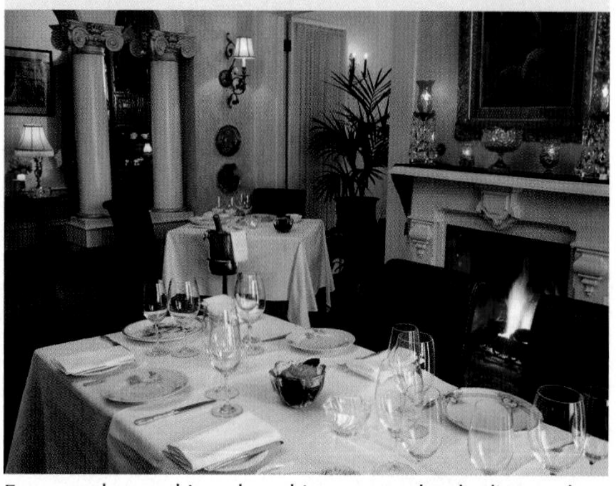

Lenny Siegel

For couples seeking the ultimate storybook dinner date, evenings at Madrona Manor practically begin with "Once upon a time." This historic Victorian mansion is resplendent with rambling gardens and a sense of grandeur. Savor the vistas from a heated covered porch, a glorious spot that marries Victoriana and Southern hospitality. Dinner guests don their evening best and the staff is appropriately professional and warm.

Chef Jesse Malgren's cuisine has grown increasingly creative, with ice cream now made tableside in the dramatic fog of liquid nitrogen. Still, refinement and finesse (along with the gels and powders of molecular gastronomy) are at the center of this excellent food. A starter of scallop sashimi and tiny lobes of uni with estate Meyer lemon and soy salt explodes with fresh flavors. Dishes of perfectly tender and flavorful Liberty Farms duck, or local petrale sole alongside an ethereal hollandaise suggest that the offerings may improve with each visit. A caviar menu and cheese course is available in addition to the seven-course tasting, and every dish is available à la carte.

Don't miss their wine pairings of exceptional value; also note their hard-to-find vintages.

Maya

Mexican

D3

101 E. Napa St. (at 1st St.), Sonoma

Phone: 707-935-3500
Web: www.mayarestaurant.com
Prices: $$

Lunch & dinner daily

Located on a corner facing Sonoma's historic town square, Maya pays homage to contemporary Mexican food and adds a dash of Californian flair. Flash-fried baby artichokes with tequila cream dipping sauce pave the way for entrées like plantain-crusted sea bass, pan-seared and set on *pasilla*-pesto corn risotto; and carne asada tacos made with marinated hanger steak dusted with a Yucatan spice rub and served with fresh *pico de gallo*.

Of course, the place to start is at the "temple of tequila," as the tiered central bar is called, with a margarita or a shot of premium tequila. Spicy toasted pumpkin seeds make a tasty accompaniment.

Bright hues, exposed stone walls, heavy wood furniture, and hammocks hanging from the ceiling give the room character and warmth.

Mirepoix 

French

B2

275 Windsor River Rd. (at Honsa Ave.), Windsor

Phone: 707-838-0162
Web: www.restaurantmirepoix.com
Prices: $$

Lunch Tue – Fri
Dinner Tue – Sun

This charming bungalow in Windsor's recently rejuvenated downtown embraces the spirit of the medieval market town of Mirepoix in Southwestern France. The restaurant's red walls are covered with black-and-white photos of its namesake city, while small bistro tables and affable service foster a convivial vibe.

Though Chef Matthew Bosquet's dishes appear rustic, this is food that deserves recognition. The offerings that truly standout here are classic bistro recipes made with local farm-raised products, such as a succulent roasted chicken served with a mushroom-turnip ragout.

The concise but smartly chosen wine list highlights a good selection of labels that changes every few days; local pinot noir and chardonnay are particularly well represented.

Monti's Rotisserie

American

B2

714 Village Court (bet. Farmer's Ln. & Hardmand Dr.), Santa Rosa

Phone: 707-568-4404 Lunch & dinner daily
Web: www.montisroti.net
Prices: $$

Carnivores delight in Mark and Terri Stark's addition to Santa Rosa's open-air Montgomery Village mall. A large wood-burning rotisserie takes center stage in the dining room, where glistening chunks of meat are roasted over the coals with exceptional skill. The mouthwatering aromas of the nightly selections are hard to resist; apple-glazed turkey may be offered one evening, pomegranate-glazed baby back ribs the next.

A long wooden bar zig-zags through the front room, packed with hungry shoppers who nosh on pasta, the addictive house-made French fries tossed with Gorgonzola and rosemary, and wood-fired pizzas. In nice weather, the spacious trellis-covered patio is an ideal spot. The Starks also run three other popular Sonoma County restaurants.

Mosaic

Californian

A2

6675 Front St. (at Mirabel Rd.), Forestville

Phone: 707-887-7503 Lunch & dinner daily
Web: www.mosaiceats.com
Prices: $$

Chef/owner Tai Olesky grew up in Sonoma County, so he's no stranger to the bountiful farms and vineyards whose products star in the Mosaic's locally-focused cuisine. The self-taught chef stirs global notes into many of his entrées, as in crispy prawns with a chile-lime glaze, or coffee-crusted filet mignon. At lunch, the humble hamburger is transformed when made from ground beef tenderloin and Italian sausage. Crown it with Manchego cheese, watercress, and horseradish mayonnaise and you've got a mouthwatering masterpiece.

The painted-brick building sits on the main drag in sleepy Forestville. A rustic canvas, the interior incorporates glazed concrete floors and velvet drapes. Out back, the trellised garden patio invites repose any time of day.

Osake

Japanese

B2

2446 Patio Ct. (at Farmer's Ln.), Santa Rosa

Phone: 707-542-8282 — Lunch Mon – Fri
Web: www.garychus.com — Dinner Mon – Sat
Prices:

Sleek lines and minimalist modern décor lure shoppers into this spacious Japanese restaurant in Montgomery Village mall. Here, they come to enjoy sushi at the welcoming bar, where a full complement of *nigiri*, sashimi, and maki rounds out the raw offerings. For those not seeking sushi, a *robata* grill turns out tantalizing skewers of Black Angus beef, chicken, yellowtail, and giant calamari cooked on the open-fire. In between these options, a generous list of kitchen dishes ranges from monkfish pâté to vegetable tempura. Fixed-price bento box lunches and dinners add a lot of bang for the buck.

The name, meaning "respect for sake," inspires an array of sake offerings, as well as a selection of Sonoma County wines, to pair with the dishes.

Ravenous Café

Californian

D1

420 Center St. (bet. North & Piper Sts.), Healdsburg

Phone: 707-431-1302 — Lunch & dinner Wed – Sun
Web: www.theravenous.com
Prices: $$

Apricot walls, worn plank floors, and a crackling fireplace lend a folksy feel to this quaint cottage, whetting appetites for a home-cooked meal. Passion resides behind the stoves of Chefs/owners John and Joyanne Pezzolo, who turn out a different roster of Californian dishes each day. Items may range from more a rustic grilled portobello sandwich topped with roasted peppers and fontina, to fish cakes accompanied with ginger, lemon, and mint-cilantro aïoli. Generous desserts are sure to squelch any plans to diet, with the likes of apple-apricot crêpes, raspberry pavlova, or—with luck and timing—a creamy pumpkin-mascarpone cheesecake.

Once the smattering of tables fills up, a line usually forms for the first-come, first-served seats at the bar.

Red Grape

D3 **Pizza**

529 1st St. W. (at Napa St.), Sonoma

Phone: 707-996-4103 Lunch & dinner daily
Web: www.theredgrape.com
Prices: ꟸ

While other types of grapes may demand the lion's share of attention in Sonoma County, the Red Grape holds its own as a wine country pizzeria. The name refers to the type of tomatoes used to make the sauce that tops the cracker-thin New Haven-style pizza that owner Sam Morphy and his family discovered during a year spent in Connecticut.

Comfortable and family-friendly, the roomy interior jams up almost as fast as the inviting outdoor garden patio does on a sunny day. In either location, an ample array of soups, salads, and appetizers only serve as a precursor to some of the more creative and tasty pizzas in these parts. Crispy pies come out of the fiery-hot, stone-lined oven in a multitude of varieties, divided simply on the menu into "red" and "white."

Rin's Thai

D3 **Thai**

139 E. Napa St. (bet. 1st & 2nd Sts.), Sonoma

Phone: 707-938-1462 Lunch & dinner Tue – Sun
Web: www.rinsthai.com
Prices: ꟸ

Warm hospitality engulfs you upon entering this quaint family-run place just off Old Sonoma Plaza. Bright yellow walls are hung with wooden carvings and colorful ceremonial masks under a high-pitched ceiling, and one of the owners is always on hand to make sure guests are handled with care.

Moderately priced dishes blend California products in nimble preparations with sauces that complement rather than dominate. Be sure to try the pleasantly plump "puffys," fried wontons stuffed with chicken, onion, and potato that have been simmered in yellow curry.

Flavorful food, coupled with the intimate ambience in this charming Victorian cottage make for an ideal first date; the place is sure to linger in your memory, even if the relationship does not.

Risibisi

Italian

B3

154 Petaluma Blvd. N. (bet. Washington St. & Western Ave.), Petaluma

Phone: 707-766-7600 Lunch Mon – Sat
Web: www.risibisirestaurant.com Dinner nightly
Prices: $$

The restaurant's namesake *risi e bisi*, a classic Venetian rice dish, changes daily and represents the deliciously rustic fare from a kitchen that never seems to miss a beat. Northern Italian recipes are interpreted with California freshness in the likes of Tuscan *ribollita* soup with white beans, chard, and Caggiano sausage; and moist, pan-roasted Fulton Farms chicken with mushrooms and four-cheese polenta.

The room is warm with exposed brick, burlap-like curtains, and stressed wood paneling, while colorful wooden chairs suspend whimsically from the ceiling. A small bar topped with alabaster sits beneath snowball-like fixtures in the back. Soothing eclectic music complements the colorful abstract paintings that line the sunny-hued walls.

Rosso

Pizza

B2

53 Montgomery Dr. (at 3rd St.), Santa Rosa

Phone: 707-544-3221 Lunch & dinner daily
Web: www.pizzeriarosso.com
Prices: $$

Fans of soccer and thin-crust pizza, rejoice: the flat-screen TV over Rosso's bar is broadcasting a match, and pizzas are emerging from the wood-burning oven. Since Rosso supports local farms and sustainable agriculture, blistered-crust pies are crowned with ingredients sourced within 100 miles, whenever possible.

Pizzas come with red or white bases, and range from the red "Goomba" topped with hand-crafted meatballs and spaghetti, to the white "Funghi" of Taleggio and fontina cheeses, local mushrooms beneath shaved fresh artichokes, and thyme. Complete your meal with a selection from their respectable list of international wines.

Reservations are only accepted for six or more, so be prepared to learn about European "football" as you wait.

Santé ✿

C3 **Californian** XXX

100 Boyes Blvd. (at Hwy. 12), Sonoma

Phone: 707-939-2415 Lunch & dinner daily
Web: www.fairmont.com/sonoma
Prices: $$$

Fairmont Sonoma Mission Inn & Spa

Disregard the somewhat industrial environs and veer off toward the Fairmont Sonoma Mission Inn & Spa, a classic pink stucco resort with sprawling manicured grounds. Pass through the lobby to Santé, a rotunda dining room with plentiful windows and a breezy vacation vibe. Rattan chairs and striped textiles lend a country chic motif, while soft yellow and earth tones illuminate the sublimely elegant yet comfortable space. Here, find mostly honeymooners and out-of-town couples enjoying the romance of the place without the stuffiness so common to fine dining. This is underscored by service so cheerful it verges on enthusiastic.

Top quality ingredients, simple concepts, and skillful preparation drive the chef's Californian menu. Boneless lamb loin is flawlessly cooked to order—its tenderness, seasoning, and flavors are paramount alongside sweet-tart roasted tomatoes and a transcendent rosemary jus; and the soufflés are models of expertise, fluffed to textbook perfection, then pierced and topped with pear anglaise.

Opt for the nine-course tasting or an array of à la carte items with no shortage of wine pairings; their leather-bound tome bursts with nearly 500 Napa and Sonoma vintages.

Scopa

Italian

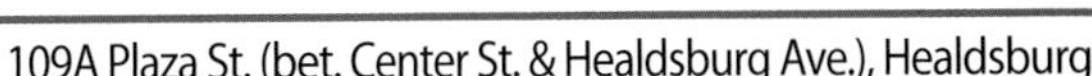

D1

109A Plaza St. (bet. Center St. & Healdsburg Ave.), Healdsburg

Phone: 707-433-5282 — Dinner Tue – Sun
Web: www.scopahealdsburg.com
Prices: $$

Named for a raucous Italian card game, Scopa packs a lot of life in a bite-size space. A genuine family affair that prides itself on hospitality, Scopa sees Chef Ari Rosen and his wife, Dawnelise, mastering the kitchen and wine program respectively. (Mom does the books; Dad helps with the baking.)

Locals feel at home in the snug setting and are often inclined to chat with their neighbors. The concrete walls are bare, but the rustic Italian menu has plenty to feast on. Small plates such as spicy meatballs in a cast iron skillet, or prosciutto-wrapped around oozing fontina encourage sharing. Handmade pastas and crusty artisan pizzas complement the local wines.

On Wednesdays, area vintners hang around to talk shop with aspiring oenophiles.

Shiso

Japanese

D3

522 Broadway (at Napa St.), Sonoma

Phone: 707-933-9331 — Dinner Tue – Sat
Web: www.shisorestaurant.com
Prices: $$

Named for the aromatic Japanese herb, Shiso arrays itself in minimal fashion with bamboo floors, lime-green tones, and round white paper lanterns that hang like moons down the center of the long room.

The well-thought-out menu offers high-quality sushi and a whole lot more. The kitchen crew's skill comes to light in creative choices such as *poke nachos* with wasabi aïoli, *tobiko*, and green onions; and the unique ahi Sunkist maki roll with ahi tuna, cilantro, avocado, and orange, and topped with peanuts and sweet eel sauce. For lunch, try the softshell crab BLT if in season; this sandwich comes with wasabi mayonnaise and Japanese potato salad.

Desserts like banana mousse crêpes; flourless chocolate cake; and coffee crème brûlée take on a Western attitude.

Sugo

Italian

B3

5 Petaluma Blvd. S. (at B St.), Petaluma

Phone: 707-782-9298 Lunch & dinner Tue – Sun
Web: www.sugopetaluma.com
Prices: $$

The strip-mall location is nothing to brag about, but the unglamorous environs melt away once you enter this welcoming spot. Softened by music, candlelight, and large wood-framed mirrors, Sugo does Petaluma proud. The restaurant is set in the town's theater district, and keeps pace by screening black-and-white movies on a wall above the kitchen.

Freshly made Italian fare at reasonable prices keeps the locals—and anyone else who is lucky enough to stumble upon this place—coming back for more. Homemade goodness fills every bite of a chicken artichoke piccata, or a simple grilled salmon dressed with lemon, garlic, and wine. Pastas, panini, and thin-crust artisan pizzas are also available. Pick any glass of wine for just $5 at lunch.

Syrah

Californian

B2

205 5th St. (at Davis St.), Santa Rosa

Phone: 707-568-4002 Lunch Tue – Sat
Web: www.syrahbistro.com Dinner nightly
Prices: $$$

This bistro celebrates and cultivates a love of wine. Chef Josh Silvers and his wife, Regina, feature a carefully selected wine list that spotlights nearly 50 different labels of syrah, with a host of other French and Californian varietals.

Pair the namesake syrah with this approachable cuisine that is dictated by the season and includes ever-changing offerings from sea, lake, or stream. The balanced menu features dishes like seared Sonoma foie gras, and red wine and mushroom braised short ribs, with horseradish crème fraîche and sour cream mashed Yukon Gold potatoes. Just remember to *finis* any meal with a delicious seasonal dessert or selection of cheese plates.

On your way in or out, visit their sibling next door, a wine shop named Petite Syrah.

the girl & the fig

Californian XX

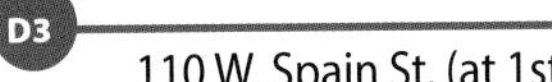

D3

110 W. Spain St. (at 1st St.), Sonoma

Phone: 707-938-3634 — Lunch & dinner daily
Web: www.thegirlandthefig.com
Prices: $$

An antique bar greets customers at this quaint restaurant, tucked inside the 1880 Sonoma Hotel. Stop here for a French aperitif before proceeding to the main dining area beyond. Wrapped in pastel hues and decorated with evocative paintings by a local artist, the room hosts a flourishing lunch business populated by a mix of locals and wine-tasting tourists.

No matter their origin, all agree that the terrific fare on the Provence-meets-California menu merits a return visit. Cheese lovers delight in sampling the selection of cow, goat, and sheep's-milk cheese; when in doubt, go for the *fromage* tower complemented by charcuterie, fruit, nuts, and house-brand condiments (available for sale). The wine list hones in on varietals from the Rhône region of France.

Underwood

International 

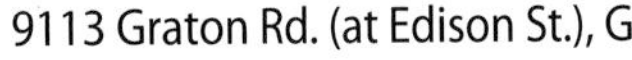

A2

9113 Graton Rd. (at Edison St.), Graton

Phone: 707-823-7023 — Lunch Tue – Sat
Web: www.underwoodgraton.com — Dinner Tue – Sun
Prices: $$

The tiny town of Graton (located about an hour north of San Francisco) centers on this block of restaurants and shops, where Underwood is found. Here, townspeople and local vintners gather over good food and wine. The nickel-topped bar lends a saloon feel, while the rest of the place conjures more of a bistro ambience. In warm weather, the patio that wraps around the side and back of the building is the preferred place to dine.

Variety is the hallmark of Underwood's menu, which travels from fresh local oysters and a selection of cheeses, to Catalan fish stew, steamed sea bass with Kaffir lime and coconut broth, or grilled New York strip steak, courtesy of Niman Ranch. Directly across the street, the Willow Wood Market Cafe is run by the same folks.

Willi's Seafood & Raw Bar

D1 — Seafood

403 Healdsburg Ave. (at North St.), Healdsburg

Phone: 707-433-9191 — Lunch & dinner daily
Web: www.starkrestaurants.com
Prices: $$

A walk through the wrought-iron archway leads diners through a quaint hedge-lined heated patio straight to Willi's entrance. This upscale tavern, a popular gathering spot just north of Healdsburg's town square, promotes sharing with its tapas-style small plates served family style. This can mean anything from a fresh ceviche made with Tasmanian salmon *crudo,* blood oranges, and black bean-chili oil, to grilled skewers of bacon-wrapped scallops paired with cilantro-pumpkin seed pesto.

At the long bar, raw oysters, clams, and other chilled seafood make a natural nosh to go with one of the creative cocktails or a glass of wine. Proprietors Mark and Terri Stark also own Willi's Wine Bar, Monti's Rotisserie, and Stark's Steakhouse, all in Santa Rosa.

Willi's Wine Bar

B2 — International

4404 Old Redwood Hwy. (at Ursuline Rd.), Santa Rosa

Phone: 707-526-3096 — Lunch Tue – Sat
Web: www.starkrestaurants.com — Dinner nightly
Prices: $$

Slow down along the Old Redwood Highway where, shrouded by a thick wall of trees, you will turn into a jammed parking lot to find Willi's Wine Bar. One of four eateries from restaurateurs Mark and Terri Stark, this obscure roadhouse is named for the first pioneering spot in Paris to serve American wines to the French. Willi's is popular among local vintners and boasts more than 40 wines by-the-glass (and half-glass). Still, international tapas mingling Asian, French, Mediterranean, and Californian flavors are the real draw, and perfect for groups looking to suit a variety of eclectic tastes.

Secure a table on the heated patio and feast upon five-spice pork belly pot stickers; foie gras "poppers" with curried chutney; and Moroccan-style lamb chops.

Willow Wood Market Cafe

Californian

A2

9020 Graton Rd. (at Edison St.), Graton

Phone: 707-823-0233
Web: www.willowwoodgraton.com
Prices: $$

Lunch daily
Dinner Mon – Sat

Good, down-home comfort food is dished up with genuine country hospitality at this tiny roadside eatery. Your first impression may be of an old-fashioned soda fountain, but it also doubles as a general store, brimming with local food items, wines, and kitschy souvenirs.

Sister to Underwood across the street, kid-friendly Willow Wood serves breakfast, lunch, and dinner, focusing on the kind of food you'd expect from a friend's mom in the good old days. Although a vast selection of salads and hot sandwiches is always at the ready, locals know to order a bowl of creamy polenta, with accompaniments such as goat cheese and house-made pesto, rock shrimp, and roasted tomatoes; or even pork tenderloin ragù. For dessert, the fresh fruit cobbler is unbeatable.

Wolf House

American

B3

13740 Arnold Dr. (near London Ranch Rd.), Glen Ellen

Phone: 707-996-4401
Web: www.jacklondonlodge.com
Prices: $$

Lunch & dinner daily

Adjoining the Jack London Lodge, Wolf House restaurant is named for the mansion of lava boulders and redwood logs that author Jack London and his wife began building in the hills above Glenn Ellen in 1911 (you can visit the ruins of the house, which burned in 1913, at nearby Jack London State Historic Park).

Service is improving, but the quality of the food makes up for any unintended gaffs. Homey main dishes such as a smoke-house pork chop with Coca-Cola yams and apples sautéed in brandy; English-style fish and chips; and house-made country meatloaf served with warm potato salad leave no doubt as to the skill in the kitchen.

The windows overlook serene tree-lined Sonoma Creek, and the outdoor patio accommodates diners as weather permits.

zazu

Californian XX

B2

3535 Guerneville Rd. (at Willowside Rd.), Santa Rosa

Phone: 707-523-4814 — Dinner Wed – Sun
Web: www.zazurestaurant.com
Prices: $$

This quaint little red roadhouse outside Santa Rosa may seem out of the way but is well worth the trip to sample Californian cuisine that comes straight from farm to table. A successful duo both in and out of the kitchen, Chefs/owners John Stewart and Duskie Edwards funnel their passion into every rustic dish. They harvest a wealth of fruits and vegetables from the organic garden behind the restaurant, and go hog-wild making their own sausages, bacon, and *salumi*. A select network of other purveyors fills in any voids with sustainably-raised meats for the Rincon Valley "sloppy goat" sliders or Southern fried Cloverdale rabbit.

Here, the staff's friendliness is genuine, the narrow room is softly illuminated by boat lights, and a good meal is guaranteed.

Zin

American 

D1

344 Center St. (at North St.), Healdsburg

Phone: 707-473-0946 — Lunch Mon – Fri
Web: www.zinrestaurant.com — Dinner nightly
Prices: $$

Winter, spring, summer, and fall each lend their bounty to the eclectic, seasonal cuisine at this Healdsburg staple, located one block north of the town square. Co-owners Jeff Mall and Scott Silva are both sons of farmers, and their pastoral upbringing shines forth in the kitchen's fresh twists on American classics, featuring produce often grown in the restaurant's own organic garden. A different Blue Plate special marks each day of the week and celebrates Americana with dishes such as chicken 'n dumplings; Yankee pot roast; or spaghetti and meatballs.

True to the restaurant's name, the wine list focuses on the best local examples of the zinfandel varietal, a grape that thrives in the soil of the surrounding Dry Creek Valley.

Where to Stay

Stanyan Park

A1

750 Stanyan St. (at Waller St.)

Phone: 415-751-1000
Web: www.stanyanpark.com
Prices: $$

30 Rooms

6 Suites

Stanyan Park Hotel

Stanyan Park's handsome three-story Queen Anne-style turret marks the corner of Stanyan and Waller streets, overlooking Golden Gate Park to the west and Haight-Ashbury to the east.

Inside, all (smoke-free) rooms and suites are quietly decorated in conventional Victorian style, and some even have glorious vistas of the park. Families and longer-term guests will appreciate the spacious suites (up to 900 square feet), appropriately equipped with a comfortable living room, full kitchen, a separate dining room, and two separate bedrooms. Free wireless Internet access throughout the property as well as phones with voice mail provide modern convenience in this historic atmosphere. The hotel's staff serves up a warm welcome, along with a complimentary breakfast and afternoon tea daily.

With Golden Gate Park at its front door, the Stanyan provides wonderful access to all of the park's cultural and natural attractions. Visitors to nearby hospitals and the University of San Francisco will find this hotel particularly convenient. While hardly hip, the Stanyan affords a comfortable stay at a reasonable price.

Inn at the Opera

333 Fulton St. (at Franklin St.)

Phone: 415-863-8400 or 800-325-2708
Web: www.shellhospitality.com
Prices: $$

30 Rooms

18 Suites

Inn at the Opera

At the heart of San Francisco's arts district, within a couple of blocks of the Opera House, Symphony Hall, and the San Francisco Ballet, this small hotel has been popular with musicians, stage performers, and audience members alike since 1927. Its 48 guestrooms are plain in their old-fashioned styling and furnishings, and they are on the small side. They do include microwaves, wet bars, small refrigerators, CD players, and bathrobes. The Ballet Studio, Concerto, and Symphony suites offer lounge or living room areas, bigger bathrooms, and kitchenettes. Ovation at the Opera, the hotel's fine-dining restaurant, puts up traditional French cuisine nightly, and a continental breakfast buffet comes gratis with your room.

The Inn at the Opera is also convenient to business and government offices in the Civic Center, while just a stone's throw away, funky Hayes Street is a good place to dine or shop. Boutiques sell unique glassware, pottery, and other crafts; eclectic restaurants and cafés provide a variety of lunch and nightlife options.

Phoenix

601 Eddy St. (at Larkin St.)

Phone: 415-776-1380 or 800-248-9466
Web: www.thephoenixhotel.com
Prices: **$$**

41 Rooms

3 Suites

Joie de Vivre Hospitality

Hip and vibrant, the Phoenix bills itself as the city's "rock and roll hotel," and indeed it is popular with entertainers in the industry as well as a cool young clientele. The building retains its 1956 motel atmosphere, though updated with high-volume color and styling. Once inside, guests will feel miles away from the seedy Tenderloin district that surrounds the hotel.

The 41 guestrooms are done up in tropical bungalow décor, aglow in bright hues, bamboo furnishings, and works by local artists. Though the rooms are ample in size, the bathrooms can be tiny (renovated bathrooms are larger). Three modern one-bedroom suites are also available. In true motel style, the rooms face—and open onto—a lushly planted courtyard where funky sculptures, Indonesian-style lounging areas, and a heated swimming pool that is itself a work of art (check out the underwater mural) offer a boisterous oasis for schmoozing or sunning.

Amenities include free parking and hotel-wide wireless Internet access. Nearby clubs and concert halls offer guests a variety of nightlife choices, from cutting-edge to classical.

Adagio

550 Geary St. (bet. Jones & Taylor Sts.)

Phone: 415-775-5000 or 800-228-8830
Web: www.thehoteladagio.com
Prices: $$$

169 Rooms

2 Suites

Joie de Vivre Hospitality

Catering to the Internet-café set, the Adagio displays a modern minimalist décor that appeals to young travelers from the U.S. and abroad. The impressive Spanish Colonial Revival structure was built in 1929 as the El Cortez, and knew several different names and owners before it was refurbished and reopened in 2003 by the Joie de Vivre Hospitality Group (whose properties include the Carlton, Hotel Kabuki, and the Hotel Vitale among others). Whether here for business or leisure, the tasteful Adagio is ideally situated in the heart of Union Square, and is perfect for shopping, dining, and exploring.

Rooms are dressed in a contemporary and sober style with earthy tones and clean lines; many of the rooms have city views. All guests will appreciate the Egyptian cotton linens, and double-paned windows to screen out the street noise. On the Executive Level, rooms boast downtown views, Frette bathrobes, hookups for iPod/MP3 players, and DVD libraries. You won't need to miss your workout here; the on-site fitness center offers Cybex equipment.

Bijou

111 Mason St. (at Eddy St.)

Phone: 415-771-1200 or 800-771-1022
Web: www.hotelbijou.com
Prices: $

65 Rooms

Joie de Vivre Hospitality

Quaint and low-key in the European tradition, the Bijou lies between Union Square and the Tenderloin, and offers good value for its convenient location. In this 1911 hotel, a theater theme and art deco-inspired décor recall the golden years of the silver screen. To illustrate this, each of the 65 rooms is named for a film that was shot in San Francisco.

Rich tones of burgundy, green, and sunny yellow color the well-maintained rooms, which are decorated with still photographs depicting their individual movie motif. Windows are not soundproofed, so if it's absolute quiet you're after, you'll have to sacrifice a street view in a front room for accommodations on the back side of the five-story building (earplugs are provided in all rooms). For security, front doors are locked at 8:00 P.M. each night; guests must show their hotel key card to get in after that time.

Amenities include complimentary wireless Internet access throughout the property, and breakfast pastries, coffee, and tea. Perhaps the best amenity of all here is the nightly double feature. These movies are screened off the lobby in a small theater decked out with vintage, folding velvet-covered seats.

Clift

495 Geary St. (at Taylor St.)

Phone: 415-775-4700 or 800-697-1791
Web: www.clifthotel.com
Prices: **$$$**

338 Rooms

25 Suites

Clift/Morgans Hotel Group

Dark meets light, antique goes modern, and eccentric cajoles conservative at this high-style hostelry. Built in 1913 and reconceived for the 21st century by Philippe Starck, the Clift surprises at every turn. Dramatic lighting, soaring ceilings, a cacophony of textures, and eclectic furnishings dress the public areas in a sleek elegance that takes equal cues from Surrealism, art deco, and a style uniquely Californian. The legendary Redwood Room, with its original 1933 redwood paneling and huge bar (said to be carved from one tree) may be the ne plus ultra, especially as reinterpreted during the renovation.

By contrast, the guestrooms are swathed in quiet tones of foggy gray, beige, and lavender. Acrylic orange nightstands and wooden wheelbarrow armchairs add whimsy to the minimalist sophistication. Standard rooms measure only 260 square feet, but more expensive chambers are larger, with deluxe one-bedroom suites topping out at 925 square feet. All of them feature luxuries from Egyptian cotton 400-thread-count sheets to DVD and CD players with an in-room disc library.

Off the lobby, glamorous Asia de Cuba serves tasty fusion fare.

Diva

440 Geary St. (bet. Mason & Taylor Sts.)

Phone: 415-885-0200 or 800-553-1900
Web: www.hoteldiva.com
Prices: $$

116 Rooms

2 Suites

Rien van Rijthoven

Steps from Union Square and across from the Curran and the American Conservatory theaters, Diva preserves its edgy Euro-tech vibe. Charcoal-gray, taupe and black lend a hip vibe to the guest rooms, which have been recently enhanced with new bedding and lighting. The ultra-contemporary look uses cobalt-blue carpets, streamlined furnishings, contemporary art, and stainless-steel accents to make its point. Upgrade your reservation to the Salon floor, and you'll enjoy amenities such as an in-room refrigerator and a complimentary continental breakfast. The Diva has no restaurant, but get your java fix next door at Starbucks.

Kids will go for the Little Diva suites, tailored to the young traveler with pop-art colors, bunk beds, kid-friendly movies, and a karaoke machine for budding American Idols. Parents get the connecting room, so they have their own space, but can easily keep track of the younger members of the family.

Even the meeting room and the Internet lounges are custom designed. The former features a golden onxy and steel underlit buffet, while the lounges credit the likes of skateboarder Pete Colpitts among their designers.

Galleria Park

191 Sutter St. (at Kearny St.)

Phone: 415-781-3060 or 800-792-9639
Web: www.jdvhotels.com
Prices: $$

169 Rooms

8 Suites

Joie de Vivre Hospitality

Both business and leisure travelers will find a quiet refuge at this 177-room property, which premiered in 1911 as the Sutter Hotel. Taken over by the Joie de Vivre group in 2005, the Galleria Park sits in the heart of the FiDi, a short walk from Union Square and all its fabulous shops.

A complete renovation in 2007 outfitted the lobby in glamorous art deco style, complete with an eclectic collection of furniture and artwork from San Francisco's Lost Art Salon. Likewise, guestrooms have been upgraded with comfy pillowtop mattresses, flat-screen TVs, and Frette linens. Shades of chartreuse and plum make a stylish color combination, especially when balanced by clean white trim.

A unique feature, an outdoor jogging track is located on the third floor. Here, you'll also find a landscaped terrace, with benches for relaxing. If jogging's not your thing, you can work out in the little fitness room. The hotel's GPS (Galleria Park Suggests) program offers set packages that provide exclusive access and behind-the-scenes scoops to sights around the city. A free 2-hour guided walking tour of the Financial District is available free of charge to all guests.

The Inn at Union Square

440 Post St. (bet. Mason & Powell Sts.)

Phone: 415-397-3510 or 800-288-4346
Web: www.unionsquare.com
Prices: $$

24 Rooms

6 Suites

The Inn at Union Square

Perfectly located just steps away from Union Square, this laid-back inn is a relatively inexpensive hotel option in the high-rent heart of the city. Its 24 adequately sized rooms, decked out in regal gold and red, all come equipped with down pillows and duvets, flat-screen TVs, a work desk, and free wireless Internet access. Compact bathrooms are well-equipped and stocked with Aveda products. In the two-room penthouse suite you'll find extra luxuries such as a wet bar, a wood-burning fireplace, and a whirlpool tub.

Each floor has a small sitting area where coffee, tea, and fresh fruit are available throughout the day. Small fireplaces in these nooks are often lit with crackling fires in the evening, when wine and hors d'oeuvres are offered on the house. Each morning, a complimentary continental breakfast (including cereal, pastries, fruit, yogurt, hard-boiled eggs, and toast) is set out here as well. The hotel also provides valet parking and access to a well-equipped fitness club with a heated pool.

Much more traditional than trendy, the Inn at Union Square stands out for its tranquility and prime location near some of the city's best shops and restaurants.

King George

334 Mason St. (bet. Geary & O'Farrell Sts.)

Phone: 415-781-5050 or 800-288-6005
Web: www.kinggeorge.com
Prices: $

151 Rooms

2 Suites

King George Hotel

Potted topiary trees and a prominent awning announce the entrance to this Anglophile's hideaway. Opened in 1914, the King George welcomes guests with European flair, beginning with the lobby, where warm tones of yellow, beige, and gold set off a full-size portrait of the hotel's namesake.

English hunting country may come to mind when you check into one of the 153 rooms, colored in a palette of green, gold and burgundy. All accommodations include fun and thoughtful touches like jars of candy. If the sweets aren't sustenance enough, the King George also offers 24-hour room service, catered by an off-site restaurant. Given these comforts, and the hotel's location—a block west of Union Square and convenient to the Moscone Center—rates here are a real deal.

The hotel no longer serves breakfast, but they do set out coffee and tea in the lobby each morning. A proper English tea is available on weekends in the Windsor Tea Room for parties of ten or more; reservations are required. For meals, there are many restaurant options nearby; but for drinks and appetizers, you need not venture farther than Winston's Bar and Lounge. Daily happy hour here features discounted beer and wine.

Mandarin Oriental

222 Sansome St. (bet. California & Pine Sts.)

Phone: 415-276-9888 or 800-622-0404
Web: www.mandarinoriental.com
Prices: **$$$$**

151 Rooms

7 Suites

Mandarin Oriental Hotel Group

From this superb hotel's ground-floor entry, high-speed elevators whisk guests to their aeries, located in the towers of the city's third-tallest building, between the 38th and 48th stories. Glass-enclosed sky bridges connect the two towers on each floor, offering spectacular views of the city and beyond. Guestroom views dazzle as well (binoculars are provided), from every angle, though corner rooms and those with a "bridge-to-bridge" perspective take top honors. Choose a city or bay view, and if tub-to-ceiling bathroom windows delight, reserve a Mandarin King room. Handsome Asian design elements, elegant fabrics, and warm colors lend a refined air to the recently refreshed rooms and suites; spacious marble bathrooms are perfectly equipped. All rooms are dressed with amenities including 24-hour room service, a minibar, and twice daily maid service.

Spacious and comfortable, the lobby includes a pleasant lounge area, a sushi bar, and live piano music beginning at 5:00 P.M. daily. The hotel features its own fitness center, and passes can be purchased for a nearby health club.

On the second floor, the elegant restaurant Silks, features contemporary cuisine with pan-Asian influences.

Monaco

501 Geary St. (at Taylor St.)

Phone: 415-292-0100 or 866-622-5284
Web: www.monaco-sf.com
Prices: $$$

169 Rooms

32 Suites

Fred Licht/Kimpton Hotels

You can count on the Kimpton group to deliver luxury, and the Monaco is no exception. Located in the midst of the Theater District, and just two blocks from Union Square shopping and dining, this hotel occupies a beautifully renovated 1910 beaux arts building. The lobby sets the tone for travel with a check-in desk styled like a steamer-trunk, and hand-painted ceiling frescoes depicting whimsical skyscapes of hot-air balloons and planes. On the landing of the grand staircase, a painting aptly entitled *Celestial Lady* clearly illustrates that the sky is the limit.

In the guestrooms, bright fabrics drape over canopy beds, cheery striped paper covers the walls, and Chinese-inspired furnishings add exotic flair. Flat-screen TVs come with a yoga channel, and there is no fee for the high-speed Internet access. Frette robes, in-room safes, hairdryers, irons and ironing boards, and L'Occitane bath amenities should provide everything you need; but if you forgot something, items like toothbrushes and razors are just a phone call away.

Enjoy a meal in the impressive surroundings of the art deco-style Grand Café, in the building's former ballroom.

Nikko

222 Mason St. (bet. Ellis & O'Farrell Sts.)

Phone: 415-394-1111 or 800-248-3308
Web: www.hotelnikkosf.com
Prices: **$$**

510 Rooms

22 Suites

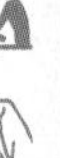

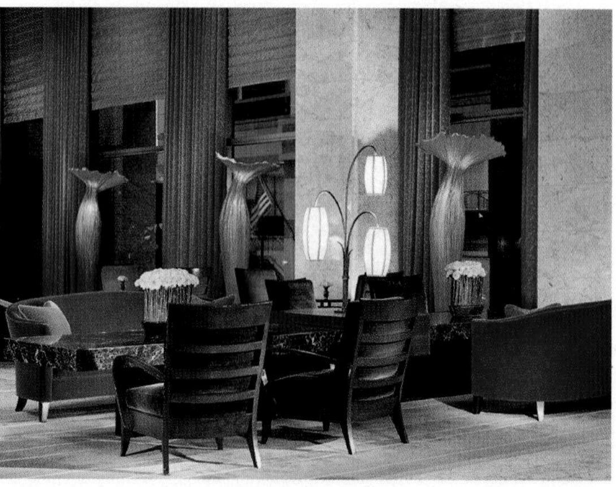

Hotel Nikko San Francisco

Though large, the Nikko offers a comfortable and convenient stay, with a choice of 12 different types of rooms and suites. At 280 square feet, the Petite queens are best for single occupancy, but may also suit two people in search of a good deal. Deluxe rooms, both king and double/doubles, occupy floors 6 through 21. The Imperial Floors (22, 23, and 24) offer added services and amenities, including restricted access and breakfast served in a private lounge. At the top end, the two-bedroom, two-bath Imperial Suite measures in at 2,635 square feet. City views are divine, especially from the higher floors. The private, aurally perfect, and sophisticated Rrazz Room theater continues to host myriad world-class entertainers such as Ashford & Simpson, Keely Smith, and the American Idols.

A lovely swimming pool, together with a fitness room and sauna, occupy the very large and bright fifth-floor atrium. For your business needs, the well-equipped business center can arrange printing, binding, faxing, translation, and secretarial services. Stop by Nikko's fine-dining restaurant, Anzu, for sushi, prime cuts of beef, and a sake martini.

Omni

500 California St. (at Montgomery St.)

Phone: 415-677-9494
Web: www.omnisanfrancisco.com
Prices: $$$$

347 Rooms

15 Suites

Omni Hotel, San Francisco

Located in the heart of the Financial District with a cable-car stop right outside, this Omni opened in 2002 in an elegantly renovated 1926 bank building. Though only the original stone and brick façade has been preserved, the spacious wood-paneled lobby, floored in rosy marble, takes its cue and its stylishness from a bygone era.

Spread over 17 stories, the 347 rooms and 15 suites follow suit. They are large and classic in style, with details to match, including Egyptian cotton sheets and well-equipped bathrooms decorated in marble and granite. Most guestrooms feature comfortable furnishings and a well-organized space. For upgraded amenities, reserve on the 16th "signature" floor, where rooms come with a Bose Wave radio and CD player, DVD player, wireless Internet, and a color copier/printer. Specialty accommodations such as Get Fit rooms (furnished with a treadmill and healthy snacks) and a Kids Fantasy Suite, where bunk beds and kids rule in the second bedroom, are also available. Bob's Steak and Chop House will draw the meat-loving guests.

Every Saturday at 10:00 A.M., a guided walking tour departs from the hotel for an overview of city history.

Rex

A2

562 Sutter St. (bet. Mason & Powell Sts.)

Phone: 415-433-4434 or 800-433-4434
Web: www.thehotelrex.com
Prices: $$

94 Rooms

Joie de Vivre Hospitality

One block off Union Square, the Rex provides a great location for a reasonable price. This member of the Joie de Vivre group styles itself after the art and literary salons rife in San Francisco in the 1920's and 30's. The lobby feels like a gentleman's study, with its dark paneling, comfortable seating, and shelves brimming with books. Quotes from various regional authors adorn the walls of the different floors as well as the hotel's cozy bistro, Café Andrée, where breakfast is served to hotel guests each morning.

In the bedrooms, gingham bedspreads and curtains lend a country feel to spaces brightened by large windows and sunny-colored walls. Pillowtop mattresses, bathrobes, CD players, and mini-refrigerators add some of the comforts of home. The hotel's business center—The Study—accomodates the needs of business travelers or lap top-less guests who may wish to check email.

Other reasons to stay here? A complimentary wine reception in the lobby bar each evening, guest access to a nearby fitness center, and even a get-oriented tour with a San Francisco Greeter—on the house.

Serrano

405 Taylor St. (at O'Farrell St.)

Phone: 415-885-2500 or 866-289-6561
Web: www.serranohotel.com
Prices: $$

217 Rooms

19 Suites

David Phelps/Kimpton Hotels

Centerpiece of this 1924 Spanish Revival building is its two-story lobby, where the majestic fireplace, beamed ceilings, wood-paneled columns, boldly patterned carpet, and leafy potted plants create a charming Old World atmosphere. It's all fun and games at the Serrano, and the games begin with the Check-In Challenge. If you can beat "the house" in a quick game of 21, you could win a free room upgrade. The fun continues once you settle in your room; you can call to order a board game from the hotel's library to be delivered to you. You can also find more board games in the lobby.

Fresh and well-maintained, rooms are adorned in sunny colors with red-and-yellow-striped drapes and Moroccan accents; leopard-print terrycloth robes add another exotic touch. If you're in the city on business, you'll appreciate the large glass-topped desk and comfy swivel chair—a perfect spot for working. There's also a 24-hour business center on-site (accessible with your room key) that keeps computers, scanners, printers, and fax machines at the ready.

And best of all for pet lovers, the Serrano—like most Kimpton properties—will welcome your four-legged friend in style.

Sir Francis Drake

B2

450 Powell St. (at Sutter St.)

Phone: 415-392-7755 or 800-795-7129
Web: www.sirfrancisdrake.com
Prices: $$$

410 Rooms

6 Suites

Kimpton Hotels & Restaurants

Named for the English explorer who landed in the Bay Area in 1579, "The Drake" enjoys a long and colorful history as one of San Francisco's landmark hostelries. When it opened in 1928, the hotel boasted such high-tech wonders as ice water on tap, an indoor golf course, and a radio in every room.

A recent $20-million restoration has put a fresh face on this dowager—now part of the Kimpton group—don't worry, the doormen retain their trademark Beefeater uniforms. Touting tons of marble, the swanky soaring lobby recalls the grandeur of a bygone era. Off the lobby, hip Bar Drake proffers cocktails with a Prohibition-era twist.

Rooms are moderately priced, given the hotel's enviable location near Union Square and the Theater District. Your accommodations will sport a sage and cream color scheme, plush carpeting, and a yoga channel on the flat-screen TV. Frosted globe overhead light fixtures are studded with gold stars—a nod to the hotel's legendary Harry Denton's Starlight Room, located on the 21st floor—where views of the city span 360 degrees. Make sure your plans include a visit to the scrumptious Scala's Bistro.

Triton

342 Grant Ave. (at Bush St.)

Phone: 415-394-0500 or 800-800-1299
Web: www.hotelrtriton.com
Prices: $$

140 Rooms

Markham Johnson/Kimpton Hotels

If you like hip and eco-friendly, head for this member of the Kimpton group. The Triton's theme—Pop Culture—jumps out at you the moment you step inside the lobby, in the form of fanciful furnishings and whimsical murals in a riot of colors. A rotating selection of work by local artists is on display in the gallery on the mezzanine.

There are no cookie-cutter-style rooms here. They come in all sizes, shapes, colors, and comfort levels, so ask for details before you book. Perhaps a standard room meets your needs; the complimentary *New York Times* will update you on world affairs as you sip your morning drink. Other features include iHome docking stations and eco-friendly bath amenities. Or maybe you prefer the panache of a Celebrity Suite, designed by the likes of comedienne Kathy Griffin or rocker Jerry Garcia. Conservation is the name of the game here, where everything is easy on the environment.

Located outside the Chinatown gate—convenient to the Financial District and Union Square—the hotel does not have its own restaurant, but Café de la Presse next door provides room service from its widely appealing French-American bistro menu.

Westin St. Francis

335 Powell St. (at Union Square)

Phone: 415-397-7000 or 866-500-0338
Web: www.westinstfrancis.com
Prices: **$$$$**

1195 Rooms

59 Suites

John Schwarzell Photography

This luxury hotel deserves its legendary status. Regally situated at the head of Union Square, the St. Francis, opened in 1904, was modeled on the grand European hotels of the period. Barely surviving the earthquake and fire in 1906, the hotel went on to build two more wings, and in 1972 a 32-story tower was added behind the main structure. Today the St. Francis remains the grand dame of West Coast hotels; visitors and residents alike rendezvous in its lobby as they have for generations.

For full effect, you may want to reserve a room in the main building, where historic materials decorate the large hallways. Rooms here are decorated in a charmingly old-fashioned Empire style, and many have good views of Union Square. More contemporary tower rooms all have bay windows for sweeping city and bay vistas. Westin's signature Heavenly Bed and Heavenly Bath come in every room. Between the spa and the acclaimed Michael Mina restaurant, you won't want for much here.

The stately 10,700 square-foot Grand Ballroom lends itself equally to society galas and business functions.

Drisco

B3

2901 Pacific Ave. (at Broderick St.)

Phone: 415-346-2880 or 800-634-7277
Web: www.hoteldrisco.com
Prices: **$$**

29 Rooms

19 Suites

Cesar Rubio

Comfortably at home in tony Pacific Heights, this 1903 hotel offers elegant accommodations surrounded by beautiful residences and quiet streets, removed from the bustle of downtown. Well dressed throughout in shades of beige accented by rich wood tones and mellow colors, this member of the Joie de Vivre group possesses a charming atmosphere that permeates each of its rooms. Accommodations, including 19 suites, vary in size but are consistently graceful in style, and well-furnished with special attention and care to ensure the guests' every comfort. Some rooms offer pleasing city views; others overlook the building's tiny courtyard.

Guests can enjoy a complimentary breakfast buffet in the sunny first-floor dining room, and coffee, tea and newspapers are available 24 hours in the hotel's lovely lobby. Each evening, wine and hors d'oeuvres come compliments of the house. An on-site workout room and complimentary access to the Presidio YMCA will appeal to fitness fiends, while the small business center provides basic services for business travelers.

Kabuki

D4

1625 Post St. (at Laguna St.)

Phone: 415-922-3200 or 800-533-4567
Web: www.hotelkabuki.com
Prices: $$

218 Rooms

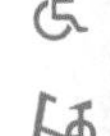

Cesar Rubio

The heart of Japantown beats right outside the door of this reasonably priced hotel. Formerly the Miyako, the property was purchased and renovated in 2007 by the Joie de Vivre group. The result appeals with a design that blends Asian and Western elements, attracting guests from both sides of the Pacific.

Clean and spacious, rooms are appointed with attractive contemporary furniture, including new Serta mattresses. Corner rooms have sliding-glass doors that open onto a private balcony.

Although this hotel lacks some of the little luxuries you'll find in more expensive properties, the Kabuki offers unique features such as a welcome tea service delivered to your room after check-in, and complimentary sake and wine set out in the lobby weekdays between 5:00 P.M. and 6:00 P.M. In keeping with Japanese tradition, guests have access to the nearby Kabuki Springs and Spa communal baths. Or you can reserve ahead with a bath butler (call 72 hours in advance), who will prepare a comforting bath for you in the deep soaking tub in your room. Afterwards, stop in at O Izakaya Lounge downstairs for a glass of sake and small plates, Japanese-style.

Laurel Inn

444 Presidio Ave. (at California St.)

Phone: 415-567-8467 or 800-552-8735
Web: www.thelaurelinn.com
Prices: $$

49 Rooms

Joie de Vivre Hospitality

The Laurel Inn, built in 1963, embraces its mid-century pedigree with gusto and good taste. Bold strokes of color enliven the interior, particularly in the artist-inspired area rugs that decorate the rooms and public spaces. Furnishings throughout are sleek and not fussy. Large windows grace the newly renovated guestrooms, which include 18 larger units with kitchenettes, much in demand by guests planning extended stays. Rooms on the back side of the hotel feature pleasant city panoramas and are quieter than those facing the street, though all are efficiently soundproofed.

Guests traveling with cars and pets will appreciate the free indoor parking and pet-friendliness of the Laurel. A small continental breakfast is served in the attractive lobby each morning. If you're content not to be in the center of downtown action, the Laurel Inn, located in residential Pacific Heights, offers good value.

Unwind at the end of the day with an expertly-prepared libation in the sexy, yet elegant, Swank Cocktail Club—ideal for a cozy tète-à-tète.

Majestic

1500 Sutter St. (at Gough St.)

Phone: 415-441-1100
Web: www.thehotelmajestic.com
Prices: $

49 Rooms

9 Suites

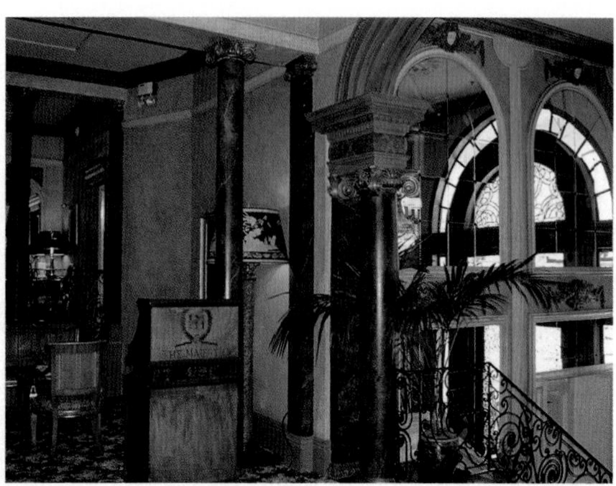

MICHELIN

The Edwardian elegance of the Majestic dates from 1902, when it was built as a private residence. Already a hotel by 1906 when the earthquake struck, the building survived to become San Francisco's oldest continuously operated hotel. Lavish public areas, set about with French and English antiques, marble columns and wrought-iron balustrades, recall a bygone era of domestic luxury which extends to the 58 rooms and suites.

Though the standard rooms are on the small side, the suites are large, pleasant and reasonably priced for their size. Sumptuously swagged canopy beds furnish each room, and bathrooms are completely equipped and beautifully tiled and marbled. All rooms come with Turkish robes and turndown service featuring cookies before bed. Though old-fashioned in style, the hotel offers modern electronic amenities, including wireless high-speed Internet and a laptop computer for guests' use.

A complimentary continental breakfast and afternoon wine and hors d'oeuvres are served in the dining room. Check out the butterfly collection in the Avalon Room off the lobby. Famished at the end of the day? There are floods of delish dining options only a stone's throw away.

Carlton

1075 Sutter St. (bet. Hyde & Larkin Sts.)

Phone: 415-673-0242 or 800-922-7586
Web: www.hotelcarltonsf.com
Prices: $

161
Rooms

Joie de Vivre Hospitality

The unassuming exterior of this 1927 hotel belies the charming and cheerful atmosphere that awaits inside. Renovated and reopened in 2004, the Carlton now features a globetrotting theme realized through furniture, photographs and objects from around the world. The eclectic result is colorful and eccentric though not overdone. Rooms are neat and tasteful, decorated in soft colors splashed with exotic accents, and the higher of the building's seven stories afford unobstructed views of the city. Though they lack air-conditioning, each room features a large ceiling fan for those rare hot days.

Guests can look forward to a nightly wine reception offered by the hotel, and business travelers will welcome the complimentary rides to the Financial District. Saha, the hotel's restaurant, serves contemporary Middle Eastern cuisine at breakfast and dinner.

Hotel employees—an international team that speaks more than a dozen languages—are singularly dedicated to the comfort of their guests. The convenience, friendliness and style of this hotel make it a good value for the money.

The Fairmont

B2

950 Mason St. (at California St.)

Phone: 415-772-5000 or 866-540-4491
Web: www.fairmont.com
Prices: $$$

528 Rooms

63 Suites

Spa

The Fairmont San Francisco

Flagship of the Fairmont hotel group, this Gilded Age palace overlooks the city from atop Nob Hill as it has since construction began in 1902, despite earthquake and fire. Recently returned to their past glory, the hotel's public spaces sparkle with turn-of-the-century splendor. The lobby alone is worth a visit, especially to see the restoration of architect Julia Morgan's original Corinthian columns, alabaster walls, marble floors, and vaulted ceilings trimmed in gold. Guests can soak up the atmosphere over a meal in Laurel Court, the hotel's original dining room. Or, for a different kind of nostalgia, visit the Tonga Room, a tiki hideaway, complete with thatched umbrellas and live music.

Rooms are dressed in pale yellows, refined fabrics, and dark wood furnishings. With their 14-foot vaulted ceilings, those around the exterior of the original seven-story structure are particularly spacious and boast nice views of city and bay. For panoramic skyline views, choose a room in the 23-story tower, opened in 1961. All guestrooms include extra-long mattresses and have been updated with modern amenities for the business traveler.

Nob Hill

835 Hyde St. (bet. Sutter & Bush Sts.)

Phone: 415-885-2987 or 877-662-4455
Web: www.nobhillhotel.com
Prices: $$

52 Rooms

Nob Hill Hotel

Decorated in a plush crush of Victoriana, the elegant Nob Hill Hotel combines stained glass, velvety fabrics, and ornate furnishings to create a cozy turn-of-the-century hideaway. The hotel was built in 1906 and restored in 1998; its 52 rooms are generally small but nicely kept and well appointed with marble baths, brass bedsteads, and richly colored wallpapers. Each is romantic and intimate, and some rooms, including two penthouse suites, have beautiful private terraces. Several suites feature whirlpool tubs. Small refrigerators and microwaves are provided, along with CD players, hairdryers, and coffeemakers—not to mention the reassuring teddy bear on each bed. The atmosphere is hushed and the rooms are quiet, whether they face the courtyard or the street. As each room is quite different, the hotel recommends that you book by phone to ensure the perfect match.

Rates include an evening wine tasting, access to a 24-hour fitness center, and a continental breakfast. Outside, all the attractions of Nob Hill await, from historic buildings to glorious views.

Orchard Garden

466 Bush St. (at Grant Ave.)

Phone: 415-399-9807 or 888-717-2881
Web: www.theorchardgardenhotel.com
Prices: $$$

86 Rooms

Orchard Garden Hotel

You can feel good about staying here in more ways than one. California's first hotel built to U.S. Green Building Council standards, Orchard Garden is environmentally friendly through and through, from the construction materials and modern, light wood furnishings to the carpets and linens. The 86-room, smoke-free hotel uses organic cleaning products, recycled paper, and an innovative key-card system that reduces energy consumption by 20 percent.

The environment is amenable as well as sustainable. Soft earth tones (a lot of green, naturally) create a serene atmosphere; the well-insulated design keeps even the street-side rooms quiet. Those eco-sheets are soft Egyptian cotton, and Aveda organic toiletries stock the bathroom. Natural and high-tech comforts—including WiFi Internet access and high-definition LCD TV with DVD—co-exist peacefully here.

The hotel restaurant, Roots, on occassion will offer a complimentary breakfast buffet. It also serves lunch and dinner using local organic produce and natural meats, and features an American Farmstead Cheese Cart.

Casually calming, comfortable, and convenient (only a few blocks from Union Square), Orchard Garden makes it easy to be green.

The Ritz-Carlton

600 Stockton St. (bet. California & Pine Sts.)

Phone: 415-296-7465 or 800-241-3333
Web: www.ritzcarlton.com
Prices: $$$$

276 Rooms

60 Suites

The Ritz-Carlton, San Francisco

This imposing neoclassical building began life as an insurance company in 1909, and since 1991 it has housed San Francisco's finest hotel. For pure class, luxury, and service, the Ritz-Carlton reigns supreme. A multimillion-dollar renovation in 2006 enhanced its cachet with upgraded technology, guestroom amenities, and new personal services for travelers with children, pets, and computers.

Decorated with a rich collection of 18th and 19th century antiques and paintings, the hotel's lobby includes a gracious lounge that serves afternoon tea, cocktails, and sushi. Due to these uncertain times, the hotel has discontinued the Champagne Cal-Med alfresco brunch on the Terrace. But don't fret—the same is now offered indoors at The Dining Room. For elegant suppers, The Dining Room also serves contemporary cuisine in a lavish setting.

Each of the guestrooms has been carefully restored with European charm and luxury in mind. All include wireless Internet access and high-definition, flat-screen TVs; marble bathrooms come with rain showerheads, double sinks, and separate water closets. On the upper floors, the amenities of the Club Level provide unexcelled ambience, privacy, and pampering.

Argonaut

495 Jefferson St. (at Hyde St.)

Phone: 415-563-0800 or 866-415-0704
Web: www.argonauthotel.com
Prices: $$

239 Rooms

13 Suites

David Phelps/Kimpton Hotels

There's no doubt about which hotel has the most character in this part of the city. Perfectly located near Ghirardelli Square, the cable-car turnaround and Fisherman's Wharf, the Argonaut occupies a 1907 waterfront warehouse at The Cannery. It shares the space with the Maritime National Historic Park Visitor Center.

There's no doubt, either, about the theme of this pet-friendly hotel: its solid, primary colors, maritime artifacts, and nautical design motifs give it away, beginning in the lobby where a lovely celestial clock hangs over the fireplace. Exposed brick walls and massive wooden beams and columns also reflect the hardworking heritage of the historic building.

Rooms and suites remain solidly in character: bold stripes and stars decorate walls, furniture, and carpets. The rooms are well soundproofed and have all the modern amenities. Some of them offer views of the bay and Alcatraz. A Kimpton group signature, six "Tall Rooms" come with extra-long beds and raised showerheads for tall guests. Room service can be ordered from the Blue Mermaid Chowder House, adjacent to the hotel.

Bohème

444 Columbus Ave. (bet. Green & Vallejo Sts.)

Phone: 415-433-9111
Web: www.hotelboheme.com
Prices: $$

15 Rooms

Hotel Bohème

This quaint boutique hotel at the foot of Telegraph Hill in the heart of North Beach takes its inspiration from the bohemian Beat Generation of the 1950s. And well it might, as poet Allen Ginsberg once slept here. Next door you'll find Vesuvio Café and City Lights Bookstore (founded by poet Lawrence Ferlinghetti), two hangouts still haunted by Beat spirits.

Built in the 1880s and rebuilt after the earthquake, the Victorian structure has been nicely adapted to its current role. Its 15 rooms reflect a certain 1950s countercultural style in their bright colors and eclectic furniture; they are small, romantic, and meticulously clean. Each has a private bath, and all the rooms offer wireless Internet access. About half face Columbus Avenue, which makes for good people-watching, but not much peace and quiet. The surrounding neighborhood is great for strolling and sipping coffee; from here you can walk up Telegraph Hill to Coit Tower and explore up and down the Filbert Steps.

The courteous staff at the Hotel Bohème is glad to help make reservations for restaurants, theater performances, and tours.

Four Seasons

757 Market St. (bet. Third & Fourth Sts.)

Phone: 415-633-3000 or 800-819-5053
Web: www.fourseasons.com
Prices: $$$$

231 Rooms

46 Suites

Mary Nichols/Four Seasons San Francisco

A testament to the burgeoning neighborhood south of Market Street, this sophisticated, modern luxury hotel caters to a loyal crowd of business travelers. Occupying the first 12 stories of a residential highrise in the Yerba Buena Arts District, the Four Seasons is convenient to Union Square, the Moscone Convention Center, and the San Francisco Museum of Modern Art.

The lobby, on the fifth floor, balances modern and classic design, blending golden wood tones with artwork for a quiet, contemporary effect. Art is everywhere, as the hotel showcases throughout its public spaces a considerable collection of paintings, sculpture, and ceramics by Bay Area artists.

Rooms, as they ascend from the 6th to the 17th floor, offer more and more stunning views of the city. Restful tones and residential touches decorate each one, the smallest of which measures a generous 450 square feet. All rooms feature large baths with a deep soaking tub and separate shower; and the large windows ensure that each gets plenty of natural light. Guests have complimentary access to the on-site Sports Club/L.A., with its junior Olympic-size pool and full-service spa.

InterContinental

888 Howard St. (at 5th St.)

Phone: 415-616-6500 or 888-811-4273
Web: www.intercontinentalsanfrancisco.com
Prices: $$$

536 Rooms

14 Suites

Rien van Rijthoven/InterContinental Hotels

San Francisco's newest InterContinental hotel rose on the scene in February 2008, piercing the SoMa skyline with its 32-story blue-glass tower. The eye-catching landmark on the corner of Howard and Fifth streets sits adjacent to the Moscone Convention Center, and just a few blocks away from Market Street—equally well situated for those visiting for business or pleasure.

Contemporary in style and voluminous in size, the hotel offers friendly, personalized service that helps make up for its corporate feel—though abundant meeting facilities do draw a large business crowd to the property.

In the rooms, colors are neutral, so as not to distract from luxuries such as feather pillows and comforters, wood paneled headboards, flat-screen TVs, and large windows for surveying the downtown landscape. Standard bathrooms are on the small side, yet well-equipped with marble countertops, Floris bath products, and fluffy towels and bathrobes.

An indoor lap pool and state-of-the-art gym are located on the 6th floor, next to the 10-room I-Spa, with a lovely terrace that wraps around the building. Off the lobby, Luce creates contemporary tastes using California products.

The Mosser

B2

54 4th St. (bet. Market & Mission Sts.)

Phone: 415-986-4400 or 800-227-3804
Web: www.themosser.com
Prices: $

166 Rooms

The Mosser

The Mosser successfully overlays a fresh modern look against the backdrop of its historic building, originally opened as a hotel in 1913. It offers a good price in a great location accessible to destinations north and south of Market Street. Best of all, the helpful, friendly staff really sets this economical property apart.

Though they are small and lack a view, the rooms on the courtyard are quiet (all have double-pane windows) and less expensive. The clean, crisp décor includes platform beds, white-washed walls, and geometrically patterned carpet for a comfortable Danish-modern effect. Some rooms feature lovely bay windows with window seats that overlook the street.

For a particular bargain, 54 of the hotel's 166 rooms share well-kept bathrooms—no more than three rooms per bath—though sinks, vanities, and bath amenities furnish all the rooms. In addition to great web rates, the hotel also offers special weekly rates, a far better value for longer stays.

The Mosser even has its own professional recording studio, a rarely found hotel amenity.

Palace

C2

2 New Montgomery St. (at Market St.)

Phone: 415-512-1111 or 888-625-5144
Web: www.sfpalace.com
Prices: $$$$

519 Rooms

34 Suites

Palace Hotel, San Francisco

Another of downtown San Francisco's grand dames, the Palace symbolized the city's meteoric rise from boomtown to world-class metropolis when it opened in 1875. Today, through earthquake, fire, and 130-plus years, the hotel withstands the test of time. Its centerpiece is the sumptuous Garden Court, beautifully restored to its 1909 condition. Here, guests can have breakfast, lunch, or brunch under a stunning canopy of intricately leaded art glass hung with Austrian glass chandeliers. In a different mood, the Pied Piper Bar displays a mural painted especially for the Palace by American illustrator Maxfield Parrish in 1909.

The rooms are more traditional in style and are done up in cheerful sunny tones with broad accents of color. The bathrooms are small and a bit out-of-date, but with 14-foot ceilings and windows that open, the rooms are spacious and airy. For business travelers, work areas are ample and well lit, with a laptop safe and dual phone lines in every room.

The fitness center features a beautiful skylit lap pool, workout room, and spa services.

Palomar

B2

12 4th St. (at Market St.)

Phone: 415-348-1111 or 866-373-4941
Web: www.hotelpalomar-sf.com
Prices: **$$$**

179 Rooms

16 Suites

David Phelps/Kimpton Hotels

Edgy, urban, artful, tranquil: this downtown addition to the Kimpton family of properties offers just enough of each in a great location. At home on the 5th through the 8th floors of a landmark 1908 building, Hotel Palomar comprises 195 guestrooms, including 16 one- and two-bedroom suites.

Some of the rooms overlook Fourth and Market streets (they are well soundproofed) while the rest face the interior courtyard. Rooms are quite spacious and strike a good balance between contemporary style and restful atmosphere, though every one sports a sassy leopard-print carpet. Rooms provide Aveda bath amenities, two plush robes, wireless Internet access, CD and DVD players, and an expanded work area. Suites and luxury rooms feature Fuji spa tubs and turreted windows with circular seating areas.

Guests can enjoy the on-site fitness center 24 hours a day, and complimentary yoga baskets are available upon request. Morning coffee is served in the lobby, and the stylish Fifth Floor restaurant—acclaimed for its French-Gascon cuisine—is open for breakfast and dinner. The adjacent bar hops at happy hour.

St. Regis

C2

125 3rd St. (at Mission St.)

Phone: 415-284-4000 or 877-787-3447
Web: www.stregis.com
Prices: $$$$

214 Rooms

46 Suites

Joe Fletcher Photography

The historic St. Regis' first incarnation in the City by the Bay is anything but stuffy. Occupying the first 20 floors of a handsome new highrise designed by Skidmore, Owings, and Merrill, the new hotel epitomizes the look and feel of classic contemporary. The oxymoron works, and it doesn't stop there. The complex also includes condos on the upper floors, a 1907 building, and the Museum of the African Diaspora. Next door is the San Francisco Museum of Modern Art.

Throughout, the hotel cultivates neutral colors, from the striated Zebrano wood of the lobby to the rich cocoa and foggy gray tones of the guestrooms. A striking 16-foot open fireplace greets guests as they enter the lobby, which also features a sleek lounge area. Cool, comfortable, spacious rooms, and suites overlook Yerba Buena Park, or have expansive city views. On the ground level, Ame serves Hiro Sone's modern fusion cuisine.

Plasma-screen TVs are standard, and a touchscreen on the nightstand controls the room's temperature, curtains, and lighting. Those familiar with St. Regis service will be cheered to know that the signature personal butlers are alive and well here.

Vitale

D1

8 Mission St. (bet. Steuart St. & The Embarcadero)

Phone: 415-278-3700 or 888-890-8688
Web: www.hotelvitale.com
Prices: $$$

180 Rooms

20 Suites

Spa

Cesar Rubio

Flagship of the Joie de Vivre group, the Vitale occupies a prime piece of real estate across the street from the Ferry Building—its marketplace teeming with gourmet delights—and the elegant Embarcadero promenade. All the attractions and eateries of Market Street, Rincon Hill, and the Financial District are easily accessible from the hotel.

An understated luxury permeates the public spaces. Rich wood paneling, rough-hewn stone columns, large softly curtained windows, and sleek furnishings create a Scandinavian modern aspect in the lobby. Luminous and well-soundproofed rooms wear soothing tones that play off the natural light that streams in from large windows. Ask for a water view room, and you'll look out on San Francisco Bay by day, and an awesome silhouette of the Bay Bridge all lit up by night.

Since the hotel's name translates to "vitality" in Italian, you'll want to save time for a trip to the YMCA next door (guests get free passes), then to the penthouse spa to unwind. Your pets will be equally pampered here with special toys and treats. When it's time to eat, you need go no farther than the hotel lobby for stylish Italian fare at Americano restaurant.

W - San Francisco

181 3rd St. (at Howard St.)

Phone: 415-777-5300
Web: www.whotels.com
Prices: $$$

404 Rooms

Starwood Hotels & Resorts Worldwide

Equally well-situated for business or pleasure, the W San Francisco sits next door to the Moscone Convention Center, the San Francisco Museum of Modern Art, and Yerba Buena Gardens. The octagonal, three-story lobby offers everything a hip, young professional could desire: contemporary artwork, a bar serving organic cocktails; live DJ music; and comfortable seating around a fireplace.

Most of the rooms boast an unobstructed view of the city, along with details such as an iPod docking station, a well-appointed mini bar, and spacious bathrooms stocked with Bliss amenities—courtesy of the hotel's 5,000-square-foot Bliss Spa. Accommodations sport a modern minimalist design with Asian accents such as a Buddha lamp. Options range from "Wonderful"—W-speak for standard—to "Fabulous," not to mention the two levels of suites. Laid-back and polite, the young staff is eager to help guests at any time of day or night; and the hotel's Pets Are Welcome policy means you don't have to leave your best friend at home.

Continuing the alphabetic W theme, XYZ restaurant indulges diners with modern Californian cuisine.

Claremont Resort & Spa

41 Tunnel Rd., Berkeley

Phone: 510-843-3000 or 800-551-7266
Web: www.claremontresort.com
Prices: $$$

263 Rooms

16 Suites

The Claremont Resort & Spa

Surrounded by 22 lovely landscaped acres in the hills overlooking San Francisco Bay, this gleaming, white, castle-like edifice has been pampering guests since 1915. The grand tradition of 19th century resort spas continues here today, as The Claremont fulfills its promise to wrap guests in elegance.

If you like lodgings with plenty of activity, the Claremont is for you. Start with the fitness facility, where weight equipment, aerobics classes, and personal training are available. Then there are the ten tennis courts (six of which are lit for evening play), and two heated pools—one dedicated to lap swimming, the other to recreation. For families, the hotel features a Kids Club, with babysitting services, games, movie nights, and other activities tailored to the young set.

Dining options include Jordan's for breakfast, lunch, dinner, and Sunday brunch overlooking the bay; and the Paragon Bar and Café, where live jazz entertains guests Thursday through Saturday nights.

Accommodations offer three degrees of comfort, all luxurious. One caveat: Request a quiet room. A few rooms face the refuse area, and any relaxation may vanish once you hear the noise made by the compactors at night.

Lafayette Park

3287 Mt. Diablo Blvd. (bet. Carol Ln. & Pleasant Hill Rd.), Lafayette

Phone: 925-283-3700 or 877-283-8787
Web: www.lafayetteparkhotel.com
Prices: $$

138 Rooms

Lafayette Park

Sister property to the Stanford Park hotel, the Lafayette Park displays all the splendor of a French château, just off the I-24 freeway. Indeed, that's what this stately structure, with its mansard roofs and turrets, brings to mind.

Beginning with the three-story domed lobby, common areas exude elegance. Wings of the hotel surround a lovely central courtyard, ideal for relaxing to the sound of a trickling fountain. Stucco walls frame the tranquil outdoor heated pool, which is flanked on one end by a small full-service spa, and on the other by a well-equipped fitness room.

Traditional American style defines the oversized guestrooms, decked out with cherrywood furnishings, granite vanity countertops, and ample work desks; many rooms have fireplaces and vaulted ceilings. Beware bargain room rates; you get what you pay for here (for a few more dollars a night you can ensure that you overlook the courtyard). Friendly service takes on a laid-back California attitude, and occasionally misses the mark, but for high style and comfort, the Lafayette Park stands out as a welcome upscale alternative to the corporate chain hotels that predominate in this area.

Casa Madrona

801 Bridgeway, Sausalito

Phone: 415-332-0502 or 800-288-0502
Web: www.casamadrona.com
Prices: $$$

63 Rooms

Casa Madrona Hotel & Spa

Whether you prefer contemporary or historic surroundings, Casa Madrona has a room for you. Tucked into a hillside rising from the Sausalito waterfront, the complex includes a 19th century mansion, a covey of quaint cottages, and a modern hotel building. From its elevated vantage point, the Victorian Mansion, built in 1885, offers lovely bay views.

This 19th century atmosphere pervades its small but charming guestrooms, each decorated individually with antique furniture and period wallpaper. Cottage-style accommodations built into the hillside since 1976 include the mid-size Garden Court rooms (decorated in contemporary or historic styles), and the Bayview rooms, each of which features a distinctive decorating theme—from the Rose Chalet to the exotic Katmandu room. Most of these offer fireplaces and large private balconies. Brick pathways and outdoor stair steps set about with gardens and scented plantings connect these chambers. Californian contemporary-style rooms occupy the most recently opened addition to the hotel in a building perched on the waterfront.

Downstairs, Poggio dishes up authentic Italian fare.

Cavallo Point

601 Murray Circle (at Fort Baker), Sausalito

Phone: 415-339-4700 or 888-651-2003
Web: www.cavallopoint.com
Prices: $$$$

142 Rooms

Michal Venera

Some hotels pin their appeal on history, others on their setting, while some tout their eco-friendly efforts. Cavallo Point boasts all of these enticements and more. On the grounds of Fort Baker, this lodge-like property offers incredible views of the Golden Gate Bridge, the bay, and the city skyline.

Rooms see-saw between classic and contemporary. The former are housed in the original fort buildings, while the latter occupy new structures. None of the facilities are air-conditioned, but who needs it when constant bay breezes cool the site? Meals at Murray Circle restaurant feature outstanding Californian cuisine, but bumbling service. Aside from eating, guests can visit the healing arts center and spa or enroll in the on-site cooking school. There's a complimentary shuttle to the center of Sausalito, but for those craving more exercise, the surrounding Marin Headlands contain a web of hiking trails.

In addition to the normal hotel taxes, Cavallo Point levies an extra 14 percent fee on its guests. This money goes toward the operation of Golden Gate National Recreation Area, in which the property is located. To save a few bucks ($20/night), insist on self versus valet parking.

The Inn Above Tide

A3

30 El Portal (at Bridgeway), Sausalito

Phone: 415-332-9535 or 800-893-8433
Web: www.innabovetide.com
Prices: **$$$**

29
Rooms

Grey Crawford

Every room in this bayfront beauty boasts spectacular water views that extend across to San Francisco, Alcatraz, and Angel Island. As you go up the price scale, king rooms add gas fireplaces, while accommodations in the deluxe category feature private decks that extend out over the bay and provide comfy teak chairs for waterside reflection.

Standard amenities encompass plush robes and slippers, Bvlgari toiletries, and DVD players with access to the hotel's film library. Another thoughtful touch, each sandy-toned room comes with a pair of binoculars for honing in on the scenery. And if that's not enough, a complimentary continental breakfast is served in the guest lounge adjacent to the small lobby—or the staff will deliver it to your room, if you prefer.

At happy hour, wine and cheese are on tap, gratis of course! A short menu of in-room spa services can be arranged for a fee.

The city is just a short ferry ride away, but there's plenty to keep you occupied in Sausalito. Stroll the waterfront and check out the shops, then have a leisurely lunch in one of the bayside restaurants. The inn's concierge can arrange a host of other activities, including biking, boating, and wine tours.

Cypress

E3

10050 S. De Anza Blvd. (at Stevens Creek Blvd), Cupertino

Phone: 408-253-8900 or 800-499-1408
Web: www.thecypresshotel.com
Prices: $$

224 Rooms

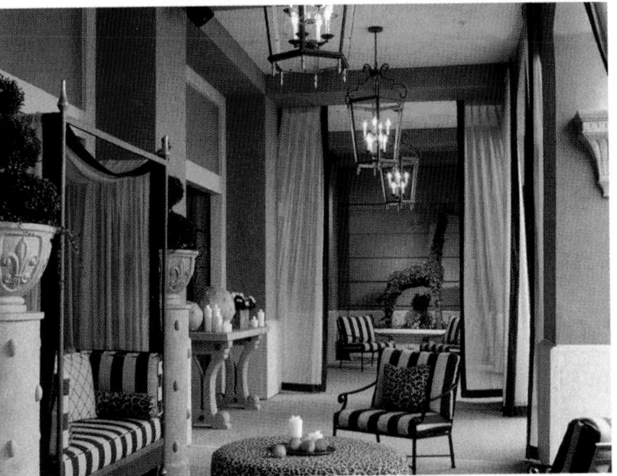

David Phelps/Kimpton Hotels

This member of the Kimpton group is set in the heart of Silicon Valley, close to major interstate arteries and a convenient launching pad for accessing local high-tech companies as well as the area's attractions.

Bold contemporary style is a Kimpton signature, and the Cypress follows suit with rooms decked out in a mélange of colors and textures, including animal-print carpeting and polka-dot wallpaper. Large windows let in natural light, but if it's tranquility you seek, simply draw the thick curtains and block the outside world. Down duvets, ample fluffy pillows, leopard-print robes, L'Occitane bath amenities, and free WiFi Internet access appeal to both leisure and business travelers.

There's a 24-hour fitness facility on-site, but if swimming is your thing, you'll have to walk a few minutes to a nearby lap pool (part of a neighboring residential complex). A complimentary wine reception each evening is part of the program here.

This pet-friendly property offers a special package that pampers your pooch with yummy treats and his own dog bed, while it caters to you with complimentary valet parking.

De Anza

B1

233 W. Santa Clara St. (bet. Almaden Blvd. & Notre Dame Ave.), San Jose

Phone: 408-286-1000 or 800-843-3700
Web: www.hoteldeanza.com
Prices: $$

80 Rooms

20 Suites

Hotel De Anza/Mary Nichols

Recognizable by its pink façade, the Hotel De Anza provides pleasant downtown San Jose digs for both business and leisure travelers. A neutral palette and blonde wood furniture warm the bedrooms without overdoing it. Two TVs, three phones, and a DVD/VCR (videos are complimentary) furnish each room. On the lower level, the business center offers a range of services, and the hotel can accommodate meetings of up to 70 people. In the rooms, a large glass-topped desk ensures adequate work space; wireless Internet access is available for an extra fee.

La Pastaia restaurant, off the lobby, serves Italian cuisine in a colorful taverna setting. Even more attractive is the Hedley Club Lounge with its sophisticated art deco design—an ideal spot for a cocktail. And lest you go hungry, cookies and fresh fruit are available throughout the day in the comfortable pastel-hued lobby; purified ice and water are on tap on each floor above. In fact, the De Anza even features a "Raid Our Pantry" service offering sandwiches and snacks to satisfy those late-night munchies.

Last but not least, your petite pet—15 pounds or less—can accompany you here.

Montgomery

211 S. 1st St. (at San Carlos St.), San Jose

Phone: 408-282-8800 or 866-823-0530
Web: www.hotelmontgomerysj.com
Prices: $$

80 Rooms

6 Suites

Hotel Montgomery

This 1911 Renaissance revival-style building was moved 186 feet from its original location in 2000, in order to save it from the wrecking ball. Today, as the Hotel Montgomery, the edifice has been refitted inside with a chic contemporary design featuring low sofas upholstered in geometric-patterned fabrics and faux-fur-covered armchairs in the lobby.

In the rooms, a warm color scheme of gold and brown is accented with Burberry plaids and splashes of red. Egyptian cotton linens and down comforters dress the beds, and the bathrooms are elegantly appointed with beige marble. Conveniences, including free high-speed Internet access, safes that fit laptops, and a 24-hour fitness center make the accommodations in this historic property thoroughly modern.

Since downtown San Jose attracts more corporate types than tourists, the low-key Montgomery attracts a lot of business travelers. In this regard, the hotel is well-located near the convention center and next to the local VTA (Valley Transportation Authority) light-rail track that heads up to Mountain View. (For a quiet stay, ask for a room that doesn't face the track.)

The Ritz-Carlton, Half Moon Bay

1 Miramontes Point Rd. (at Hwy. 1), Half Moon Bay

Phone: 650-712-7000 or 800-241-3333
Web: www.ritzcarlton.com/hmb
Prices: **$$$$**

239 Rooms

22 Suites

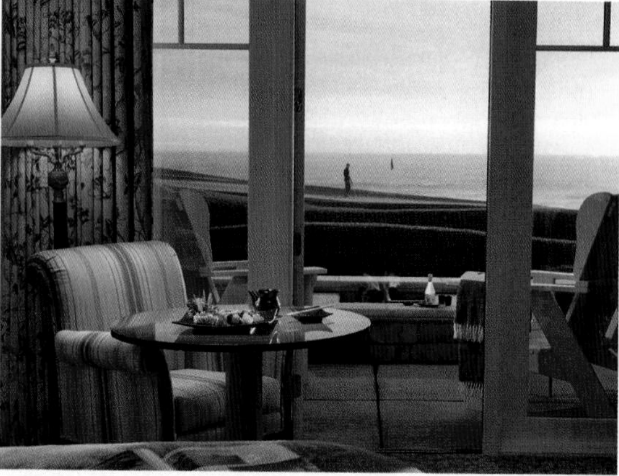

The Ritz-Carlton, Half Moon Bay

Elegant décor, luxurious amenities, impeccable service—everything you would expect from a Ritz-Carlton is here. But as good as this hotel is, everything pales next to the view. And that's exactly how it was planned. Sitting atop a bluff overlooking the Pacific coastline, the resort takes full advantage of its setting. Guestroom décor in subdued tones creates a calming frame for the coastal views that most rooms feature. Baths follow suit in white polished marble. Some rooms have terraces with fire pits.

Navio restaurant offers formal dining, while The Conservatory Lounge dishes up more casual fare with its floor-to-ceiling ocean vistas. Keep your eye on the Pacific in the custom-built wine room, where 5,000 bottles await, or on the Ocean Terrace. If all the drama at sea gets to be too much, afternoon tea is served in the paneled library.

Nearly flawless service makes it challenging to do anything yourself here. If you must be on the go, tennis courts, jogging trails, a fitness center, a full activity schedule, and two oceanside golf courses oblige. Or relax in the spa's Roman bath. Better yet, just sit back and enjoy the view.

Stanford Park

B2-3

100 El Camino Real (at Sand Hill Rd.), Menlo Park

Phone: 650-322-1234 or 866-241-2431
Web: www.stanfordparkhotel.com
Prices: $$$

134 Rooms

29 Suites

Stanford Park Hotel

Situated next to Stanford University and the Stanford Shopping Center, this English colonial-style hotel offers a civilized retreat from research or retail. Stately palm trees and a fountain announce the entrance to the four-story hotel. Cedar shingles and white trim cover the exterior, while antiques and museum-quality *objets d'art* grace the lobby. The latter, incidentally contains a library of literary masterpieces for guests' use—this is still Stanford, after all.

Spacious guestrooms, some with fireplaces, canopied beds, and vaulted ceilings radiate traditional elegance. Bathrooms boast granite counters and make-up mirrors. Other appointments include full-length mirrors, large closets, and separate dressing areas. Put on one of the plush robes and curl up with a book—or your computer and complimentary WiFi access.

With manicured garden courtyards blooming with bright flowers and lush foliage, the public grounds of the Stanford Park make a serene park-like setting in which to relax. If active is your style, you can swim laps in the heated pool, pump some iron in the on-site gym, then savor the American fare at the Duck Club Restaurant.

Valencia

355 Santana Row (bet. Olin Ave. & Tatum Ln.), San Jose

Phone: 408-551-0010 or 866-842-0100
Web: www.hotelvalencia-santanarow.com
Prices: $$$

196 Rooms

16 Suites

Mark Knight/Mark Knight Photography

Myriad shopping, dining, and entertainment options lie just outside your door when you check into this gracious hacienda, set smack in the middle of Santana Row. Shopping is the draw for many of the guests here, but young Silicon Valley business types also find the Valencia a fitting and well-located haven.

Contemporary Cal-Med describes the hotel's shiny style, including the spacious third floor lobby, which feels like a lounge with its low lighting, comfy couches, and hidden nooks. Service is friendly and informal, in keeping with a young Californian sensibility.

Whether your stay is for business or pleasure, you'll find ample room in the well-kept accommodations that sport plenty of counter space for the paper chase, as well as a leather club chair and ottoman for chilling out. Soundproofing is a minus; light sleepers may be bothered by hallway noise or clamor from the street outside.

Best perks? The complimentary breakfast served at the glorious open-air restaurant (Citrus), and the sunny rooftop pool. On the seventh floor, Cielo lounge serves up impressive Silicon Valley views with its cocktails, a buzzing happy hour spot in warm weather.

Auberge du Soleil

B1

180 Rutherford Hill Rd. (off the Silverado Trail), Rutherford

Phone: 707-963-1211 or 800-348-5406
Web: www.aubergedusoleil.com
Prices: $$$$

31 Rooms

21 Suites

Spa

Erhardt Pfeffer

The quintessential wine country hideaway, the "Inn of the Sun" tucks into 33 hilly acres overlooking the Napa Valley. It was the valley's first luxury hotel when it opened its rooms to guests in 1985. More than 20 years later, silvery olive trees and sunny colors still create a rustic Mediterranean feel, while flat-screen TVs, DVD players, and complimentary wireless Internet access provide all the modern amenities you could desire.

Scrambling down the hillsides, newly renovated rooms and suites, all housed in "sun and earth" cottages, feature Italian linens, down pillows and duvets, robes, slippers, private terraces, and minibars stocked with beverages and snacks—compliments of the house. Spacious bathrooms are equipped with skylights, separate showers, and LCD flat-panel TVs to watch while you soak in the tub.

Be sure to savor a meal at The Restaurant at Auberge du Soleil, which is renowned as much for its breezy terrace and sweeping views as for its excellent Cal-Med cuisine. And pamper yourself with a Napa-themed treatment (a warm grapeseed-oil massage or the Vineyard Head to Toe) at the 7,000 square foot Spa du Soleil.

Bardessono

6526 Young St. (at Finnell Rd.), Yountville

Phone: 707-204-6000 or 877-932-5333
Web: www.bardessono.com
Prices: **$$$$**

62 Suites

Sammy Dyess Todd

What's new in the Napa Valley? Bardessono, a 62-room hotel that stands out as a feat of eco-engineering. Constructed with 100,000 square feet of salvaged wood, the hotel uses photovoltaic solar collectors to create electricity, and geothermal wells to heat the rooms and the water. Motion sensors turn off lights when guests are not in residence; settings are automatically restored when they return. Stone paths lined with flowering plants meander between the low-rise buildings that compose the complex.

Guest suites serve as tranquil sanctuaries, well-appointed with organic cotton bed linens, deep soaking tubs, and private patios or balconies. The carefully thought-out design places a comfy sitting area in front of the gas fireplace and the flat-screen TV. Bathrooms conceal a massage table for in-room spa treatments, but there's also a full-service spa for those who desire a more in-depth experience.

For exercise, you can swim in the rooftop lap pool, or use one of the complimentary bicycles to explore the valley. And while the hotel lies within an easy walk of some stellar restaurants, you won't go wrong if you stay on-site to dine on contemporary Californian fare at The Restaurant.

The Carneros Inn

B3

4048 Sonoma Hwy., Napa

Phone: 707-299-4900 or 888-400-9000
Web: www.thecarnerosinn.com
Prices: $$$$

76 Rooms

10 Suites

Mark Hundley

Perched at the crossroads between Napa and Sonoma, The Carneros Inn is a PlumpJack resort—part of the group that owns the PlumpJack winery, as well as the Balboa Cafe and renovated Plumpjack Café in San Francisco.

The concept here takes its cue from the surrounding countryside, fitting a complex of individual cottages into a 27-acre vineyard setting. Natural light bathes tastefully decorated cottages, with French doors leading onto an enclosed patio. Here, reclining lounge chairs promote stargazing, and a table with a heat lamp over it makes the ideal stage for a private alfresco wine tasting.

In the bathrooms, heated slate floors warm your feet, and sunken tubs provide places for soaking. Guests even have the option of indoor or outdoor showers. Two inviting pool areas, a spa, and a terrific gym featuring yoga and fitness classes (schedule changes seasonally) will keep you in top shape.

With its breathtaking view, Hilltop restaurant is the place for breakfast, while fine-dining Farm has a great outdoor lounge for cocktails. Boon Fly Café dishes up a casual menu of sandwiches and flatbread pizzas.

Lavender

C2

2020 Webber St. (bet. Yount & Jefferson Sts.), Yountville

Phone: 707-944-1388 or 800-522-4140
Web: www.lavendernapa.com
Prices: $$

8 Rooms

Four Sisters Inns

Nested in a profusion of lavender and roses, this country inn offers a comfortable, rustic stay in the heart of Napa. A wraparound porch embraces the main farmhouse, and inside, the small entry parlor and sunny breakfast room welcome guests. A full complimentary breakfast is served each morning, to be enjoyed here or in the lovely terrace garden.

Two guestrooms also occupy the main house, one with a private spa tub tucked onto an enclosed outdoor deck. Six cottage rooms surround the house and garden, each with its own private entrance and patio. All the accommodations are spacious and decorated with sophisticated country charm in the Provençal style; they include king beds and fireplaces. Glazed tile glistens in the gracious bathrooms, set off pleasingly by brightly painted walls. Double sinks and a generous-size tub make these baths particularly pleasant, though soaking tubs have no showers. Wireless Internet access is available throughout the hotel.

Guests at Lavender can borrow house bicycles for a spin, and enjoy pool privileges (for a fee) at nearby Maison Fleurie. Or, try your hand at *boules*, the French version of lawn bowling.

Maison Fleurie

6529 Yount St. (at Washington St.), Yountville

Phone: 707-944-2056 or 800-788-0369
Web: www.maisonfleurienapa.com
Prices: **$$$**

13 Rooms

Four Sisters Inns

Oozing French country charm inside and out, the "Flowering House" makes the perfect romantic wine country getaway. This member of the Four Sisters Inns welcomes guests amid Provençal-inspired fabrics and furnishings, and a huge stone fireplace in the lobby. Constructed in 1849, back when the valley was known for growing walnuts and olives, the rustic main house contains 7 of the property's 13 rooms. Elsewhere on the grounds, two Carriage House rooms have private entrances, while those in the Bakery Building boast fireplaces and whirlpool tubs.

Before setting out to explore the valley, whether by car or complimentary mountain bike, you'll need a hearty breakfast. The inn complies with a spread of hot and cold dishes—perhaps a quiche, a potato casserole and soft-boiled eggs, along with fresh fruit, cakes, toast, and English muffins. Drop by the lobby lounge for wine and hors d'oeuvres each evening. A small refrigerator in the common area offers complimentary soft drinks all day.

True to its name, Maison Fleurie abounds in lovely landscaped flora, from the roses that surround the hot tub area, to the grape vines that climb the walls and trellises scattered around the pastoral grounds.

Meadowood

900 Meadowood Ln. (off the Silverado Trail), St. Helena

Phone: 707-963-3646 or 800-458-8080
Web: www.meadowood.com
Prices: $$$$

41 Rooms

44 Suites

Meadowood Napa

Set on 250 exquisite acres a mile east of downtown St. Helena, this world-class resort off the Silverado Trail nestles amid wooded hills, where accommodations take the form of individual cottages. A country-club ambience pervades this recently renovated property. White wainscoting, wood-burning fireplaces, spacious bathrooms, and French doors leading onto private terraces highlight the room décor. (The resort doubles as a private country club for Napa Valley residents.)

While Meadowood makes the perfect perch for wine country adventures, between the nine-hole golf course, seven tennis courts, two croquet lawns, two lap pools, the fitness center, and the new full-service spa, you may never want to leave the grounds. There's even a wine center (ask the staff to arrange vineyard picnics), where the resort's wine tutor holds tastings and seminars for guests. Meals can be either casual at The Grill (where an English-style breakfast is served) overlooking the golf course, or more formal at the excellent Restaurant at Meadowood, lauded for its ambitious, product-driven cuisine.

Napa River Inn

500 Main St. (at 5th St.), Napa

Phone: 877-251-8500
Web: www.napariverinn.com
Prices: $$$

68 Rooms

Napa River Inn

The Historic Napa Mill (1884), with its present-day complex of shops and restaurants, forms a convenient setting for this downtown boutique hotel. Rooms at the Napa River Inn are divided among three structures and are distinguished by three different design themes. Full of vintage charm, eight rooms in the 1884 Hatt Building are done in Victorian style with canopy beds, fireplaces, and old-fashioned slipper tubs. In the Plaza Building, 34 rooms sport a rustic wine country décor and creature comforts such as marble bathrooms and balconies with river views. The remaining quarters are housed in the 1862 Embarcadero Building, where they are decked out in a maritime motif, complete with cherrywood wainscoting, porthole mirrors, and carved-rope frames. Grapeseed-oil-based bath products are de rigueur for this wine country inn.

The Inn doesn't have a restaurant, but delivers a California-style breakfast to your room each morning, and stocks each one with coffees and teas to get things started.

The town's points of interest lie close by, and if you don't feel like walking, the city trolley stops in front of the hotel every 15 minutes to transport you around the downtown area.

Rancho Caymus Inn

B2

1140 Rutherford Rd. (off Hwy. 29), Rutherford

Phone: 707-963-1777 or 800-845-1777
Web: www.ranchocaymus.com
Prices: $$

25 Rooms

1 Suite

Rancho Caymus

Perfectly located between St. Helena and Yountville, Rancho Caymus Inn blends a bit of old California with wine country convenience and unpretentious western hospitality. All the rooms and suites are housed in the rambling hacienda-style building. Each bears the name of a Napa Valley personality, from Lillie Langtry to Black Bart.

Mexican-style wooden furniture, hand-carved walnut bedsteads, wrought-iron details, and colorful woolen rugs impart a genuine Old West ranch feeling to the spacious rooms. Massive century-old oak ceiling beams and trim of walnut, fir, and redwood add a natural warmth. Designed as "split levels," the sleeping areas are set up a step in each room. Standard amenities include televisions, air conditioning, wet bar, and refrigerator, and some rooms have mission-style fireplaces and private outdoor balconies or sitting areas. More elaborate Master Suites feature whirlpool tubs against a stained-glass backdrop in their bathrooms. All the rooms are quiet, well maintained, and clean, and breakfast is included in the room rate.

Solage

755 Silverado Trail (at Rosedale Rd.), Calistoga

Phone: 707-226-0800 or 866-942-7442
Web: www.solagecalistoga.com
Prices: $$$$

83 Rooms

6 Suites

Solage Calistoga

There's no place like wine country to indulge in the good life, and Solage capitalizes on what is best about this area. The first property from Auberge Resorts' new Solage Hotels & Resorts brand, this eco-friendly cottage-style resort and spa spreads out over 20 acres off the Silverado Trail.

The resort's 89 rooms are tucked inside bungalows that fashion urban lofts in a pastoral environment. Modern amenities (WiFi, flat-screen TV, iPod docking station, mini refrigerator) mix with vaulted ceilings, contemporary furniture, polished concrete floors, and semi-private patios. Colors run to leafy greens, and sizes range from one-bedroom studios to spacious suites. Each cottage is equipped with a pair of bikes for exploring.

Guests want for little here. There's a large outdoor heated pool flanked by cabanas, and a state-of-the-art fitness center where classes are complimentary. Solbar restaurant serves up healthy Californian cuisine for breakfast, lunch, and dinner. But the pièce de résistance is the resort's 20,000 square foot spa. And this being Calistoga—a small town with a big reputation for its mineral-rich mud—a visit to the spa's signature Mud Bar is an absolute must.

Villagio Inn & Spa

C3

6481 Washington St., Yountville

Phone: 707-944-8877 or 800-351-1133
Web: www.villagio.com
Prices: $$$

86 Rooms

26 Suites

Spa

Villagio Inn & Spa

Villagio brings to mind a Tuscan village; two-story villas range through lush gardens and vineyards that share a 23-acre family-owned estate with the Vintage Inn. A stroll around the grounds here reveals tranquil pools and fountains, vivid flowers, and cypress, olive, and Meyer lemon trees.

Accommodations are done in Tuscan style with warm tones, wrought-iron accents, plantation shutters, and wood-burning fireplaces. Rooms on the upper levels have domed ceilings and furnished balconies (ground-level rooms have patios). Villagio accommodates business functions with 10,000 square feet of meeting space. In the morning, breakfast takes the form of a complimentary gourmet buffet (complete with Champagne) served off the lobby. Also included in the room rate is the afternoon tea and Friday evening wine tastings, sponsored by local vineyards.

At the end of a long day spent cycling or visiting wineries, a Napa River stone massage at the Spa at Villagio is a great way to unwind. (A new expanded spa is in the works.) Weddings are memorable events at Villagio, especially with the addition of the new outdoor pavilion surrounded by grassy lawns and bright plantings.

Vintage Inn

6541 Washington St., Yountville

Phone: 707-944-1112 or 800-351-1133
Web: www.vintageinn.com
Prices: $$$

72
Rooms

8
Suites

Vintage Estate

Opened in 1985, this lovely property lines Yountville's main street with French country charm. Paths and footbridges connect the two-story buildings, where French antiques, toile de Jouy fabrics, plush robes, and down duvets set the tone for luxurious comfort. Each room features a wood-burning fireplace, and bathrooms are equipped with dual sinks and an oversize whirlpool tub; suites add wet bars and eating areas.

Rates include a bottle of wine in your room, a gourmet breakfast buffet, and afternoon tea. If you tire of touring wineries, the inn offers an outdoor heated lap pool, tennis courts, and bicycle rentals. Not to mention the fact that guests have access to the spa at sibling Villagio and to the Yountville Fitness Center (at no charge). Pets are welcomed here with their own goodies (no wine, but some yummy treats).

Shoppers can stroll next door to explore "V Marketplace." Once the Groezinger Winery, this brick complex now houses shops, galleries, and eateries. Foodies will love the fact that some of Napa Valley's most renowned restaurants—Bouchon, Bottega, Redd, and The French Laundry—lie within easy walking distance of the resort.

Duchamp

421 Foss St. (at North St.), Healdsburg

Phone: 707-431-1300 or 800-431-9341
Web: www.duchamphotel.com
Prices: $$$

6 Rooms

David Duncan Douglas

This unusual small hotel is located within minutes of Healdsburg's downtown plaza, convenient to the wineries of the Russian River, Dry Creek, and Alexander Valley. The owners also run a small winery of the same name. Their affection for French Dada artist Marcel Duchamp manifests itself in wonderful, whimsical ways at both locations.

The hotel comprises seven small bungalows: one for reception and six housing one guestroom each. The grouping surrounds a heated swimming pool equipped with a sundeck and Jacuzzi. Each room is large, but minimalist in style, with whitewashed walls and decorative murals to add just a touch of color. Floors are polished concrete, the furniture contemporary. French doors let in the light, and each cottage features a private patio. King beds furnish the rooms, along with a high-definition flat-screen TV, a CD player, and free wireless Internet access. White walls and tiles dress the very large bathrooms, which include two washbasins and a roomy shower.

Guests are treated to a continental breakfast buffet in the reception cottage, and the hotel staff will gladly arrange for private tours and tastings at Duchamp Estate Winery.

El Dorado

405 1st St. W. (at W. Spain St.), Sonoma

Phone: 707-996-3220 or 800-289-3031
Web: www.eldoradosonoma.com
Prices: $$

27 Rooms

Erin Kunkel

The El Dorado occupies a spot at the heart of historic Sonoma, located directly on Spanish Plaza in a recently renovated historic building. Laid out by Mariano Vallejo in 1835, the eight-acre site is the largest Mexican-era plaza in California.

Light and color set the hotel's 27 rooms aglow, while cool tile floors suggest the town's Spanish origins and four-poster beds made up with fine linens add romance. French doors open onto private balconies or terraces and admit a wash of sunlight into the rooms. Some look over the historic plaza; others face the restaurant terrace, which is shaded by a fig tree. Though most bathrooms offer only showers, they are well appointed. The pool may be small but offers a satisfying splash after a hot day of Cab tasting.

If you don't mind casual service, the El Dorado presents good value for the money, as well as an alternative to the Provençal or Tuscany style that predominate in other wine country hostelries. Savor seasonal Californian cuisine at the stylish and scrumptious El Dorado Kitchen.

The Fairmont
Sonoma Mission Inn & Spa

100 Boyes Blvd. (bet. Arnold Dr. & Hwy. 12), Sonoma

Phone: 707-938-9000 or 800-441-1414
Web: www.fairmont.com
Prices: **$$$**

166 Rooms

60 Suites

Fairmont Sonoma Mission Inn & Spa

Tile roofs, adobe walls, and the historic character of a Sonoma Valley mission create the perfect backdrop for a relaxing weekend getaway or a visit to wine country. Originally built around an ancient hot springs in 1895, the resort was rebuilt in 1927 after fire destroyed the property. Renovated and greatly expanded since then, the facility retains its gracious 1920s atmosphere with all the comforts of a modern hotel and spa.

Nowadays, guests can still "take the waters," as well as enjoy the many services offered at the luxurious spa. They can also play the private 18-hole championship golf course, hike the countryside, lounge by the pool, take fitness classes, or join bike tours. The sprawling resort comprises a central "living room" with a variety of accommodations spread among an assortment of buildings. Done up in French country décor, standard rooms tend to be small; wood-burning fireplaces furnish about half of them. Signature Mission Suites, the most recent additions to the property, foster romance with two-person Jacuzzi tubs and private patios or balconies.

Gaige House Inn

13540 Arnold Dr. (at Railroad St.), Glen Ellen

Phone: 707-935-0237 or 800-935-0237
Web: www.gaige.com
Prices: $$$

12 Rooms

11 Suites

Erin Derby & Paul Davis

The Gaige House Inn offers a complete departure from typical wine country accommodations. Here, serenity trumps country or western charm; Japanese influences replace French and Spanish inside an 1890 Queen Anne Victorian. Tucked away on three wooded creekside acres, this intimate inn features a full menu of spa services, a particularly fine breakfast, and a lovely swimming pool.

Guests can reserve a room in the main house or a garden or creek suite in separate cottage settings. Though all 23 rooms and suites share a similar palette of earthy browns and grays with design details inspired by nature, each one has been thoughtfully furnished, decorated, and arranged individually. In some, tatami mats cover hardwood floors, and rice-paper screens decorate the walls; others feature fireplaces. In the eight spa suites, beautifully hewn granite soaking tubs, and Japanese *tsubo* gardens for massage services turn your room into a spa. All cottage rooms feature private terraces or a little garden by the creek. This secluded inn promises quiet nights and peaceful days.

Healdsburg

25 Matheson St. (at Healdsburg Ave.), Healdsburg

Phone: 707-431-2800 or 800-889-7188
Web: www.hotelhealdsburg.com
Prices: $$$$

51 Rooms

4 Suites

Cesar Rubio

Natural elements of wine country combine in this three-story garden hotel to create a serene retreat on Healdsburg's town square. Spacious rooms are decorated with soothing wine country tones, Tibetan wool carpets, and pecan wood floors; most have French doors leading to private balconies. Teak platform beds dress in down duvets and Frette linens. In the oversize bathrooms, you'll find Italian glass tile, walk-in showers, separate soaking tubs, and organic bath amenities courtesy of the hotel's full-service spa.

A hearty breakfast comes with your stay. Whether you plan on wine-tasting, getting acquainted with the shops and wine bars around the square, or working out in the hotel's fitness room and relaxing by the olive- and cypress-tree-shrouded pool afterwards, the selection of baked goods, smoked salmon, eggs, cereals, and fruit will fortify you for the day's activities.

Dining options abound in downtown Healdsburg, but you can eat just as well on-site. Check out the grappa bar in the lobby before retiring to Charlie Palmer's Dry Creek Kitchen for seasonal Californian fare. If it's just a nosh you need, light refreshments are served on the screened porch that adjoins the lobby.

Honor Mansion

14891 Grove St. (bet. Dry Creek Rd. & Grand St.), Healdsburg

Phone: 707-433-4277 or 800-554-4667
Web: www.honormansion.com
Prices: $$$

13 Rooms

The Honor Mansion

Romance waits behind the façade of this restored 1883 house, located less than a mile away from the tony boutiques, tasting rooms, and fine restaurants lining Healdsburg's downtown plaza. Owners Cathi and Steve Fowler have anticipated guests' every need in the 13 individually decorated rooms and suites. Rooms in the main house vary in size and style, while four separate Vineyard Suites (the priciest accommodations) foster *amore* with king-size beds, gas fireplaces, and private patios complete with your own whirlpool (robes and rubber ducky included). On the four-acre grounds, landscaped with rose gardens and zinfandel vines, you'll find a lap pool, a PGA putting green, bocce and tennis courts, a croquet lawn, and a half-basketball court.

Following the Fowlers' hospitable lead, the staff will provide you with a picnic basket and a list of places to pick up picnic fare. They'll also make arrangements for everything from private winery visits to poolside massages. A hearty multicourse breakfast, and an afternoon wine and hors d'ouevres reception are included in the room rate.

On weekends, count on a minimum stay of two nights in low season, and four nights in high season.

Les Mars

D1

27 North St. (bet. Foss St. & Healdsburg Ave.), Healdsburg

Phone: 707-433-4211 or 877-431-1700
Web: www.lesmarshotel.com
Prices: **$$$$**

16 Rooms

Les Mars Hotel

Picture the limestone façade of a 19th century French chateau just off Healdsburg's plaza, and you've got Les Mars. Step inside and you'll be instantly awash in luxury, from the 17th century Flemish tapestry that hangs in the lobby to the hand-carved walnut panels and leather-bound books that line the library.

Sumptuous antiques fill the 16 individually designed rooms with the likes of Louis XV armoires, draped four-poster beds, and chaise longues. Italian linens, reading lights, and switch-operated fireplaces provide extra thoughtful touches. In the bathrooms, lined with salt and pepper marble, you can pamper yourself with deep soaking tubs, lavender bath salts, and Bulgari amenities. Third-floor rooms boast high ceilings with exposed wood beams. Yes, the prices are steep, but this level of luxury doesn't come cheap.

The adjoining Cyrus restaurant, a separate venture, makes an equally elegant setting in which to linger over Chef Douglas Keane's contemporary cooking.

Note that there's a minimum stay of two nights on weekends, and this family-owned hotel is not recommended for children under 12 years of age.

Madrona Manor

1001 Westside Rd. (at West Dry Creek Rd.), Healdsburg

Phone: 707-433-4231 or 800-258-4003
Web: www.madronamanor.com
Prices: **$$$**

17 Rooms

5 Suites

Ben Davidson

Eight wooded acres form the backdrop for Madrona Manor. A short drive from downtown Healdsburg, this 19th century estate oozes with romantic cachet. It's a serene place to retire to after a day of wine tasting.

Built for San Francisco businessman John Paxton, the stately, three-story Victorian mansion has graced this site since 1881. Of the 22 handsome rooms on-site, 9 are located in the mansion itself; all of these have king-size beds and fireplaces. The remainder of the rooms and suites are scattered around the grounds in buildings such as the original carriage house. All rooms are individually decorated and fitted with soft linens and terry robes. WiFi is available in most areas of the inn, and rates include a buffet breakfast each morning. If it's seclusion you seek, reserve the Garden Cottage with its own private garden and sheltered deck. And be sure your stay includes an intimate dinner at the mansion's lovely restaurant.

To foster romance, there are no TVs in any of the rooms, but with a heated pool on-site, the boutiques of Healdsburg, and the Dry Creek Valley wineries so close by, you won't want for things to do.

Vintners Inn

4350 Barnes Rd. (at River Rd.), Santa Rosa

Phone: 707-575-7350 or 800-421-2584
Web: www.vintnersinn.com
Prices: $$$

44 Rooms

Vintners Inn

Nestled in 92 acres of vineyards, Vintners Inn welcomes guests with a bottle of wine. The inn, owned by Dan and Rhonda Carano of Ferrari-Carano Winery, is located just north of Santa Rosa and convenient to Highway 101.

Four two-story Tuscan-style buildings with red-tile roofs range around a landscaped courtyard. Each room enjoys its own private balcony or small patio. Country décor is rustic and refined, and Internet access and a copy of the local newspaper come compliments of the house. Rooms on the second floor boast vaulted ceilings with exposed wood beams; some are equipped with fireplaces. If you want a bit more space, reserve a junior suite, outfitted with a king-size featherbed, a fireplace, and a sitting area with a sleeper sofa. There's a two-mile path through the surrounding vineyards for an early morning stroll or jog.

Rates include a buffet breakfast each morning; for lunch or dinner, you need only walk next door to John Ash & Co. for a meal that highlights Sonoma County products.

The inn has an events and conference center which offers more than 6,000 square feet of meeting space for a relaxed yet productive working session.

Your link to sublime taste
U.S.A. [Change]
ubiubi
ubiubi
Welcome, Alessandra Van Huys
1. Pick Your City:
New York
Add My Spot | Edit My Spots
2. Search By:
KEYWORD
BROWSE
REVIEWER
THE DAILY 3
YOUR ACCOUNT
You are a Premium User
My Favorites
My Account
About Me
Settings | Legal | Help | About | Sign In

Indexes

Where to Eat

Alphabetical List of Restaurants

C

D

E

F

Restaurants by Cuisine

Cambodian

Chinese

Contemporary

Filipino

French

Fusion

Gastropub

Moroccan

Persian

Peruvian

Pizza

Portuguese

Seafood

Singaporean

Southern

Spanish

Steakhouse

Thai

Turkish

Vegan

Vegetarian

Vietnamese

Look for our new symbol 🍸, spotlighting restaurants with a notable cocktail list.

Cuisines by Neighborhood

SAN FRANCISCO

SoMa

East of San Francisco

Starred Restaurants

Within the selection we offer you, some restaurants deserve to be highlighted for their particularly good cuisine. When giving one, two, or three Michelin stars, there are a number of elements that we consider including the quality of the ingredients, the technical skill and flair that goes into their preparation, the blend and clarity of flavours, and the balance of the menu. Just as important is the ability to produce excellent cooking time and again. We make as many visits as we need, so that our readers may be assured of quality and consistency.

A two or three-star restaurant has to offer something very special in its cuisine; a real element of creativity, originality, or "personality" that sets it apart from the rest. Three stars – our highest award – are given to the choicest restaurants, where the whole dining experience is superb.

Cuisine in any style, modern or traditional, may be eligible for a star. Due to the fact we apply the same independent standards everywhere, the awards have become benchmarks of reliability and excellence in over 20 countries in Europe and Asia, particularly in France, where we have awarded stars for 100 years, and where the phrase "Now that's real three-star quality!" has entered into the language.

The awarding of a star is based solely on the quality of the cuisine.

✿✿✿

Exceptional cuisine, worth a special journey.

One always eats here extremely well, sometimes superbly. Distinctive dishes are precisely executed, using superlative ingredients.

✿✿

Excellent cuisine, worth a detour.

Skillfully and carefully crafted dishes of outsanding quality.

✿

A very good restaurant in its category.

A place offering cuisine prepared to a consistently high standard.

Bib Gourmand

This symbol indicates our inspector's favorites for good value. For $40 or less, you can enjoy two courses and a glass of wine or a dessert (not including tax or gratuity).

Under $25

Feast for under $25 at all restaurants with .

Brunch

Look for our new category small plates icon, small plates.

Late Dining

Indexes

Where to **Stay**

Notes

Michelin

Notes

Michelin

Notes

Michelin

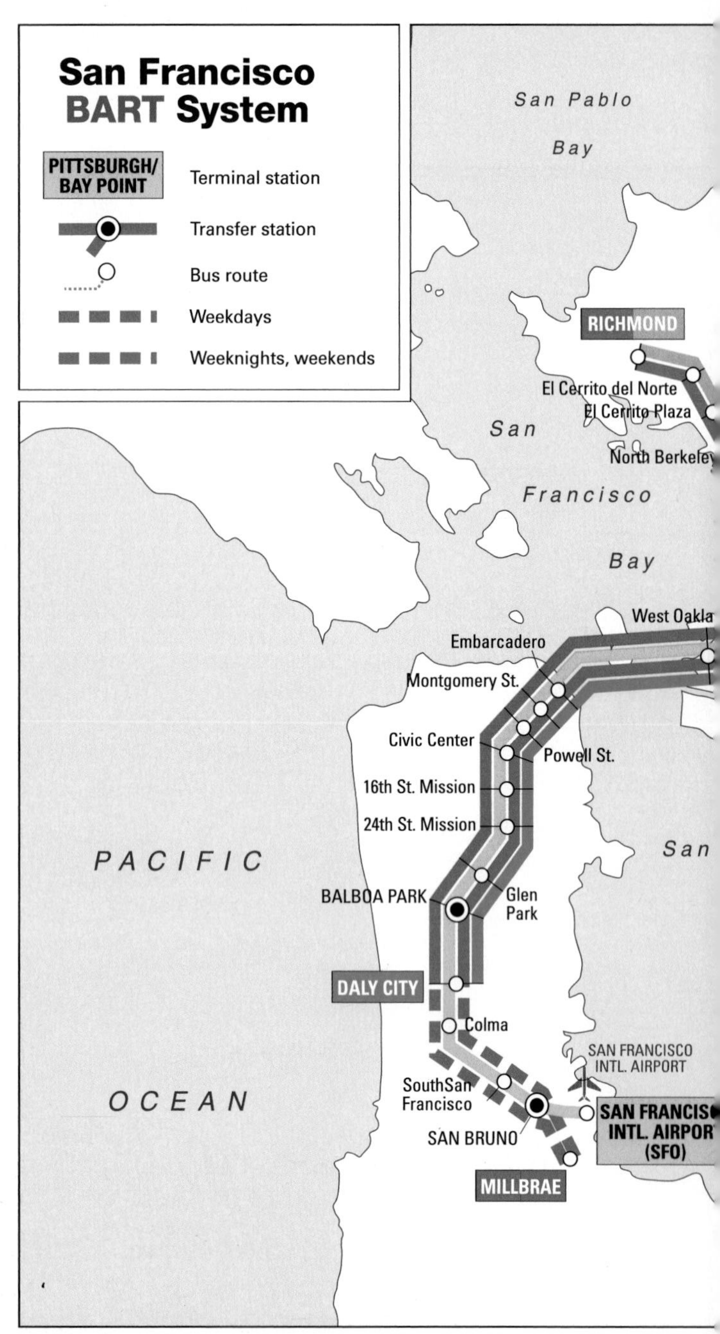
San Francisco
BART System
PITTSBURGH/
BAY POINT
Terminal station
Transfer station
Bus route
Weekdays
Weeknights, weekends
San Pablo
Bay
RICHMOND
El Cerrito del Norte
El Cerrito Plaza
North Berkeley
San
Francisco
Bay
West Oakla
Embarcadero
Montgomery St.
Civic Center
Powell St.
16th St. Mission
24th St. Mission
PACIFIC
San
BALBOA PARK
Glen
Park
DALY CITY
Colma
SAN FRANCISCO
INTL. AIRPORT
SouthSan
Francisco
OCEAN
SAN BRUNO
SAN FRANCIS
INTL. AIRPOR
(SFO)
MILLBRAE

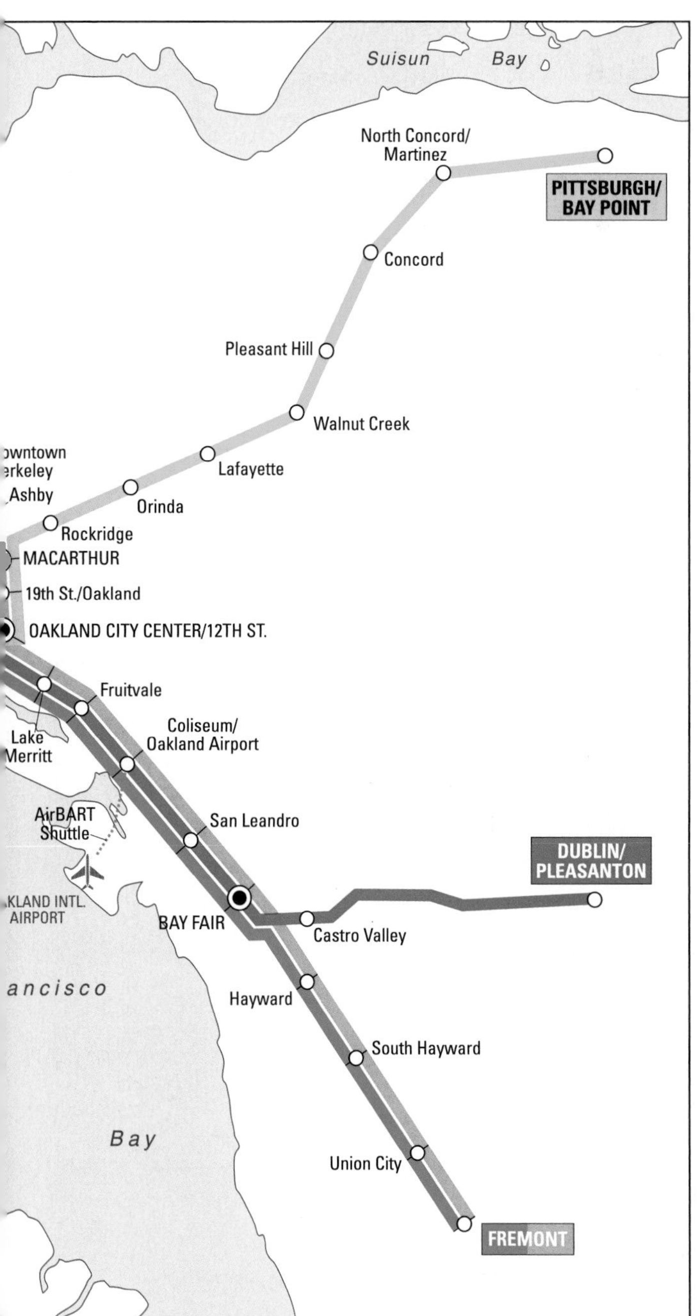
Suisun Bay
North Concord/
Martinez
PITTSBURGH/
BAY POINT
Concord
Pleasant Hill
Walnut Creek
Lafayette
Orinda
Rockridge
Ashby
MACARTHUR
19th St./Oakland
OAKLAND CITY CENTER/12TH ST.
Fruitvale
Lake Merritt
Coliseum/
Oakland Airport
AirBART
Shuttle
AIRPORT
San Leandro
DUBLIN/
PLEASANTON
BAY FAIR
Castro Valley
Hayward
South Hayward
Bay
Union City
FREMONT

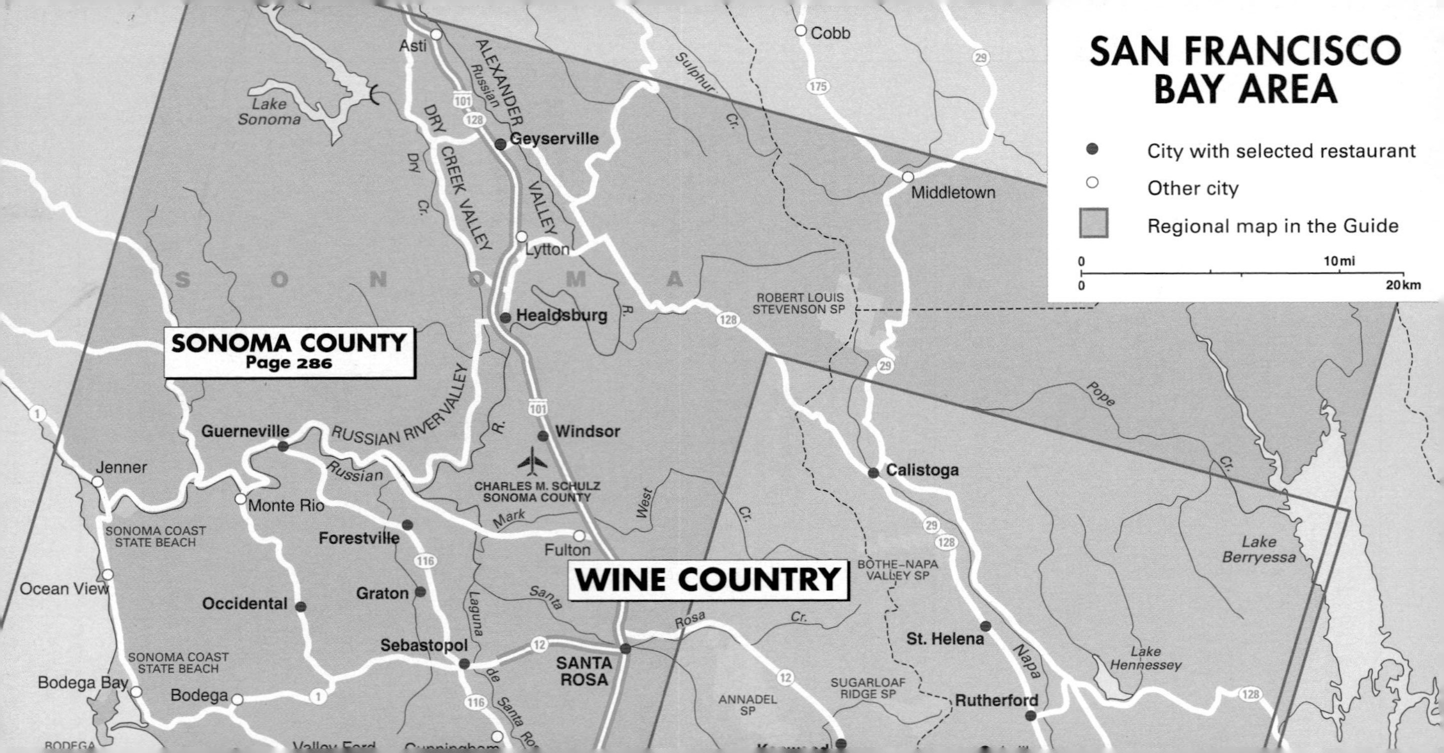
SAN FRANCISCO BAY AREA
City with selected restaurant
Other city
Regional map in the Guide
0
10 mi
0
20 km
SONOMA COUNTY
Page 286
WINE COUNTRY
SONOMA
Asti
Cobb
Middletown
Geyserville
Lytton
Healdsburg
Windsor
Guerneville
Jenner
Monte Rio
Forestville
Fulton
Graton
Occidental
Sebastopol
SANTA ROSA
Ocean View
Bodega Bay
Bodega
Calistoga
St. Helena
Rutherford
ALEXANDER VALLEY
DRY CREEK VALLEY
RUSSIAN RIVER VALLEY
Lake Sonoma
Lake Berryessa
Lake Hennessey
CHARLES M. SCHULZ SONOMA COUNTY
ROBERT LOUIS STEVENSON SP
BOTHE-NAPA VALLEY SP
SUGARLOAF RIDGE SP
ANNADEL SP
SONOMA COAST STATE BEACH
SONOMA COAST STATE BEACH
Russian
Dry Cr.
Sulphur Cr.
Pope Cr.
Mark West
Santa Rosa Cr.
Laguna de Santa Rosa
Napa
R.
101
128
175
29
116
12
1